BEHAVIOUR ANALYSIS AND CONTEMPORARY PSYCHOLOGY

Edited by:
C. F. Lowe, M. Richelle, D. E. Blackman, C. M. Bradshaw

Lawrence Erlbaum Associates Ltd., Publishers
Chancery House
319 City Road
London EC1V 1LJ

British Library Cataloguing in Publication Data

Behaviour analysis and contemporary psychology.
1. Psychology
I. Lowe, C. F.
150 BF199

ISBN 0-86377-025-8

Typeset by Acorn Bookwork, Salisbury, Wiltshire
Printed and bound by A. Wheaton & Co. Ltd., Exeter

Contents

List of Contributors

E. Alleva, Laboratorio di Fisiopatologia di Organo e di Sistema, Istituto Superiore di Sanita, Viale Regina Elena 299, I-00161 Rome, Italy

G. Bignami, Laboratorio di Fisiopatologia di Organo e di Sistema, Istituto Superiore di Sanita, Viale Regina Elena 299, I-00161 Rome, Italy

D. E. Blackman, Department of Psychology, University College, Cardiff, P.O. Box 78, Cardiff, Wales CF1 1XL, U.K.

A. Brekstad, Institute of Psychology, University of Oslo, Box 1094, Blindern, Oslo 3, Norway

A. C. Catania, Department of Psychology, University of Maryland Baltimore County, 5401 Wilkens Ave, Catonsville, Maryland 21228, U.S.A.

F. C. Colpaert, Department of Pharmacology, Janssen Pharmaceutica, Beerse, B-2340 Belgium

J. D. Delius, Experimentelle Tierpsychologie, Psychologishes Institut, Ruhr-Universität, Universitätsstr. 150, D 4630 Bochum, F.R.G.

J. L. Evenden, Department of Experimental Psychology, University of Cambridge, Downing Street, Cambridge CB2 3EB, U.K.

V. Giardini, Laboratorio di Fisiopatologia di Organo e di Sistema, Istituto Superiore di Sanita, Viale Regina Elena 299, I-00161 Rome, Italy

P. J. Horne, Department of Psychology, University College of North Wales, Bangor, Gwynedd LL57 2DG, U.K.

S. E. G. Lea, University of Exeter, Exeter, Devon EX4 4QJ, U.K.

J.-F. Le Ny, Centre d'Etudes de Psychologie Cognitive, Université de Paris-sud, Bâtiment 335, Centre Scientifique d'Orsay, 91405 Orsay Cedex, France

C. F. Lowe, Department of Psychology, University College of North Wales, Bangor, Gwynedd LL57 2DG, U.K.

J. Michael, Department of Psychology, Western Michigan University, Kalamazoo, Michigan 49008, U.S.A.

E. Ribes, Escuela Nacional de Estudios Profesionales Iztacala, Coordinacion General de Investigation, Apartado Postal 314, Tlalnepantla, Estado de Mexico

M. N. Richelle, Institut de Psychologie et des Sciences de l'Education, Psychologie Experimentale, Université de Liège, 5 Bolevard du Rectorat (B32), Sart-Tilman, B4000 Liège par Liège 1, Belgium

T. W. Robbins, Department of Experimental Psychology, University of Cambridge, Downing Street, Cambridge CB2 3EB, U.K.

X. Seron, Unité de Neuropsychologie Expérimentale de l'Adult (NEXA), Cliniques Universitaires St. Luc, Avenue Hippocrate, 10/1350, B-1200 Brussels, Belgium

B. F. Skinner, Department of Psychology, William James Hall, Harvard University, Cambridge, Mass. 02138, U.S.A.

J. E. R. Staddon, Department of Psychology, Duke University, Durham, North Carolina 27706, U.S.A.

I INTRODUCTION

1 Behaviour Analysis and Contemporary Psychology

Marc N. Richelle
Laboratoire de Psychologie Experimentale, Université de Liège, Belgium

Behaviour analysis and contemporary psychology was the title we chose to give the First European Meeting on the Experimental Analysis of Behaviour. Behaviour analysis stands as the conventional short form of the experimental analysis of behaviour.

These three words do not have the same connotation for everyone. They might be thought of as referring, in a straightforward manner, to the activities of those psychologists who study behaviour with experimental methods. This would have included all experimental psychologists when, in the years immediately following the behaviourist revolution, most people defined psychology as the science of behaviour. Things are slightly different now, as a number of experimental psychologists think of themselves as studying mental processes such as cognition, information processing, and representations, rather than behaviour. Labelling oneself as a student of behaviour, in this context, may sound close to confessing a preposterous attachment to an outdated view of psychology, and maintaining oneself deliberately in what Bunge (1980) has called the "long and boring night of behaviourism." In spite of such contemptuous or hostile judgements many psychologists still devote their scientific activity to the experimental analysis of behaviour in the more restricted sense of the expression that it has had since the 50s, when it came to designate a specific approach to the study of behaviour derived essentially from Skinner's work. Whatever their differences in other respects these people share a common methodological and epistemological view, sometimes referred to as radical behaviourism.

A detailed account of this position would exceed the limits of this introductory chapter. But some important points should be mentioned: the emphasis on functional analysis; the much favoured use of operant techniques; a conception of the organism-environment interaction that attributes to the latter *selective* action (a conception that allows for the emergence of complex recombinations and constructions in individual behaviour just as the dynamics of variation and selection account for the emergence of new living forms through biological evolution); and, finally, a definition of psychology as being in the realm of biology that does not imply any reductionism, nor dispense with the task of explaining the most complex or elusive aspects of behaviour such as awareness and consciousness, verbal behaviour, and creativity.

Clearly, some of these and other points that might be listed also characterise or are the concern of other psychologists. These latter might feel, not totally without justification, that the experimental study of behaviour has been usurped by a self-assertive group of people who have duly claimed exclusivity. Enthusiasm was the rule among the American psychologists who founded the Society of the Experimental Analysis of Behavior a quarter of a century ago. Enthusiasm is close to triumphalism and was often perceived as such from the outside. Could these territorial aspects of the development of the field fully account for the misrepresentations and the criticisms to which behaviour analysis has been exposed? More basic factors might be involved and become clear to any observer (especially if he or she has a European background) who takes a historical look at the behaviour analysis movement. Two important points emerge that can be summarised in the following statements:

1. However impressive the achievements of thousands of laboratory studies in a variety of topics—many of them previously unexplored—one is struck by the long, if not persistent, neglect of a number of dimensions that can hardly be ignored in a scientific study of behaviour.
2. If B. F. Skinner, who inspired the movement, can be held responsible for some of its traits—and possibly for some of its limitations—it appears that, more often than not, seminal views expressed in his writings *did not* lead to the experimental or theoretical work one would have expected from his followers.

Let us briefly document these judgements.

The laboratory procedures originally designed by Skinner and further developed by his followers are an unquestionable contribution to scientific psychology. Operant techniques have established animal psychophysics as a sophisticated, highly precise, field of research; they have, from 1950 or so, provided an efficient tool for the newly fledged experimental psychopharmacology; they have been put to work to analyse in depth problems related, in traditional handbook categories, to perception, motivation, memory, time sense, cognition and so on; they have fostered formal and mathematical models such as the matching law and its variants, resorting to the econometric concepts of maximisation and optimisation. Major dimensions of behaviour, however, have been given little, if any, attention.

The importance of species-specific behaviour remained almost completely ignored until the late 60s and it was not until the 70s that ethological thinking penetrated into operant circles. Now it has become fashionable to talk about species-specific constraints on stimuli and responses, and to observe animal subjects in the conditioning chamber with the naked eye, as a field naturalist would do, while the microcomputer is controlling and recording all possible experimental events. The shift has resulted from observations made by experimenters themselves, who came across "natural repertoires" in the conditioning situation, and from the objections made by ethologists to the claim of universality for behavioural laws that have not been submitted to comparative test. There has been a surprisingly long delay between the findings of Breland and Breland (1961) that went almost unnoticed and the full recognition (albeit accompanied by a climate of rupture and tension—see Herrnstein, 1977a, b; Skinner, 1977) of species-specific behaviour. We are now on the way to an integrative view of behaviour that reconciles and combines ethology and experimental analysis, as reflected in the contributions of Lea, Delius, and Staddon to the present volume. That it has taken so long to reach this stage looks strange to European psychologists whose training has usually included more than a superficial grounding in ethology. Some, back in the 60s, were aware of the fruitfulness of a multi-faceted approach to animal behaviour (for example, Richelle & Ruwet, 1972, based on a symposium that took place in 1969 on the same site as the First European Meeting on the Experimental Analysis of Behaviour).

Neglecting ethology meant, of course, neglecting the phylogenic sources of behaviour and the evolutionary approach that is central in modern ethological thinking. The experimental behaviour analyst might have argued, however, that he was not concerned with the long history of behaviour through biological evolution but with mechanisms at work at the level of the individual organism, insofar as it is able to learn something. How will he, however, justify another, no less surprising neglect, namely development? Up to now, the index of the *Journal of the Experimental Analysis of Behavior* has no entry whatsoever for development or the related terms—growth, ontogenesis, age, etc. Little reference is made to work done by others on young animals or infants, though it might seem that everyone interested in learning should be interested in development. The impressive work of Piaget—not to speak of other European developmentally oriented psychologists such as Wallon, Rey, Zazzo—that came to influence American psychology only after a long latency period is still now almost totally ignored by behaviour analysts who leave Piaget to cognitivists.

There are, however, at least two good reasons for looking at development and more specifically at Piaget's contribution to its study. On the one hand, developmental constraints on learning might be just as important as species-specific constraints in accounting for behavioural changes in an individual organism. No one interested in learning can ignore notions such as critical or favourable periods, developmental sequences or stages, the role of early experience, imprinting in birds, and the formation of attachment in primates. On the other hand, if we look at the problems which confront us, rather than stick to the particular formulations of great theorists in both fields, developmental theory and learning theory appear to be complementary rather than antagonistic, and, on several sometimes unexpected points, convergent rather than incompatible.

Piaget's and Skinner's theories have a number of basic points in common, in spite of the fact that the great European epistemologist and the leading figure of American radical behaviourism made little or no reference to each other in all their prodigious writings. Both consider psychology as a part of biology (a view that is not, by any means, shared by all contemporary psychologists); both provide an interactionist account of behaviour; both resort to the variation–selection analogy model to explain changes in the individual organism; and both, being equally opposed to crude empiricism, view knowledge as action (for a detailed discussion of these points of convergence between the Skinnerian brand of behaviorism and Piaget's constructivism, see Richelle, 1976). Problems left unsolved by Piaget's theory, especially the transition from one stage of intellectual development to the next, can undoubtedly benefit from a methodological approach borrowed from the laboratory of behaviour analysis. Conversely, if we deal with infant or child behaviour in terms of operant, contingencies, and the like, we shall not avoid structural characterisations as described by Piaget. It has been admitted by scientists within Piaget's circle that methods from the learning laboratory are recommended in the study of developmental transitions (Inhelder, Sinclair, & Bovet, 1974). Use of the controlled and rigorous methods proposed by the experimental analysis of behaviour would provide the strongest possible test of some crucial points in Piaget's theory (Richelle, 1977). Experimental work along these lines has shown the constructivist account to be especially frail on some points (for example, the coherence of developmental stages) but to be especially strong on others (for example, the reality of developmental constraints with respect to a given operation or set of operations such as transitive reasoning [Botson & Deliege, 1975; Botson, 1976; Richelle, 1982]). Besides the intrinsic scientific interest of a synthesis between learning and development, which have been kept apart artificially by existing in different scientific traditions, the advantages of such a rapprochement are obvious in the applied field of education where the student is currently presented with two allegedly irreconcilable views which he or she is supposed to use in practice.

Let us now turn to the second statement, that experimental behaviour analysts have missed the opportunity to pioneer the study of some problems on which Skinner had clearly opened new vistas. For the sake of symmetry, I shall illustrate this by two examples: the study of language; and the study of behavioural variability and novel behaviour.

The basic proposal of *Verbal Behavior* (Skinner, 1957) that one should look at the "global episode," involving speaker, listener, and contextual events, was completely overlooked by most of Skinner's students. Replies to Chomsky's irrelevant, unfair though successful, review of Skinner's book (Chomsky, 1959) were rare and slow to come from behaviourally oriented psychologists (MacCorquodale, 1970; Catania, 1972; Richelle, 1971, 1972) and experimental work on verbal behaviour initiated by them in the early 60s was scarce, theoretically naive, and was not a serious counterweight to the claims of the nativistic and formal approaches. Skinner's project has eventually been carried out by psychologists working on children's acquisition of language, though most of them would certainly not acknowledge the affiliation. Having encountered the methodological blind alleys and the theoretical inadequacies of the Chomskyan approach to language acquisition, developmental psycholinguists have turned to a detailed analysis of the verbal and non-verbal interaction between children and adults, and of the "speech acts" in their relation to context. In the various brands of modern pragmatics, theories of enunciation, and the like, the emphasis has clearly shifted away from the formal characterisations of a child's utterances, considered as the manifestation of an innate device or "organ," as Chomsky puts it in a more than metaphorical way (Piatelli-Palmarini, 1979), to a functional account of what appears now as an essentially interactive process. The role of the immediate linguistic community, once reduced to a general stimulating input triggering the language-acquisition device to produce French rather than Spanish or Dutch, is now given extensive attention.

Though much remains to be described and understood, we know enough to reject the idea that the child is exposed to a chaotic linguistic model, composed of often ill-formed sentences filling his/her ears with little relevance to his or her present existence. On the contrary, adults addressing infants and children spontaneously resort to a typical sub-language, which is sometimes referred to as "baby talk," but that we prefer to call "language modulé" (Moreau & Richelle, 1982), characterised by a number of structural and functional features which can plausibly be considered as *implicit teaching procedures* (mécanismes implicites d'apprentissage). Functional categories of verbal utterances, related to verbal and non-verbal consequences in the social environment, have been proposed which were clearly foreshadowed, in spirit, by Skinner's account. Interestingly enough, recent work along these lines often refers to Austin, and completely ignores Skinner. This probably reflects the fact that most psycholinguists (and psychologists as well) rely on Chomsky's destructive criticisms to spare themselves the reading of *Verbal Behavior*. We leave it to the historians of psychology to clarify this point. As far as the progress of a science is concerned, it does not matter where a good problem is identified and fruitfully dealt with. It is to be welcomed if people of other persuasions are doing now exactly what Skinner had in mind, just as M. Jourdain was speaking prose without being aware of it. Indeed, the behaviourist revolution in the study of language is taking place under our eyes outside the behaviourist tradition. It would be unwise for behaviour analysts not to recognise it and not to integrate in their theoretical endeavours these contributions from outsiders.

How to account for novel behaviour, or more generally for creativity, was also an early concern for Skinner. He viewed the dynamics of behavioural change as a dialectical process involving both variations and selective action. Selective action, as translated in terms of reinforcement and contingencies of reinforcement, has been given the almost exclusive attention of experimenters at the expense of variation. There are many reasons for this, including (possibly): the technical sophistication of operant methods that induced experimenters to favour the analysis of environmental control; the intrinsic difficulty of any valid study of variability; the concern of psychologists with gaining full scientific recognition by avoiding hazardous enterprises, epistemological notions concerning the place of chance in nature, etc. This leaves us, after half a century of research, with only one half of the subject matter of behaviour analysis thoroughly explored.

The second half, the study of the role and the sources of variation, has only recently been given the attention it deserves (Staddon & Simmelhag, 1971; Segal, 1972) and even now, it often attracts theoretical, rather than experimental, contributions. Similarly, work on creative behaviour is scarce (Richelle & Botson, 1974). It is no wonder that the confusion between an operant response and stereotyped behaviour is a persistent one among outsiders and that there is a widespread reluctance to consider behaviour analysis as a valuable tool in the understanding and the conduct of human affairs. If we bring into the picture the central concept of behavioural variability and give it status equal to the concept of control by consequences (which, in any case, does not make sense if there is no variation to start with) we shall come closer to a theory of behaviour that will fit within the general framework of evolutionary thinking (Skinner, 1981), we will embrace higher-level processes and account for the apparently unlimited emergence of novel activities in the human species. This may provide us with a key to cultural evolution and some insight into the vital question it has generated, that is, "vital" in the sense of "crucial for survival": How can we bring human behaviour under the control of temporally distant consequences when immediate consequences, possibly lethal for the species, are so powerful? This is the very question to which Skinner addresses himself in the special invited lecture reproduced in this volume. It is, certainly, a deeply troublesome and distressing question, but one that can not be set aside by any student of behaviour.

These comments, which might appropriately be summed up in the phrase "Behaviour analysis as a European psychologist views it," will throw some light on the content of the present book, that, in its turn, reflects the spirit of what was intended as a European scientific event. Though not all the relevant problems and areas could possibly be covered in the limited time and space, topics were selected to be representative of those domains where dialogue with other traditions of research is both desirable and fruitful: ethology, psychopharmacology, human behaviour. Language, development, creative behaviour, etc., would have served equally well and are kept in reserve for another meeting and publication. Dialogue involves different points of view. Some contributors to the following chapters would certainly not identify themselves as belonging to the experimental analysis of behaviour tradition. In some cases, they make expert use of operant techniques in their laboratory but do not commit themselves to the theoretical tenets of behaviour analysis. In other cases, they use different techniques, resort to different concepts, but raise valuable questions which cannot be ignored.

One section is devoted to the relation between fundamental research and behaviour modification. With respect to applied analysis of behaviour, the European psychology map exhibits an interesting feature. While there are very few laboratories specialising in the experimental analysis of behaviour as such, especially on the European continent, most western European countries have very active societies of behaviour therapy or modification. To some extent, this is an encouraging situation. It is also a matter of concern, however, that such a wide expansion of application is not always grounded in the experimental and theoretical research that should be the distinctive feature of applied behaviour analysis. The permanent flow of information from researchers in the laboratory to practitioners, and vice versa, is needed if applied behaviour analysis is to develop as something different from the numerous kinds of more or less fanciful treatment methods flourishing in present-day psychology.

Behavioural research in Europe may well be far behind American research for a number of reasons: it took some time before it crossed the Atlantic; it was not always accepted in the context of dominant trends in European psychology; the behavioural approach was so often misrepresented (Richelle, 1978); and because the resources for psychological research have been (with few exceptions) very limited. In the peculiar economic situation of the 80s, and insofar as we are able to foresee the immediate future, European behaviour analysis will have difficulty catching up. This makes it all the more important that those who are engaged in behavioural research combine their efforts and exchange their ideas. As could be seen from more than 150 volunteer papers and posters presented at the Liege conference, the experimental output of European behaviour analysts is far from negligible, even if it is too often neglected, possibly because it is expressed in one of those Indo-European languages in disgrace among the international scientific community. Quantity, however, is not a crucial factor in scientific progress. A genuine European contribution to the field might be toward an integrative synthesis that would lead us beyond the artificial separation—theoretical, methodological, geographical—that has dominated mid-century psychology.

ACKNOWLEDGEMENT

The author is grateful to Fergus Lowe and Derek Blackman for their expert work in improving the grammar and the style of this chapter.

REFERENCES

Botson, C. (1976) *Analyse experimentale de l'operation concrete*. Unpublished PhD Thesis, Liege.

Botson, C. & Deliége, M. (1975) *Le développement intellectuel de l'enfant. II. Une methode d'approche; les apprentissages sans erreurs*. Brussels: Ministére de l'Education Nationale.

Breland, K. & Breland, M. (1961) The misbehavior of organisms. *American Psychologist*, **16**, 681–684.

Bunge, M. (1980) *The mind-body problems: A psychobiological approach*. Oxford: Pergamon.

Catania, A. C. (1972) Chomsky's formal analysis of natural languages: a behavioural translation. *Behaviorism*, **I**, 1–15.

Chomsky, N. (1959) Review of B. F. Skinner, Verbal Behavior. *Language*, **35**, 26–58.

Herrnstein, R. J. (1977a) The evolution of behaviorism. *American Psychologist*, **32**, 593–603.

Herrnstein, R. J. (1977b) Doing what comes naturally. A reply to Professor Skinner. *American Psychologist*, **32**, 1013–1016.

Inhelder, B., Sinclair, H., & Bovet, M. (1974) *Apprentissage et structures de la connaissance*. Paris: PUF.

MacCorquodale, K. (1970) On Chomsky's review of Skinner's Verbal Behavior. *Journal of the Experimental Analysis of Behavior*, **13**, 89–99.

Moreau, M. L. & Richelle, M. (1982) *L'acquisition du langage*. Brussels: Mardaga.

Piatelli-Palmarini, M. (Ed.) (1979) *Théories du langage, Théories de l'apprentissage*. Paris: Seuil.

Richelle, M. (1971) *L'acquisition du langage*. Brussels: Dessart-Mardaga.

Richelle, M. (1972) Analyse formelle et analyse fonctionelle du comportement verbal: note sur le débat entre Chomsky et Skinner. *Bulletin de Psychologie*, **26**, 252–259. English translation by Foster, W. S. & Rondal, J. A., *Behaviorism*, 1976, **4**, 209–221.

Richelle, M. (1976) Constructivisme et behaviorisme. *Revue Europeénne de sciences sociales et Cahiers Vilfredo Pareto*. Numero spécial Hommage à J. Piaget, **14**, 291–303.

Richelle, M. (1977) A propos d'apprentissages. *Bulletin de Psychologie*, **30**, 341–345. Numero spéciale Hommage à Piaget.

Richelle, M. (1978) *B. F. Skinner ou le Péril behavioriste*. Brussels: Mardaga. Spanish translation: *Skinner o el peligro behaviorista* (1981) Barcelona: Herder.

Richelle, M. (1982) La intelligencia humana: Reconciliacion entre desarollo y apprendisaje. In A. Morles (Ed.) *Educacion y desarollo de la Intelligencia*, Caracas: Cinterplan.

Richelle, M. & Botson, C. (1974) *Les conduites créatives—Essai d'exploration expérimentale*. Brussels: Ministère de l'Education et de la Culture Française.

Richelle, M. & Ruwet, J. C. (Eds.) (1972) *Problèmes de méthodes en psychologie comparée*. Colloque de Liège, 1969. Paris: Masson, 1972.

Segal, E. (1972) Induction and the provenance of operants. In R. M. Gilbert & J. R. Millenson (Eds.) *Reinforcement, Behavioral Analysis*, New York: Academic Press.

Skinner, B. F. (1957) *Verbal Behavior*. New York: Appleton-Century-Crofts.

Skinner, B. F. (1977) Herrnstein and the evolution of behavior. *American Psychologist*, **32**, 1006–1012.

Skinner, B. F. (1981) Selection by consequences. *Science*, **213**, 501–504.

Staddon, J. E. R. & Simmelhag, V. L. (1971) The "superstition" experiment: a reexamination of its implications for the principles of adaptive behavior. *Psychological Review*, **78**, 3–43.

2 European Roots of Behaviourism and Recent Developments

Jean-François Le Ny
Centre d'Etudes de Psychologie Cognitive, Université de Paris-sud, Orsay, France

It is not my purpose to present a historical view of European roots of behaviourism. I hope that all readers will be indulgent towards the incompleteness, the failings and the biases in the first part of my paper. In this part, I only intend to identify some conceptual views that seem to have been present in European psychology before the advent of American behaviourism, and to relate these to behaviourism itself. In the second part of my lecture, I should like to discuss some present issues in the field of scientific psychology.

BEHAVIOUR AND BEHAVIOURISM

"Behaviour" and "behaviourism" cannot be taken as unambiguous words. They need to be characterised precisely to put them into perspective.

There is no doubt that behaviourism is primarily American. Its first important public expression may be taken to be the well-known article by Watson (1913): *Psychology as a behaviorist views it*. According to Watson, the first expression of behaviourism in private conversations was around 1903.

The words "behaviour" in English, "Verhalten" in German, and "comportement" in French[1], were, however, used before. I am only able to trace back this use in French, but I think it may be of some interest.

[1]The word has been attested since 1475 in French.

The first technical use of "comportement" was made by Henri Pieron in 1907 (Pieron, 1951). He presents it as an equivalent of "behaviour" and "Verhalten" and says that the word was previously used by Blaise Pascal. I have looked for the meaning and the context of "comportement" in the *Pensées* of Blaise Pascal (1670). I found this sentence: "In order to know whether it is God who makes us move, it is much better to examine ourselves by our behaviours outside than by our motives inside." The opposition between "outside" and "inside" is undoubtedly very meaningful. Moreover, Pascal is not dealing in this text with the well-known moral problem of acts and intentions but with the problem of causality in psychological activity: Who "makes us move?"

Anyway, the word "comportement" was not very much used in French in 1907: French dictionaries published at the beginning of the 20th century say that the word was "old", i.e., almost out of use at this time. Pieron claimed to have reintroduced it into French.

Possibly the shortest characterisation of behaviour is in a sentence of Watson's *Behaviorism* (1925). Behaviour there is simply "what an organism does and says." Pieron gave a definition of behaviour as: "the way of being and doing in animal and man, objective manifestation of their global activity." I am not sure I understand what "global" means in this definition. We shall discuss this problem again.

But with more detailed definitions new problems arise. In his book *Le Behaviourisme*, André Tilquin (1942) described several trends of American behaviourism. And he wrote just after: "Beyond disagreements between schools, there is a definition upon which every behaviourist agrees: behaviour is the set of adaptive reactions, objectively observable, which an organism, as a rule equipped with a nervous system, performs as a response to stimuli, objectively observable too, coming from the environment in which it lives."

Clearly, not every behaviourist would agree with this definition, since it implies that any behaviour should be respondent. Assuming Tilquin's definition is correct, Skinner and most psychologists employing analysis of behaviour would not be behaviourists. This role of stimuli is one of the important questions settled by the notion of emitted behaviour. So I shall discard this role from the characterisation I adopt for "behaviour."

Thus, according to my characterisation, the core meaning of the word "behaviour" involves three components:

1. It is an event or a set of events that takes place in the physical world outside the organism.
2. This is brought about by an organism in an adaptive way.
3. It is publicly observable.

It follows from (1) that I should not consider as behaviour, for example, an electroencephalographic record. Such a record can provide very interesting data for psychophysiology, of course, and has several features in common with behaviour without being behaviour itself.

As a consequence of (2), I should not, and presumably nobody would, consider as behaviour the heat emitted by an organism, although this might be recorded and be useful for psychology.

The consequences of (3) are much more basic. In conjunction with (1), i.e., with the distinction between "inside" and "outside", point (3) i.e., the requirement of public observability, excludes introspection from scientific psychology. But as indicated in Watson's characterisation of behaviour as "what an organism does and *says*," the requirement of public observability leaves psychology free to observe verbal behaviour, including sentences about some internal events in a subject. Although this possibility remains open, we shall see that this has less importance than it may first seem in the choices made by several categories of psychologists.

Regarding point (3), I should like to note another possibility that turned out to be widely used: We can consider as a behaviour the fact of *not* doing something in certain circumstances, as a rule in contrast with the fact of doing something in comparable circumstances.

A LOOK AT HISTORY

I shall try to identify the main features in some important works in the early history of European psychology.

It is clear that the first steps in scientific psychology did not involve the complete notion of behaviour properly speaking. It is interesting to examine what parts of its content and which additional features were present in these early stages.

If we begin with the oldest field, psychophysics, it turns out that Weber and Fechner, and Helmholtz and Bouguer who preceded them, were interested in sensation or perception as conscious events, not in behaviour itself. Their step towards objectivity was in their attempt to establish relationships between sensation and physical stimuli. Of course, they could not measure sensation and perception itself—nobody can. They used behaviour, especially verbal behaviour, and they initiated the discovery of many behavioural methods in psychophysics. But they did not rely on a behavioural methodology. This is even more striking in the case of Wundt. In his laboratory, the first psychological laboratory in Europe, and with William James' laboratory, the first in the world, experimental methodology coexisted with the use of introspection. Although I have a liberal attitude towards attempts to describe internal states, in so far as this is done through behavioural observations, I consider that Watson was right when he later criticised the followers of Wundt because their middle way proved unfruitful, even after decades of work.

In France, the advent of scientific psychology was strongly dependent on the development of psychopathology, and mainly of neurology. The convergence of neuropathology and philosophy prevented the clear emergence of the three ideas I have mentioned. States of consciousness featured in most conceptions of this early time. I have often been surprised to see how frequently in France the debate on "scientificity" focussed, up to recent times, on quantification. This may be understood if we take into account the role of applied psychology. The construction by Binet and Simon of the first scale intended to "measure" mental development and intelligence was an important step towards an objective psychology. The notion of IQ and the use of testing without consideration of environmental conditions, however, may have impaired rather than helped the development of a true scientific psychology in France. It is amazing and amusing to see how emotional, even these days, the behaviour evoked by the word "behaviourism" is.

Historically, the most interesting substitute for the notion of "behaviour" was presumably the notion of "conduct" developed by Pierre Janet. Conduct was different from behaviour in two distinct ways. One was the way segmentation of what an organism does (or says) was conceived: "a conduct" is a much larger segment or unit than are "a response," "a reaction," or, as a rule, "an operant". As Richelle points out (Chapter 1, this volume), "an operant" could possibly be a large segment: for example, a whole lecture[2]. The notion of "behaviour" as characterised here and used by psychologists does not involve any particular way of segmentation. But behaviourism typically led to segmentation into small units. Instead, the notion of "conduct" as used by Janet[3] and several French psychologists after him involved a large segmentation. This was directly related to their assumption of "plans," a notion that was later reintroduced into American psychology by the successful book of Miller, Galanter and Pribram (1960). Nevertheless, the important disadvantage of Janet's notion of "conduct" lay in the second way it was different from behaviour, i.e., in the fact that it did not involve a sharp

---

[2]Being supposed that the reinforcing device, human or artificial, is able to tell the difference between a lecture and a long narrative or scenic monologue, a sermon, a political speech. I do not see how this could be done without resorting to some sort of topic and meaning detection, i.e., of semantic characterisation.

[3]See, for instance, Janet (1946).

distinction between the outside and the inside, nor between publicly observable and unobservable events.

I have mentioned that the clear notion of "behaviour" was reintroduced into French psychology by Henri Piéron. But in Pieron's work this notion was mostly associated with psychophysics, testing, and psychophysiology. I shall now examine the psychophysiological roots of European behaviourism, especially outside France, in connection with the work of Pavlov and his predecessor Setchenov.

BEHAVIOUR AND PHYSIOLOGY

Nobody underestimates the importance of Pavlov's work. But the man who was considered by Pavlov himself as having given the main impetus for this work is not so well known. This man was Setchenov.

The main influential work of Setchenov was published as early as 1863 under the title: *Reflexes of the brain*. But the true original title was *Attempt to ground psychological processes on a physiological basis*. This title, and for some time the publication of the book itself, was forbidden by Tsarist censorship. In the second page of the book, there is the following passage: "Psychological activity of man is expressed, as is known, by external signs, and, as a rule, everybody, the people at large as well as scientists, naturalists and those dealing with spirituality by profession, form a judgment on the first after the latter, i.e. after these external signs. But laws regarding external manifestations of psychological activity are still not well known, even by physiologists who, as we shall see, should precisely know them."

This passage seems to me particularly important for three different reasons.

First, it may be taken as giving a full characterisation of behaviour, different from the classical one, such as has been adopted in the beginning of this paper and has been historically prevalent in behaviourism. But, in my opinion, Setchenov's characterisation is acceptable.

Remember he speaks of "external manifestations," or "signs of psychological activity." This amounts to saying that one component must then be added to the three mentioned before. This component would be: (4) observable behaviour is not only brought about by an organism, as previously said in point (2), not only a manifestation of its "global" activity, as Pieron said; behaviour is brought about by a special kind of activity *inside* an organism, and is a manifestation of this internal activity.

This is, of course, a basic issue for behaviourism and for psychology in general. I elaborate this issue later.

Let us now examine the second reason why Setchenov's passage is important. I have said that the original title of Setchenov's book was: *Attempt to ground psychological processes on a physiological basis*. Ten years later, Setchenov (1873) published an article entitled: *Who must think out psychology, and how to do it*?, and he answered, in short: Psychology must be done by physiologists.

This is important because it sheds light on what Setchenov meant by "psychological activity" in the passage I previously quoted. This was not consciousness nor subjective activity but the brain's activity, to be studied in the framework of physiology.

This idea was by no means isolated at that time, and it still exists today. In the same year (1873) as this second important work of Setchenov, Wundt published his *Elements of physiological psychology*. One year later, the biological ideas of Darwin were extended to the forthcoming comparative and differential psychology in Britain by Galton (1874)[4]. In France too, the first psychological laboratory was created in 1889 at the Sorbonne by Beaunis, with Alfred Binet as codirector shortly after, was called "Laboratory of physiological psychology."

But the third important point, maybe the most important concerning Setchenov's view, was that Pavlov took it seriously. Pavlov did what Setchenov said must be done. Moreover, Pavlov did what Watson later said must be done. Pavlovian conditioning fed Watson's behaviourism with a scientific content and provided psychology with the first set of structured knowledge.

Was it behaviour? Surely. Was it behaviourism? Probably not. Was it psychology? This is what we must now examine.

Pavlov himself (1922, 1927) always called what he was studying "higher nervous activity": in fact, it was the phenomena of classical conditioning as a body of facts and the related field of facts discovered using classical conditioning as a methodological tool. Pavlov always considered that these fields applied to physiology.

In my opinion, this is a characterisation that can hardly be maintained if we use modern concepts. Pavlov cannot, of course, be considered to have studied the physiology of conditioning simply because he was a former physiologist who had obtained a Nobel prize for his work on digestive glands—even though he had to open a fistula in every dog he observed.

Pavlov was a typical psychologist who worked at two interrelated levels. First, the level of observable data, among them pure behavioural data; and

---

[4]Galton's work involved the germs of a socially conservative, and maybe racialist interpretation of Darwinism. However, Karl Marx had shortly before unsuccessfully dedicated his "Capital" (1867) to Darwin. Darwin's influence upon Setchenov, via Spencer (1855)—that is before publication of "Origin of Species"—is also a matter of fact.

second, the level of theoretical explanation, that he called physiology but which we should nowadays call an explanatory functional model.

On the first level, Pavlov only used behaviour to discover laws or relationships between determined classes of behaviour and determined classes of conditions. He was lucky or clever enough to discover many of them. Sometimes he did not recognise facts, as when he refused to admit the specificity of Miller and Konorski's second type of conditioning—simultaneously discovered by Skinner and later extensively studied by the latter. This was undoubtedly a lack of shrewdness in Pavlov's work.

On the second level, Pavlov attempted to build a general model, explanatory and not only descriptive, of the data he observed and of their relationships. He tried to make this model compatible with physiological knowledge of his time.

But he always stressed the requirement to deal with the animal organism as a whole. In doing so, he was led to think as a psychologist, not as a physiologist. This was precisely the point Watson later mentioned as distinguishing between physiology and psychology. Watson (1925) wrote: "The behaviourist is largely concerned with the central nervous system, but only as a system integrated into the body as a whole." Pavlov used a very particular behaviour, salivation. But at that time he was clearly not interested in salivation per se, but only in salivation as a manifestation of internal activity, according to Setchenov's view. Pavlov did not even work as a psychophysiologist in the modern sense, i.e., by relating data about behaviour (in determined environmental conditions) to data about observed events in the nervous system. In this respect, Pavlov was rather unsuccessful, partly because knowledge about the brain was then so poor and partly because Pavlov was not fully informed about, or attentive enough to, progress being made in the physiology of the nervous system, in particular on the neuronal structure of the brain.

I believe that the main features of the forthcoming notion of "behaviour" were already present under the guise of physiology in the philosophical work of Setchenov and that they were later actualised in the experimental and theoretical work of Pavlov, whatever we may think of certain ideas appearing in this work. The evidence of that judgement is, of course, the use Watson made of classical conditioning both in his conceptualisation and in his own experimental studies.

But, in spite of the late developments in Pavlov's work towards experimental and observational psychopathology, or the theory of "nervous types," etc., human psychology received little attention in this work.

If we try to find a proper forerunner of the later use of the behavioural approach to human psychology, we presumably have to return to Germany. I should readily consider Ebbinghaus as the author closest to modern psychology. He moved experimental psychology out of the field of

Wundt's experimental introspection and put it more firmly on the ground of observation, looking for regular relationships between observational data and objective factors. I particularly appreciate the idea of driving meaning out of the study of memory. It is my deep conviction that this was the most important thing to do a century ago, for the same reasons that the most important thing to do 15 years ago was to reintroduce meaning into the study of memory and into psychology in general. The centenary of Ebbinghaus' book *Uber das Gedächtnis* (*About Memory*) (1885) is in 1985. I hope that this will be an excellent opportunity to hear more about Ebbinghaus.

RECENT DEVELOPMENTS

I now jump to the present time, disregarding the long period during which behaviourism, methodological or radical, helped to collect so many results, and was the framework, or the matter, of so many discussions.

Two points of view may now be taken towards behaviourism: retrospective or historical, and prospective. Let us begin with a brief historical look at it to establish a firmer prospective view later.

In a retrospective judgement on behaviourism, it is necessary to treat separately questions on methodology, and even epistemology, and those on strategy.

Since methodological and epistemological questions are so important, I postpone their examination and restrict myself, at the moment, to strategic aspects.

Behaviourism has involved strategic considerations, in particular on the nature and the extent of fields open to scientific investigation. Such scientific strategy in psychology consisted of restricting oneself to fields upon which experimental or observational data could afford objective information, given the technical and conceptual tools available at a particular time. In these fields, behaviourists extensively used the principle of parsimony. Taken in this way, apart from ideological prohibitions or taboos, such restrictions may be considered as having played a favourable role in simplifying psychology. Some people can indeed say that this was oversimplification, and it was. But this may also be seen as a historical application of the third Cartesian general rule of method in which René Descartes (1628) advises us to begin research with the objects that are simplest and easiest to know, and to gradually ascend, by degrees, up to the knowledge of the most compound objects.

This latter view was exemplified when I expressed my opinion about exclusion of meaning from the study of memory by Ebbinghaus. Other relevant examples are: preference given to the study of animals over the study of man; restriction in human psychology to problems that may be solved by establishing direct relationships between environmental factors and classes of behaviour. It is also possible to put under this heading avoidance of premature theorising, as recommended by Skinner in his well-known article of 1950: "Are theories of learning necessary?" Certainly, they were not necessary.

But we can now ask two different questions. First, have the theories proposed in the past been useful? The answer to this question depends on how we appreciate the outcome of research based on this class of theories. Presumably, all of us could agree upon the outcome itself: These old theories of learning have turned out to be incorrect in their detailed forms. So, do we have to consider them as having been useless? My answer is no. This early overall failure in theoretical work about learning constituted the first time in the history of humanity that the ideas people form about themselves have had their weaknesses shown up by experimentation. To a certain extent, the fate of the standard Chomskyan theory has illustrated a second similar episode. But much particular and general knowledge has survived these theoretical failures. From this point of view, theories of learning may be considered as having been very useful, not in producing complete unrevisable knowledge, but by exemplifying the hypothetico-deductive experimental approach (construct a theory or a model, derive predictions, test with empirical data, make a—hopefully—better model) and by stimulating empirical and conceptual research and helping to grasp facts that might otherwise not even have been noticed.

My second question is: Are theories of psychology useful now? From what I have said, this question has already received a positive answer. All the more so, as long as we get rid of ideological prohibitions or taboos mentioned earlier, which are particularly unadapted to our times.

INTERNAL ACTIVITY AND STRUCTURES

Let us now examine the question of restrictions in using three notions: behaviour, internal activity and structures, and conscious experience. Later we distinguish two terms: observable and knowable.

First, what about consciousness and behaviour? Undoubtedly, modern scientific psychology has developed a strong opposition to introspection. I believe that the right point, in this respect, was to put subjective experience into the background of psychology. This was not easy since subjectivity has long been, and often still is, in the foreground. "Subjective" is a highly salient property of certain psychological phenomena, and we can see every day how difficult it is to inhibit consideration of this property, even in people familiar with various forms of scientific practice. In a sense, psychoanalysis, and common knowledge of it, are mainly based on this property via its negation, namely the unconscious.

Elaboration and use of the notion of behaviour was an important step towards scientific psychology. But another very important step forward has been taken in the last two decades: It consisted of telling apart subjective experience on the one hand and internal activity and structures on the other. This has been difficult too, maybe for the reason I just mentioned: Subjectivity might be so salient a property in considering internal activity that it can hardly be dissociated from it. Paradoxically, it appears that some behaviourists do not discriminate between internal activity or states, and subjective experience: When questioned about "internal," they respond with "private," "conscious," or "aware"—which involve several other issues.

But theoretical and practical use of "information" as an objective notion has made it much easier to cope with these ideas. We can easily understand that a computer has internal operations, an internal organisation, and can contain internal representations—if they have been put into it—without possessing any kind of subjective experience. I do not believe that this state of affairs nullifies in any way the question of human consciousness[5] or awareness. But it helps to understand that the problems regarding internal activity and structures in man (and in animals) are completely different from the problems regarding consciousness and subjectivity.

Now what, from this point of view, about internal activity and behaviour? This is a problem of behavioural methodology. Many computer scientists, even among those studying artificial intelligence, insist that they do not mind about similarities in internal activity between machine and man, and that they are only attempting to achieve an external behaviour of the machine that is similar to human behaviour. It might be argued that nothing can be learnt about internal activity in man from work with the computer. I do not believe this but we can disregard the problem here.

Another consequence of this observation could possibly be: Because a determined behaviour (for example grasping, or emitting pieces of speech) may be achieved as a result of very dissimilar sub-processes in man and in machine, how could we hope to discover knowledge about internal activity and structures from observation of behaviour? Perhaps we had better rely on neurosciences and direct observational or experimental data regarding the actual (and not the conceptual) nervous system.

From neurophysiology and more generally, from neurosciences, very detailed knowledge is now available about some internal activities of the nervous system. But little is known about higher activities. For example,

---

[5]See, *inter alia*, Hofstadter and Dennett (1982), Mandler (1983).

no well established neurophysiological model of classical conditioning is yet available. And this is even more true in the case of the highest activities, such as language, reasoning or thinking. If, as seems plausible, such particular activity as say comprehension of a given sentence involves the activation of an assembly of neurones with several million synapses whereas comprehension of a slightly different but incompatible sentence involves the activation of another assembly comprising some millions of synapses identical with the former and some millions different, then it is difficult to see how neuroscience could cope with a detailed neural description of this in the not too distant future. But this does not matter. We need a functional, rather than neural, description of the processes taking place in comprehension.

For now, we can see how neuropsychological phenomena (such as those pertaining to aphasia or to human amnesia) can hardly be related to neurophysiological data except via models of cognitive psychology, as shown in Seron's paper.

COGNITIVE PSYCHOLOGY AND BEHAVIOURISM

"Cognitive psychology" is an ambiguous expression too. In one sense, it means a domain of investigation: perception, memory, language, and thinking. Presumably, this domain may best be characterised as opposite to the general domain of affective phenomena and structures: motivations, emotions, personality, etc. The latter is usually dealt with by conventional clinical psychology. In this sense we have to consider cognitive psychology versus psychology of affectivity (Le Ny, 1982).

In another sense "cognitive psychology" has come to be understood as equivalent to "cognitivism", considered as a theoretical and methodological frame of reference. This may be because the recent strategic issue has been for psychologists: Either let us refrain from investigating such important sub-domains of psychology as semantic memory, mental image, meaning, concept formation, inferences, or let us investigate them in a cognitivistic way.

I should like to defend a view that may seem unacceptable to the most radical behaviourists (cf Blackman, 1980, 1983) but which I consider right, particularly in a European context: Cognitive psychology is the best heir of this scientific lineage of which behaviourism has been a branch.

Admittedly, a universal agreement has existed in scientific psychology on three main issues:

1. Scientific psychology can only be established upon observable data.
2. Behaviour constitutes the first class of observable data that

psychology can be established upon, the second class being present or past environmental conditions.

3. Introspection does not provide observable data, according to the criterion "public versus non-public." Verbal reports regarding internal conscious states must be treated exactly as any kind of public data.

Those agreeing with these three ideas comprise, among others, behaviourists of any school and cognitive psychologists. This is in agreement with the sentence quoted by Blackman in his paper in this book: In this respect, "we are all behaviourists now."

Looking at the progressive development of American cognitive psychology and at all these polemical controversies coming from it in the last 20 years, would these three ideas continue in the cognitivistic school, in particular as long as intuition was so highly prized in it? During the first half of this period, they did. At present, it is clear that the matter is settled.

Now, it remains to be seen to what extent the sentence: "Scientific psychology can only be established on observable data" may be understood as leading further than observable data or direct relationships between them.

Being asked this question, it seems that the radical behaviourists respond: To no extent at all. This is no longer a strategic, but an epistemological, or philosophical response.

Cognitive psychologists give their own response in three stages:

1. They assume that behaviour is caused by an internal activity taking place in accordance with internal structures that "exist", in the proper sense[6] of this term, inside an organism.

2. They consider that this internal reality is knowable.

3. They think that it is specifically psychological—or even, if they are broad-minded, "mental"—and not strictly reducible by physiology, biochemistry or any other science. This specificity refers to a level of analysis, not to a different substance.

I shall not try to completely characterise internal activity and structures here. But I should like to emphasise that, in my view, internal activity is not "covert behaviour"; it is not behaviour at all, according to my previous characterisation. Similarly, internal activity does not involve such things as "private stimuli," provided that we adopt a clear definition of what the word "stimulus" means, in the same way as for "behaviour." I consider

[6]Their modes of existence must be viewed as somewhat dissimilar: Activity is a sub-set of events whereas structures are a subset of lasting invariants. But this makes no difference as regards their reality (discussed later).

the word "private" to be ambiguous as it may be taken as referring to subjective experience, to consciousness or awareness, or merely to internal activity that must be distinguished, as already stated.

I consider that the terms "covert behaviour" and "private stimuli or events" express concepts that have unfortunately been derived by analogy from strictly observational concepts, i.e., "behaviour" and "stimuli". "Internal activity and structures" expresses a concept, or a family of concepts, that are avowedly theoretical, constructed and elaborated in connection with empirical data but not in a one-to-one relationship.

SOME ELABORATIONS

On account of some objections, it would be useful to be more precise on these points. Apparently one reason, and maybe the main reason, that makes some radical behaviourists call "behaviour" what I call "internal activity" is their wish to avoid any concept implying features such as "immaterial," "spiritual," "insubstantial," or intended for naming special substances similar to the Cartesian "thought," as opposed to "stuff." I am concerned about this too. It must be explicitly stated that "psychological activity" as used in this paper involves no such feature or content and has to be understood without any such connotation.

This is the reason why three notions were introduced previously: subjective experience, internal activity and structures, and behaviour. Subjective experience has to be put aside, as its merely phenomenal, inexpressible content is clearly not attainable by scientific investigation. In my classification, "consciousness," or "awareness," as expressible in verbal reports or, more precisely, as inferred from verbal reports, are internal activities (or states).

It stems from this that "internal activity or structures" and "behaviour" can be viewed as referring to a common category of objective realities, as opposed to strict "subjectivity." Presumably, internal activity and structures will, in the long run, be analysed in a more and more detailed way, especially in their relationships with environmental characteristics. The notion of "representation" should be a central one in this analysis. The specificity of psychological activity in man lies in its very large capacity for using representations of the world, or of various parts or properties of it, in particular when the stimuli concerned are absent. There is no room for a discussion of "representations" in this chapter, although I should like to emphasise that this word does not refer here to conscious, subjective representations but to hypothesised internal structures (having, of course, a neural substrate) viewed as existing even when not activated.

Nevertheless, even though "internal activities and structures" on the one hand and "behaviour" on the other are considered, in this view, as belonging to the general conceptual category of objective "things" or entities the distinction between them must be maintained. There are two very strong reasons for this.

The first is that "observable versus unobservable" is such an important dichotomy in science, especially in psychology. It must be neither underestimated nor overestimated, as we see later. In the present case, I believe that radical behaviourists underestimate this dichotomy, as "behaviour" is typically observable and, in my view, is nothing but observable, whereas internal psychological activity is by definition unobservable. If some neural correlate of an internal activity or state becomes observable, then we have a new basis for the analysis of psychological activities or structures into lower level entities. There is no problem with the possibility of such different levels. It has often been exemplified in other domains in the history of science. But identity, i.e., reduction of a level to a lower level is another matter. Anyway, the dichotomy between "observable" and "unobservable" remains the first epistemological basis of the distinction between "behaviour" and "internal psychological activity and structures".

The second reason why we have to maintain this distinction concerns the role of inference in psychology. It was possible to develop scientific psychology, originally, with a minimal use of inference, mainly of what may be called "one-step inferences." They were, as a rule, backward, inductive inferences, going from a class of observations, or of relationships between classes of observations, to a given concept. Their general form was: "If we observe such and such things or events, then we can subsume this under the concept A." In the history of theories of learning there have been sharp discussions over the status of these concepts: for example, as "intervening variables" or as "hypothetical constructs" (MacCorquodale & Meehl, 1948). It may be soundly argued (Skinner, 1977; Blackman, 1983) that, in determined cases—for example "association"—this status makes no difference at all in real knowledge. But this question is confused if consideration of conscious experience is mixed with inferences drawn from behaviour, as is done in Skinner's text.

Let us take a simple example of one step inference in analysis of behaviour. Suppose we consider the sentence: (1) "If a given class of behaviour B is, in determined conditions C, followed by a stimulus E, and if we observe that the frequency of B increases, then E is 'a reinforcer'."

This sentence describes the necessary and sufficient conditions under which we can call any stimulus E_i "a reinforcer," irrespective of the many differences that may exist among the various Es, if only they have the common functional property described in (1). This is, of course, a conceptual assignation of the term and of the concept "reinforcer" to a particular stimulus event E_i. This is what I call a one-step inference. A more commonplace example is: (2) "If a car collides with another car, then this is 'an accident'." (For a more detailed experimental analysis, see Le Ny, Carfantan & Verstiggel, 1982).

What I am claiming here is that it has been possible for psychologists to restrict themselves for many years to such a mode of reasoning by one-step inferences. This mode of reasoning was intended to comply, and actually complied, as a rule, with the principle of parsimony.

But this is not always the case. It may be considered that "covert behaviour" also involves a one-step or one-attribute change of meaning. This notion is explicitly intended to mean: events that are in every respect similar to behaviour, except that they are "covert", i.e. unobservable. What evidence can be provided that such events exist? In this case, parsimony is only apparent. The work of Skinner on verbal and social behaviour provides many such cases. It shows that it is rather difficult to stick to short inferences.

What I am also claiming is that it is no longer possible or fruitful to restrict psychology to such a mode of reasoning. We must accept many-step reasoning and be careful that every step is made explicit. This is a historical point of view. It comes down to: No matter how scientific psychologists have previously considered their own concepts—which may have been actually more similar than they seemed to be—the present state of the research requires another mode of reasoning. This is typically expressed in the statement: (3) "If H1, H2, . . . and Hn are true, and if a subject S is set in appropriate environmental conditions C, then we must logically predict observation of the behaviour B."[7]

In this statement, H1, H2, . . . , Hn stands for a set of interrelated hypotheses. First, we can construct a one-step hypothesis as H1: "Correct use of the word 'tiger' implies that the subject has in his or her head the meaning of 'tiger'." I have, for the present, no counter-objection to such a would-be objection as "to say that the subject has the meaning of 'tiger' tells nothing more than: He is able to use 'tiger' properly in his verbal behaviour". And I have, of course, no objection either to: "If he is able to use 'tiger' properly, it is, *inter alia*, because he has been steadily approved, or understood, whenever he used this word properly, and disapproved, or misunderstood, or laughed at, whenever he used it improperly."

Similarly, we can construct another one-step hypothesis as H2: "Emission of the word 'tiger' by a subject implies activation of the motor causes of the word 'tiger,' the so called response (or operant) 'tiger'." The same remarks made regarding H1 are also true in this case.

Things become very different if we want to introduce more distant inferences, in particular relational ones. These are of the type: $H_k = R(H_i, H_j)$. In plain language, such a hypothesis concerns a relationship between

---

[7]B can of course stand for: a determined value, or range of values, of a variable characterising a given behaviour.

two hypotheses. The best case we can choose is a case in which the relationship is supposed to take in a hypothesised process P_i and a hypothesised representation Z_j. As an example of this, it might be assumed that, during comprehension of a sentence containing the word "tiger," H3: "The meaning of 'tiger' is activated." In this simple example, a process P_i—activation—is supposed to apply to a representational structure Z_j—word meaning. This type of relational hypothesis may be used several times, or recursively, i.e., relational hypotheses may take in lower level relational hypotheses, as in: "Speed of a given word meaning activation depends on the semantic relatedness of this word meaning with the core of the previous sentence's meaning."

I shall not elaborate this mode of reasoning, but restrict myself to three remarks. First, it is possible to derive precise behavioural predictions from such hypotheses and to state rules permitting, under appropriate conditions, an evaluation of their plausibility. Second, such hypotheses must be formulated only in so far as precise behavioural predictions can be derived from them. Third, I do not see how it could be possible to deal with these new domains in psychology without such a use of interrelated many-step hypotheses.

I am, of course, prepared to give in to experimental evidence on this matter as for others. But a clear reason to use the approach outlined above is that every human complex activity, and consequently all complex behaviour, must involve a large number of interrelated sub-processes and structures. This compels psychologists to elaborate explicit sets of hypotheses, organised in general or specific models. If so, fruitful use of minimal hypotheses and of one-step inferences is presumably a thing of the past.

This view may itself be considered as a metahypothesis to be submitted to the sanction of future psychological research. In behavioristic form, this meta-hypothesis comes to: (4) "Suppose that psychologists whose research behaviour is in accordance with the mode of reasoning described above turn out to be more successful—in particular as regards complex human activity—than psychologists whose research behaviour is based upon one-step inferences, or radical behaviourism; then the former behaviour would increase, and the latter would extinguish." So, the structure of the world, as regards behaviour and causes of behaviour, could possibly be a source of reinforcement for cognitivistic research behaviour rather than for radical behaviourism.

CONCEPTS AND REALITY

Now, I should like to give a brief answer to an important question asked by Richelle (Chapter I) on previous formulations of mine: (5) "If internal activity[8] is a notion, or a concept, and if internal activity is viewed as a cause of behaviour, how can a concept be a cause of behaviour?''

The answer requires use of more types of quotation mark than used up to now. It may be written that 'internal activity' (with single quotation marks) is a concept, of which ''internal activity'' (with double quotation marks) is the verbal expression, and of which internal activity (without quotation marks) is supposed to be the real referent. It is internal activity that is supposed to cause the subject's behaviour, and to exist in the subject's head. But it is the concept 'internal activity' that is in the psychologist's head, if he uses a cognitivistic point of view, and it is this concept that he expresses in using the words ''internal activity'' in his behaviour.

Now, what about ''to exist''? Consider the following: 'Pencil' is a concept, of which ''pencil'' is the verbal expression (name), and of which any pencil is a real referent; pencils really exist. When I say: ''Movements of my pencil (instrumentally) cause this written manuscript,'' it is the pencil that I infer (by a short inference) to really cause the manuscript. It is 'pencil' that I use in my head, and it is ''pencil'' that I use in my discourse.

Of course, most people accept as warranted the real existence of pencils because it is close to observation, whereas the existence of such or such type of psychological activity, or the existence of psychological activity as a whole, as viewed by cognitive psychology, is far from observation, and is thus uneasy to warrant. I should like to emphasise the following: The type of existence internal activity is hypothetically accredited is the same as for pencils, that is, real existence.

About internal activity, we have at our disposal another source of knowledge, because more and more results are now collected from neurosciences. But, as already stated, mapping complex human activities and structures on to corresponding neural activities and structures is only possible if psychology is able to identify cognitive processes and organisation from a functional point of view.

OBSERVABLE AND KNOWABLE

Let us now get to the last point: Internal activity and structures are actually ''knowable'' (in a non-introspective way). This is the point on which I believe that the opposition between ''observable'' and ''unobservable'' must not be overestimated.

''Unobservable'' must not be confused with ''unknowable''. This seems a general principle of contemporary science. In this respect, the epistemological status of cognitive activity and structure is not different from, say, structure and processes in a molecule, an atom, an atomic nucleus, or the

[8]For the sake of brevity, I neglect ''and structures'' in this passage.

whole universe. For example, scientific progress has only recently made it possible to observe directly photographs of some crystals' structure. It turned out that this structure could be, in these cases, perfectly mapped on to the previously calculated structure of these crystals. But in other cases indirect knowledge remains superior to observational knowledge. Fields in which knowledge must be entirely constructed, that is judged as true from remote observational data, are many in the physical and chemical sciences. I do not see why the situation should be judged to be different in psychology.

Consider the field of language. A number of observations can be made about speech, hearing, or emitting verbal behaviour. Many regularities can be discovered from behavioural, phonological, or distributional data in language. But one question cannot be escaped: the question of meaning. Moreover, in spite of all attempts to dodge the issue—and I have read very many such attempts indeed—a conclusion cannot be escaped either: Meaning must somehow be in people's heads. Maybe (this is my thesis) it is *really* nowhere else.

Can we come to know of meaning from introspection? Clearly not. If we ask ourselves: "What is going on when we understand the sentence: 'There is a cat in the hall of this building'?" no introspective report can tell us what exactly is going on. Introspection can only tell the hearer, at best, that he *has understood* the sentence.

This does not amount to saying that nothing can be substantiated by philosophical or linguistic reflexive analysis of meaning. But the very new situation in the history of thought and science is that, for the first time now and presumably more in the future, important knowledge can be extracted from experimental study about what meaning is and about how it is generated or used in comprehension and production of discourse.

Similar judgements can be held about image, reasoning, perception, etc, and similarly about all those mental disorders that involve content and beliefs.

In brief, contemporary experimental study necessarily involves experimentation and observation of behaviour or of behavioural productions. But this approach is fundamentally different from psychology conceived as a science *of* behaviour. It requires elaboration of complex models and use of behavioural observations as a means of testing them in detail, as theoretical and experimental physics or chemistry do in their own fields.

Surely, this approach, when used in psychology, implies taking risks on the epistemological, methodological and conceptual levels. Words such as "meaning," "representation," or "processing" carry true risks of misinterpretation, of misconceptions, or of vagueness. This approach also requires us to take a number of precautions. The general principle is to keep the notions tied as closely as possible to behaviour and observation.

But I do not see why psychology cannot take both risks and precautions to open new fields to scientific investigation. The notion of behaviour is now firm enough to make possible such an opening, by which psychology will be able to substantially extend its domain.

ACKNOWLEDGEMENT

I am very grateful to D. E. Blackman, A. C. Catania, and M. Richelle for their comments on a first draft of this paper and to C. M. Bradshaw for a careful revision of it.

REFERENCES

Blackman, D. E. (1980) Images of man in contemporary behaviourism: In A. J. Chapman & D. W. Jones (Eds.), *Models of man*. Leicester: The British Psychological Society. 99–112.

Blackman, D. E. (1983) On cognitive theories of animal learning: Extrapolations from humans to animals. In G. C. L. Davey (Ed.), *Animal models of human behavior*. New York: Wiley. 37–50.

Descartes, R. (1628) *Regulae ad directionem ingenii*. Paris; (1701) Amsterdam.

Ebbinghaus, H. (1885) *Ueber das gedächtniss*. Berlin.

Galton, F. (1874) *English men of science, their nature and nurture*. London.

Hofstadter, D. R. & Dennett, D. C. (1982) *The Mind's I*. Harmondsworth: Penguin Books.

Janet, P. (1946) Autobiographie, *Etudes philosophiques*, 80–92.

Le Ny, J. F. (1982) Psychologie cognitive et psychologie de l'affectivité: In P. Fraisse (Ed.), *Psychologie de demain*. Paris: Presses Universitaires de France. 97–118.

Le Ny, J. F., Carfantan, M., & Verstiggel, J. C. (1982) Accessibility from working memory and role of reprocessing in sentence comprehension: In J. F. Le Ny & W. Kintsch (Eds.), *Language and comprehension*. Amsterdam: North-Holland. 112–134.

MacCorquodale, K. & Meehl, P. E. (1948) On a distinction between hypothetical constructs and intervening variables. *Psychological Review*, **55**, 95–107.

Mandler, G. (1984) *Mind and body:* Psychology of emotion and stress. New York: Norton.

Marx, K. (1867) *Das kapital*, **1**.

Miller, G. A., Galanter, E., & Pribram, K. H. (1960) *Plans and the structure of behavior*. New York: Holt.

Pascal, B. (1670) *Pensées*. Port-Royal.

Pavlov, I. (1922) (in Russian), *Twenty years of experiments in the field of higher nervous activity in animals*. Moscow.

Pavlov, I. (1927) *Conditioned reflexes*. Oxford: Oxford University Press.

Pieron, H. (1951) *Vocabulaire de la psychologie*. Paris: Presses Universitaires de France.

Setchenov, I. (1863) (in Russian), Reflexes of the brain. Moscow. Translated into French in I. Setchenov (1957). *Oeuvres philosophiques et psychologiques choisies*. Moscow: Editions en langues étrangères. 29–136.

Setchenov, I. (1873) (in Russian), Who must think out psychology, and how to do it, Moscow. Translated into French in I. Setchenov (1957). *Oeuvres philosophiques et psychologiques choisies*. Moscow: Editions en langues étrangères. 176–260.

Skinner, B. F. (1950) Are theories of learning necessary? *Psychological Review*, **57**, 193–216.

Skinner, B. F. (1977) Why I am not a cognitive psychologist. *Behaviorism*, **5**, 1–10.

Spencer, H. (1855) *Principles of psychology*. London.
Tilquin, A. (1942) *Le behaviourisme*. Paris: Vrin.
Watson, J. B. (1913) Psychology as a behaviorist views it, *Psychological Review*.
Watson, J. B. (1925) *Behaviorism*. New York: Norton.
Wundt, W. (1873) *Grundzüge der physiologischen psychologie*. Leipzig.

3 The Evolution of Behaviour[1]

B. F. Skinner
Harvard University, Cambridge, Mass., U.S.A.

Evolutionary theorists not only point to the survival value of the present structure and function of an organism, they try to reconstruct earlier stages which should also have had survival value. An example of current interest is the flight of birds. Feathers may have evolved first as thermal insulation, but what about wings? Were they adaptations of forelimbs which first helped animals run faster or that helped tree animals leap from branch to branch or branch to ground? (Even when a feature first evolved because of consequences quite different from those which explain its current survival value, a plausible early history is still needed.) Among the features to be explained in this way is behaviour. The current survival value of reflexes and the released patterns of behaviour studied by ethologists may be clear, but can we construct plausible sequences through which they could have evolved, with survival value at every stage?

The first behaviour was presumably simple movement—like that of the amoeba reaching out into new territory and hence increasing its chances of finding materials necessary for its survival. To account for behaviour a plausible second step was sensing, as the result of which movement could take the organism away from harmful stimuli and closer to useful materials.

---

[1]This paper was read at the First European Meeting on the Experimental Analysis of Behaviour, Liège, Belgium, August 1983. Reprints may be obtained from B. F. Skinner, Department of Psychology and Social Relations, Harvard University, 740 William James Hall, 33 Kirkland Street, Cambridge, MA 02138.

Previously published in the *Journal of the Experimental Analysis of Behavior*, March, 1984.

The assignment of different organs to sensing and moving should have led to the evolution of connecting structures, and eventually to tropisms and reflexes.

The released behaviour patterns studied by ethologists also presumably evolved through increasingly complex stages. It is unlikely that many current instances occurred first in their present state as variations which were then selected by survival. In my paper "The Shaping of Phylogenic Behavior" (Skinner, 1975), I suggested that well-established geological changes could have supplied some of the necessary sequences of contingencies. It would not be hard to teach a fish to jump from a lower level to a higher one. One could reinforce swimming across an underwater barrier, slowly raise the barrier until it reached the surface, and then raise it so that it became the wall of a second tank. As the levels of water slowly separated, the fish would jump with greater and greater force. Something of the same sort, over a very different time span, may have happened if the shallow, gravelled bottom of a river in which salmon breed moved upstream as the river changed and as rapids and falls intervened between the gravelled bottom and the ocean.

A different geological change has been suggested (Carr, 1966) to explain the behaviour of the turtles which feed along the coast of Brazil but swim more than a thousand miles to Ascension Island where they breed. Apparently they once swam to nearer islands which have disappeared. As a third example I cited the behaviour of the Atlantic eel, which travels from either American or European rivers to a breeding ground near the Sargasso Sea. These long journeys are taken only once, and it is quite unlikely that they could have occurred first in their present form as variations. Before North America and Europe separated, however, the distances must have been very short. The present behaviour could have evolved as each generation went at most a few centimetres farther than the preceding.

Like most evolutionary theories these are speculations, but they appeal to known geological changes which could have provided the conditions under which complex innate behaviour was shaped. So far as I know, ethologists have not given much attention to plausible histories of this sort. Some, indeed, have questioned whether reproduction with variation can explain complex behaviour without appeal to mental processes. There is a heron, for example, that fishes by touching the surface of the water with a feather and seizing the fish that rises to this simulation of an insect. Does the heron not show some of the thought processes of the human angler? But the journey of the eel from the Nile River to the Sargasso Sea, a quarter of the way around the earth, is a much more complex example of innate behaviour and is much harder to explain in "cognitive" terms. Anyone who has seen a slip of a plant grow into a complete plant with flowers and fruit, an achievement also hard to attribute to mental life, will have no difficulty in accepting the role of natural selection in the origin of behaviour, no matter how complex.

Social behaviour raises a special problem, as two interrelated but different kinds of behaviour appear to evolve together. If bees returning to the hive dance in ways used by other bees in finding sources of food, what could have been the survival value of the dance before the response of the other bees had evolved, and how could it have evolved before returning bees danced? We must assume that returning bees behaved in ways related to the location of food for other reasons. A bee that had come a long way might show fatigue, a bee coming in a particular direction might make circular phototropic movements, and so on. Once the responses of other bees to these stimuli had evolved, further refinements could occur.

BEHAVIOURAL PROCESSES: IMITATION AND MODELLING

The evolution of the processes through which behaviour changes also needs to be explained. An early example must have been imitation. A structural definition (behaving as another organism is behaving) will not suffice; the dog chasing the rabbit is not imitating the rabbit. Phylogenic imitation could be defined as behaving as another organism is behaving for no identifiable environmental reason. But some other reason may first have been necessary. Consider a group of grazing animals subject to frequent predation. They all exhibit a strong tendency to run, in response not only to predation but to stimuli correlated with predators. An example of the latter should have been the sudden running of one or more other members of the group, already responding to the predator. At that stage the behaviour would not be imitation; it would be released by either of two stimuli—the sight of a predator or the sight of another animal suddenly running. But a variation as a result of which one organism imitated another would then have had survival value as redundant support. As the process developed, the imitative model could take full control, and the imitator would then simply do what another animal was doing and for no other reason.

Once imitation has evolved, contingencies of selection exist which should produce *modelling*. A young bird will eventually fly by itself, but if it flies sooner when parent birds fly, and if early flying has survival value, then parental modelling should evolve, the parent birds flying often and in particularly conspicuous ways that are easily imitated.

RESPONDENT CONDITIONING

As evolved processes through which behaviour changes during the lifetime of the individual, imitation and modelling prepare the individual only for behaviour that has already been acquired by the organisms that model it. Other processes have evolved which bring the individual under the control of environments to which the individual alone is exposed. One is respondent (Pavlovian or classical) conditioning. Under what conditions could it have evolved?

Let us consider Pavlov's classical example: A bell frequently followed by the delivery of food eventually begins to elicit salivation. The unconditioned salivation is an evolved reflex. The commonest stimuli are substances in the mouth, but in a stable environment salivation to the mere appearance of a particular food should also have evolved, as seizing and eating the food evolved to the same stimuli. The contingencies would favour a stronger response to taste, however. Respondent conditioning could have begun as a variation which made the visible features of food slightly more likely to elicit salivation. Saliva would then have been secreted in response to the sight of food, both as a weak reflex arising from natural selection and as a conditioned reflex. The conditioned version could take over in response to a stimulus (e.g., a bell) which had no effect due to natural selection.

Salivation does not suggest strong survival value, and the argument is more convincing for sweating and the acceleration in pulse rate associated with vigorous action. An evolved tendency to fight or run away at the sight of a predator could be accompanied by an evolved tendency to sweat and increase the pulse rate, but there would be more sweating and a more rapid pulse during the actual flight or attack. If early sweating and an increased pulse rate helped in preparing for effective flight or attack, variations leading to the process of respondent conditioning would have had survival value.

In these examples, respondent conditioning is explained as a supplementary increase in the strength of reflexes which have not fully evolved. The explanation is supported by certain features of respondent conditioning that are often overlooked. The Pavlovian conditioned reflex has no survival value unless it is followed by the unconditioned. Although one can demonstrate that salivation is eventually elicited by a bell, there is no advantage to the organism unless food follows. Similarly, an inclination to sweat or increase heart rate in response to the appearance of a predator also has no value unless vigorous action follows.

The scope of respondent conditioning is much broader than its role in the conditioned reflex. Releasers, studied by ethologists, are conditioned in more or less the same way, and imprinting is at least similar. There is obvious survival value in the behaviour of a young duckling as it follows its mother. The features of the releasing object could have been sharply defined, but a lesser demand is placed on the genes if following is released by any large moving object. In the world of the duckling that object is almost always the mother. The looser specification suffices, because it is a consistent feature of the natural environment. The imprinting is a kind of statistical confirmation of a less than specific genetic instruction.

OPERANT CONDITIONING

A different explanation is needed for operant conditioning. Under what conditions could the smallest possible variation contribute to the evolution of the process? Innate behaviour has consequences which are ultimately related to survival. The hand is withdrawn from a painful stimulus, presumably because the painful stimulus is potentially damaging; the response promotes survival by preventing damage. Any slight change as the result of which subsequent damage would be more quickly terminated should have had survival value, and operant conditioning through negative reinforcement would be such a change. The operant response would be an exact duplicate of the phylogenic response, and the strengthening consequence would be the same, contributing to the survival of the individual and hence of the species through both natural selection and an evolved susceptibility to reinforcement by a reduction in painful stimuli.

A similar argument can be made for positive reinforcement. If eating a particular kind of food has had survival value (such as that which explains the behaviour of eating the food), an increased tendency to eat because the taste of the food has become a reinforcer should have had survival value. Both the topography of the behaviour and the immediate consequence (ingestion of a particular food) would be the same, but the consequence would have two effects—one related to natural selection and the other to an evolved susceptibility to operant reinforcement by a particular taste. Once the process of operant conditioning had evolved, topographies of behaviour with less and less resemblance to phylogenic behaviour could have been affected, and eventually behaviour could have emerged in novel environments which were not stable enough to support it through natural selection.

Two other stages in the evolution of operant behaviour need to be considered. Once the process existed, a susceptibility to reinforcement by new forms of stimulation could have evolved. It would have been supplemented by a new role for respondent conditioning—the conditioning of reinforcers. Stimuli which frequently precede unconditioned reinforcers could begin to have reinforcing effects in both respondent and operant conditioning.

A second stage may have been the evolution of unconditioned behaviour having no survival value of its own but available for selection through operant reinforcement. It would enable the individual to develop a much wider repertoire of behaviour appropriate to novel environments. The human infant shows a large repertoire of uncommitted behaviour.

Many current contingencies of reinforcement resemble contingencies of survival. We behave in a given way both because we are members of a given species and because we live in a world in which certain contingencies of reinforcement prevail. Thus, we avoid going over a cliff, we dodge objects, we imitate others, we struggle against restraint, we turn toward a movement seen out of the corner of an eye—and all for two kinds of reasons; contingencies of survival and contingencies of reinforcement. It would be hard to say how much of the strength of the behaviour is due to each. Only a first instance can be said to be necessarily innate, and first instances are hard to spot. An example of current interest is aggression. We may have an innate repertoire of aggressive behaviour, but similar behaviour is generated by many contingencies of reinforcement. It does not matter whether a given instance is phylogenic or ontogenic unless we are concerned with doing something about it. When we are, the variables to be changed must be identified.

In the human species operant conditioning has very largely replaced natural selection. A long infancy gives the ontogenic process greater scope, and its role in adapting to very unstable environments is a great advantage. Nevertheless, the process is not untouched by environmental changes. As I have pointed out (1966), the human susceptibilities to reinforcement by sweet and salt, sexual contact, and signs of aggressive damage may once have had much greater survival values than they have now. Technological advances in the production, storage, and distribution of foodstuffs, in the control of famine and pestilence, and in the improvement of weapons may have made these susceptibilities more likely to be lethal.

Just as very complex innate behaviour has led to an appeal to cognitive processes, so it is often argued that operant conditioning cannot account for complex learned behaviour. Animals as well as people are said to transcend the shaping and maintenance of behaviour by contingencies of reinforcement and to show insight, the development of concepts, and other cognitive processes. Such claims are vulnerable to demonstrations that operant conditioning will suffice. Robert Epstein, Robert Lanza, and I (1980, 1981), Epstein and I (1981), and Lanza, Star, and I (1982) have recently simulated a variety of complex cognitive processes in pigeons. Not only can such behaviour be explained by pointing to fortuitous contingencies of reinforcement, it can be produced by arranging the necessary contingencies.

It has also been said (by Thorndike, for example) that things reinforce because of the way they feel, but certainly the reinforcing effect must have evolved first. Only when that had happened would things have been felt as, and called, pleasing and satisfying. Perhaps we should speak of feelings only when what is felt is reinforcing. If we pull our hand away from a hot plate simply as a reflex, the reduction in painful stimulation plays no current role. Perhaps it is only because the behaviour is reinforced by the same reduction that we say that the stimulation hurts. The same may be true of positive reinforcers. Insects copulating simply as phylogenic behaviour may not be "enjoying themselves."

The conditions under which operant conditioning evolved are helpful in understanding its nature. Selection did not need to respect how a bit of behaviour produced a consequence; any immediate consequence would have sufficed. Immediacy was essential for other reasons. Deferred reinforcers have a more powerful effect upon intervening behaviour, and behaviour must be in progress if it is to be changed by a consequence. The claim that behaviour is affected by a general melioration, optimisation, or maximisation of a reinforcing condition conflicts with these principles, and the evidence should be re-examined—to make sure, for example, that gaps between behaviour and deferred consequences are not bridged by conditioned reinforcers.

A concept of optimisation is like the concept of health. The healing of a wound restores a normal condition of the body and the normal condition favours survival. But healing does not occur because it promotes survival; it occurs because certain structures in the individual have evolved because they have promoted survival. Similarly, in a hungry organism an operant is reinforced by the receipt of food. The food reduces a state of hunger and contributes to the survival of the individual and species. But the operant does not occur because it reduces hunger; it occurs because certain behavioral processes have evolved when a reduction in hunger has contributed to the survival of the species. Behaviour is not reinforced by the melioration, optimisation, or maximisation of anything. It is reinforced through evolved processes, to the ultimate effects of which those terms refer.

THE EVOLUTION OF CULTURAL PRACTICES

Operant imitation requires no new evolved process. When organisms are behaving because of prevailing contingencies of reinforcement, similar behaviour in another organism is likely to be reinforced by the same contingencies. A general conditioned tendency to behave as others behave supplements phylogenic imitation. Operant modelling then follows: When the behaviour of another person is important, modelling is reinforced when the other person imitates.

Imitation and modelling play important roles in transmitting the results of exceptional contingencies of reinforcement. Some of the great human achievements were due to extraordinarily lucky accidents, and other people came under the control of the same fortuitous contingencies through imitation. The behaviour was even more rapidly transmitted by modelling. The human species made further progress in the transmission of what had already been learned when its vocal apparatus came under operant control.

A culture may be defined as the contingencies of social reinforcement maintained by a group. As such it evolves in its own way, as new cultural practices, however they arise, contribute to the survival of the group and are perpetuated because they do so. The evolution of cultures is of no further relevance here because no new behavioural processes are involved.

REFERENCES

Carr, A. (1966) Adaptive aspects of the scheduled travel of *Chelonia*. In *Animal orientation and navigation*. Corvallis: Oregon State University Press.

Epstein, R., Lanza, R. P., & Skinner, B. F. (1980) Symbolic communication between two pigeons (*Columba livia domestica*). *Science*, **207**, 543–545.

Epstein, R., Lanza, R. P., & Skinner, B. F. (1981) "Self-awareness" in the pigeon. *Science*, **212**, 695–696.

Epstein, R. & Skinner, B. F. (1981) The spontaneous use of memoranda by pigeons. *Behaviour Analysis Letters*, **1**, 241–246.

Lanza, R. P., Starr, J., & Skinner, B. F. (1982) "Lying" in the pigeon. *Journal of the Experimental Analysis of Behavior*, **38**, 201–203.

Skinner, B. F. (1966) Contingencies of reinforcement in the design of a culture. *Behavioral Science*, **11**, 159–166. Also published in: Skinner, B. F. (1978) *Reflections on behaviorism and society*. Englewood Cliffs, N.J.: Prentice Hall.

Skinner, B. F. (1975) The shaping of phylogenic behavior. *Acta Neurobiologiae Experimentalis*, **35**, 409–415. Also published as: Skinner, B. F. (1968) The environmental solution, in *Contingencies of reinforcement*. New York: Appleton-Century-Crofts.

II BEHAVIOURIST AND ETHOLOGICAL APPROACHES: COMPLEMENTARY OR ANTAGONISTIC?

4 Operant Psychology and Ethology: Failures and Successes in Interdisciplinary Interaction

S. E. G. Lea
University of Exeter, Devon

It is always unwise for a mere practitioner in a subject to attempt to comment on its history; even more unwise for someone who has the status of a visiting amateur from another discipline. Caricature seems to be the inevitable result. A standing joke among academics is the undergraduate essay that begins, "Learning was first studied by Pavlov," or, alternatively, "Learning was well known to the ancients." But in introducing this section of the book, I feel bound to comment at least briefly on the history of the relation between operant psychology and ethology. If there is something of caricature in the result, at least I can claim whatever modest degree of pardon is afforded to those who confess their sins before committing them.

Not so very long ago, we should have thought in terms of two totally distinct and largely opposed ways of studying the behaviour of animals. There was "learning theory," a mainly American creation, committed to a radical empiricism, working in artificial, laboratory situations, with a restricted range of species and a rigorous scientific/statistical methodology, unmistakably a part of the wider social science of psychology and claiming to be fundamental to it. And there was "instinct theory," mainly coming from Europe, firmly committed to the heritability of behaviour, studying animals in their natural conditions or as near them as could be managed, claiming the entire animal kingdom as its sphere of study, utterly dependent on the skill and persistence of expert observers, and vigorously claiming its place as a part of zoology. The opposition between these two schools was felt by their members. Lorenz records his disgust at the lack of anything he could recognise as "expertise" among the comparative psychologists of the 1930s: Learning theorists perceived ethological phenomena such as the properties of innate releasing mechanisms as nothing but the effects of known psychological processes such as stimulus generalisation.

The opposition between these two disciplines had its uses. Confrontation sharpens wits and attracts attention. Besides, psychologists of other persuasions wielded "instinct theory" to good effect as a weapon against the unhealthy pre-eminence of learning theory within psychology: How could an approach to animal behaviour that ignored the Lorenzians claim to be valid, let alone to predict human behaviour? For a while ethology even became part of the fashionable radical's armoury—though having served its turn in dethroning "ratology," it soon dropped as far out of favour among the non-psychological public as the Skinnerism to which it was opposed.

Unfortunately, confrontation all too easily also leads to the participants digging themselves in to entrenched positions. It is the great good fortune of everyone who studies animal behaviour that this has not happened in the case of ethology and operant psychology. From the isolation of the past, we have moved to a situation where almost any psychology course will pay at least a nodding reference to ethology, and an increasing number of researchers trained in a more or less classical psychological tradition have come to incorporate ethological methods and insights into their work. It is as a result of this increasing broadmindedness on the psychological side, that, in rather more recent years, some ethologists and (especially) behavioural ecologists have started to recognise that the huge collections of data that operant psychologists have made, albeit on a few species in a few highly artificial situations, are relevant to their own concerns; and that operant techniques, and operant vocabulary, may be applicable well beyond laboratory conditions and laboratory species.

How has this fortunate situation come about? To understand that, we need to look at the specific ways in which ethology and operant psychology have interacted over the past 20 years; and, almost as important, the ways in which they have not interacted. I shall argue that in each case of successful interaction, one discipline has turned out to contain elements that corresponded to the most progressive developments in the other. Failed interactions, on the other hand, have involved mere graftings of randomly chosen branches from one discipline to the other; failures to interact occur where any interaction would in fact take that form. Let us look at some examples of all three. As a psychologist, I have chosen to mention the abuses committed by psychologists, but doubtless ethologists could find their own.

FAILED INTERACTIONS

Consider first the most notorious kind of failed interaction—for historical reasons, let us refer to it as the "porcupine experiment." The conscientious but unimaginative graduate student in comparative psychology takes some well-known psychological phenomenon, and goes away to investigate whether it occurs in porcupines. With a little more time (but no more imagination), our student may well run a control group of rats, so as to be able to make a quantitative comparison between the two species. We could all think of examples of this kind of thing, and it would be invidious to single out any particular one, so I shall leave the references to your imagination. Our knowledge of either psychology or ethology is not advanced one whit by this kind of experiment. Even our knowledge of porcupines does not get very much further forward. The reasons are stated very clearly by Bitterman (1965). Whether the porcupines and rats behave the same or differently, we do not know whether that is because they are fundamentally the same (or different) or because of a lucky, or unlucky, choice of experimental procedures or parameters, which cannot be made equivalent for the two species since we do not know what such equivalence would mean. As Bitterman (1975) stresses, even identical results from two species might spring from quite different underlying mechanisms which a single, isolated experiment is powerless to discover.

This is not to say that operant psychologists ought to continue confining their attention to rats and pigeons. There is everything to be said for a systematic exploration of a few well-chosen learning capacities in a more representative range of animals, in the manner of Bitterman's early work, or the extension of detailed analysis to a few well-chosen species, as in his more recent studies of honey-bee learning (Couvillon & Bitterman, 1980, 1982). But Bitterman's work stands in an older tradition of comparative psychology, and cannot really be claimed as part of the operant school. Furthermore, even his work has not yet achieved much in the way of real integration with a more biological approach to the study of behaviour, perhaps because of an apparently cavalier approach to taxonomy in its early days: What could a biologist, aware of the 20,000 different known species of fish, make of a paper called "Probability-matching in the fish" (Behrend & Bitterman, 1961)?

Another failed interaction is the case where, surrounding a classic porcupine experiment, we find an introduction and discussion purporting to relate the differences between rats and porcupines to their taxonomic status or ecological niche. This is usually meaningless. The two species concerned are too separate, both ecologically and taxonomically, for us to ascribe any differences in their behaviour to any particular one of the thousands of evolutionary differences between them (cf. Gould & Lewontin, 1979). Furthermore, at least the rats used will probably be laboratory strains with a hundred or so generations of artificial and natural selection for laboratory conditions separating them from their true niche and their true relatives.

There is nothing original in criticising porcupine papers, but they do still turn up. Anyone who has a reputation among journal editors as a psychologist with biological interests will get them to review with depressing regularity. But let us turn from failed interactions to the rather different class of simple failures to interact.

FAILURES TO INTERACT

One of the points ethologists made against comparative psychology, during the era of confrontation, was that learning theorists restricted themselves to a few apparently rather inefficient forms of learning. Nothing that psychology has discovered about habituation, or classical conditioning, or operant conditioning, prepares us for the way in which a digger wasp finds its nest unerringly using landmarks it has seen for only 9 seconds, or a day-old duckling learns the characteristics of the first moving, noisy object it sees, or a Manx shearwater finds its way back to its burrow after being removed to the wrong side of the Atlantic, or a marsh wren learns over a hundred different songs, or a rat becomes "bait-shy" after a poisoning attempt, or a three-year-old human child adds words to his or her vocabulary.

I am not saying that all these learning phenomena are necessarily inconsistent with conventional learning theory. But the most fervent advocates of comparative and operant psychology could not seriously claim that any of them would have been discovered without a very substantial nudge from ethology, simply because the prominence of these kinds of learning comes from their importance in the animal's adaptation to its physical or social environment. Furthermore, even though Tinbergen (1951) called attention to the anomalies over 30 years ago, many of these biologically important kinds of learning remain outside the scope of learning psychology. Although there are many psychologists who now work on imprinting, attempts (e.g., Hoffman & Ratner, 1973) to integrate it into our general understanding of animal learning are still controversial. There are plenty of psychologists working on language acquisition, but most of their work ignores conditioning theory. (The exception, of course, is some of the "ape language" research; but though that has been successful in attracting scientific and public interest, it is questionable how much it has yet contributed to a comparative analysis of language.)

The one special kind of learning that might be counted as involving a successful interaction between ethology and psychology is taste aversion learning, now firmly established as one of the standard ways of studying learning in the laboratory (though in this case one might question how much enduring interest there is from the ethological side). In my view, there is a clear reason why there has been some degree of successful interaction in this one case. Taste aversion learning involves the subject focussing on the novel aspect of the mixture of flavours that comprises the "dangerous" food; that is to say, it is at least as much a problem in stimulus selectivity as in long-delay learning. It thus responded to one of the progressive aspects of learning theory at the time it appeared. The origins of the still continuing interest in stimulus selection in Pavlovian conditioning, the observation of the "blocking effect" by Kamin (1969) and the theoretical account of it given by Rescorla and Wagner (1972), lie close in time to the first report in the psychological literature of long-delay taste avoidance learning (Garcia & Koelling, 1966). The phenomenon was of course known to ethologists long before (Chitty, 1954). It is easy to see how this stimulus selection aspect of taste aversion dominated early discussions of it (McFarland, 1973).

The starkest failure to interact concerns current work in Pavlovian conditioning. This is one of the liveliest areas in animal psychology now. But apart from some use of taste aversion learning (generally stripped of its original ecological concerns), it totally lacks ethological or comparative interest, or, one is tempted to say, ecological validity. Entire issues of journals (e.g., Volume 34B, Part 2, of the *Quarterly Journal of Experimental Psychology*), and entire and excellent books (e.g., Dickinson, 1980), have been devoted to analytic work on classical conditioning, without including a single citation of an ethological paper, or anything that I might want to encourage my ethological friends to read. Only Hollis (1982) and Rashotte, O'Connell and Beidler (1982) have tried to bring all this to bear on current ecological issues.

Why this continued isolationism on the part of some of the cleverest people working on learning now? The optimistic answer is that we really are now getting to grips with the abstract mechanisms of learning, or at least of classical conditioning, so that it really does not matter what species or what response system we use to study them. The pessimistic answer is the same, but sounds different: The study of classical conditioning has now become so abstract that it is irrelevant to the actual behaviour of any actual species. The true answer, it seems, is that there is simply nothing in current ethology that corresponds to the growth points in modern classical conditioning theory and nothing in modern classical conditioning theory that corresponds to the growth points in ethology. It is as hard to prove this as any other negative, of course. But can anyone disprove it for me by pointing to the interaction that ought to be taking place but is not?

SUCCESSFUL INTERACTIONS

I will give four examples of situations where I think there has been a more fruitful encounter between psychology and ethology.

The first, historically, was the introduction into psychology of ethogrammatic analysis—and, at a simpler level, the sheer idea of becoming expert in your animal's behaviour and just watching it. This way of doing things has revolutionised the study of, for example, deprivation effects (Shettleworth, 1975) and adjunctive behaviour (Roper, 1978). Even a small amount of looking into the Skinner box enabled Barrera (1974) to make a decisive contribution to the "autoshaping" debate. My argument is that ethograms succeeded in psychology because they corresponded to a growing interest within psychology in measuring more than a single behaviour. We can see this in the development of the technology of "multiple response baselines" in studies in human operant psychology (Bernstein & Ebbesen, 1978; Findley, 1966) and applied behaviour analysis (Winkler, 1971), which were right outside the sphere of ethological influence.

A second successful interaction is the use of niche considerations in the study of spatial learning. This has not produced a literature explosion in the same way as the next examples, but it has produced some very elegant research. The work of Kamil and his collaborators (Kamil, 1978; Kamil, Jones, Pietrewicz & Mauldin, 1977) on win-stay/lose-shift strategies in the learning of corvids and nectarivores must, in my estimation, stand as one of the most fruitful introductions of biological ideas into the study of learning; and it is leading on to some powerful general ideas about the biology of learning (Kamil & Yoerg, 1982). Once again, I see the same general pattern: Spatial learning became a growth point within animal psychology with the behavioural work of Olton and Samuelson (1976) and the physiological work of O'Keefe (1976), and Kamil was able to find an ecological key to unlock some of its problems.

A third successful interaction is, of course, the area of foraging theory. There is no need to expound this example in detail; I have already done so several times (Lea, 1979, 1981, 1982), the 1983 Harvard Symposium on the Quantitative Analysis of Behavior was wholly devoted to it, and Shettleworth (1984) provides an up-to-date summary. But let me again draw out my main theme. Psychologists were beginning to think about optimising models (Staddon, 1979) and economic analyses (Rachlin, Green, Kagel &

Battalio, 1976; Lea, 1978) before the current stream of psychological papers about optimal foraging began. Furthermore, behavioural ecologists had begun to use operant techniques (Krebs, Kacelnik & Taylor, 1978) before they realised that that was what they were doing. Here the evidence is clear that functional analysis needed experimental analysis and vice versa. Each discipline was in a position to contribute something that corresponded to the growth points in the other.

My final example is more in the way of a hope and a belief than a confirmed success story. Over the past 8 years, the "sociobiological revolution" has swept across ethology in true Kuhnian fashion, and most of us who work on animal behaviour have been caught up in it, either as proponents or opponents. Its most exciting recent twist has been the growth of interest in cultural evolution as a supplement, complement, or alternative to genetic evolution. The basic ideas were there in the final chapters of Dawkins' (1976) original popularisation of sociobiology, and they have received added impetus from Pulliam and Dunford's (1980) popular treatment. It is not the idea of cultural evolution that is new, of course: Evolutionary biologists have always given it some consideration (Dobzhansky, 1955, pp338–341); Darwin (1890) quotes Lyell (1863) for the parallels between the evolution of species and the evolution of languages. From Darwin's time to the present, anthropologists have tried to adapt evolutionary ideas to the comparison of cultures (e.g., Murdock, 1965, Chapter 9). What is new is that cultural evolution is now the growth point of evolutionary thinking within biology. According to the historical generalisation that I have been developing in this chapter, therefore, the time is ripe for a successful interdisciplinary interaction. Furthermore, to discuss cultural evolution requires a theory of learning.

Will learning psychologists be able to grasp the opportunity this gives us? I see one reason for pessimism and one for optimism. Pessimistically, I have to point out that most theories of cultural evolution rely on learning by observation and imitation. Of all kinds of learning, this is the one that psychologists have most consistently ignored: Of the major learning theorists, only Bandura (1977) has taken it really seriously, and we cannot claim him as a comparative psychologist, still less an experimental analyst of behaviour. But optimistically, we must remember the strain within the experimental analysis of behaviour which has always asked about the relative survival of cultures. I am no great advocate of treating Skinner's writings as some kind of holy writ to which those working in operant psychology should keep returning. But perhaps the time has now come to blow the dust off Skinner (1969, chapter 2), and, in the hope of another successful interaction with the biological approach, consider what operant psychology has to say about the evolution of cultures.

REFERENCES

Bandura, A. (1977) *Social learning theory*. Englewood Cliffs, NJ: Prentice-Hall.

Barrera, F. J. (1974) Centrifugal selection of signal-directed pecking. *Journal of the Experimental Analysis of Behavior*, **22**, 341–355.

Behrend, E. R. & Bitterman, M. E. (1961) Probability-matching in the fish. *American Journal of Psychology*, **74**, 542–551.

Bernstein, D. J. & Ebbesen, E. B. (1978) Reinforcement and substitution in humans: a multiple-response analysis. *Journal of the Experimental Analysis of Behavior*, **30**, 243–253.

Bitterman, M. E. (1965) Phyletic differences in learning. *American Psychologist*, **20**, 396–410.

Bitterman, M. E. (1975) The comparative analysis of learning. *Science*, **188**, 699–709.

Chitty, D. (1954) *Control of rats and mice* (Volume 1). Oxford: Clarendon.

Couvillon, P. A. & Bitterman, M. E. (1980) Compound conditioning in honeybees. *Journal of Comparative and Physiological Pscyhology*, **94**, 878–885.

Couvillon, P. A. & Bitterman, M. E. (1982) Some phenomena of associative learning in honeybees. *Journal of Comparative and Physiological Psychology*, **96**, 192–199.

Darwin, C. (1890) *The descent of man* (2nd edn.). London: Murray.

Dawkins, R. (1976) *The selfish gene*. Oxford: Oxford University Press.

Dickinson, A. (1980) *Contemporary animal learning theory*. Cambridge: Cambridge University Press.

Dobzhansky, T. (1955) *Evolution, genetics and man*. New York: Wiley.

Findley, J. D. (1966) Programmed environments for the experimental analysis of human behavior. In W. K. Honig (Ed.), *Operant Behavior* New York: Appleton-Century-Crofts, pp. 827–848.

Garcia, J. & Koelling, R. A. (1966). Relation of cue to consequence in avoidance learning. *Psychonomic Science*, 123–124.

Gould, S. J. & Lewontin, R. C. (1979) The spandrels of San Marco and the Panglossian paradigm: a critique of the adaptationist programme. *Proceedings of the Royal Society, Series B*, **205**, 581–598.

Hoffman, H. S. & Ratner, A. M. (1973) A reinforcement model of imprinting: implications for socialization in monkeys and men. *Psychological Review*, **80**, 527–544.

Hollis, K. L. (1982) Pavlovian conditioning of signal-centered action patterns and autonomic behavior: A biological analysis of function. In J. S. Rosenblatt, R. A. Hinde, C. Beer & M. C. Busnel (Eds.), *Advances in the study of behavior* (Volume 12). New York: Academic Press.

Kamil, A. C. (1978) Systematic foraging by a nectar-feeding bird, the amakihi (*Loxops virens*). *Journal of Comparative and Physiological Psychology*, **92**, 388–396.

Kamil, A. C., Jones, T. B., Pietrewicz, A. T., & Mauldin, J. E. (1977) Positive transfer from successive reversal training to learning set in blue jays (*Cyanocitta cristata*). *Journal of Comparative and Physiological Psychology*, **91**, 79–86.

Kamil, A. C. & Yoerg, S. I. (1982) Learning and foraging behavior. In P. P. G. Bateson & P. Klopfer (Eds.), *Perspectives in ethology* (Volume 5). New York: Plenum.

Kamin, L. J. (1969). Predictability, surprise, attention and conditioning. In B. A. Campbell & R. M. Church (Eds.). *Punishment and aversive behavior*. New York: Appleton-Century-Crofts, pp. 279–296.

Krebs, J. R., Kacelnik, A., & Taylor, P. (1978) Test of optimal sampling by foraging great tits. *Nature*, **275**, 27–31.

Lea, S. E. G. (1978) The psychology and economics of demand. *Psychological Bulletin*, **85**, 441–466.

Lea, S. E. G. (1979) Foraging and reinforcement schedules in the pigeon: optimal and non-optimal aspects of choice. *Animal Behaviour*, **27**, 875–886.

Lea, S. E. G. (1981) Correlation and contiguity in foraging theory. In P. Harzem & M. D. Zeiler (Eds.), *Advances in analysis of behaviour* (*Volume 2: Predictability, correlation and contiguity*). Chichester: Wiley, pp. 355–406.

Lea, S. E. G. (1982) The mechanism of optimality in foraging. In M. L. Commons, R. J. Herrnstein & H. Rachlin (Eds.), *Quantitative analyses of behavior* (Volume 2). Cambridge, MA: Ballinger, pp. 169–188.

Lyell, C. (1863) *The geological evidences of the antiquity of man*. London: Murray.

McFarland, D. J. (1973) Stimulus relevance and homeostasis. In R. A. Hinde & J. Stevenson-Hinde (Eds.), *Constraints on learning*. London: Academic Press, pp. 141–155.

Murdock, G. P. (1965) *Culture and society*. Pittsburgh, PA: Pittsburgh University Press.

O'Keefe, J. (1976) Place units in the hippocampus of the freely moving rat. *Experimental Neurology*, **51**, 78–109.

Olton, D. S. & Samuelson, R. J. (1976) Rememberance of places passed: spatial memory in rats. *Journal of Experimental Psychology: Animal Behavior Processes*, **2**, 97–116.

Pulliam, H. R. & Dunford, C. (1980) *Programmed to learn*. New York: Columbia University Press.

Rachlin, H., Green, L., Kagel, J. H., & Battalio, R. C. (1976) Economic demand theory and psychological studies of choice. In G. H. Bower (Ed.), *The psychology of learning and motivation* (Volume 10). New York: Academic Press, pp. 129–154.

Rashotte, M. E., O'Connell, J. M., & Beidler, D. L. (1982) Associative influence on the foraging behavior of pigeons (*Columba livia*). *Journal of Experimental Psychology: Animal Behavior Processes*, **8**, 142–153.

Rescorla, R. A. & Wagner, A. R. (1972) A theory of classical conditioning: variations in the effectiveness of reinforcement and non-reinforcement. In A. H. Black & W. F. Prokasy (Eds.), *Classical conditioning II: Current research and theory*. New York: Appleton-Century-Crofts, pp. 64–99.

Roper, T. J. (1978) Diversity and substitutability of adjunctive activities under fixed-interval schedules of food reinforcement. *Journal of the Experimental Analysis of Behavior*, **30**, 83–96.

Shettleworth, S. J. (1975) Reinforcement and the organization of behavior in golden hamsters: Hunger, environment and food reinforcement. *Journal of Experimental Psychology: Animal Behavior Processes*, **1**, 56–87.

Shettleworth, S. J. (1984) Learning and behavioural ecology. In J. R. Krebs & N. B. Davies (Eds.), *Behavioural Ecology* (2nd edn.). Oxford: Blackwell, pp. 170–194.

Skinner, B. F. (1969) *Contingencies of reinforcement*. New York: Appleton-Century-Crofts.

Staddon, J. E. R. (1979) Operant behavior as adaptation to constraint. *Journal of Experimental Psychology: Animal Behavior Processes*, **108**, 48–67.

Tinbergen, N. (1951) *The study of instinct*. New York: Oxford University Press.

Winkler, R. C. (1971) The relevance of economic theory and technology to token reinforcement systems. *Behaviour Research and Therapy*, **9**, 81–88.

5 The Peck of the Pigeon: Free for All

Juan D. Delius
Experimentelle Tierpsychologie, Psychologisches Institut, Ruhr-Universität, D4630 Bochum, F.R.G.

There seem to be four discernible areas of conflict between behaviourism, especially the experimental analysis variety, and other scientific schools of behavioural studies. I would like to discuss these briefly before introducing some factual information that hopefully will illustrate how I conceive a free-for-all analysis of behaviour. It is inevitable that I shall need to set up straw men to deal with these initial generalities. The diversity of standpoints among individual representatives of the various traditions is great and has doubtlessly increased recently. An eclectic attitude, for which I shall be pleading, seems to be spreading. Gradations rather than divisions of opinion are the rule. Schools of thought are no longer as monolithic as they once were. Other branches of the natural sciences appear to have gone through a similar dissolution of factions as the volume of positive knowledge they could command increased.

One of the areas of conflict has to do with the range of behaviours that the various schools study. I consider that for an ambitious general account of behaviour, the "experimental analysis" school of behaviourism studies a too restricted range of phenomena. We have been told that a botanising of behaviour is not needed but it would seem that this can no longer be taken for granted. What is, for example, the experimental behaviour analysis account of the sexual behaviour of the female rat or the singing behaviour of song birds? One should in principle be able to deduce from lever-pressing rats and key-pecking pigeons, but can one? The account offered by behavioural endocrinologists for the first case and by neuroethologists for the second is likely to be closer to the truth by any definition than one behaviourists could offer. It might be argued that the demand is unfair but consider even such a classical experimental analysis item as concurrent schedule responding for food. I am not sure if the account offered by behavioural ecologists is not by now similarly superior. At the very least, the optimal foraging based approach has made the schedule literature a lot less arid than it used to be.

The next area of conflict is one that has gradually receded into history but at one time it caused much acrimony between ethologists and behaviourists. It is the age old nature versus nurture dispute where even only a decade or two ago one could still take a theoretical stand one way or another without being appreciably constrained by facts. Meanwhile the field of behaviour ontogeny has been flooded by evidence that supports an interactionist mode of behaviour development, and more fundamentally of neural development. The plurality and complexity of the interactions between genetic and environmental factors that have been revealed meantime dwarf all the conceptions that classical ethologists and behaviourists had about the ontogeny of behaviour. This new position also agrees well with the theoretical reasoning that derives from first principles of molecular biology. Together they constitute a knowledge network that cannot any longer be reasonably ignored, not even by psychologists.

More recently the dispute between behaviourism and ethology has shifted to the issue of the adaptedness of learning versus the general laws of learning. I hope that nobody doubts that the neural structures and processes that are the basis of the learning phenomena we study are the product of the historical process that started several billion years ago with the emergence of the first replicating molecules. Learning phenomena have repeatedly been shown to be critically dependent on the modern versions of these molecules, the genes. Biological evolution thus cannot be ignored when discussing conditioning. It is also an undeniable fact that we know a great deal about the processes underlying biological evolution. For example, it inherently tends towards fitness maximisation. There are no reasonable grounds for believing that learning is exempt from the consequences of this principle. It follows that the ways different organisms learn must on the whole match the ecological demands that they face.

That does not contravene the assumption that there are general principles underlying learning. For one thing we apply the term "learning" to a set of phenomena that exhibit certain similarities. It is likely that only a restricted set of causal processes is capable of yielding phenomena that fit this particular semantic category. Also, all animals whose learning we study live on the same macrohabitat, Earth, and that makes for evolutionary convergence. Not least, all species very probably have a common ancestry which together with phylogenetic inertia, another inherent trait of evolution, makes for similarities.

A fourth area of dispute is not concerned primarily with ethology. Rather the conflict is with both cognitive behaviourism and physiological psychology. It stems from a tradition among behaviourists that studiously, if not stubbornly, avoids getting too involved with the processes within the organism that intervene between stimuli and responses. But a full account of behaviour must obviously include a description of these processes. Two approaches have proven eminently viable in studying intervening processes, among other areas in biology and engineering: inferential deduction from input–output analysis and direct-access identification and measurement. I see modern cognitive psychology doing the first, and behavioural neuroscience doing the second, and both as having accumulated a large amount of firm complementary knowledge. One can no longer reasonably ignore that the nervous system with its associated systems transduces, transmits, processes, and, particularly, stores and reproduces information in the course of behaviour production. The ways in which it does so incontrovertibly affect the relationships between stimuli and responses that behaviourists are interested in.

Summarising after a fashion, an ideally complete account of any behaviour has to include descriptions of its phylogeny, its ontogeny, and its physiogeny. The latter term is a neologism introduced here to replace the more common but cumbersome formulations "short-term causation" or "physiology in the wider sense" with which the triad is usually completed. These three elements of such a "complete" account are, however, hierarchically dependent simply because any behaviour we look at is necessarily the historical end-product of its phylogeny, ontogeny and physiogeny in that order. An account of the ontogeny of an organism's behaviour must square up with the evolutionary past of that organism. Similarly the description of the physiogeny of a behaviour must be in agreement with its developmental history. Behaviour is a biological phenomenon and the central fact of biology is evolution. Any "true" theory about behaviour must in a certain way always be a subset of evolutionary theory.

Rather than continuing with abstract assertions I now present a summary of some research on the behaviour of the pigeon (*Columba livia*), a classical subject of both the behaviourist and the ethological traditions. Our work has, however, been conducted with no particular regard for either position. It is motivated by an eclectic curiosity, a desire to "understand" the behavioural phenomena at hand, and is conceived as a contribution towards some future, all-embracing biology of the pigeon (Abs, 1983). It should demonstrate that an interdisciplinary approach can be enlightening, or if not that, entertaining.

CONSTRAINTS ON A DISCRIMINATION

First I deal with an issue that has already been touched upon. It concerns the fact that a given stimulus class is often effective in controlling responses in certain conditioning situations but not in others. I came upon this problem in a rather oblique way in connection with a neurophysiological experiment I was involved with while spending a year at the department of neurosciences at the University of California, San Diego. Anne Biederman-Thorson was recording the activity of single neurones in the main telencephalic auditory projection of birds, the so-called area L of the neostriatum caudale (Biederman-Thorson, 1970). In ring doves (*Streptopelia risoria*) she occasionally found neurones that appeared to respond specifically to particular species-specific vocalisations. As one test for specificity she played the tape recording of the relevant dove calls backwards and found, disappointingly, that the neurones were often also activated by these stimuli, thus making it doubtful whether they really were call-specific detectors. But we had to be certain that ring doves could behaviourally distinguish between forward and backward species-typical vocalisations.

We set up a successive instrumental discrimination experiment in which forward and backward played "bow-coo" calls were the conditional cues for the ring doves to peck either the right or the left key of a Skinner-box for food reward. In spite of extensive training and various methodological improvements the ring doves did not learn the discrimination that, to the human ear at least, seemed easy enough. About the same time Krasnegor (1971) had, in spite of an even more intensive and expert application of behavioural technology, found that pigeons would not discriminate two temporal tone patterns in an instrumental food reinforced situation. If I remember correctly my conclusions and those of Krasnegor's supervisor (William Hodos) regarding these analogous negative results differed markedly at the time. While Hodos was inclined to believe that these birds were fundamentally incapable of such discriminations I, based on admittedly weak collateral ethological evidence, was convinced that both doves and pigeons could distinguish between forward and backward auditory patterns but that the conditioning procedures that we had used were not adequate to demonstrate this.

On return to the department of psychology at Durham, England, I requested the cooperation of Roger Tarpy, a visiting fellow. His summary opinion was that recalcitrant conditioning debilities were always best resolved by the use of aversive reinforcers! And indeed, within a few days he had pigeons discriminating tones differing in pitch by only small frequency differences using an aversive classical heart rate differentiation procedure. I took over his method and quickly accumulated data showing that pigeons have indeed no difficulty discriminating between the same tone pattern played forward and backward (Delius & Tarpy, 1974). Subsequently, evidence was obtained that a proportion of avian area L neurones are also capable of the corresponding discriminations (Leppelsack, 1978).

When, however, my collaborator Jacky Emmerton attempted to apply the apparently so efficient Tarpy method to the psychophysical measurement of the wavelength discrimination function of pigeons (Emmerton & Delius, 1980) she obtained results that seemed to indicate that pigeons were colour-blind! Of course they are not, as is well known from many appetitive instrumental key-pecking hue discrimination experiments. On the contrary, pigeons have exceptionally sophisticated colour vision capabilities (Emmerton, 1983b). In a formal experiment we then confirmed these asymmetric stimulus control results. The same pigeons were trained to discriminate both two different colours and two different tones, each in an appetitive conditional successive instrumental discrimination paradigm and an aversive classical successive heart rate–differentiation procedure. The results showed that the colours came to control the key pecking in the appetitive instrumental paradigm but not the heart rate in the aversive classical procedure and that the tones yielded control of tachycardia in the aversive classical but not of key pecking in the appetitive instrumental procedure (Fig. 5.1, Delius & Emmerton 1978).

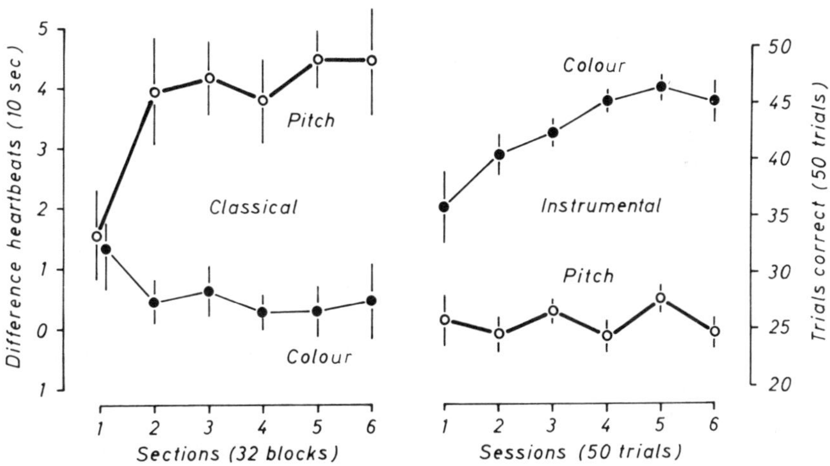

FIG. 5.1. Mean learning curves of pigeons on different tasks. The same subjects (N = 4) had to discriminate two diffuse lights differing in hue and two tones differing in pitch. In an instrumental, food-reinforced, successive conditional key pecking paradigm the pigeons easily discriminated the lights but not the tones. In a classical, shock-reinforced heart-rate conditioning paradigm they easily discriminated the tones but not the lights (Delius & Emmerton, 1978).

Taking into account other evidence (LoLordo & Furrow, 1976) showing that the relative control exerted by the light or the tone component of a compound stimulus in an instrumental treadle pressing conditioning situation switched according to whether food delivery or shock avoidance was used as a reinforcer, we surmised that the important factor for the asymmetry observed in our experiment was the aversive (shock)–appetitive (food) disparity. Also, a survey of the literature indicated that what auditory psychophysical investigations demanding fine discriminations had been done using pigeons, had almost exclusively used shock reinforcement. On the other hand, research on colour vision of pigeons as already remarked, had almost exclusively employed food reinforcement. That the classical cardiac conditioning per se is not responsible for the absence of colour discrimination was established in a recent heart rate–conditioning experiment employing an appetitive unconditional stimulus (water) (UCS) (Klinkenberg, Delius & Emmerton, 1984). Colours yielded good stimulus control, provided that the water reinforcement yielded a cardioacclerative unconditional response (UCR), which in some birds it did not.

We interpreted these stimulus-reinforcement compatibilities-incompatibilities in terms of a constraint of learning of phylogenetic origin. In the normal environment of pigeons, sounds are unlikely predictors of food (grains are mostly silent) whereas tones are likely predictors of pain (predators are often noisy). Pigeons with only two millilitres of brain, compared with, for example, humans with 1200 ml, are bound to be too short of neuronal structures to be able to relate and store all the possible associations between the multitude of events they can perceive. It is inevitable that natural selection will apportion such memory space as is available to the registration of contingencies that are particularly conducive to fitness promotion. Thus bird species that feed on noisy prey should differ from pigeons in auditory-alimentary conditionability and indeed in at least one instance we know that it is so. Barn owls (*Tyto alba*) are exceedingly proficient at learning fine auditory discriminations with food reward (Konishi, 1973, & personal communication).

An incidental observation, auditory evoked potentials recorded from the frontal forebrain of a pigeon, made during an electrophysiological study of the somatosensory forebrain projections of pigeons (Delius & Benetto, 1972), eventually somewhat upset our conception. When we recently reinvestigated these potentials, we found that they originated from the nucleus basalis telencephali or its immediate neighbourhood, and had a very short latency (5–8 msec, Fig. 5.2) as compared with the latencies of auditory potentials in the more orthodox acoustic projection in area L (12–14 msec, Delius, Runge & Oeckinghaus, 1979). This was already known (Naumov & Iljitschew, 1964) but it had been disregarded by later authors because of their inability at that time to find an anatomical correlate, an auditory

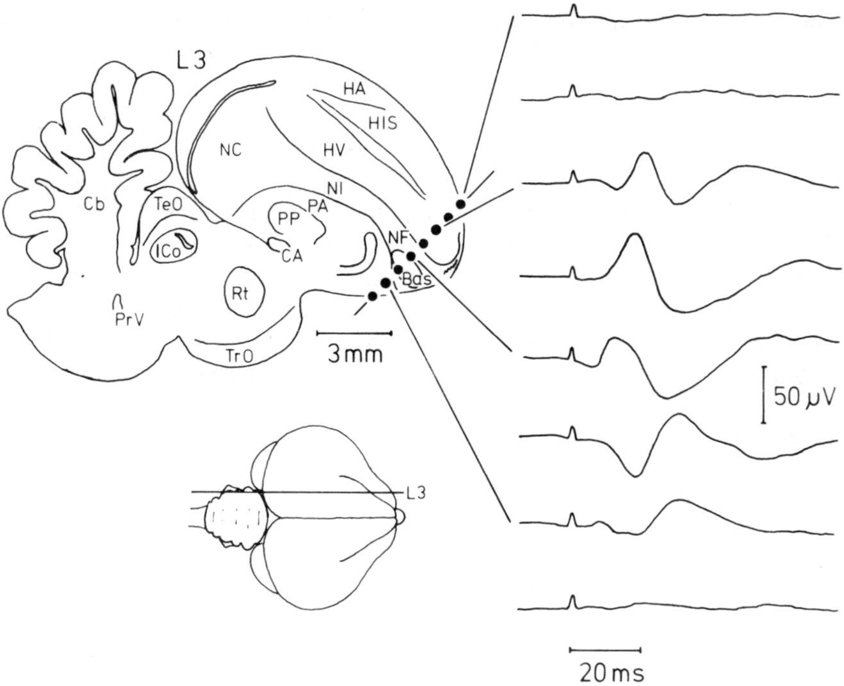

FIG. 5.2. Averaged auditory evoked potentials from the nucleus basalis of the pigeon. The anterior forebrain of anaesthetised pigeons was explored with a bipolar recording electrode for electroencephalographic responses to a click-tone. Short latency potentials were recorded in the neighbourhood of the nucleus basalis (Bas). Other abbreviations: Cb cerebellum, CA commissura anterior, HA hyperstriatum accessorium, HIS h. intercalatus superior, HV h. ventrale; ICO nucleus intercollicularis, NC neostriatum caudale, NI n. intermedium, NF n. frontale, PA paleostriatum augmentatum, PP p. primitivum, PrV nucleus principalis nervus quintus, Rt n. rotundus, TeO tectum opticum, TrO tractus opticus. (Modified from Delius, Runge, & Oeckinghas, 1979).

pathway to the nucleus basalis (Karten, 1968). This nucleus, which is an avian speciality, was only known to receive fast somatosensory afferences from the beak and face via the trigeminal nerve and the quinto-frontal tract with a synaptic relay in the medulla (Wallenberg 1903; Witkowsky, Zeigler & Silver, 1973). The auditory pathway reaching the basalis, we now know (Kirsch, personal communication; Schall, Güntürkün & Delius, 1985), has its origin in the nucleus of the lateral lemniscus, which itself receives direct input from the medular auditory nuclei (Karten, 1968).

The nucleus basalis has been implicated in the motivational/motor control of feeding in birds (Zeigler, 1976). It is at the head of a descending neural pathway consisting of the tractus fronto-archistriaticus that reaches the archistriatum mediale (as well as the overlying neostriatum caudale) and the tractus occipito-mesencephalicus that from thence reaches various diencephalic, mesencephalic, and rhombencephalic structures (Fig. 5.3). The evidence for the involvement of the nucleus basalis in feeding behaviour stems from comparative studies showing that bird species with complex feeding behaviour have a large basalis complex (Stingelin, 1962), from a study in which lesions of the nucleus itself and structures of its efferent pathway affect food intake (Zeigler, Green & Karten, 1969; Levine & Zeigler, 1981) even though some of this evidence is in dispute (Martin Ramirez, 1979), and from a study in which electrical stimulation of the nucleus basalis and neighbouring structures yielded feeding related behaviour in herring gulls (*Larus argentatus*, Delius, 1971). We shall be commenting upon the role of the nucleus basalis later in this paper.

The fact that auditory information reaches a forebrain "centre" implicated in the control of feeding with an exceptionally short conduction-time

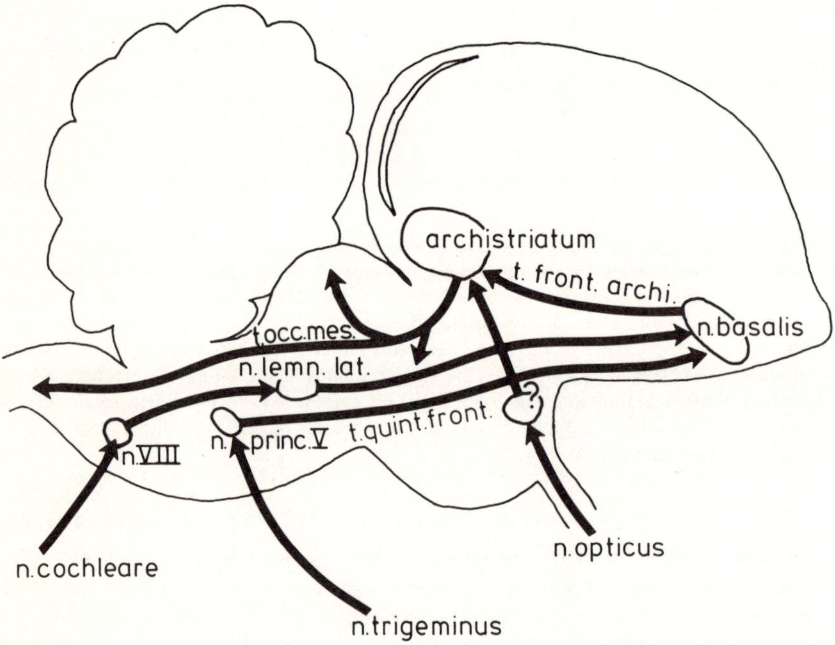

FIG. 5.3. Neural structures related to the nucleus basalis. Somatosensory afferences from the beak (trigeminal nerve) reach the nucleus basalis via the quintofrontal tract after synaptic relay in the principal sensory nucleus of the trigeminal (fifth) nerve. Auditory afferences (cochlear nerve) reach the nucleus basalis after relays in the medular nuclei of the eighth nerve and the nucleus of the lateral lemniscus. Efferences of the nucleus basalis reach the anterodorsal archistriatum via the frontoarchistriatal tract. This area also receives visual input via the optic nerve through an unidentified relay nucleus. The occipito-mesencephalic tract that originates the archistriatum descends to various di-, mes-, and rhombencephalic structures and also reaches the upper spinal levels.

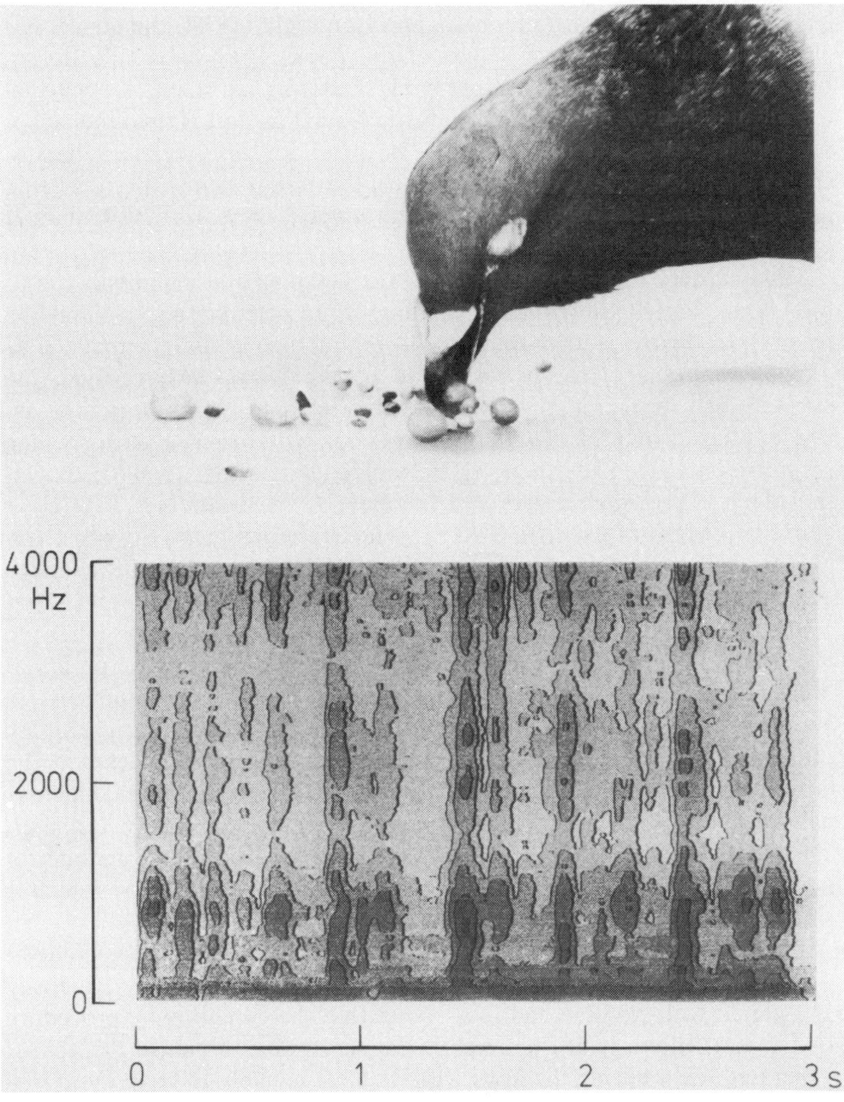

FIG. 5.4. Sonogram of noise produced by a pigeon as it pecked for grains among grit. Note that pigeons close their eyes in the terminal phases of pecking (courtesy of H. J. Jahnke).

clearly runs counter to our earlier argument that sounds are not important for feeding in pigeons. A brief reconsideration reveals that, though grains are silent by themselves, they generate a good deal of noise when they are pecked at. Figure 5.4 shows a sonogram of sounds recorded while a pigeon pecked at a heap of grains and sand. Notice that, as already described for key-pecking by Hodos, Leibowitz, and Bonbright (1976), the animal has closed its eye in the final stages of the peck. They habitually do so, presumably as protection against back-scattering particles. A peck that reaches its target yields massive acoustic feedback. Part of this feedback is mediated by bone-conducted sound. The avian skull is especially suited for such bone-transmission as the jaw bones, the osseus elements of the beak, link up with the middle-ear bones that support the eardrums (Schall & Delius, 1985).

This auditory feedback could steer the grasping and mandibulation of food items, and possibly further pecking. If the latter were so it should be feasible to devise a food reinforced conditioning paradigm that yields efficient tone control over pecking. And that is just what we have done. The subjects had to discriminate between a brief tone (90 ms) and an even briefer tone (10 ms). In a two-key Skinner box, within a trial, each pecking response on a given key immediately yielded an S+ tone, while pecks on the other key always triggered S− tones. A fixed number (FR 16) of consecutive responses on the S+ key yielded reinforcement. Responses on the S− key never yielded reinforcement (EXT) and reset the FR count of correct responses to zero. After a reinforcement the allocation of S+ and S− to the two keys was determined according to a quasi-random sequence.

In one control condition the two tones were triggered by the programming equipment independently of the subject's pecking responses. In another control condition, the discriminative tones were still triggered by the key-pecks but with a delay of 600 msec. Pigeons only learned the discrimination when the tones followed directly upon the pecks, much as natural auditory feedback does, but not otherwise (Delius & Gebauer, 1985). Incidentally, Kinchla (1970), searching for an efficient method for auditory psychophysics in the pigeon, had devised a procedure which is similar to that reported here.

We conclude that if the tone stimuli to be discriminated are presented to the pigeons in a way that resembles the natural situation they are easily associated with pecking and food. Note that the conditioning procedure that was effective is not optimal in the sense that the noise the animal generated upon hitting the keys with its beak is likely to have interfered with the perception of the discriminative tones produced by the loudspeakers. Notice also that an analogous discrimination of light-flashes is unlikely to succeed with this paradigm as pigeons have their eyes closed at the relevant instant. But pigeons are quite efficient at discriminating the duration of light-flashes in a more conventional food rewarded discrimination procedure as Servière (1979), for example, has shown. Interestingly the same author (personal communication) could not obtain even gross tone duration discrimination using the same conventional procedure in spite of very extended training.

There is a further anomaly. Lab-lore has it that hungry pigeons become excited on hearing the noises of food handling and feeding equipment. On the basis of casual experimentation I believe that the observation is correct and that pigeons are acutely discriminating in this situation. It suggests that pigeons can associate auditory stimuli with food in a quite conventional conditioning context. Indeed, I believe that this has been demonstrated by Leyland (1977) and Nairn and Rescorla (1981) who showed that tones can act as mediators (conditioned reinforcers) in second order classical conditioning of pecking to a light CS with food as UCS even though tone stimuli as CS do not yield pecking as CR (Boe & Winokour, 1979). To put it in another way, if the response measured in classical conditioning of pigeons was motor restlessness and not the conventional key-pecking, tones may prove quite effective as first order CS. I also risk the opinion that if this response was made the operant in an instrumental discrimination of tones, pigeons will turn out to be well capable of fine auditory stimulus distinction under food reinforcement. This can easily be reconciled with normal foraging behaviour of pigeons. They are highly social feeders and it is apparent that the behaviour of other pigeons is used as a distant cue for food finding (Murton, Coombs & Thearle, 1972). Food-lucky pigeons generate both visual and auditory stimuli. In hungry conspecifics however these cues elicit approach rather than pecking.

PHYSIOLOGY OF AN OPERANT

Although our interest in responses has ranged more widely (Sieland, Delius, Rautenberg & May, 1981; Mallin & Delius, 1983) for present purposes I concentrate on pecking. Pigeons have their hands in the face, the "limb" capable of the finest manipulative motions being the beak. Zweers (1982b) has described in detail pecking as it is most frequently used by pigeons, for grasping grains. His description deals principally with late stages of this motion but it can be supplemented with accounts of the earlier stages by others (Friedman, 1975; Zeigler, Levitt & Levine, 1980; Goodale, 1983; Jahnke, 1984). Not all pecking acts seen in the context of feeding terminate individually in the swallowing of food (appetitive or search pecking, scattering [Timberlake, 1983], "begging"), and some may serve other unknown functions (adjunctive behaviour; Palya & Zacny, 1980). Also note that besides feeding-related pecking there are other kinds of pecking such as that employed in intra- and interspecific fighting (Martin Ramirez & Delius, 1979), in courtship, in preening, and in what ethologists have called displacement activity contexts. There is finally a pecking-like motion, beak-dipping, that subserves drinking (Zweers, 1982a). It seems clear that when behaviourists get pigeons to peck manipulanda, most often a key, they are not really dealing with arbitrary behaviour. Rather it is a derivative of one of the various kinds of pecking that we have mentioned. This is best documented for the different forms of key-pecking that arise with food and water reinforcement: a grasping and a dipping peck (Jenkins & Moore, 1973). We have recently observed that pigeons may also activate a suitably designed manipulandum, a rubber bulb connected to pressure transducer with an action that is suspiciously similar to aggressive, wide-gape biting. This is particularly the case if a partial schedule of reinforcement is used suggesting that schedule-induced, frustrative aggression (Staddon, 1977) may be involved.

Our interest, however, has been in elucidating the neural bases of pecking. The starting point was a psychopharmacological approach developed in collaboration with Pierre Deviche, of the University of Liège. The drug apomorphine, a potent dopamine receptor agonist, is known to elicit persistent fits of pecking in pigeons when injected peripherally (Amsler, 1923; Brunelli, Magni, Morruzi & Musumeci, 1975). The drug-induced pecking is facilitated and guided by external stimuli, the pigeons preferring to peck contrasting, small-sized features (Fig. 5.5, Deviche, 1985). That this pecking is at least partly related to the operant pecking studied in instrumental conditioning situations is suggested by the fact that food reinforcement induced responding can sometimes be augmented with apomorphine injections (Graeff & Oliveira, 1975). But it is common for individual pigeons to develop idiosyncratic pecking stereotypies that do not always coincide with key-pecking and in fact can markedly interfere with it (own observations, Abelson & Woods, 1980). Even though the drug promotes pecking it does not facilitate feeding. Apomorphine-treated pigeons eat less, but do not drink less, than saline-injected controls. Interestingly this suppression is greater in the afternoon than in the morning. The food intake suppression occurs even with doses of apomorphine that do not induce pecking (e.g., 50 μg subject; Deviche, 1984). Intracerebroventricular injections of apomorphine do not yield pecking, however, suggesting that the site of action relating to this behaviour is not situated close to the ventricles (Deviche, 1983).

This issue is being investigated with the (14)C-2-deoxyglucose autoradiography technique in collaboration with H. Scheich, at the Technical University of Darmstadt. Glucose is the prime energy source for neurones. 2-deoxyglucose, a chemically denatured glucose, is taken up by cells in the same way as glucose is but it cannot be metabolised further. It accumulates selectively in highly active neurones that normally would utilise more glucose than average. As apomorphine triggers fits of pecking, the population of neurones that controls this motor act should be activated and selectively take up 2-deoxyglucose. Pigeons were thus injected with both 0.5 mg apomorphine and 70 μCi radioactively labelled deoxyglucose. After

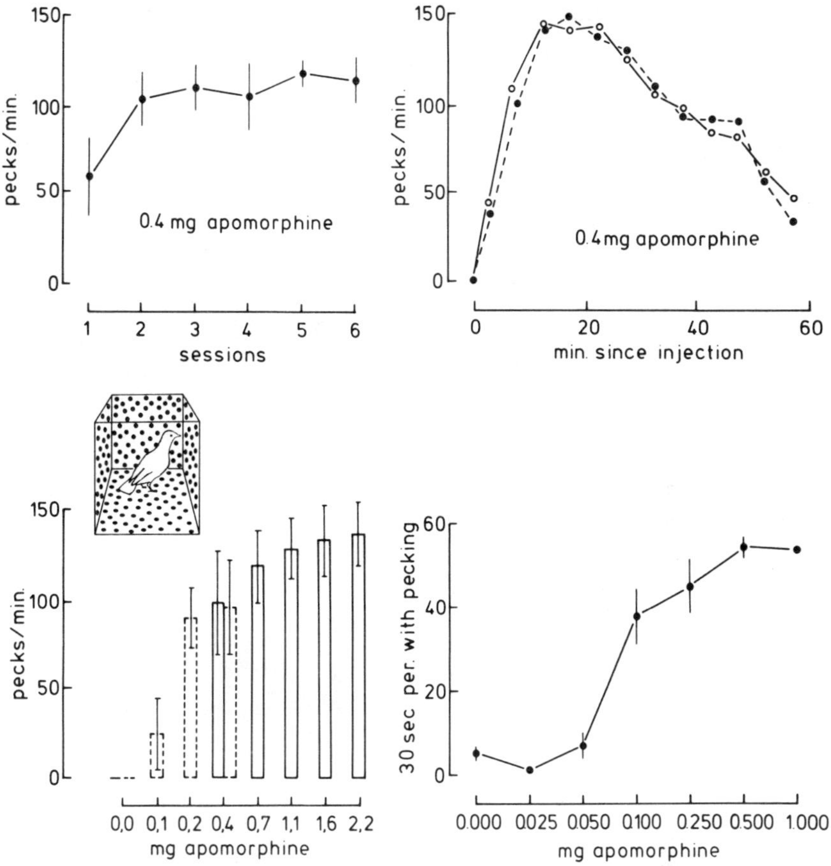

FIG. 5.5. Systemic injections of the dopaminereceptor agonist drug apomorphine elicit pecking in pigeons. The response is facilitated by providing a profusion of suitable targets. Top left: There is a sensitisation effect with repeated daily drug administration (N = 6). Top right: The pecking persists at high rates for over an hour; repeated experiments (N = 6). Bottom left: Dose-response curves; two separate experiments (doses mg/kg, N = 6). Bottom right: Alternative dose-response curve (doses mg/subject, N = 9). (Basten-Krefft & Delius unpublished; Deviche, 1985).

they had exhibited frantic pecking for one hour they were sacrificed and their brains were extracted from the skull, rapidly frozen and sectioned at 30 μm. The dry-mounted tissue sections were pressed against photographic film and kept in the dark for 14 days. The brain sites that have accumulated the radioactive deoxyglucose expose the film locally, this becoming visible on development. The autoradiographs can be matched up with the corresponding, conventionally stained brain sections.

We find that several different brain areas are marked in animals that have been treated with apomorphine and have shown pecking as compared with saline treated controls, among them also the nucleus basalis (Fig. 5.6, Delius & Scheich, 1985). One cannot automatically conclude that all differentially marked structures are involved in the control of pecking since

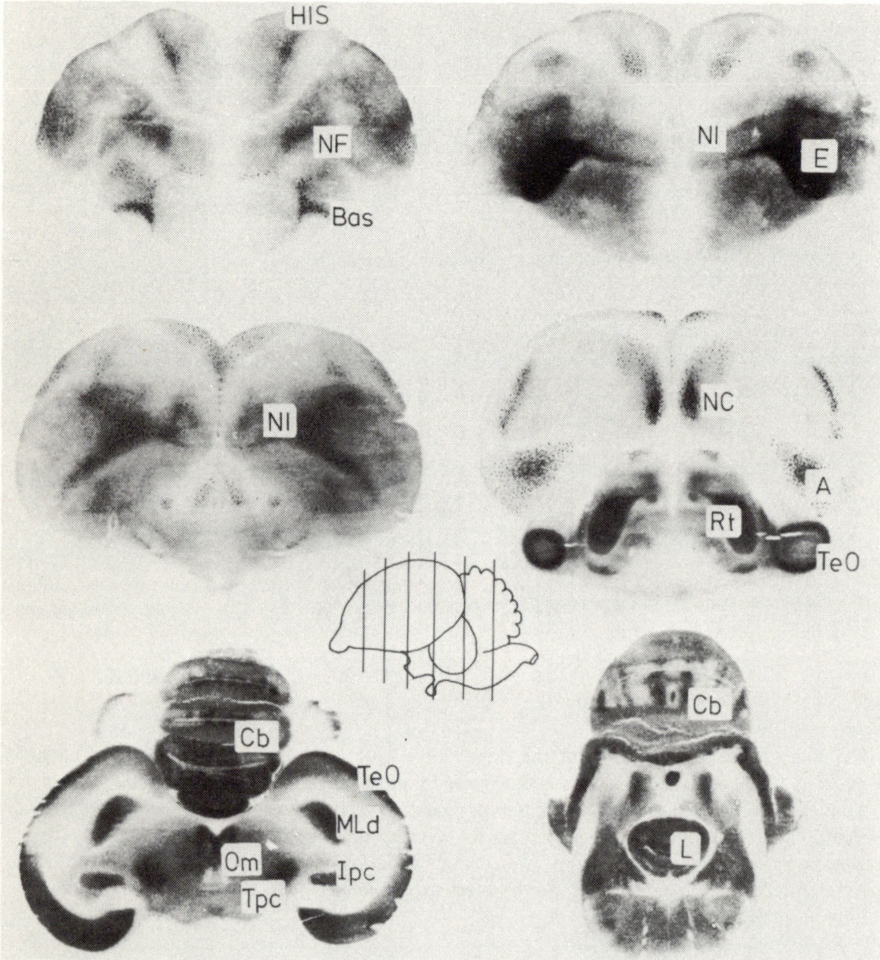

FIG. 5.6. Some examples of pigeon brain autoradiographs after apomorphine and radioactive deoxyglucose injections. Darker areas indicate above average, lighter areas below average uptake of glucose, an indication of the level of neuronal activity. Through comparison with brain autoradiographs of pigeons not injected with apomorphine it can be shown that a number of different brain structures are activated by the pecking-inducing drug, among them the nucleus basalis area (Bas; Delius & Scheich, 1985, retouched). Other abbreviations as in Fig. 5.2 and: A archistriatum, E ectostriatum, Ipc nucleus isthmi parvocellularis, L lingula, Tpc nucleus tegmenti peduncularis pontinus, MLd n. mesencephalicus lateralis dorsalis, Om nucleus nervi occulomotorii.

it is possible that apomorphine also activates subliminally other neural systems. It also remains uncertain whether a structure is marked because of direct excitation by apomorphine or because it is indirectly activated by another dopaminoceptive structure or even because it receives reafferent tactile, auditory or visual sensory input generated by the act of pecking. Visual stimulation can be avoided by carrying out the procedure in the absolute dark, as pigeons will continue to peck under this condition. Auditory feedback can be prevented by surgical removal of the cochleae, tactile afferences by sectioning the trigeminal nerve branches innervating the beak but we have not yet completed these experiments. Even so all the structures marked can be initially considered candidates for involvement in the control of pecking.

To check out more precisely the role of the various candidate brain sites, one can now proceed to inject into them micro-quantities of apomorphine. If the relevant structures are involved in the control of pecking such injections should elicit this response. This is exactly what happens in the case of the nucleus basalis (Lindenblatt, 1985). Pigeons were stereotaxically implanted with guide cannulae through which we then injected 2 μl of drug solution into the nucleus basalis. The effective dose of apomorphine is below 20 μg, about 1/10 of the standard systemic dose necessary to elicit pecking. As suggested by the apomorphine/deoxyglucose autoradiography, other brain structures probably also yield pecking upon such microinjections but our work has not yet defined them sufficiently enough to make comment on them worthwhile. Goodman and Stitzel (1977), however, have described that such injections in the paleostriatum reliably elicit pecking. It is clear though, that, even with respect to dopaminoceptive neurones alone, the neural substrate of pecking is a distributed control system.

If, as it seems, apomorphine activates specific brain areas while eliciting pecking then one should be able to demonstrate an electrophysiological activation concomitant with pecking. With chronically implanted bipolar electrodes and a head-mounted preamplifier we have been able to show that while the animal pecks under the influence of the drug the electrocephalogram recorded from the nucleus basalis and its neighbourhood shows quite obvious changes in activity consisting of waves that apparently have the same rhythm as the pecks. Several other telencephalic locations that have so far been checked do not show such obvious peck-related activation.

Because of the difficulty of obtaining an accurate timing of the apomorphine induced pecks that could be cross-correlated with these local brain potentials, and with the intention of comparing the pharmacologically induced pecking with conditioned pecking we autoshaped the pigeons to peck a key providing a convenient signal. Although this kind of analysis has not yet proceeded very far it is clear that nucleus basalis related locations do indeed often yield a rhythmic electrocephalographic activity that is phase related to the pecks. Of course, since pecking elicits auditory and tactile stimuli we can expect evoked potentials following these. But it seems likely that some loci show activation preceding these responses, indicating that it may be involved in the neuronal initiation of pecking commands (Delius, unpublished).

If that is so, electrical brain stimulation through electrodes implanted in such sites should elicit pecking. And indeed, even though head shaking, beak scratching and retching are the most common responses evoked, presumably due to trigeminal hallucinations, occasional locations are found that yield stimulus-bound pecking upon low current stimulation. As far as we can tell at present, such pecking is similar to apomorphine induced pecking insofar as it is not particulary directed at food. The nucleus basalis may thus be on the one hand the source of neuronal motor command components for pecking while at the same time it receives auditory and tactile afferences that are relevant for the control of pecking.

To this it must be added that, as discovered by Zeigler, Hollard, Wild and Webster (1978), electrical stimulation of the nucleus basalis, among other structures, has reinforcing properties. Delius, Williams and Wootton (1976) had previously found that the tracti quinto-frontalis and fronto-archistriaticus, both as described earlier associated with the nucleus basalis, supported brain self-stimulation (Fig. 5.7). Delius and Pellander (1982) noted an association between dopaminergic structures and self-stimulation sites in the pigeon, much as it has been reported in mammals. The dopamine agonist apomorphine is obviously capable of activating the nucleus basalis and histochemical investigations indicate that this, and other structures that support self-stimulation, are naturally rich in dopamine (Minelli, 1970; Brauth, Ferguson & Kitt, 1978). However, the coincidence of reinforcement pathways, sensory afferences and motor efferences in this area seems suggestive that this area may be directly involved in conditioning processes associated with pecking.

The pecking of pigeons, pursuing this line of thought, is undoubtedly under close and very plastic, in the sense of conditionable, control of visual stimuli. Where if at all, could visual information enter the presumed peck-steering nucleus basalis related system? I once speculated, simply on grounds of neighbourhood, that it did so via the optic thalamofugal projection reaching the fronto-dorsal telencephalon, the hyperstriatum or Wulst, a probable homologue of the mammalian visual cortex (Delius, 1971). But that is probably not so since large bilateral lesions in this area do not produce appreciable deficits in visually conditioned discriminative key-pecking (Parker & Delius, 1980) nor in visually guided unconditioned pecking (Parker, unpublished experiments). The fact that unilateral Wulst

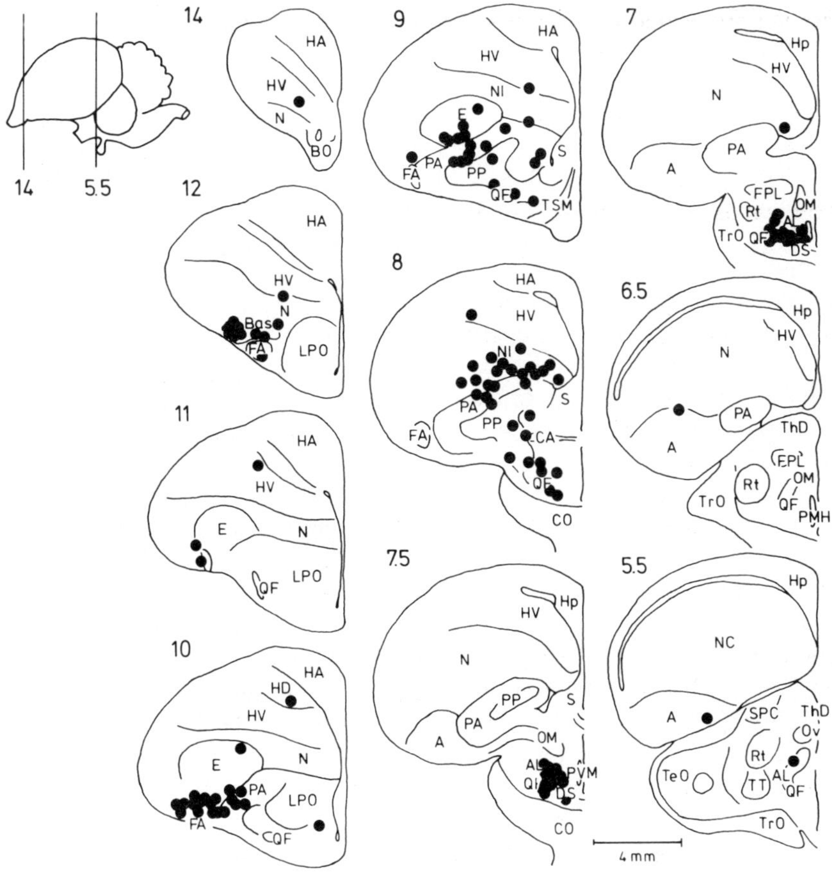

FIG. 5.7. Brain sites that have yielded instrumental electrical self-stimulation in pigeons. Note that among other structures the nucleus basalis (Bas) yields reinforcement effects (compilation, modified after Delius & Pellander, 1982). Abbreviations as in Figs. 5.2 and 5.6 and: BO bulbus olfactorius, CO chiasma opticum, DS decussatio supraoptica, FA tractus fronto-archistriaticus, FPL fasciculus prosencephali lateralis, Hp hippocampus, LPO lobus paraolfactorius, N neostriatum, OM tractus occipitomesencephalicus, Ov n. ovoidalis, PMH n. medialis hypothalami posterioris, PVM n. periventricularis magnocellularis, QF tractus quintofrontalis, S septum, SPC n. superficialis parvocellularis, ThD thalamus dorsalis, TSM tractus septomesencephalicus, TT tractus tectothalamicus.

lesions can affect monocularly guided instrumental pecking (Nau & Delius, 1981) does not alter this assessment since the imbalance so created is likely to have this effect by mediating a dysfunction at lower visual centres through descending pathways.

Rather we have found that lesions of the lateral forebrain markedly impair visual hue, intensity and pattern discriminations both proactively and retroactively in an instrumental food rewarded pecking paradigm (Delius, Jäger & Friesel, 1984). Ritchie (1979) has reported that the posterolateral aspect of the telencephalon of the pigeon receives secondary visual projections from the Wulst and the ectostriatum. Furthermore, a visual evoked potential study done in our laboratory confirmed and extended to pigeons findings by Phillips (1966) who had described short latency flash evoked responses in the archistriatum of chickens (*Gallus gallus*). Using animals with chronic implanted electrodes Güntürkün (1984) found in our laboratory that visual evoked potentials of short latency (15–18 msec) could be recorded from the archistriatum mediale/neostriatum caudale border suggesting a direct input from di- or mesencephalic visual nuclei. This is just where the tractus fronto-archistriaticus coming from the nucleus basalis terminates (Fig. 5.3). It is possible that the visual information that controls pecking may enter the network at the archistriatal level.

In this context we have become aware that in the pigeon, as has been known for some time to be the case in the domestic chicken (Rogers, 1982; Andrew, Mench & Rainey, 1982), the visual control of pecking is lateralised such that the right eye and left brain play a dominant role (the optic nerve is totally crossed in birds). The effect of unilateral lesions is accordingly markedly non-symmetrical when pigeons are allowed the use of only one or the other eye (Güntürkün, 1985). This applies also to the lesions of the lateral telencephalon to which I have just referred (Jäger, 1985).

COGNITION CONTROLLED RESPONDING

We now concentrate on the control exerted by complex visual stimuli over the pecking of pigeons. First, however, I would like to remind readers of the fact that the vision of pigeons has some remarkable features: a sensitivity spectrum extending from the near-ultraviolet (300 nm) to the deep-red (700 nm), detection of the polarisation plane of light, an at least tetrachromatic colour vision system, and a division of the retina into two histologically different areas possibly associated with two different kinds of vision (Delius & Emmerton, 1979; Emmerton & Delius, 1980; Delius, Jahnke-Funk & Hawker, 1980; Emmerton, 1983a, 1983b, 1983c; Emmerton & Remy, 1983).

Here, however, we will deal with the visual pattern recognition capabilities of pigeons. An object in the environment can, depending on its relative distance and orientation with respect to the observer, cast very different retinal images. Differing lighting conditions will also yield different images. The image of a given object may on different occasions fall on sections of the retina that have different transducing properties. Also such an object may cast an image on both retinae or on only one as the pigeons' binocular field is of restricted extent while the monocular fields are nearly panoramic (Jahnke, 1985). The effective information about the retinal image that is transmitted to the brain further varies due to the previous stimulation history of the retina (adaptation phenomena).

In spite of this it seems probable that the pigeon's central visual system can recognise such variable information as it receives through the optic nerves as belonging to one and the same object or to different objects. It is capable of what is known as invariance of object recognition. The information processing operations that bring this about are by no means trivial as we know from engineers who attempt to furnish artificial vision systems with similar performance. We have begun to systematically explore pigeons' capabilities in this respect. First we needed a flexible method. In the matching-to-sample paradigm a pigeon is presented first with a visual stimulus on the centre key of a Skinner box which it has to peck for two comparison stimuli to appear on side keys. The pigeon has to choose the comparison stimulus identical to the sample in order to be reinforced. The problem was that we needed to be sure that the animals would do so on the basis of a general same/different principle and not, as some authors have argued, by having learned a collection of stimulus specific rules (Carter & Werner, 1978). We reasoned that if the number of stimuli involved in training the matching-to-sample, or rather the converse oddity from sample, performance was large, then a stimulus-by-stimulus solution would be impractical for pigeons and the application of a concept-like rule would be promoted. To test for the existence of such a general rule we used transfer trials under extinction conditions involving new stimuli. An above chance performance in these test trials indicates that, since pigeons could not apply stimulus specific rules as the stimuli were unknown to them, they must have used a general rule (Fig. 5.8, Lombardi, Fachinelli & Delius, 1983).

This concept-like same-different principle used by pigeons gives us the possibility of investigating the invariance of pattern recognition. For example, will pigeons recognise the identity of a given visual form when it is shown in different sizes, that is will they evince size invariance of pattern recognition? In current work at our laboratory Celia Lombardi has been looking at this. She trained the pigeons on the oddity-from-sample task using patterns of the different sizes but in any given trial both the sample and the comparison stimuli were of the same size. In test trials the pigeons were faced with instances where the comparison stimuli were larger or smaller than the sample stimulus by a scale factor of about two. When the comparison stimuli were small the performance of the pigeons was excellent showing that they recognised the equivalence/non-

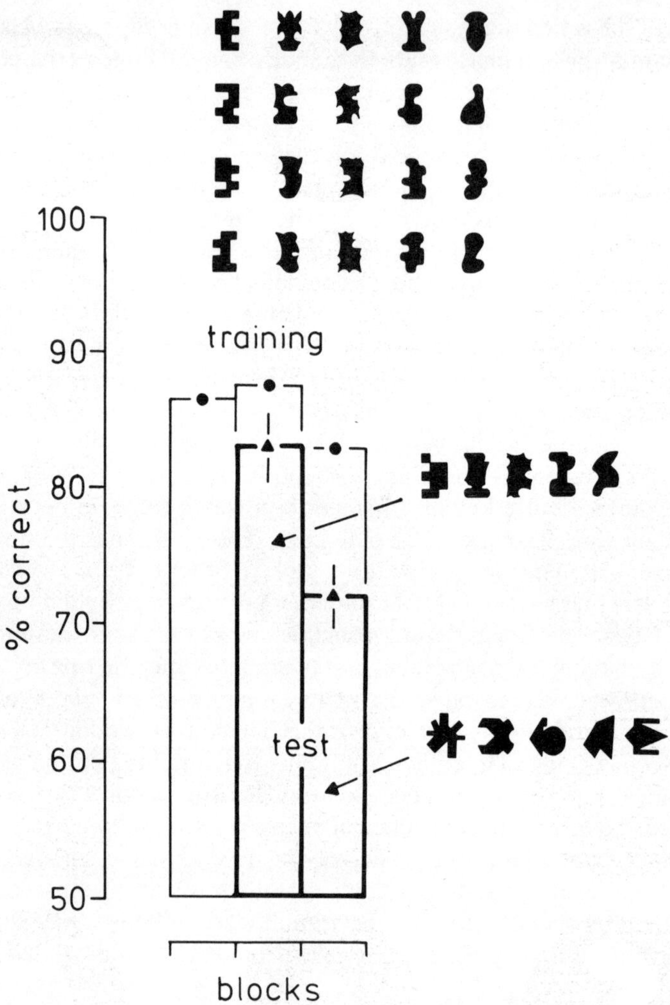

FIG. 5.8. Generalised oddity-from-sample performance of pigeons. The subjects (N = 5) learned the task with 160 three-stimulus configurations based on the 20 pattern (training, top). They were then tested for transfer of performance to totally new patterns in interspersed extinction trials using 40 configurations based first on the top five patterns, and then on the bottom five patterns (modified from Lombardi, Fachinelli & Delius, 1983).

equivalence of shapes in spite of size differences. When the comparison stimuli were large the discrimination of the subjects, though still above chance, was less good. At present we entertain two hypotheses about this latter result. Either pigeons are reluctant to peck at large stimuli and this interferes with discriminative behaviour or they only have a small visual-angle field of attention within which they can recognize a shape as a whole (Fig. 5.9).

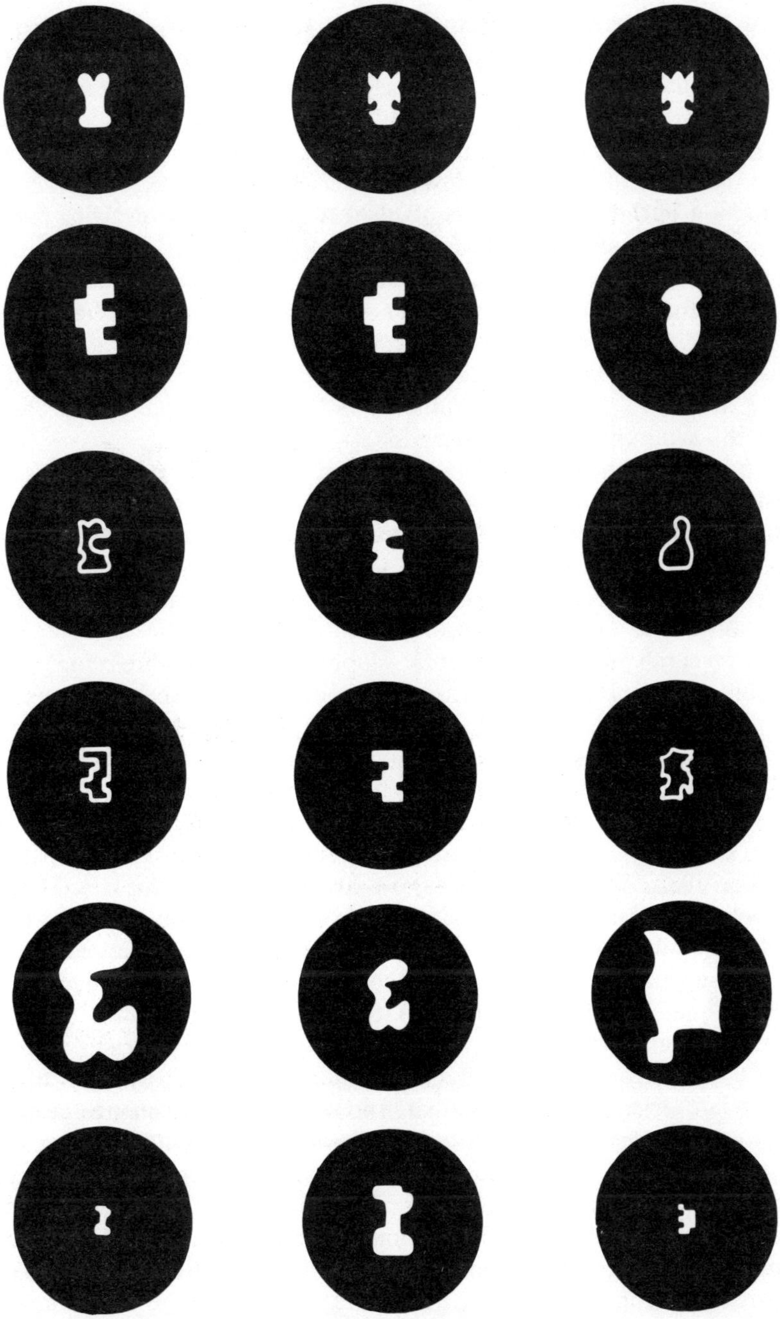

FIG. 5.9. Examples of oddity-from-sample stimulus configurations to study shape recognition invariance. Top: training configurations, middle: outline invariance, bottom: size invariance, test configurations (from Lombardi, unpublished; Lombardi and Delius, 1985).

Another invariance-of-pattern-recognition feat of which pigeons are quite capable is that of identifying the equivalence/non-equivalence of shapes and their outlines. That is what we do when we recognise objects represented in line-drawings. Since in nature such invariance is probably rarely in demand it is remarkable that pigeons should show this capacity. We suppose that as artificial vision designers (Duff, 1983) have found out, the extraction of the information equivalent to that of a line drawing from a visual scene is an almost essential basis for later scene interpretation, because it implies a considerable reduction of redundancy. There is good evidence that the mammalian visual system performs such outline extraction (Marr, 1982; Creutzfeldt & Nothdurft, 1978). Our evidence is that the avian visual system, though anatomically quite differently organised in being midbrain, optic tectum rather than forebrain, visual cortex based, does the same (but see Cerella, 1982).

A further instance of perceptual invariance performance by pigeons is of some interest because it is one that humans have difficulties with. R. N. Shepard and collaborators found that if humans were asked to decide whether two visual shapes are the same or different when the different shape is a mirror image of the original shape, the reaction times increase as a function of the orientation misalignment of the forms to be compared. Later research has revealed that the slope of this "mental rotation" function of a person correlates with his visuo-spatial abilities score measured by standard intelligence tests. The subjective impression while doing this task is that to solve the more difficult instances one has to think hard. There is more objective evidence that serial processing of information is involved where the number of successive steps until solution is greater when the angle of the orientation disparity between shapes is larger (Shepard & Cooper, 1982). We have looked at how pigeons deal with this task (Hollard & Delius, 1982). Using the matching-to-sample technique as described earlier the subjects were confronted on each trial with a sample geometrical form and subsequently with two comparison forms, one identical to sample, the other a mirror image of it. In the "mental rotation" tests the comparison patterns were rotated in the frontal plane by various amounts from 0 to 180 degrees against the sample shape that was always presented in a standard orientation. The animals showed better than chance performance on these tests and, importantly, showed no sign, either with respect to the error rates or the reaction times, that they found the increasing angular misalignments of samples and comparison shapes more difficult. Humans tested with the same shapes and apparatus showed a strong effect, reaction times in particular lengthening markedly with increasing angular mismatches (Fig. 5.10, Delius, 1985).

Pigeons thus performed better on this invariance task than intelligent humans. It seems obvious that pigeons do not utilise a serial mode of information processing as humans do but a parallel one. Humans can do

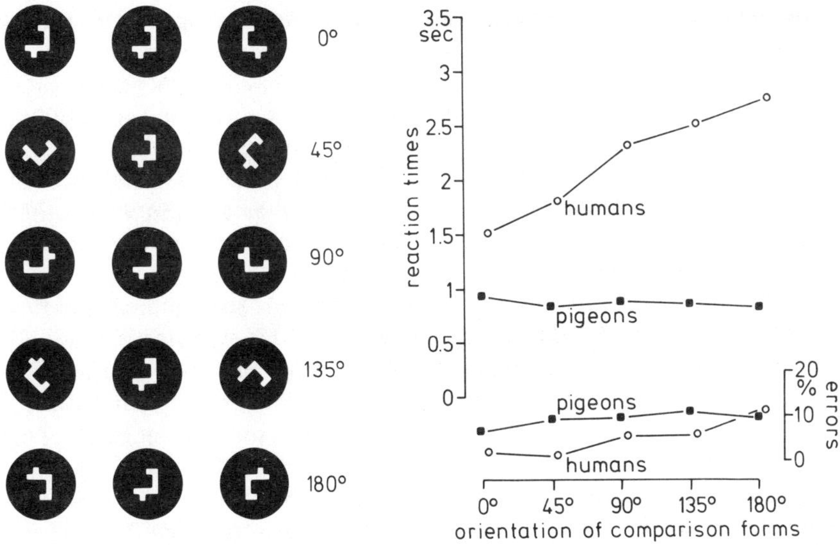

FIG. 5.10. Performance of pigeons and humans in a task involving the rotational invariance of shape recognition (right: examples). Humans (N = 22) yielded a typical "mental rotation" performance (longer reaction times with increasing orientation disparities), pigeons (N = 9) did not show such effect (modified from Hollard & Delius, 1982).

that too but only when the rotation invariance tasks involve arbitrarily different shapes rather than mirror image shapes. It is known that mirror image shapes are peculiarly difficult for humans to discriminate (Corballis & Beale, 1976). An explanation could be that pigeons find mirror image shapes just as easy as arbitrarily different patterns to distinguish and thus do not need to resort to the time consuming serial processing to which humans seem to be forced. Recent work of ours shows this not to be likely. Pigeons were taught to discriminate several pairs of visual patterns with a successive free operant method. Half of the pairs were mirror images, the other half were arbitrarily different shapes. The pigeons' performance was markedly worse on the mirror images (Lohmann, Delius, Hollard & Friesel, 1985). The other explanation that we offered is that pigeons may tend to store information about visual patterns in an orientation free mode because, differently from humans, they operate visually predominantly on the horizontal rather than the vertical plane. Whereas in the latter plane objects and observers usually have definite orientations with respect to gravity and the horizon, in the former neither objects nor observers have any preferred orientations. But how are we to imagine an orientation-free engram? Certain complex mathematical transformations of spatial patterns are said to yield this property (Hord, 1982). Perhaps the pigeon's brain is making use of such image information conversions.

Beyond the fact that a given object can cast different images on the retina it can also change its appearance by itself, particularly if it is a live organism. We know that pigeons are at a premium to recognise such objects in spite of their variable appearance, as they may be competitors, mates, offspring and suchlike. Herrnstein, Loveland and Cable (1976) demonstrated that they can indeed easily learn to identify such kinds of variable objects, a particular person for example, as different from other persons on a collection of slides and that they are then capable of extending this recognition to new, previously unseen slides. A further step is the recognition of different objects as belonging to a particular class. For pigeons this might be predators, conspecifics, trees, nesting sites, all categories whose recognition is likely to be important for Darwinian fitness. Again Herrnstein, Loveland and Cable (1976) have demonstrated that pigeons can learn to recognise items belonging to such categories. For example, they showed that pigeons would learn to pick slides showing water in its various forms (puddles, lakes, rivers, seas, etc.) from slides not showing water and that again they were capable of extending this distinction to novel slides.

We have been interested in finding out whether pigeons would be able to learn about a more abstract category, bilaterally symmetrical shapes as different from non-symmetrical shapes. We used a free operant successive discrimination technique to train the discrimination using 52 different shapes. The acquisition of the discrimination was so efficient that we are inclined to think that we did not teach the pigeons the perceptual concept symmetry/asymmetry but rather only to apply one that they already had, perhaps even innately. Later we inserted transfer trials under extinction conditions with over 200 novel stimuli. Even when the test stimuli were quite different in geometrical style from the training stimuli the pigeons' performance was excellent. This was also so when the orientation of the symmetry axis of the test stimuli differed from that of the consistently vertical orientation of the training stimuli. Pigeons also mastered the concept-like discrimination of symmetric versus non-symmetric stimuli when they could use only one eye. This indicates that the recognition of bilaterally symmetrical patterns has little to do with the gross symmetrical organisation of the visual system (Delius & Nowak, 1982). We have rather hypothesised that the recognition of symmetry is based on the fine, multiple-symmetric structure at the histological level seen in tangential sections of the optic tectum. We contend that systems that analyse in parallel surface information like pictorial images in a largely homogeneous manner must have such a structure. If this reasoning is correct, the salience that bilateral symmetry has for humans and apparently for pigeons moves into the neighbourhood of many visual illusions, useless side-products of otherwise useful information processing networks. If so it is perhaps better to talk of bilateral symmetry as a feature rather than a concept (Delius & Habers, 1978).

CONCLUSION

I have described phenomena and processes that have caught our interest in the recent past. All were related to just one kind of behaviour, the pecking of pigeons. Nonetheless the tale meandered through various scientific fields. Probably most of the few explanations offered are wrong, but can it be conceived that the problems raised can all be answered by just one discipline, just a single tradition? It is my contention that besides experimental analysis and ethology there are a multitude of other branches of knowledge, from genetics to robotics, from economics to ecology, from histochemistry to sociobiology, that contribute or can contribute to the description, explanation, understanding of behaviour. I have yet to hear convincing reasons why they should not. After all, even the microcephalic pigeon has a brain that contains some 10^8 neurones times some 10^3 synapses, a remarkable high performance biological nano-computer dedicated to the very special purpose of maximising its owners fitness. That allows for no mean complexity and makes the task of accounting for behaviour so difficult that any useful suggestions must always be welcome. Everybody should join the melee!

ACKNOWLEDGEMENTS

Thanks are due to Mrs D. Hagenkötter, Mrs P. Ohmann-Jamal, Miss A. Lohmann and Miss J. A. Delius for excellent assistance. Dr P. Deviche, Dr V. D. Hollard, R. Jäger, H. J. Jahnke and O. Güntürkün kindly allowed me to refer to as yet unpublished work of theirs. Dr J. Emmerton criticised an earlier version and made useful suggestions. The research reviewed was supported by the Deutsche Forschungsgemeinschaft through its Sonderforschungsbereich 114, the Heinrich Hertz Stiftung and the Research Fund of the Ruhr-University.

REFERENCES

Abelson, J. S. & Woods, J. H. (1980) Effects of apomorphine on elicited and operant pecking in pigeons. *Psychopharmacology*, **71**, 237–241.

Abs, M. (Ed.) (1983) *Physiology and behaviour of the pigeon*. London: Academic Press.

Amsler, C. (1923) Ueber einige Wirkungen des Apomorphins. *Experimentelle Pathologie und Pharmakologie*, **97**, 1–27.

Andrew, R. J., Mench, J., & Rainey, C. (1982) Right-left asymmetry of response to visual stimuli in the domestic chick. In D. J. Ingle, M. A. Goodale and R. J. W. Mansfield (Eds.), *Analysis of visual behavior*. Cambridge, Mass: MIT Press.

Biederman-Thorson, M., (1970) Auditory responses of units in the ovoid nucleus and cerebrum (Field L) of the ring dove. *Brain Research*, **24**, 247–256.

Boe, R. B. & Winokour, S. (1979) Positive automaintenance does not produce sustained pecking to a tone. *Bulletin of the psychonomic Society*, **14**, 67–70.

Brauth, S. E., Ferguson, J. L., & Kitt, C. A. (1978) Prosencephalic pathways related to the paleostriatum of the pigeon. *Brain Research*, **147**, 205–221.

Brunelli, M., Magni, F., Morruzi, G., & Musumeci, D. (1975) Apomorphine pecking in the pigeon. *Archive Italienne de Biologie*, **113**, 303–325.

Carter, D. E. & Werner, T. J. (1978) Complex learning and information processing by pigeons: a critical analysis. *Journal of the Experimental Analysis of Behavior*, **29**, 565–601.

Cerella, J. (1982) Mechanisms of concept formation in the pigeon. In: D. J. Ingle, M. A. Goodale & R. J. W. Mansfield (Eds.), *Analysis of Visual Behavior*. Cambridge, Mass: MIT Press.

Corballis, M. C. & Beale, I. L. (1976) *The Psychology of Left and Right*. Hillsdale: Lawrence Erlbaum Associates.

Creutzfeld, O. D. & Nothdurft, H. C. (1978) Representation of complex visual stimuli in the brain. *Die Naturwissenschaften*, **65**, 307–318.

Delius, J. D. (1971) Foraging behaviour patterns of herring gulls elicited by electrical forebrain stimulation. *Experientia*, **27**, 1287–1289.

Delius, J. D. (1985) Complex visual information processing in the pigeon. *Acta 18th International Ornithological Congress Moscow*, in press.

Delius, J. D. & Bennetto, K. (1972) Cutaneous sensory projections to the avian forebrain. *Brain Research*, **37**, 205–221.

Delius, J. D. & Emmerton, J. (1978) Stimulus-dependent asymmetry and instrumental discrimination learning by pigeons. *Psychological Record*, **28**, 425–434.

Delius, J. D. & Emmerton, J. (1979) Visual performance of pigeons. In: A. M. Granda & J. H. Maxwell (Eds.), *Neural Mechanisms of Behavior in the Pigeon*. New York: Plenum.

Delius, J. D. & Gebauer, W. (1985) *Discrimination of peck-elicited sounds by pigeons* (in preparation).

Delius, J. D. & Habers, G. (1978) Symmetry: can pigeons conceptualize it? *Behavioral Biology*, **22**, 336–342.

Delius, J. D., Jäger, R., & Friesel, M. (1984) Lateral telencephalic lesions affect visual discriminations in the pigeons. *Behavioural Brain Research*, **11**, 249–258.

Delius, J. D., Jahnke-Funk, E., & Hawker, A. (1980) Stimulus display geometry and colour discrimination learning by pigeons. *Current Psychological Research*, **1**, 203–214.

Delius, J. D. & Nowak, B. (1982) Visual symmetry recognition by pigeons. *Psychological Research*, **44**, 199–212.

Delius, J. D. & Pellander, K. (1982) Hunger dependence of electrical brain self-stimulation in the pigeon. *Physiology and Behavior*, **28**, 63–66.

Delius, J. D., Runge, T. E., & Oeckinghaus, H. (1979) Short latency auditory projection to the frontal telencephalon of the pigeon. *Experimental Neurology*, **63**, 594–609.

Delius, J. D. & Tarpy, R. M. (1974) Stimulus control of heart rate by auditory frequency and auditory pattern in pigeons. *Journal of the Experimental Analysis of Behavior*, **21**, 297–306.

Delius, J. D., Williams, A. S., & Wootton, R. J. (1976) Motivation dependence of brain self stimulation in the pigeon. *Behavioural Processes*, **1**, 15–27.

Deviche, P. (1983) Stereotyped behaviour affected by peripheral and intracerebroventricular apomorphine administration in pigeons. *Pharmacology, Biochemistry and Behaviour*, **18**, 323–326.

Deviche, P. (1984) Administration of small doses of apomorphine attenuates feeding in non-deprived pigeons. *Physiology and Behaviour*, **33**, 581–585.

Deviche, P. (1985) Behavioural response to apomorphine and its interaction with opiates in domestic pigeons. *Pharmacology, Biochemistry and Behaviour*, **22**, 209–214.

Duff, M. J. B. (1983) Neighbourhood operators. In: O. J. Braddick and A. C. Sleigh (Eds.), *Physical and Biological Processing of Images*. Berlin: Springer.

Emmerton, J. (1983a) Functional morphology of the visual system. In: M. Abs (Ed.), *Physiology and Behaviour of the Pigeon*. London: Academic Press.

Emmerton, J. (1983b) Vision. In: M. Abs (Ed.), *Physiology and Behaviour of the Pigeon*. London: Academic Press.

Emmerton, J. (1983c) Pattern discrimination in the near ultraviolet by pigeons. *Perception and Psychophysics*, **34**, 555–559.

Emmerton, J. & Delius, J. D. (1980) Wavelength discrimination in the 'visible' and ultraviolet spectrum by pigeons. *Journal of Comparative Physiology*, **141**, 47–52.

Emmerton, J. & Remy, M. (1983) The pigeon's sensitivity to ultraviolet and 'visible' light. *Experientia*, **39**, 1161–1163.

Friedman, M. (1975) How birds use their eyes. In: P. Wright, P. C. Caryl & D. M. Vowles (Eds.), *Neural and Endocrine Aspects of Behaviour in Birds*. Amsterdam: Elsevier.

Goodale, M. A. (1983) Visually guided pecking in the pigeon (*Columba livia*). *Brain, Behavior and Evolution*, **22**, 22–41.

Goodmann, I. J. & Stitzel, R. E. (1977) Corpus striatum (paleostriatal complex) interventions and stereotyped behaviours in pigeons. *Neuroscience Abstracts*.

Graeff, F. G. & Oliveira, L. de (1975) Influence of response topography on the effect of apomorphine and amphetamine on operant behaviour of pigeons. *Psychopharmacology*, **41**, 127–132.

Güntürkün, O. (1984) Evidence for a third primary visual area in the telencephalon of the pigeon. *Brain Research*, **294**, 247–254.

Güntürkün, O. (1985) Lateralization of visually controlled behavior in pigeons. *Physiology and Behavior*, **34**, 575–577.

Herrnstein, R. J., Loveland, D. H., & Cable, C. (1976) Natural concepts in pigeons. *Journal of Experimental Psychology: Animal Behavior Processes*, **2**, 285–311.

Hodos, W., Leibowitz, R. W., & Bonbright, J. C. (1976) Near field acuity of pigeons: effects of head location and stimulus luminance. *Journal of the Experimental Analysis of Behavior*, **25**, 129–141.

Hollard, V. D. & Delius, J. D. (1982) Rotational invariance in visual pattern recognition by pigeons and humans. *Science*, **218**, 804–806.

Hord, R. M. (1982) *Digital Image Processing of Remotely Sensed Data*. New York: Academic Press.

Jäger, R. (1985) *Lateralization reversal following unilateral forebrain lesions in pigeons* (in preparation).

Jahnke, H. J. (1984) Binocular visual field differences among various breeds of pigeons. *Bird Behavior*, **5**, 96–102.

Jenkins, H. M. & Moore, B. R. (1973) The form of the autoshaped response with food or water reinforcers. *Journal of the Experimental Analysis of Behavior*, **20**, 163–181.

Karten, H. J. (1968) The ascending auditory pathway in the pigeon (*Columba livia*): Telencephalic projections of the nucleus ovoidalis thalami. *Brain Research*, **11**, 134–153.

Kinchla, J. (1970) Discrimination of two auditory durations by pigeons. *Perception and Psychophysics*, **8**, 299–307.

Klinkenberg, T., Delius, J. D., & Emmerton, J. A. (1984) Classical heart-rate conditioning and differentiation of visual CS with an appetitive UCS in pigeons. *Behavioural Processes*, **9**, 23–30.

Konishi, M. (1973) Locatable and nonlocatable acoustic signals for barn owls. *American Naturalist*, **107**, 775–785.

Krasnegor, N. A. (1971) The effects of telencephalic lesions on auditory discriminations in the pigeon. *Dissertation Abstracts International*, **31**, 5029 B.

Leppelsack, H. J. (1978) Unit responses to species specific sounds in the auditory forebrain center of birds. *Federation Proceedings*, **37**, 2336–2341.

Levine, R. R. & Zeigler, H. P. (1981) Extratelencephalic pathways and feeding behaviour in the pigeon (*Columba livia*). *Brain, Behavior and Evolution*, **19**, 56–92.

Leyland, C. M. (1977) Higher-order autoshaping. *The Quarterly Journal of Experimental Psychology*, **29**, 607–619.

Lindenblatt, U. (1985) *Apomorphine microinjections into the nucleus basalis prosencephali of pigeons elicit pecking fits* (in preparation).

Lohmann, A., Delius, J. D., Hollard, V. D., & Friesel, M. (1985) *Discrimination of mirror images by pigeons* (in preparation).

Lolordo, V. M. & Furrow, D. R. (1976) Control by the auditory or the visual element of compound stimulus: Effects of feedback. *Journal of Experimental Analysis of Behavior*, **25**, 251–256.

Lombardi, C. M. & Delius, J. D. (1985) Size invariance in visual pattern recognition in pigeons. In M. L. Commons, R. J. Herrenstein & S. Kosslyn (Eds.) *Pattern Recognition and Concepts*. Hillsdale, N.J.: Lawrence Erlbaum Associates.

Lombardi, C. M., Fachinelli, C. C., & Delius, J. D. (1983) Oddity of visual patterns conceptualized by pigeons. *Animal Learning and Behavior*, **12**, 2–6.

Mallin, H. D. & Delius, J. D. (1983) Inter- and intraocular transfer of colour discriminations with mandibulation as an operant in the head fixed pigeon. *Behaviour Analysis Letters*, **3**, 297–309.

Marr, D. (1982) *Vision. A computational investigation on processing of visual information*. San Francisco: Freeman.

Martin Ramirez, J. (1979) Forebrain lesions and food intake in pigeons. *Physiology and Behavior*, **23**, 981–984.

Martin Ramirez, J. & Delius, J. D. (1979) Aggressive behaviour of pigeons: suppression by archistriatal lesions. *Aggressive Behavior*, **5**, 3–17.

Minelli, G. (1970) Ricerche istochimiche dell' encephalo di *Testudo graeca* e *Coturnix coturnix*. *Rivista di Biologia*, **63**, 61–86.

Murton, R. K., Coombs, C. F. B., & Thearle, J. P. (1972) Ecological studies of the feral pigeon *Columba livia var*. Flock behaviour and social organization. *Journal of Applied Ecology*, **9**, 875–889.

Nairn, J. S. & Rescorla, R. A. (1981) Second order conditioning with diffuse auditory reinforcers in the pigeon. *Learning and Motivation*, **12**, 65–91.

Nau, F. & Delius, J. D. (1981) Discrepant effects of unilateral and bilateral forebrain lesions on the visual performance of pigeons. *Behavioural Brain Research*, **2**, 119–224.

Naumov, N. P. & Iljitschew, W. D. (1964) Klanganalyse im Grosshirn der Vögel. *Die Naturwissenschaften*, **51**, 644.

Palya, W. L. & Zacny, J. P. (1980) Stereotyped adjunctive pecking by caged pigeons. *Animal Learning and Behavior*, **8**, 293–303.

Parker, D. M. & Delius, J. D. (1980) The effects of Wulst lesions on simple visual discrimination performance in the pigeon. *Behavioural Processes*, **5**, 151–159.

Phillips, R. E. (1966) Evoked potential study of connections of avian archistriatum and caudal neostriatum. *Journal of Comparative Neurology*, **127**, 89–99.

Ritchie, T. L. C. (1979) Intratelencephalic visual connections and their relationship to the archistriatum in the pigeon (*Columba livia*). PhD thesis. University of Virginia, Charlottesville.

Rogers, L. J. (1982) Light experience and asymmetry of brain function in chickens. *Nature*, **297**, 223–225.

Schall, U. & Delius, J. D. (1985) *Sensory input to the nucleus basalis prosencephali, a feeding-pecking center in the pigeon* (in preparation).

Schall, U., Güntürkün, O., & Delius, J. D. (1985) *Sensory projections to the nucleus basalis prosencephali of the pigeon* (in preparation).

Servière, J. (1979) Psychophysiological correlates of time perception in the pigeon. In: A. M. Granda & J. H. Maxwell (Eds.), *Neural Mechanisms of Behavior in Pigeons*. New York: Plenum Press.

Shepard, R. N. & Cooper, L. A. (1982) *Mental Images and their Transformations*. Cambridge, Mass: MIT Press.

Sieland, M., Delius, J. D., Rautenberg, W., & May, B. (1981) Thermoregulation mediated by conditioned heart-rate changes in pigeons. *Journal of Comparative Physiology*, **144**, 375–379.

Staddon, J. E. R. (1977) Schedule induced behaviour. In: W. K. Honig & J. E. R. Staddon (Eds.), *Handbook of Operant Conditioning*. Englewood Cliffs: Prentice Hall.

Stingelin, W. (1962) Ergebnisse der Vogelhirnforschung. *Verhandlungen der Naturforschenden Gesellschaft Basel*, **73**, 300–317.

Timberlake, W. (1983) Rats' responses to a moving object related to food or water: a behaviour-systems analysis. *Animal Learning Behaviour*, **11**, 309–320.

Wallenberg, A. (1903) Der Ursprung Des Tractus isthmo-striatus (oder bulbo-striatus) der Taube. *Neurologisches Central-blatt*, **22**, 98–101.

Witkowsky, P., Zeigler, H. P., & Silver, R. (1973) The nucleus basalis of the pigeon, a single unit analysis. *Journal of Comparative Neurology*, **147**, 119–128.

Zeigler, H. P. (1976) Feeding behaviour of the pigeon. *Advances in the Study of Behaviour*, **7**, 285–389.

Zeigler, H. P., Green, H. L., & Karten, H. J. (1969) Neural control of feeding behaviour in the pigeon. *Psychonomic Science*, **15**, 156–157.

Zeigler, H. P., Hollard, V. D., Wild, J. M., & Webster, D. M. (1978) Intracranial self-stimulation from endbrain nuclei in the pigeon. *Physiology and Behavior*, **21**, 387–394.

Zeigler, H. P., Levitt, P. W., & Levine, R. R. (1980) Eating in the pigeon *Columba livia*: Movement patterns, stereotypy and stimulus control. *Journal of Comparative Physiological Psychology*, **94**, 783–794.

Zweers, G. (1982a) Drinking in the pigeon (*Columba livia L.*), *Behaviour*, **80**, 274–317.

Zweers, G. (1982b) Pecking in the pigeon (*Columba livia L.*), *Behaviour*, **81**, 173–230.

6 The Comparative Psychology of Operant Behaviour

J. E. R. Staddon
Duke University, Durham, North Carolina

The theme of this session, Behaviouristic and Ethological Approaches: Complementary or Antagonistic? seemed to me at first merely rhetorical. Behaviourists and ethologists study similar animals, often in very similar situations. Assuming both groups follow generally agreed scientific principles, how can there be any real opposition between them? To study animals without deep awareness of evolutionary principles seems ludicrous, so ethology's roots in Darwinian theory are surely unassailable. And history has shown the futility of basing psychology, especially animal psychology, on anything other than behaviour, so behaviourism, at least of the nonradical variety, seems equally well based[1].

Yet further reading began to raise doubts. In the USA the *Comparative Psychology Newsletter*, a widely circulated mimeographed periodical, contains much of interest to ethologists and animal psychologists. When I first saw it, it seemed to me an admirable organ giving animal psychology a boost much needed in these days when apparent human relevance is a major requirement for research funding in psychology. Yet further acquaintance soon revealed that the newsletter had a rather different agenda, namely to promote 'comparative psychology,' defined as quite

[1]Basing psychology on behavioural data does not limit theory to the same level. Particle physicists study streaks and dots on film, and *Drosophila* geneticists count fruit flies of different colors and shapes, but both deal with theories at levels remote from these data. The difference between methodological behaviourism and some varieties of cognitivism is that concepts such as "representation" and "information processing' are for the behaviourist inferences from, or theories of, behaviour, not a subject matter prior and superordinate to what can be directly observed.

distinct from behavioural psychology, ethology, and, especially, sociobiology (I have since learned that this tendency is a characteristic of some contributors to the newsletter, not of its editor). Clearly, not everyone shares my naïve assumption that all who study the behaviour of animals are in essential accord.

This persistence, even widening, of divisions within our field got me thinking about the historical origins of behavioural psychology and the relations, or lack of relations, between biology and psychology. In the remainder of my paper, I want to speak about the historical origins of modern behaviourism and how they may have led to an unnecessary divergence between behaviourism and ethology. If history had taken a slightly different turn, our field might have developed along different and possibly more fruitful lines. There is a promising alternative, as yet undeveloped, which was foreshadowed in the dawn of behaviourism, but failed to catch the attention of its most vocal advocates.

THE ORIGINS OF BEHAVIOURISTIC THEORY

Behaviourism developed out of reflex physiology. John Watson was strongly influenced by Pavlov and Sechenov; Skinner by Sherrington, Crozier, and Magnus. Stimulus-response psychology and its various neobehaviouristic successors also derives from a simplified reflex model. Skinner was one of the first to see serious problems with this approach. But his *Behaviour of organisms* is a curiously schizophrenic work, in that it attempts to reconcile two opposing notions: the concept of the reflex, which implies a stimulus for every response, and the concept of the operant, which implies spontaneous "emission" of behaviour. This opposition was dealt with in two ways, neither wholly satisfactory. At an empirical level, Skinner and his students resolved the contradiction by studying almost exclusively *asymptotic behaviour*, that is established habits, for which a controlling stimulus could invariably be found (Staddon, 1967). At a theoretical level, it was resolved by a form of words: Controlling stimuli were said to "set the occasion for" their responses, not to elicit them—although often no quantitative difference can be found between the stimulus-response relations set up by operant conditioning and comparable reflex relations.

The reflex model has been something of a red herring in the development of behavioural psychology. It has been distracting for two reasons. First, psychologists emphasised the wrong aspect of reflexology, attending to the stimulus-response property of reflexes, and not to reflex integration—the principles by which tendencies to action combine to produce overt behaviour. Second, by focussing on reflex-like behaviour, psychologists were led to neglect behaviour that could not easily be tied to a stimulus.

A look at the history of behavioural biology reveals an alternative which, had psychologists paid more attention to it, might have led us on a more fruitful path. What is the essential feature of operant behaviour? I believe Skinner had the right answer when he defined operant behaviour as behaviour controlled by its *consequences*[2]: Consequences, not reflexes, are the key. Nearly 80 years ago, when behavioural psychology was yet unborn, H. S. Jennings, a little-known zoologist, was working on the effects of consequences manifested in their most primitive form, in the behaviour of single-celled animals. Jennings' work with these simple creatures provides a model for the operant behaviour of higher organisms more appropriate than reflex-based models. Following this alternative path leads to what might be called a *comparative behaviourism* that eliminates the current divisions between behavioural and cognitive psychologists and raises no barriers between behavioural psychology and its sister (should one these days say "sibling"?) disciplines of ethology and sociobiology.

OPERANT BEHAVIOUR OF SIMPLE ORGANISMS

If we concentrate on control-by-consequences as the defining feature, then essentially every organism shows operant behaviour. In the late 19th century, two German biologists, Engelmann and Pfeffer showed that bacteria will congregate in the vicinity of a capillary tube containing a nutrient solution. Still earlier, Darwin (1880) studied the orienting movements of plants that allow them to seek light. Recently, Daniel Koshland (1980) and his students have analysed the mechanism of bacterial chemotaxis. In all these cases, consequences have their effects through a process of behavioural variation accompanied by selection of favoured variants. In chemotaxis (actually a klino*kinesis* in the terminology of Fraenkel & Gunn, 1940), for example, *Salmonella* bacteria find their way up a nutrient gradient by alternating between two modes, "tumbling," in which they turn rapidly and follow no consistent direction, and straight swimming. Under resting conditions, tumbling is the mode, but if by accident the animal moves up the gradient, tumbling ceases and the animal swims straight. If swimming straight causes the animal to move down the gradient, it begins to tumble again: "By taking giant steps in the right direction and small steps

[2]Skinner defined operant behaviour in at least two other ways, of course: as linked stimulus and response classes that show "orderly changes" as a function of "third variables" (this is the reflex-like definition, Staddon, 1967); and by exclusion, as behaviour for which "no correlated stimulus can be detected on occasions when it is observed to occur. (Skinner, 1938, p21)" Which definition was to be used depended on what aspect of behaviour was being studied, but implicit was the assumption of a single, unique class of behavior having all three characteristics.

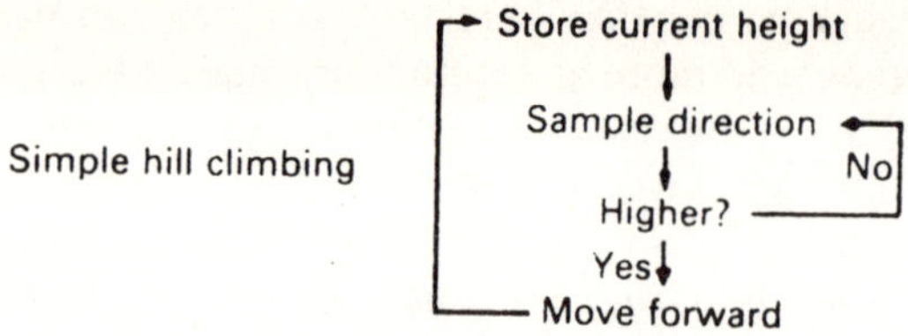

FIG. 6.1. The logic of simple hill climbing.

in the wrong direction, it biases its walk very effectively in the direction which aids its survival. (Koshland, 1977, p.1057).''

Tumbling serves the function of sampling different directions (behavioural variation); the selection criterion is the time derivative of nutrient concentration. When the derivative is positive (things are getting better), the animal swims straight; when it is not (things are unchanging or getting worse), it tumbles. The process is an example of hill climbing, illustrated schematically in Fig. 6.1. More on hill-climbing later.

Jennings described numerous examples of simple operant behaviour. His account of the avoidance reactions of the ciliate *Stentor* is perhaps the most revealing. His experimental situation is shown in Fig.6.2: The animal is attached to its tube on a substrate and a weak irritant suspension of carmine is introduced into the vicinity. The animal at first just turns away,

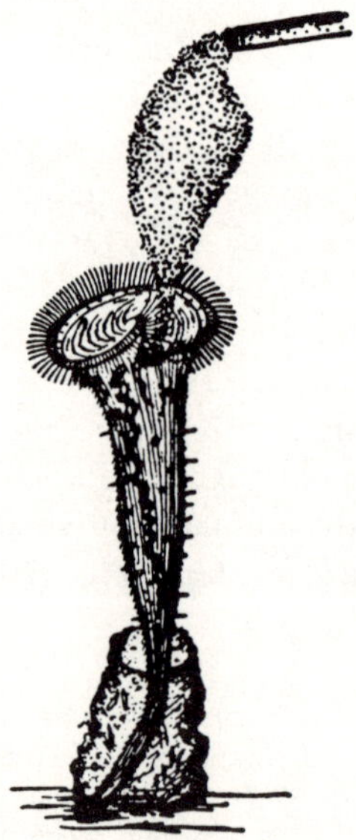

FIG. 6.2. *Stentor roeselii* attached to its tube and drawing a cloud of carmine particles into the ciliary disk as part of its normal feeding pattern. (After Jennings, 1906, Fig. 111).

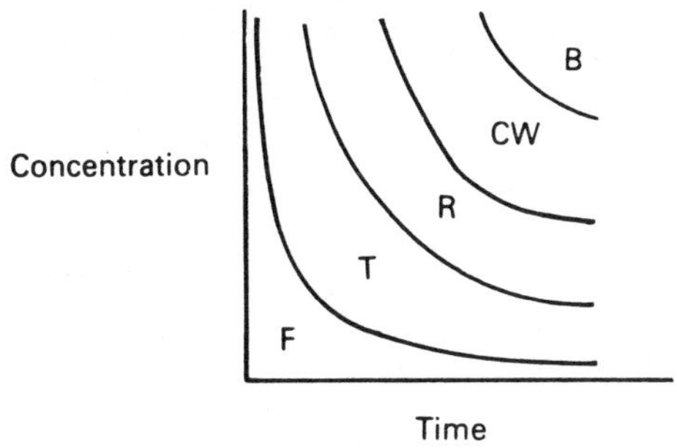

FIG. 6.3. Economic analysis of *Stentor* escape behaviour. Each contour line represents the combination of concentration and time sufficient to cause a transition from one escape behaviour to the next. Codes: F = feeding; T = turning away; R = ciliary reversal; CW = retraction into tube + waiting; B = breaking away.

the movement being repeated several times. If this is ineffective, the animal next reverses the direction of ciliary movement, blowing rather than sucking. This also is repeated a few times. If this also fails to work, *Stentor* may then contract into its tube and wait for some time. This may also be repeated if the irritating condition is still present when the beast reemerges. Finally, if all else fails, the animal detaches itself from its tube and swims away.

This example of simple adaptive behaviour by a single-celled animal embodies every property of the operant behaviour of higher animals save one. It fits into the variation-selection idea: The animal has a repertoire of five acts (feeding, F, turning away, T, ciliary reversal, CR, contract and wait, CW, and breaking away, B). Feeding is preferred, but if a noxious stimulus is presented, then the other four activities occur, usually in the sequence described, until the aversive condition is relieved. The behaviour is more complicated than the kinetic movement of Koshland's bacteria only in that five activities rather than two are involved.

What determines when *Stentor* will change from one escape activity to another, or from feeding to escape? Jennings does not give enough information to be sure, but we can guess that at least two factors are likely to be involved: time and stimulus intensity (density of carmine)[3]. How do these combine to determine the animal's behaviour? Again, we don't know for sure, but we can imagine two ways of dealing with the question: an economic analysis, or an analysis in terms of mechanism—the same two methods that have been used to explain the operant behaviour of mammals and birds.

A simplified economic analysis is illustrated in Fig. 6.3. The figure shows

[3]Undoubtedly rate of change of intensity will also be a factor, but for simplicity I ignore dynamics here.

a set of curves, convex to the origin, that describe when the animal should change from one activity to the next. The rationale for the curves is that the four escape activities are progressively more costly to the animal (ciliary reversal—an interruption of feeding—is more costly than turning way; contract–and–wait is more costly than ciliary reversal, and so on) so that the animal should switch from one to the next only when the damage-potential of the aversive stimulus is higher than some predetermined level. Presumably danger is directly related to both the duration and intensity of the stimulus, hence the approximately hyperbolic curves[4].

The escape behaviour of *Stentor* can also be analysed mechanistically. The traditional behaviouristic explanation for sequences of behaviour like this is the *chain reflex*, but this won't work for several reasons (none of which relate to *Stentor*'s conspicuous lack of synapses—physiology is irrelevant to this argument). *Stentor* repeats each escape activity several times, so that the essential property of a chain, that each link depends only on the preceding one, is violated. Escape activities occasionally occur out of the order I have described—this also argues against chaining. Strict serial dependence makes chain reflexes highly vulnerable to disruption (if activity N is blocked, activity N+1 cannot occur)—a functional argument against the principle. Early dominance of chain-reflex explanations in the history of behaviourism is an example of the misplaced emphasis on stimulus-response relations that I mentioned earlier.

There are other reflex-type models that do much better. For example, suppose that each of the various activities of which *Stentor* is capable competes for access to the "behavioural final common path," while each is simultaneously facilitated by appropriate stimuli. This situation is illus-

---

[4]Fig. 6.3 applies only when carmine concentration is constant. The formal analysis is as follows. Suppose that concentration changes with time according to some function, C(t). The simplest assumption is that damage-potential, D, depends upon the cumulative effect of the dangerous substance, that is, on its time integral:

$$D = \int_0^t C(t)dt.$$

If $C(t) = C$ (i.e., concentration is constant), then integration between the limits shows:

$$D = Ct.$$

Thus the hyperbolic boundaries in Fig. 6.3 (which have the equation Ct = constant, where C is concentration and t is time) correspond to lines of constant cumulative effect for fixed concentrations of irritant substance.

A more realistic model would presumably need to weight recent concentration values more than old ones, to incorporate a threshold (below which damage potential is negligible) and to give greater weight to rapid changes in concentration.

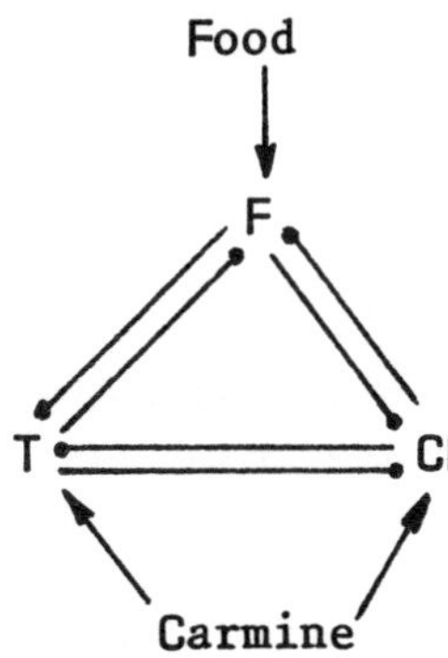

FIG. 6.4. A parallel reflex-type model sufficient to explain *Stentor* escape behaviour. Activities T (turning away), F (feeding) and CR (ciliary reversal) are mutually inhibitory; F is facilitated by food stimuli, T and CR by aversive stimuli (carmine).

trated for just three activities in Fig. 6.4. A process sufficient to generate the escape behaviour I have described might work as follows: (1) the animal can only do one thing at a time, and which occurs is determined by its "strength," highest wins; (2) strength depends on facilitating effects from stimuli, inhibiting effects from other tendencies (the net strength of T [say] depends on the positive effect of carmine, less the inhibiting effects from F and CR); (3) activities are self-inhibiting, that is, occurrence of an activity tends to weaken it (an equivalent assumption is that nonoccurrence of an activity tends to strengthen it). Without this assumption, the dominant activity would persist indefinitely. If the effect of carmine on T is relatively greater than its effect on CR, then when first presented, T will occur, to be followed by CR, and so on. Simple assumptions about dynamic properties, thresholds, and differences in inhibitory and excitatory strengths, allow this system to mimic almost any escape sequence.

Reflex models of this sort rest much more on the integrative properties of reflexes than their stimulus-response properties; are not limited to the rigid sequences implied by chains; and can account in principle for quite complex serial organisation (for example, the theoretical work of Ludlow, 1980; Grossberg, 1982).

Jennings' account of *Stentor* behaviour provides a better model for operant behaviour than naïve stimulus-response theory: it shows behavioural variation and environmental selection, the key features of operant behaviour; and the dynamics of variation can be analysed in reflex terms. The proper role for reflex theory is to explain how tendencies to action interact, the mechanics of behavioural variation, rather than provide a stimulus-response model for the habits of mammals and birds.

STIMULUS CONTROL

If *Stentor* are so smart, why don't we use them in operant conditioning experiments? Subject cost would be much reduced, the Japanese would soon come up with the appropriate miniaturised operant chamber (Suzuki box?), and space savings would be substantial. What does the operant behaviour of a ciliate lack? The obvious answer is learning (or memory). Left alone for a few hours, a *Stentor* will remember nothing of its former experience with carmine. If it gets the stimulus again, it will again cycle through the same escape sequence but repetition brings no increase in efficiency. The animal is not completely devoid of memory, of course, since the same stimulus, carmine, produces one effect at one time (turning, say), a different effect (ciliary reversal) at a slightly later time. Something must have changed in the meantime. The salient fact about this memory, however, is that it is transient or local. The animal has no long-term memory.

Why not? The answer to this question can tell us something about the real differences between "higher" and "lower" animals, and provides an interpretation for the effects of discriminative stimuli that is quite different from the reflex account. The first thing to dispose of is the tacit assumption of many early behaviourists that there is something intrinsically demanding in the faculty of memory. Not so. Abundant contemporary acquaintance with computers and tape recorders should convince anyone that the process of reversible storage is no technical challenge, for man or, presumably, for nature. "Storage," in this trivial sense, is not the problem. The real problem is one of information.

Consider what is involved in *Stentor* learning to respond more rapidly to succeeding carmine presentations, that is, learning that the first few seconds of carmine are a reliable signal for prolonged exposure, so that instead of waiting to cycle through its whole escape repertoire, the beast can just break away at once. Every stimulus has hedonic and nonhedonic properties. Carmine is aversive, but it also has a certain colour, particle size, chemical composition, and so on. Associative learning implies using the nonhedonic properties (the conditioned or discriminative stimulus) as a signal for the hedonic ones (the US or reinforcer). An animal encounters numerous stimuli, positive, negative and neutral, each with its own set of nonhedonic properties. Learning is worthwhile only if a given stimulus, like carmine, is sufficiently different in its *non*hedonic aspects from other stimuli, encountered before and after, that the animal can detect a correlation between that stimulus and its associated hedonic effect.

For example, imagine an animal that is sensitive to only one nonhedonic dimension, say intensity, and can only distinguish two values, A and B. For learning to be worthwhile, there must be some real correlation between

TABLE 6.1

	Hedonic Category	
Physical Category	*Bad*	*Good*
A	$p(b \mid A)$	$p(g \mid A)$
B	$p(b \mid B)$	$p(g \mid B)$

hedonic value (good and bad) and the animal's experience with stimuli falling into categories A and B. The problem is illustrated in Table 6.1: For learning to be worthwhile, this table must show some real contingency, $p(g \mid A) \neq p(g \mid B)$. If carmine is similar in its nonhedonic properties to many other stimuli daily encountered by *Stentor*, then the animal is in no position even to detect that repeated exposures to carmine are "the same." Its cognitive world is so primitive that it cannot reliably distinguish carmine from other things, so cannot learn that this particular constellation of nonhedonic properties is a signal for any particular hedonic outcome. Under these conditions, the animal will not learn—not because it cannot "remember," but because its representation of the world is too crude to allow it to detect a real correlation. It fails to learn because, from its point of view, there is nothing *to* learn[5].

This cognitive limitation is no impediment to local memory, because time–since–an–event will always have strong predictive value. *Stentor* may not recognise carmine when it encounters it a second time after long delay, but, the world now being much as it was a moment ago, can infer that stimuli in the same category that follow one another closely in time are in fact the same event. Thus, if carmine is withdrawn after the animal has shown activity CW (contraction), but is then reintroduced after not-too-long a delay, the animal will contract again at once, rather than beginning its whole escape sequence from the beginning.

I draw two conclusions from this simple example. First, the real con-

[5]There is related limitation on the learning of simple animals that is more difficult to demonstrate. Even if we could show that the receptor response of *Stentor* to carmine is much different from receptor response to other stimuli, the animal would still need information-processing machinery sufficient to keep separate the record of carmine and the animal's history of experience with it. The problem here is not so much the laying down of the record, as the existence of a system for keeping the various records separate from one another and ensuring that recurrence of the same environment reinstates the appropriate internal state. The evolutionary task is to create a database management system, not just a reel of tape, a library, not a pile of books. This problem becomes more acute the more sensitive the animal's receptor apparatus: The more states of the world the animal can distinguish, the more difficult the task of organising the resulting information.

straint under which primitive animals labour is not one of memory but one of cognition. It is not that they cannot retain an impression over time, it is that they cannot differentiate among objects in the world with sufficient resolution to make remembering worthwhile. Second, a discriminative stimulus is not really a stimulus, in the sense of something that exists to provoke a response, at all. A discriminative stimulus causes an animal to go into a particular state, and that state is defined not by psychophysical relations but solely by being different from all other states. Stimulus control is primarily control of state, not of response. In other words, the discriminative stimulus for an operant is just whatever it is about the situation that differentiates it for the animal from all other situations. A discriminative stimulus is more like a category, than like the goad of a reflex.

The set of states—large for mammals and birds, small for ciliates—defines what Von Uexkull called the animal's "Umwelt," its world view. Animals' world views will differ and will reflect differences in their niches (innate differences) and perhaps differences in their individual experiences (learned differences). Comparative psychology becomes then in large measure the study of cognitive differences among species and among individual animals.

SELECTION RULES AND COGNITIVE CONSTRAINTS

Operant conditioning, the meat and potatoes of behaviourism, fits into this kind of scheme as hill-climbing. The animal can identify states of the world. Some states are better than others. The animal behaves in such a way as to improve his state. *Salmonella* or pigeon, the selection criterion is essentially the same: the time derivative of hedonic value. Positive reinforcement is a change for the better. The difference between bird and bacterium is not the raw rule, but the complexity of the material with which it must operate; the animal's world view, which, in protists comprises only the present and immediate past, but in mammals and birds can reflect remote past experience in such a way that when a situation recurs, the animal need not repeat its entire prior variation-selection sequence, but can at once pick the best behaviour. Mammals and birds choose among richer alternatives than protists, and are aided in their choice by cumulative effects of past experience.

I conclude with an example of how cognitive constraints limit animals' ability to behave optimally, so must be included in any realistic account. John Hinson and I have shown in several experiments (e.g., 1983a, 1983b) that pigeons pecking two keys on concurrent variable-interval schedules respond according to a momentary-maximising (hill-climbing) decision rule: When they peck, they tend to choose the key most likely to pay off. This requires that they attend to the relevant stimulus features, which in this simple situation are just the time-since-last-peck to each choice. It turns out that this hill-climbing rule is quite close to optimal in this situation.

Mazur (1981) published a paper describing a situation where hill-climbing based on postresponse times is not optimal. In his experiment a single variable-interval schedule allocated brief timeouts to one response key or the other. Once the VI timer had "set up," a response to the selected alternative was necessary to restart the timer and permit food to be allocated to the other key. Mazur varied the proportion of timeouts associated with food delivery. In one condition, for example, only 10 per cent of timeouts were paired with food for pecks on one key, whereas 100 percent of timeouts were paired with food for pecks on the other key. because food allocation to the two keys was not independent, reward maximisation required the pigeons not to stray too far from equality in their allocation of pecks to the two keys. Of course, they failed to do this, and instead approximately matched choice and payoff proportions—the result to be expected from almost any simple hill-climbing rule based on the hypothesis that the two choices are independent (Hinson & Staddon, 1983b). Stephen Lea (1976) some years ago reported similar nonoptimal choice behaviour in a choice experiment using ratio schedules.

These results show how our understanding of reward mechanisms depends inevitably on what we assume about animals' cognitive capacities. From one point of view—the assumption that pigeons have no difficulty attending to overall payoff rate, as distinct from payoffs associated with each choice—Mazur's animals were behaving irrationally; consistently picking the worse alternative. From another point of view—which assumes that his animals were constrained to treat two physically distinct choices as independent—they were behaving rationally and consistently picking the best option (Staddon & Hinson, 1983).

For many years, the cognitive problem was evaded by restricting experiment to known, simple situations. This work has been very successful: We now know a great deal about how rewards and punishments work. The next step is to tackle the much more difficult task of understanding the cognitive capacities that differentiate individuals and species from one another—what they are, how they develop, and how they can be modified. This work obviously touches on both human cognitive psychology (although not in some of its narrower mechanomorphic forms) and behavioural ecology. There is no antagonism between behaviourism and ethology[6].

---

[6]Research supported by grants from the National Science Foundation to Duke University. Some of the arguments in this chapter are elaborated from Staddon (1983).

REFERENCES

Darwin, C. (1880) *The power of movement in plants*. London: John Murray.

Fraenkel, G. S. & Gunn, D. L. (1940) *The orientation of animals*. Fair Lawn, NJ: Oxford University Press. (Dover edition: 1961)

Grossberg, S. (1982) *Studies of mind and brain*. Boston: D. Reidel.

Hinson, J. M. & Staddon, J. E. R. (1983a) Hill-climbing by pigeons. *Journal of the Experimental Analysis of Behaviour*, **39**, 25–47.

Hinson, J. M. & Staddon, J. E. R. (1983b) Matching, maximizing and hill climbing. *Journal of the Experimental Analysis of Behaviour*, **40**, 321–31.

Koshland, D. E. (1977) A response regulator model in a simple sensory system. *Science*, **196**, 1055–1063.

Koshland, D. E. (1980) *Bacterial chemotaxis as a model behavioural system*. New York: Raven Press.

Jennings, H. S. (1976) *Behaviour of the lower organisms*. Bloomington: Indiana University Press. (Reprint of the 1906 edition).

Lea, S. E. G. (1976) Titration of schedule parameters by pigeons. *Journal of the Experimental Analysis of Behaviour*, **25**, 43–54.

Ludlow, A. R. (1980) The evolution and simulation of a decision maker. In F. M. Toates & T. R. Halliday (Eds.), *The analysis of motivational processes*. London: Academic Press.

Mazur, J. E. (1981) Optimization theory fails to predict performance of pigeons in a two-response situation. *Science*, **214**, 823–825.

Skinner, B. F. (1938) *The behaviour of organisms*. New York: Appleton-Century.

Staddon, J. E. R. (1967) Asymptotic behaviour: The concept of the operant. *Psychological Review*, **74**, 377–391.

Staddon, J. E. R. (1983) *Adaptive behaviour and learning*. New York: Cambridge University Press.

Staddon, J. E. R. & Hinson, J. M. (1983) Optimization: A result or a mechanism? *Science*, **221**, 976–7.

III DETERMINANTS OF HUMAN OPERANT BEHAVIOUR

7 On the Generality of Behavioural Principles: Human Choice and the Matching Law

C. F. Lowe and P. J. Horne
Department of Psychology, University College of North Wales, Bangor

In his book *Behavior of Organisms*, Skinner (1938) argued that the importance of his science of behaviour, then based upon research with animals, lay in the possibility of its eventual extension to human affairs. In the decades that have elapsed since the publication of this seminal book, the approach which has come to be known as the experimental analysis of behaviour has been a major influence in applied work with humans, particularly in the areas of clinical and educational psychology. The achievements of "applied analysis" in these areas are well documented; they need not be reiterated here. But the precise nature of the relationship between the behavioural principles derived from animal research and these applied studies remains controversial. For although the success of various behaviour modification procedures has often been taken as direct evidence that human behaviour is subject to the same laws of learning as apply to animals, a number of authors have argued that the efficacy of such procedures owes little to conditioning principles, and indeed, some have said that there is no convincing evidence for operant or classical conditioning in humans (see Beech, 1974; Bloomfield, 1976; Boulgouris, 1982; Brewer, 1974; Dietz, 1978). Evidence derived from studies in the applied area does little to clarify the issue since these studies were designed, not systematically to isolate the determinants of human learning, but to provide effective therapy and to change behaviour on a pragmatic basis. Skinner suggested in 1938 that whether or not one could extrapolate from animal to human was a question that could be resolved "only by closing in upon the problem in an orderly way and by following the customary procedures of an experimental science".

An issue of such moment for the new science of behaviour should, of course, have merited urgent and rigorous experimental study, all the more so as Skinner had enjoined it. Yet, remarkably, research with human subjects within behaviour analysis has been singularly sparse and, until recently, no systematic attempt has been made to validate the notion that human and animal behaviour have similar determinants and are governed by the same general principles. Instead researchers in the area have tended to dedicate themselves to an exhaustive consideration of a number of aspects of animal behaviour; in the past two decades there has been an increasing concern with detailed mathematical descriptions and abstract models of animal performance under a variety of reinforcement conditions (see Lea, Chapter 4). With major areas of human functioning thus ignored there has been an obvious vacuum that "cognitive" psychologists have not been disinclined to fill. Those involved in applied analysis, armed with not much more than the notion of the three-term contingency, have struggled to deal with the complexities of human behaviour, but have increasingly bemoaned the fact that most basic research makes little contact with their concerns and hence does not inform their practice (Branch & Malagodi, 1980; Dietz, 1978; Hayes, Rincover & Solnick, 1980; Michael, 1980; Michael, Chapter 10).

A justification of this neglect of human behaviour could take a number of forms. First, it could be argued that conditioning principles are applicable only to non-human animal species, and that entirely different laws operate at the human level; human behaviour then ought properly to be studied within the framework of a different paradigm, using different theoretical concepts and methods. According to this view, which might be termed the *discontinuity assumption*, the study of animal behaviour is of intrinsic interest and does not need to justify itself by claiming any relevance, directly or indirectly, to human affairs.

The polar opposite of this position is the view that there are no qualitative differences between human and animal behaviour. There may be differences of degree or complexity but, it is argued, in studying animal behaviour we are, essentially, studying the behaviour of humans. This *continuity assumption* is very widely held and takes one of two forms. According to one school of thought the principles of conditioning derived from the study of animal behaviour, as outlined by Skinner and others, are in themselves sufficient to account for human behaviour; having explored the fundamental workings of the three-term contingency with sub-human species we now need merely to construct a technology of behaviour to deal with the educational, clinical, and social problems that beset mankind. This essentially zoomorphic view has its anthropomorphic counterpart in "cognitive" theories that attempt to explain animal performance with concepts derived from observations of human behaviour. Dickinson (1980, 1984), for example, maintains that animals "acquire knowledge" and are "rational," and that they use a "propositional model" for these purposes. In describing animal operant behaviour he argues that "the knowledge about the action-goal relationship must be encoded in propositional-like form so that it can be operated on by a practical inference process to generate the instrumental performance. In this sense actions (of animals) are truly rational in a way that responses can never be" (1984). According to this account (see also Mackintosh & Dickinson, 1979; Roitblat, Bever & Terrace, 1984) the central concern of learning theorists should not be with behaviour but with the ways in which knowledge acquisition by animals takes place (1980, pxi). (For a critique of this approach, see Blackman, 1983.)

The continuity position in both its forms has held great sway among psychologists and has provided the framework, if not straitjacket, within which most researchers in the area of animal learning have operated, as the following quotation from Honig (1978) illustrates:

> If psychologists were consistent in applying the principle of biological continuity amongst species, they would find it easier to adopt concepts based on human experience to characterize behavior in other species and to suggest theoretical formulations. The principle of continuity implies the possibility of moving in both directions along the phylogenetic continuum. Traditionally psychologists have started with a S-R analysis founded on animal behavior and have moved "up" the scale for the analysis of human behavior. The study of cognitive processes in animals may open the way to movement in the other direction. Once the behavioral analysis has been soundly established, subjective or mentalistic concepts arising from human experience can perhaps be used for explanation or theory (p13).

But the choice for psychologists need not be bounded by the simple continuity or discontinuity perspectives. An alternative, more dialectical, view for which evidence has been accumulating in recent years, is one that acknowledges that there is a biological, and indeed psychological, continuity between animals and humans but also that there are qualitative differences (Vygotsky, 1962, 1978; Luria, 1961, 1982). Much of this evidence comes from developmental studies, for long a neglected area of operant research, and it supports the notion that the development of language in humans and the consequent emergence of *rule-governed*, as opposed to *contingency-shaped*, behaviour, has a profound effect on behavioural relationships (cf. Skinner, 1966). Although this literature has been reviewed in detail elsewhere (Lowe, 1979, 1983), the main findings will be summarised here.

Several studies have shown that, in terms of response patterning and sensitivity to schedule parameters, the behaviour of adult humans on basic schedules of reinforcement, such as fixed-interval (FI) and fixed-ratio (FR), bears little resemblance to animal performance under comparable conditions. Studies by Lowe, Harzem and Bagshaw (1978) and Lowe, Harzem and Hughes (1978), which introduced response-produced clock stimuli to attenuate covert counting strategies on interval schedules, are possible exceptions to this general rule. In addition to these gross differences in performance on the basic schedules, humans also differ from animals in the way they are affected by their previous history of reinforcement. Human subjects exposed to different schedules frequently show a "rigidity" of performance in the face of altered reinforcement contingencies that is often maladaptive in terms of reinforcement gain or response output, and is also uncharacteristic of animal behaviour. A series of studies by one of the present authors and colleagues (Bentall, Lowe, & Beasty, 1983, 1985; Lowe, 1983; Lowe, Beasty, & Bentall, 1983) has shown that these distinctive features of adult human operant behaviour are absent in pre-verbal infants, who perform on FI, FR and differential-reinforcement-of-low-rate (DRL) schedules in a manner indistinguishable from that of animals. By the time children reach the age of two-and-a-half to four years, however, and have some verbal behaviour, their performance is no longer like that of animals, but neither does it resemble the behaviour of adults. By the age of five to six-and-a-half years children have acquired the verbal skills which enable them to describe schedule contingencies accurately to themselves and to formulate rules for responding. At this age they show much the same behaviour as adults, with similar response patterning and similar insensitivity to alterations in schedule of reinforcement. Further evidence that the acquisition of linguistic skills is the variable responsible for these age-related changes in operant behaviour is shown by the finding that the developmental sequence can be accelerated by appropriate verbal instruction (Lowe, 1983; Bem, 1967; Luria, 1961).

Whatever the explanation of these findings, they are consistent in showing major differences between the performance of humans, at least those who are verbally accomplished, and animals. There is one area of human operant research, however, which has yielded data which supports the continuity position. This work has centred around Herrnstein's (1970) equations, particularly the Matching Law and its derivations, which aim to quantify the effects of reinforcement on behaviour. In particular the findings of a number of studies have led to the claim that both human and animal performance on variable-interval (VI) schedules, presented either singly or "concurrently," is characterised by a lawful relationship between rate of responding and rate of reinforcement that, like animal behaviour, closely conforms to these equations (Baum, 1979; Bradshaw, Ruddle & Szabadi, 1981; Bradshaw, Szabadi & Bevan, 1976, 1977, 1979;

Bradshaw, Szabadi, Bevan & Ruddle, 1979; de Villiers, 1977; Ruddle, Bradshaw, Szabadi & Bevan, 1979). Indeed, some authors have been so impressed by this evidence that they have suggested that this may be an area of contemporary animal research of direct relevance to applied behaviour analysis, with profound implications for the study of, for example, human economic behaviour, or the behaviour of people in clinical, educational, and social settings (Epling & Pierce, 1983; Hamblin, 1979; McDowell, 1981, 1982; Pierce & Epling, 1980, 1983; Rachlin, 1980; Schwartz, 1984; Winkler, 1980). These findings, or at least the common interpretation of them, are at odds with much of the human operant literature and are potentially problematic for accounts that accept that qualitatively different variables operate at the human level. Can it be that in the case of performance on concurrent VI schedules there is a behavioural "black hole" where the laws governing human behaviour in the rest of the universe of reinforcement conditions no longer hold? We will attempt to show in what follows that this is not in fact the case.

INTO THE BLACK HOLE

In order to evaluate the research that has been done in this area it is necessary to outline the procedures in some detail. Many of the studies have employed variable-interval schedules that have either been presented singly or as two schedules simultaneously available to the subject. In the latter, *concurrent schedule*, procedure the subject can "choose" to respond on either of the two alternatives. Within the context of animal choice behaviour, Herrnstein (1970) proposed that when two explicitly programmed sources of reinforcement are available independently and concurrently the allocation of responding to these two sources is governed by the Matching Law, in such a way that relative response rates approximately equal the relative reinforcement frequencies for the two alternatives. This is described mathematically in Equation 1:

$$\frac{R_A}{R_A + R_B} = \frac{r_A}{r_A + r_B} \qquad 1$$

where R_A and R_B are the number of responses per session to alternatives A and B respectively and r_A and r_B are the obtained frequencies of reinforcement for the alternative responses.

In order to account for deviations from the ideal matching relationship,

Baum (1974) proposed a modification to Equation 1 which has become known as the Generalised Matching Law, Equation 2:

$$\frac{R_A}{R_B} = k\left[\frac{r_A}{r_B}\right]^a \qquad 2$$

where R_A, R_B, r_A and r_B are as defined in Equation 1, and *k* and *a* are two free parameters, estimated empirically by fitting a straight line to a logarithmic transformation of response and reinforcement ratios. The slope of the line *a* provides an index of the sensitivity with which response ratios change when reinforcement ratios are varied. If the value of *a* is greater than one, as a result of a disproportionately greater preference for the richer reinforcement schedules, performance is described as over-matching. In the case of a disproportionate preference for the poorer schedules, *a* is less than one and there is said to be undermatching. The intercept *k* provides an index of *bias* and a value of *k* different from one signifies a constant proportional bias toward responding on one alternative versus the other (e.g., a positional bias). When both *a* and *k* are equal to one, there is "ideal" or "perfect" matching and Equation 2 reduces to Equation 1.

Many studies of concurrent schedule performance have employed a *changeover delay* which is a time penalty during which no scheduled reinforcement is delivered for a specified time following a change in responding on one alternative to responding on the other. This is designed to prevent adventitious reinforcement of changeover responses though its precise role in determining performance on concurrent schedules is not well understood (Catania, 1966; Heyman, 1979).

Several recent reviews of the literature have shown that animal performance conforms closely to the Generalised Matching Law, with values of *a* falling between 0.6 and 1.2 in the great majority of cases (Baum, 1979, 1983; de Villiers, 1977; Taylor & Davison, 1983; Wearden & Burgess, 1982). A number of instances of matching have been reported in human studies (Baum, 1975; Bradshaw, Szabadi & Bevan, 1976; Bradshaw, Szabadi and Bevan, 1979; Bradshaw, Szabadi, Bevan and Ruddle, 1979; Bradshaw, Ruddle & Szabadi, 1981; Buskist & Miller, 1981; Ruddle, Bradshaw, Szabadi & Bevan, 1979) but also some gross departures (Navarick & Chellsen, 1983; Oscar-Berman, Heyman, Bonner & Ryder, 1980; Pierce, Epling & Greer, 1981; Schmitt, 1974). There are a number of procedural differences between the human experiments, however, that has made it difficult to account for the variability in results. For example, some studies: (1) considered only group data (Conger & Killeen, 1974; Schroeder & Holland, 1969); (2) varied magnitude of reinforcement at the same time as reinforcement frequency (Schmitt, 1974); (3) included a response-cost contingency (Baum, 1975); (4) employed different changeover delay values within and across subjects (Schroeder & Holland, 1969); (5) arranged for subjects to have only very brief exposure to the contingencies (Conger & Killeen, 1974; Pierce, Epling & Greer, 1981; Schmitt, 1974).

Some of the most highly regarded, and certainly the most widely cited, research in this area has been conducted by Bradshaw and colleagues, who have reported for several human subjects, in a number of studies, a conformity to the Generalised Matching Law comparable to that of animals. These studies employed a 5-ply multiple concurrent VI VI procedure wherein each of five different concurrent VI pairs were alternated with 5-minute rest periods. In one version of the procedure, successive 10-minute presentations of each of the following VI schedules occurred, in pseudo-random order on the right-hand manipulandum (Component A): 8 sec, 17 sec, 51 sec, 171 sec and 720 sec, with VI 51 sec concurrently operative on the left-hand manipulandum (Component B). Each VI schedule on the right-hand manipulandum was signalled by a different stimulus, consisting of a row of five lights one of which was illuminated for the 10 minutes that the schedule was in operation. An alternative version of the Bradshaw procedure entailed the use of a single response manipulandum and a changeover button enabling subjects to switch between components. No changeover delay was employed in any of the experiments. The subjects were human adults and responding was reinforced by the delivery to a counter of points which were later exchanged for money. Sixteen sessions were conducted with each subject.

An interesting procedural aspect of these studies concerns the stimuli that were used to signal the schedules in operation. The position of the light that was illuminated was ordinally related to the reinforcement frequency signalled. Thus, when the VI 8-sec schedule was operative the left-most light was lit, when VI 17-sec was operative the next to left-most light was lit and so on. Moreover, for the first experimental session subjects were presented only with the VI schedules on the right-hand manipulandum, the other manipulandum being inoperative for that session, and these schedules were presented in ascending order of interval value. So in addition to the kinds of stimuli usually provided in multiple schedules, this ordinal information, albeit implicit, may have led subjects to describe the schedules to themselves in a manner which would favour the emergence of matching-like behaviour. For example, the schedule signalled by the left-most light (VI 8) might be described as "best" and, those to the right, as progressively "worse". Because these studies have produced some of the best evidence for matching in humans, and in favour of the continuity hypothesis, we decided to carry out a series of experiments with the purpose of analysing the determinants of human performance under these conditions.

In our first experiment we attempted to eliminate ordinal cues by employing individual geometric shapes to signal the VI schedules. Five adults, three female and two male, with various occupational backgrounds took part in the study. The response operanda were two Lehigh Valley human response panels spaced 20 cm apart. A points counter was mounted midway between the response panels and each reinforcement consisted of the addition of one point to the counter, with the monetary exchange rate being one penny per point earned. This yielded an average earning per session of approximately £1.50 to £1.90. A VI 50-sec schedule was operative on the left panel throughout each 10-minute stimulus presentation while on the right panel one of the following VI schedules was presented in pseudorandom order: 10, 20, 50, 175, 500, and 720 sec. During the operation of each schedule the response panel was illuminated by the appropriate geometric shape, i.e., one of the following: a cross, open circle, triangle, horizontal line, filled circle, square. These 10-minute schedule presentations alternated with 5-minute rest periods.

Sixteen one-and-a-half hour sessions were conducted with each subject and, in line with the Bradshaw procedure, no changeover delay was in operation. The instructions to subjects were also closely based upon those of Ruddle, Bradshaw, Szabadi and Bevan (1979) but in addition, all taking part were asked not to speak to anyone, other than the experimenter, about the study. At the end of the experiment each subject completed a questionnaire.

Data from the last three experimental sessions were used to calculate mean response rates and mean frequency of obtained reinforcement on each schedule value. Figure 7.1 shows for each subject, the ratios of response rates in the two components (R_A/R_B) as a function of the ratios of reinforcement frequencies delivered in the two components (r_A/r_B), using double logarithmic coordinates (Baum, 1974). Linear functions were derived by the method of least squares. The slope of the fitted line is a measure of the exponent a, and the intercept is a measure of k, in Equation 2.

The behaviour of none of the five subjects conformed to Herrnstein's Matching Law (Equation 1) and only one, CT, might be said to conform to the Generalised Matching Law (Equation 2), and even this subject undermatched considerably the value of a being 0.53. The remaining four subjects had values of a not significantly different from zero. These findings differ greatly from those of the Bradshaw experiments but are consistent with other studies of human performance on concurrent schedules (Navarick & Chellsen, 1983; Oscar-Berman, Heyman, Bonner & Ryder, 1980; Pierce, Epling & Greer, 1981; Schmitt, 1974; Poppen, 1982).

The verbal reports revealed that three of the four subjects with zero values of a were unable to rank accurately the geometric shapes in order of scheduled reinforcement frequency. They had idiosyncratic formulations

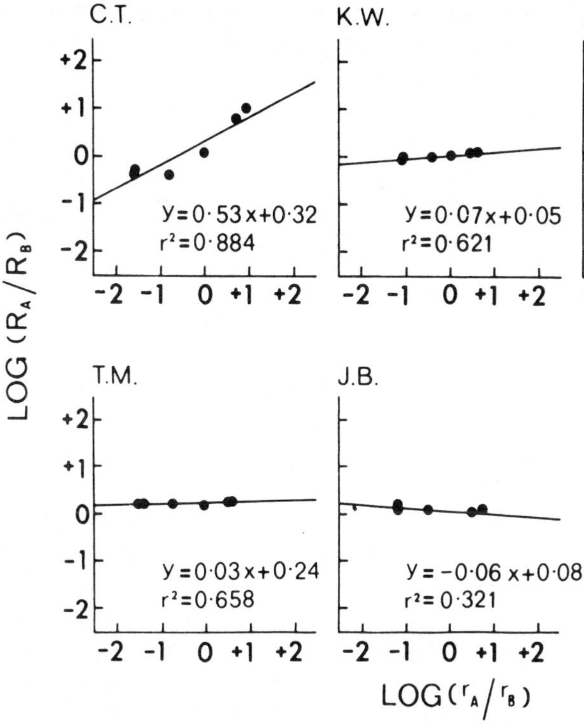

FIG. 7.1. Ratios of response rates in the two components (R_A/R_B) plotted against ratios of reinforcement frequencies in the two components (r_A/r_B), using double logarithmic coordinates, for each subject in Experiment 1. The straight lines are the best-fit linear functions obtained by least squares method. Equations for linear functions are shown in each panel together with r^2 values (proportions of data variance accounted for by linear functions).

of the contingencies and strategies for elaborate response sequences that were reflected in their performance. The fourth subject, KW, accurately ranked the six schedules but he reported that he decided to "respond randomly" on the two panels. The remaining subject in the group, CT, came closest to formulating a "matching hypothesis" in that she accurately ranked the three richest schedules and considered that she should press more often the shape which "held more points in relation to the triangle" (i.e., the shape corresponding to the VI 50 sec schedule operative on the left-hand panel). For the other three schedule values, relative response rates were in accord with her stated preferences though the latter did not correspond to scheduled reinforcement frequency. These reports suggested that subjects' formulations of the contingencies and rules for responding strongly influenced their performance.

Experiment 2 investigated the extent to which the absence of a changeover delay might have contributed to the results obtained in the first experiment. The procedure was identical to that of Experiment 1 except that a 3-sec changeover delay was employed throughout (cf. McSweeney, Melville, Buck & Whipple, 1983). Five additional subjects, three female and two male, took part. With respect to Equation 2, the linear regression analysis produced the following values of a, for each of the five subjects; the coefficient of determination (r^2) is given in parenthesis: 0.62 (0.92), 0.59 (0.94), 0.45 (0.78), 0.37 (0.77), 0.15 (0.25). This shows that, even with an added changeover delay, some subjects showed gross undermatching and insensitivity to the reinforcement parameter of a kind not recorded in animal experimentation.

One reason why the findings of Experiments 1 and 2 were not in agreement with those of Bradshaw and colleagues might be the presence of ordinal cues in the Bradshaw procedure. We tested this possibility in the next experiment. The procedure was the same as that employed in the first two experiments except that the geometric shapes which were illuminated on the right-hand panel were replaced by a row of six filled circles, one of which was red and the remainder black. The position of the red circle was ordinally related to scheduled reinforcement frequency in the manner of Bradshaw's stimuli. No changeover delay was employed in this experiment.

The regression analyses for the five subjects in Experiment 3 are shown in Fig. 7.2. With the exception of Subject CL, these results are based upon the last three sessions of responding; the function for CL excludes data obtained on the last day of the study and represents the mean of the preceding three sessions. The reason for this omission is discussed below. The data for three of the five subjects (NL, SP, SC) are well described by Equation 2 with values of a comparable to those reported by Bradshaw and colleagues. But this was not true of the remaining two subjects, CL and PB, whose performance failed to conform to either of the matching equations.

The performance of one of these subjects, CL, together with her verbal reports, is informative about the variables controlling behaviour, not only in this experiment, but in human operant studies in general. Following her completion of the post-experimental questionnaire, CL revealed that she spent the night before her last session with another subject, NL; his performance over the last three sessions of this experiment approximated ideal matching. The following morning, Subject CL's performance was also close to ideal matching (see Fig. 7.3), although previously it was insensitive to relative reinforcement frequency (Fig. 7.2). One could speculate about the mechanisms responsible for this sudden transformation in behaviour, but Subject CL reported that, in a final attempt to increase her point score, she had persuaded Subject NL to divulge his response strategy.

We are not suggesting that all of the subjects in the Bradshaw studies

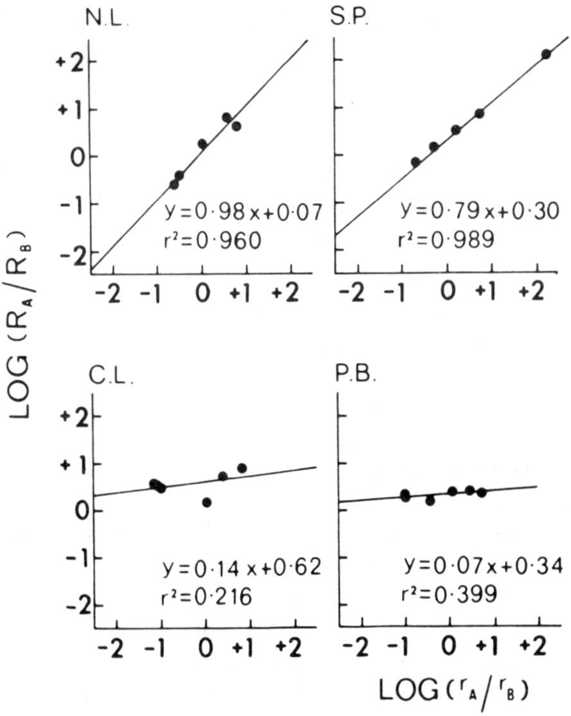

FIG. 7.2. Ratios of response rates in the two components (R_A/R_B) plotted against ratios of reinforcement frequencies in the two components (r_A/r_B), using double logarithmic coordinates, for each subject in Experiment 3. The straight lines are the best-fit linear functions obtained by least squares method.

behaved in just this fashion but many of their subjects, who were domestic, technical and secretarial staff working in the same institution, may have talked to one another about their performance in the experiments. Clearly, it only needs one subject in the group to discover the nature of the task, and an "appropriate" strategy, and that subject can convey the rule to everyone else in the group.

Verbal reports at the end of the experiment suggested that all four subjects whose behaviour conformed to the Matching Law used the ordinal cue stimuli in formulating a matching hypothesis; they reported, correctly, that they could rank the panel stimuli with respect to scheduled reinforcement frequency and that they had decided to respond more on the richer schedules. The verbal reports of the remaining subject, PB, suggested that she used the ordinal cue stimuli as a basis for the construction of elaborate mathematical rules to generate complex sequences of responding bearing little relation to the programmed contingencies.

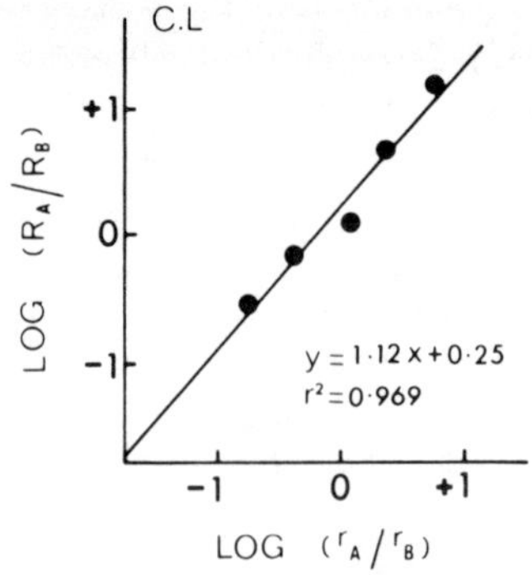

FIG. 7.3. Ratios of response rates in the two components (R_A/R_B) plotted against ratios of reinforcement frequencies in the two components (r_A/r_B), using double logarithmic coordinates, for Subject CL on the last session of Experiment 3. The straight line is the best-fit linear function obtained by least squares method.

The results from these three experiments suggest that the presence of an ordinal cue, signalling reinforcement frequency, is more effective than a changeover delay in producing behaviour that is formally similar to that of animals, although this finding, together with subjects' verbal reports, suggests that the controlling relations are very different. In our fourth experiment, adding a 3-sec changeover delay to the procedure used in Experiment 3 did not result in further improvements in matching but instead appeared to generate more complex hypotheses and rules for responding. Two subjects showed good animal-like matching, one grossly undermatched, one was completely insensitive to reinforcement frequency, and the fifth subject showed exclusive preference for the richer schedule of each concurrent VI VI pair, a behaviour pattern not previously reported in the animal literature.

In two further experiments we provided explicit instructions concerning the relative reinforcement values of the different schedules. When the procedure was otherwise the same as that of Experiment 1 (i.e., geometric shapes and no changeover delay), the performance of three of the five subjects conformed to the Generalised Matching Law but two of these showed gross overmatching of a kind not normally seen in animal studies of concurrent performance. Adding a changeover delay to this procedure, in Experiment 6, did not enhance matching; two subjects showed exclusive preference for the richer of each pair of VI schedules, one grossly overmatched, one considerably undermatched and only one showed undermatching like that of animals.

Of the 30 subjects who took part in the six experiments, the performance of only seven could be said to conform to Equation 2 with parameter values typical of animals, that is, values of a ranging from 0.6 to 1.2; more than

90% of animal subjects' performance falls within this range (Baum, 1979; Wearden & Burgess, 1982). These findings show that the type of procedure employed by the Bradshaw group, that, in their studies, has generated some of the best data from humans in favour of the Matching Law, also yields results that cannot be described by any of the matching equations and are without comparison in the animal literature. In the case of many of our subjects, it was not that there were mere "deviations" from typical animal matching—performance was qualitatively different. As such the results are entirely consistent with the literature on human performance under single schedules of reinforcement which has revealed differences of a comparably gross nature between human and animal responding (Lowe, 1979, 1983; Matthews, Shimoff, Catania & Sagvolden, 1977; Weiner, 1969). The present experiments are also consistent with other studies of human behaviour on concurrent schedules which have reported marked departures from typical animal performance and failures of the Matching Law.[1]

Human operant behaviour under some conditions can formally resemble that of animals and a number of subjects in our experiments showed good conformity to Equation 2. Our results, however, suggest that whether matching occurs is dependent upon a number of factors, particularly the provision of information which enables the subject to form a matching hypothesis or rule. The ordinal cues, which are implicit in the apparatus and procedures of the Bradshaw studies and our Experiments 3 and 4, provide just this type of information. Experimental instructions may also be employed for this purpose (Experiments 5 and 6) and verbal exchanges with other subjects (e.g., CL and NL in Experiment 3). Presumably, explicit teaching of matching law relationships or a reading of Herrnstein's paper would be even more effective! But what can be concluded if, under any of these conditions, human subjects show matching?

It is at this point that many researchers in the operant area fall victim to the *formalistic fallacy* of placing an undue emphasis upon the formal characteristics of behaviour at the expense of controlling relations (Lowe & Harzem, 1977; Skinner, 1969). The fallacy in this case is to assume that, because plots of relative response rate and relative reinforcement frequency on logarithmic coordinates look the same for both animals and humans, the determinants of their behaviour are also the same. For this reason, and particularly in the context of the rest of the human operant

[1]One might also speculate about the number of studies conducted in other laboratories (and some are known to the present authors) which have "failed" to show matching and, because of the problems that often beset studies that are considered to show "negative results," have not been published. But whether failure to show matching in humans should be considered as a negative result depends upon the point of reference—the literature on animal or on human operant behaviour.

literature, when subjects show ideal matching it should not be assumed that this poses any fewer problems for behavioural theory than when they fail to conform. Together with her testimony, the overnight conversion of CL's behaviour (Experiment 3) from almost complete insensitivity to excellent conformity to the Generalised Matching Law, is as damning for an account of human choice in terms of the operation of a simple matching principle, common to both animals and humans, as is the worst "failure" of any of the other subjects.

The case of CL may also be instructive for those who continue to deny the usefulness of verbal reports in research of this kind and, indeed, of any attempt to infer the existence of behaviour that is not publicly observable. Instead, it is argued, the experimental analysis of behaviour should confine itself to dealing with overt behaviour and environmental events (Baron & Galizio, 1983; Baron & Perone, 1982; Branch & Malagodi, 1980; Weiner, 1983). It has also been suggested that subjects' verbal reports cannot be taken into account unless they are experimentally validated (Shimoff, 1984). One of the present authors (Lowe, 1983, and see also Skinner, 1945) has outlined some of the philosophical and practical problems inherent in such an approach. In the context of the present experiments, and we shall deal here with only one subject to illustrate the point, how is it possible to make sense of the sudden change in CL's behaviour without taking into account what she had to say about it? And how would it be possible, experimentally, to establish the veracity of what was reported? Clearly, as has been recognised by many psychologists from Watson onwards, introspective evidence may be problematic (Nisbett & Wilson, 1977). But studies have shown that it is both possible, and indeed, fruitful, to test experimentally hypotheses which are based upon subjects' verbal reports (Bentall, Lowe & Beasty, 1985; Lowe, 1979, 1983). This evidence shows that to ignore what subjects tell us (and the fact that they can tell), even when particular reports cannot be directly verified, is a crippling limitation on behaviour analysis. Such positivistic excesses are now comparatively rare in the rest of science and they no longer can be justified, if they ever could, in psychology.

The evidence indicates that continuity theories of animal and human learning are untenable. Our experiments show that this is as obviously true for performance on concurrent schedules as it is for other areas of operant behaviour. On the other hand, these results do not disprove discontinuity accounts, and may even seem to furnish positive support for them. Developmental studies show, however, that conditioning relationships are very similar in both animals and humans at some stage in human development (Bentall, Lowe & Beasty, 1985; Lancioni, 1980; Lowe, Beasty & Bentall, 1983; Rovée-Collier & Gekoski, 1979). We would also expect the performance of pre-verbal children on concurrent schedules to show matching and, indeed, there is evidence (Horne & Lowe, 1983) that infant performance on single VI schedules conforms to Herrnstein's equation, derived from the Matching Law, which specifies the relationship between response rate and reinforcement frequency on single schedules (cf. Herrnstein, 1970). In addition, some studies have shown that when experimental procedures are designed to attenuate the intrusion of rule-governed behaviour into conditioning relationships, then human operant performance more closely resembles that of animals (Hefferline, Keenan & Harford, 1959; Lowe, Harzem & Bagshaw, 1978; Lowe, Harzem & Hughes, 1978).

Clearly, the issues at stake do not lie in any clear cut way within the confines of either the continuity or the discontinuity approach. The following questions, though fundamental, elude the nets of both: To what extent and under what conditions is human behaviour under direct contingency control and governed by reinforcement principles as we know them in animals? How do humans learn to be "conscious" of their behaviour and to formulate rules for responding, and how does this type of behaviour interact with existing conditioning relationships? Although some attempt has been made to address these problems in theoretical papers (Skinner, 1945, 1966) they have been almost completely ignored by researchers in behaviour analysis (but see Catania, Matthews & Shimoff, 1982).

The results of the present experiments give little comfort to those who, assuming that human choice conforms to the Matching Law, have confidently asserted that such principles should be applied directly to the study of economic, social, and clinical problems. This is not to say that matching equations, and related animal research, are without relevance for applied behaviour analysis. There may be situations in the board room, commodities market, shop, or hospital where people act without reflecting on their behaviour and its consequences, and without being affected by a plan, hypothesis, theory, or ideology. On such occasions, if they can be identified, there may be a role for the straightforward application of the principles established in animal research. In a similar vein, Lea (1981) has suggested that animal studies may contribute to the study of human economic behaviour, provided they are coupled with a theory as to what extent "habit" rather than "reason" will govern behaviour. According to Lea, approaches in economic psychology which have had most success have been those which have elaborated just such a theory (Katona, 1975; Reynaud, 1981).

Attempts to apply the Matching Law in clinical settings will almost certainly be problematic. Indeed, it has been argued elsewhere (Lowe & Higson, 1981, 1983) that in many "behaviour modification" studies the time delay between responses and putative reinforcers is such that any change in behaviour *cannot* be the result of direct reinforcing operations alone; in order for the programmed consequences to be effective the behaviour must, to some extent, be rule-governed. As Michael (1980) has observed, the subjects' verbal behaviour in these situations is typically neither mentioned nor analysed. If rule-governed behaviour is as pervasive and potent a variable in clinical settings as our account suggests (and see Zettle & Hayes, 1982) then it is folly for applied behaviour analysis to ignore it. It is our contention that until a consideration of verbal behaviour and its interactions with other behaviour is placed at the centre of the agenda for behaviour analysis, little progress can be made in constructing a psychology that is fit for humans.

ACKNOWLEDGEMENTS

We would like to thank Llio Ellis Williams for her help in the preparation of the manuscript.

REFERENCES

Baron, A. & Galizio, M. (1983) Instructional control of human operant behavior. *The Psychological Record*, **33**, 495–620.

Baron, A. & Perone, M. (1982) The place of the human subject in the operant laboratory. *The Behavior Analyst*, **5**, 142–158.

Baum, W. M. (1974) On two types of deviation from the matching law: Bias and undermatching. *Journal of the Experimental Analysis of Behavior*, **22**, 231–242.

Baum, W. M. (1975) Time allocation in human vigilance. *Journal of the Experimental Analysis of Behavior*, **23**, 45–53.

Baum, W. M. (1979) Matching, undermatching, and overmatching in studies of choice. *Journal of the Experimental Analysis of Behavior*, **32**, 269–281.

Baum, W. M. (1983) Comment: Matching, statistics, and common sense. *Journal of the Experimental Analysis of Behavior*, **39**, 499–501.

Beech, H. R. (1974) Behaviour therapy: In P. Morris (Ed.), *Behaviourism*. Milton Keynes, UK: The Open University Press.

Bem, S. L. (1967) Verbal self-control: The establishment of effective self-instruction. *Journal of Experimental Psychology*, **74**, 485–491.

Bentall, R. P., Lowe, C. F., & Beasty, A. (1983) Does language produce behavioural rigidity in humans? *Behaviour Analysis Letters*, **3**, 251.

Bentall, R. P., Lowe, C. F., & Beasty, A. (1985) The role of verbal behavior in human learning II: Developmental differences. *Journal of the Experimental Analysis of Behavior*, **43**, 165–181.

Blackman, D. E. (1983) On cognitive theories of animal learning: Extrapolation from humans to animals?: In G. C. L. Davey (Ed.) *Animal models of human behavior*. Chichester, UK: Wiley. 37–50.

Bloomfield, T. M. (1976) About Skinner: Notes on the theory and practice of 'Radical Behaviourism'. *Philosophy of the Social Sciences*, **6**, 75–82.

Boulgouris, J. C. (Ed.) (1982) *Learning theory approaches to psychiatry*. Chichester, UK: Wiley.

Bradshaw, C. M., Ruddle, H. V., & Szabadi, E. (1981) Studies of concurrent performances in humans: In C. M. Bradshaw, E. Szabadi, & C. F. Lowe (Eds.) *Quantification of steady-state operant behaviour*. Amsterdam: Elsevier/North Holland Biomedical Press. 79–90.

Bradshaw, C. M., Szabadi, E., & Bevan, P. (1976) Behavior of humans in variable-interval schedules of reinforcement. *Journal of the Experimental Analysis of Behavior*, **26**, 135–141.

Bradshaw, C. M., Szabadi, E., & Bevan, P. (1977) Effect of punishment on human variable-interval performance. *Journal of the Experimental Analysis of Behavior*, **27**, 275–279.

Bradshaw, C. M., Szabadi, E., & Bevan, P. (1979) The effect of punishment on free-operant behavior in humans. *Journal of the Experimental Analysis of Behavior*, **31**, 71–81.

Bradshaw, C. M., Szabadi, E., Bevan, P., & Ruddle, H. V. (1979) The effect of signalled reinforcement availability on concurrent performances in humans. *Journal of the Experimental Analysis of Behavior*, **32**, 65–74.

Branch, M. N. & Malagodi, E. F. (1980) Where have all the behaviorists gone? *The Behavior Analyst*, **3**, 31–38.

Brewer, W. P. (1974) There is no convincing evidence for operant or classical conditioning in adult humans: In W. B. Weiner & D. S. Palermo (Eds.) *Cognition and the symbolic processes*. Hillsdale, NJ: Lawrence Erlbaum Associates. 1–42.

Buskist, W. F. & Miller, H. L. Jr. (1981) Concurrent operant performance in humans: Matching when food is the reinforcer. *The Psychological Record*, **31**, 95–100.

Catania, A. C. (1966) Concurrent operants: In W. K. Honig (Ed.) *Operant behavior: Areas of research and application*. New York: Appleton-Century-Crofts. 213–270.

Catania, A. C., Matthews, B. A., & Shimoff, E. (1982) Instructed versus shaped human verbal behavior: Interactions with non-verbal responding. *Journal of the Experimental Analysis of Behavior*, **38**, 233–248.

Conger, R. & Killeen, P. (1974) Use of concurrent operants in small group research. *Pacific Sociological Review*, **17**, 399–416.

de Villiers, P. A. (1977) Choice in concurrent schedules and a quantitative formulation of the law of effect: In W. K. Honig & J. E. R. Staddon (Eds.). *Handbook of operant behavior*. New York: Prentice Hall. 233–287.

Dickinson, A. (1980) *Contemporary animal learning theory*. Cambridge, UK: Cambridge University Press.

Dickinson, A. (1984) Actions and habits: The development of behavioural autonomy. Paper presented to a meeting of the Royal Society on *Animal Intelligence*. London.

Dietz, S. M. (1978) Current status of applied behavior analysis: Science versus technology. *American Psychologist*, **33**, 805–814.

Epling, W. F. & Pierce, W. D. (1983) Applied behavior analysis: New directions from the laboratory. *The Behavior Analyst*, **6**, 27–37.

Hamblin, R. L. (1979) Behavioral choice and social reinforcement: Step function versus matching. *Social Forces*, **57**, 1141–1156.

Hayes, S. C., Rincover, A., & Solnick, J. (1980) The technical drift of applied behavior analysis. *Journal of Applied Behavior Analysis*, **13**, 275–286.

Hefferline, R. F., Keenan, B., & Harford, R. A. (1959) Escape and avoidance conditioning in human subjects without their observation of the response. *Science*, **130**, 1338–1339.

Herrnstein, R. J. (1970) On the law of effect. *Journal of the Experimental Analysis of Behavior*, **13**, 243–266.

Heyman, G. M. (1979) A Markov model description of changeover probabilities on concurrent VI schedules. *Journal of the Experimental Analysis of Behavior*, **31**, 41–51.

Honig, W. K. (1978) Studies of working memory in the pigeon: In S. H. Hulse, H. Fowler, & W. K. Honig (Eds.) *Cognitive processes in animal behavior*. Hillsdale, NJ: Lawrence Erlbaum Associates. 1–14.

Horne, P. J. & Lowe, C. F. (1983) On the application of Herrnstein's equation to human behaviour. Paper presented to the First European Meeting on the Experimental Analysis of Behaviour, Liège.

Katona, G. (1975) *Psychological economics*. New York: Elsevier.

Lancioni, G. E. (1980) Infant operant conditioning and its implications for early intervention. *Psychological Bulletin*, **88**, 516–534.

Lea, S. E. G. (1981) Animal experiments in economic psychology. *Journal of Economic Psychology*, **1**, 245–271.

Lowe, C. F. (1979) Determinants of human operant behaviour: In M. D. Zeiler & P. Harzem (Eds.) *Advances in analysis of behaviour (Volume 1). Reinforcement and the organisation of behaviour*. Chichester, UK, and New York: Wiley. 159–192.

Lowe, C. F. (1983) Radical behaviourism and human psychology: In G. C. L. Davey (Ed.) *Animal models of human behaviour*. Chichester, UK: Wiley. 71–93.

Lowe, C. F., Beasty, A., & Bentall, R. P. (1983) The role of verbal behavior in human learning: Infant performance on fixed-interval schedules. *Journal of the Experimental Analysis of Behavior*. **39**, 157–164.

Lowe, C. F. & Harzem, P. (1977) Species differences in temporal control of behavior. *Journal of the Experimental Analysis of Behavior*, **28**, 189–201.

Lowe, C. F., Harzem, P., & Bagshaw, M. (1978) Species differences in temporal control of behavior: II. Human performance. *Journal of the Experimental Analysis of Behavior*, **29**, 351–361.

Lowe, C. F., Harzem, P., & Hughes, S. (1978) Determinants of operant behaviour in humans: Some differences from animals. *Quarterly Journal of Experimental Psychology*, **30**, 373–386.

Lowe, C. F. & Higson, P. J. (1981) Self-instructional training and cognitive behaviour modification: A behavioural analysis: In G. C. L. Davey (Ed.) *Applications of conditioning theory*. London: Methuen. 162–188.

Lowe, C. F. & Higson, P. J. (1983) Is all behaviour modification "cognitive"?: In E. Karans (Ed.) *Current issues in clinical psychology*. London: Plenum. 207–227.

Luria, A. (1961) *The role of speech in the regulation of normal and abnormal behavior*. New York: Liveright.

Luria, A. (1982) *Language and cognition*. New York: Wiley.

Mackintosh, N. J. & Dickinson, A. (1979) Instrumental (Type 11) conditioning: In *Mechanisms of learning and motivation: A memorial volume to Jerzy Konorski*. Hillsdale, NJ: Lawrence Erlbaum Associates, 143–169.

Matthews, B. A., Shimoff, E., Catania, A. C., & Sagvolden, T. (1977) Uninstructed human responding: Sensitivity to ratio and interval contingencies. *Journal of the Experimental Analysis of Behavior*, **27**, 453–467.

McDowell, J. J. (1981) On the validity and utility of Herrnstein's hyperbola in applied behavior analysis. In C. M. Bradshaw, E. Szabadi, & C. F. Lowe (Eds.) *Quantification of steady-state operant behaviour*. Amsterdam: Elsevier/North Holland Biomedical Press.

McDowell, J. J. (1982) The importance of Herrnstein's mathematical statement of the law of effect for behavior therapy. *American Psychologist*, **37**, 771–779.

McSweeney, F. K., Melville, C. L., Buck, M. A., & Whipple, J. E. (1983) Local rates of responding and reinforcement during concurrent schedules. *Journal of the Experimental Analysis of Behavior*, **40**, 79–98.

Michael, J. L. (1980) Flight from behavior analysis. *The Behavior Analyst*, **3**, 1–21.

Navarick, D. J. & Chellsen, J. (1983) Matching versus under-matching in the choice behavior of humans. *Behaviour Analysis Letters*, **3**, 325–335.

Nisbett, R. E. & Wilson, T. D. (1977) Telling more than we can know: Verbal reports on mental processes. *Psychological Review*, **84**, 231–259.

Oscar-Berman, M., Heyman, G. M., Bonner, R. T., & Ryder, J. (1980) Human neuropsychology: Some differences between Korsakoff and normal operant performance. *Psychological Research*, **41**, 235–247.

Pierce, W. D. & Epling, W. F. (1980) What happened to analysis in applied behavior analysis? *The Behavior Analyst*, **3**, 1–9.

Pierce, W. D. & Epling, W. F. (1983) Choice, matching and human behavior: A review of the literature. *The Behavior Analyst*, **6**, 27–37.
Pierce, W. D., Epling, W. F., & Greer, S. M. (1981) Human communication and the matching law: In C. M. Bradshaw, E. Szabadi, & C. F. Lowe (Eds.) *Quantification of steady-state operant behaviour*. Amsterdam: Elsevier/North Holland Biomedical Press. 345–348.
Poppen, R. (1982) Human fixed-interval performance with concurrently programmed schedules: A parametric analysis. *Journal of the Experimental Analysis of Behavior*, **37**, 251–266.
Rachlin, H. (1980) Economics and behavioral psychology: In J. E. R. Staddon (Ed.) *Limits to action: The allocation of individual behavior*. London, UK: Academic Press. 205–236.
Reynaud, P. L. (1981) *Economic psychology*. New York: Praeger.
Roitblat, H. L., Bever, T. G., & Terrace, H. S. (Eds.) (1984) *Animal cognition*. Hillsdale, NJ: Lawrence Erlbaum Associates.
Rovée-Collier, C. K. & Gekoski, M. J. (1979) The economics of infancy: A review of conjugate reinforcement. *Advances in Child Development and Behavior*, **13**, 195–255.
Ruddle, H. V., Bradshaw, C. M., Szabadi, E., & Bevan, P. (1979) Behavior of humans in concurrent schedules programmed on spatially separated operanda. *Quarterly Journal of Experimental Psychology*, **31**, 509–517.
Schmitt, D. R. (1974) Effects of reinforcement rate and reinforcer magnitude on choice behavior of humans. *Journal of the Experimental Analysis of Behavior*, **21**, 409–419.
Schroeder, S. R. & Holland, J. G. (1969) Reinforcement of eye movement with concurrent schedules. *Journal of the Experimental Analysis of Behavior*, **12**, 897–903.
Schwartz, B. (1984) *Psychology of learning and behavior*. (2nd edition). New York & London: W. W. Norton.
Shimoff, E. (1984) Post-session questionnaires. *Experimental Analysis of Human Behavior Bulletin*, **2**, 1.
Skinner, B. F. (1938) *The behavior of organisms*. New York: Appleton-Century-Crofts.
Skinner, B. F. (1945) The operational analysis of psychological terms. *Psychological Review*, **52**, 270–277.
Skinner, B. F. (1966) An operant analysis of problem solving: In B. Kleinmuntz (Ed.) *Problem solving: Research, method and theory*. New York: Wiley. 225–257.
Skinner, B. F. (1969) *Contingencies of reinforcement: A theoretical analysis*. New York: Appleton-Century-Crofts.
Taylor, R. & Davison, M. (1983) Sensitivity to reinforcement in concurrent arithmetic and exponential schedules. *Journal of the Experimental Analysis of Behavior*, **39**, 191–198.
Vygotsky, L. (1962) *Thought and language*. New York: Wiley.
Vygotsky, L. (1978) *Mind in society: The development of higher psychological processes*. London, UK: Harvard University Press.
Wearden, J. H. & Burgess, I. S. (1982) Matching since Baum (1979). *Journal of the Experimental Analysis of Behavior*, **38**, 339–348.
Weiner, H. (1969) Controlling human fixed-interval performance. *Journal of the Experimental Analysis of Behavior*, **12**, 349–373.
Weiner, H. (1983) Some thoughts on discrepant human-animal performances under schedules of reinforcement. *The Psychological Record*, **33**, 521–532.
Winkler, R. C. (1980) Behavioral economics, token economies, and applied behavior analysis: In J. E. R. Staddon (Ed.) *Limits to action: the allocation of individual behavior*. London: Academic Press, 269–297.
Zettle, R. D. & Hayes, S. C. (1982) Rule-governed behavior: A potential theoretical framework for cognitive therapy: In P. C. Kendall (Ed.) *Advances in cognitive-behavioral research and therapy, Vol. 1*. New York: Academic Press, 76–118.

8 Human Behaviour as Operant Behaviour: An Empirical or Conceptual Issue?

Emilio Ribes
National University of Mexico-Iztacala

In Skinner's writings (1953, 1957, 1969) there is a basic assumption that all human behaviour, even that which is complex, is operant behaviour: "Tradition and expedience seem to agree in confining the analysis of human thought to operant behaviour . . ." and only "for practical purposes a special field has been set apart in terms of characteristics imparted to it by special controlling variables. It is in terms of these variables—of the contingencies arranged by the verbal community—that verbal behaviour can be defined and analysed (Skinner, 1957, pp449–452)." Because of this assumption the experimental analysis of human behaviour has proceeded in accordance with the concepts, problems, and procedures developed for the study of animal behaviour, mostly simple animal behaviour, and although (as Buskist and Miller (1982) have reported) there is a substantial increase in the number of experimental studies of human behaviour, there is well founded scepticism about the actual meaning of this research (Baron & Perone, 1982). Is it experimental research about human behaviour or is it only traditional operant research using human subjects? Recent reviews of the literature suggest that it is the latter (Baron & Galizio, 1976; Bradshaw, Szabadi & Bevan, 1976, 1978; Duvinsky & Poppen, 1982).

In order to examine the issue of the determinants of human operant behaviour it is first necessary to distinguish the conceptual aspects from the empirical questions. Is human behaviour operant behaviour? Does it conform narrowly to the conceptual relations embodied in operant theory? Has human behaviour as operant behaviour special features distinct from those found in the experimental research of operant behaviour with non-human subjects? Are the categories customarily employed to analyse operant behaviour sufficient to describe possible emerging functions brought about by the complex contingencies involved in the social interaction of human beings? These and other questions need thorough discussion before we can entertain the possibility of studying the empirical determinants of human behaviour, whether they are conceived of as being within the operant framework or otherwise.

The study of human behaviour by behaviour analysts has developed in two main directions. One has involved the use, with human subjects, of procedures originally employed in animal research, especially those related to schedule effects and complex discrimination. The other has been the implementation of applied procedures in natural social settings in order to produce practical outcomes or to demonstrate the feasibility of using operant techniques in typically human environments.

In the former approach, recent literature begins to show differences between human and infrahuman experimental subjects with regard to schedule performances, variations that seem important since inter-species uniformity of processes is one of the assumptions set forth by Skinner (1956) to justify the convenience of carrying out research with simpler organisms. The studies by Harzem, Lowe and Bagshaw (1978) and Lowe, Beasty and Bentall (1983), suggest that responding in interval schedules by humans is controlled not by direct programmed contingencies but by covert verbal responses related to expected or assumed working contingencies. Similarly, Shimoff, Catania and Matthews (1981) found that instructed human responding under low-rate contingencies showed insensitivity to changes in random interval and ratio scheduling. Verbal behaviour was assumed again to be responsible for this effect. Poppen (1982) also pointed out the problems in extrapolating scallop-like response patterns when analysing human behaviour under what were assumed to be fixed-interval contingencies. The evidence reported rests on two basic arguments. First, verbal behaviour seems to introduce new parameters into the operant behaviour situations typical of infrahuman research, and second, parameter interactions and contingency complexity in human social settings cannot be analysed adequately in terms of the contrived conditions of response and stimulus restriction which are characteristic of the free-operant methodology. The findings point to the possibility that differences found between the behaviour of human subjects and infrahuman organisms, in experimental situations which have been designed for the study of simple relations, might be due to processes peculiar to human behaviour which are not amenable to experimental analysis in such restricted circumstances.

In the applied approach, two main problems may be identified. First, without a theory of human behaviour it is difficult to analyse which variables and interactions are operating in the application of procedures which have been designed by extrapolating from basic animal research or from principles derived from the study of animal learning. Outcomes, positive or negative, do not provide any logical or empirical support for the conceptual assumptions guiding the solution of practical problems (Dietz, 1978; Ribes, 1977, 1980). Second, in the absence of well-established experimental facts about human behaviour under complex contingencies, such as those operating in social settings, applied research becomes isolated from any theoretical effort to explain human behaviour according to scientific rules. Technology is replaced by pragmatics. Basic research about specifically human behaviour is needed to link and give meaning to the relation between present knowledge about operant animal behaviour and applied procedures in social settings (Hake, 1982).

Conceptual simplification is a major problem. Operant theory consists in the analysis of contingency relations between antecedents, responses and consequences. The concepts used to describe the elements of these contingency relationships are bound to special assumptions about behaviour and the logic and methods employed to account for it. Although later on we shall try to pin-point other limitations and inadequacies of these special assumptions, it is important to mention here the two main shortcomings. Operant concepts have been formulated to describe punctate, repetitive, linearly sequenced events in simple situations (Schoenfeld, 1972). Their use to describe behaviour and contingency relations which do not conform with these restrictions becomes a violation of the logic of the theory. The loose and *ad hoc* usage of the concepts of "reinforcement," "discriminative stimuli" and so on, renders them meaningless. Not only does it seem contradictory to talk about the reinforcement of behaviours such as following rules or problem solving, but it is also unsound to describe low-rate and non-prescribed response schedules in terms equivalent to those specifying discrete, identifiable responses. As we shall see, not every antecedent and consequent event may be correctly described in terms of discriminative stimuli and reinforcers.

Another problem is that human behaviour is considered to be primarily operant behaviour. Although respondent behaviour is recognised as a second process, its importance is secondary and only in interaction with operant contingencies. Human behaviour is approached as a single-process phenomenon in which all behaviour is explained as relations between occasions, responses, and consequences, with reinforcers playing a decisive role, even in terms of an assumed history or of deferred consequences. There is no piece of human behaviour that is not susceptible to analysis in terms of the three-element contingency relationship, though most of the time this simplifies the behaviour interaction being depicted, or strains the concepts as they are forced to account for situations which empirically do not support their usage.

Vygotsky (1925, 1979 English translation) pointed out this trend towards simplification in the objectivistic psychology of his time. If we substitute the word "operant" for "reflex" we may get a fair picture of the present state of affairs in our discipline: "Indeed, in the sense in which we use the term reflex, it resembles very closely the story of Kannitfershtan, whose name a poor foreigner heard in response to any question no matter what he asked: Whom are they burying? Whose house is this? . . . etc. He naively thought that everything in this country was done by Kannitfershtan, whereas actually the word simply meant that the Dutchman he met did not understand the questions. Patent evidence of our lack of understanding of these phenomena may be seen in a "reflex of purpose" or a "freedom reflex." That these are not reflexes in the usual sense, i.e., in the sense that a salivary reflex is a reflex, but rather are some sort of structurally distinct mechanism of behaviour is clear to everyone. Only if we reduce everything to one common denominator can we explain everything in the same way: then a reflex is like this Kannitfershtan. But then the very term reflex is deprived of any meaning." (p10).

THE REFLEX PARADIGM AND THE OPERANT CONCEPTION

Although the use of the term "reflex" for the first time is not clearly attributable to Descartes, it is accepted that the concept of the reflex as a movement reflecting an impulse to the organism was introduced by Descartes in his theory of automatic action (Fearing, 1930; Canguilhem, 1955). The use of the term "reflex" in *Passions of the Soul* is not of primary importance. The significant contribution of Descartes was the conception of animal movement as mechanical movement, through the action of animal spirits, similar to fluids, in the nerves. These animal spirits were put into action as a reflexion of the excitation of an external object. The brain, the heart, the liver, and the stomach played various roles in the functioning of these animal spirits, but they were autonomous and free of the soul with respect to involuntary action or movement. The soul, in any case, could exert indirect influence on voluntary movement through interaction with the body in the pineal gland. With Descartes, biological functions were incorporated as a special case of mechanical laws, and the interactions of soul and body became paramechanical relations (Ryle, 1949).

Kepler and Galileo transformed the scholastic-religious conceptions of celestial bodies, giving rise to a new philosophy of nature. In this philosophy the concept of *force* laid down the foundations of Mechanics as a philosophy of science. Through the concept of *magnitude* the difference between matter and form was eliminated and mathematical representation as geometry became the central core of the new physics. Substances, as an ontological concern, were substituted for the analysis of geometrical functions, and it was through the formulation of mathematical dependencies in the theory of gravitation that scientific abstraction became independent of discussion about the being and the confirmation of divinity by the order of celestial bodies. Ultimate causes were exchanged for mathematical dependencies and functions. It was in this context that Descartes proposed a systematisation of the rules of scientific knowledge through the use of his method. Descartes viewed scientific knowledge as pure relations and proportions on the foundations of his theory of geometrical space. This theory was based on the concept of the point as the ultimate element of geometrical forms and relations.

Although accepting the importance of empirical confirmation of mathematical descriptions, Descartes asserted that bodies were not known through the senses but by understanding. The contents of mathematical abstractions never could be grasped through direct observation. They were, in this sense, constructed through pure understanding. And it is in the identification of the concept and the being, according to Cassirer (1906; 1953 Spanish translation), that Descartes transformed the new philosophy of nature into a metaphysical doctrine. It is in the discussion of the concept of the infinite that there appears "a total inversion of the relations between thought and being. The 'eternal truths' of geometry and logic are only valid because God has given them this value and this sanction (p505)." As methodic doubt is the basis of all truthful knowledge, the idea is no longer trustworthy "if we have not acquired full certainty about the 'creator of our existence.' Knowledge is not its own valid and authentic origin; it needs confirmation and support by a metaphysical foundation of existence (p506)." Innate ideas as fixed and definite forms allowed for the postulation of the soul (the entity of understanding) as a separate substance from the body. Dualism in Descartes contains two mutually antagonistic conceptions. On one hand, there was the possibility of a scientific knowledge of physics by means of mathematical relations and functions foreign to ontological concerns for the bodies. On the other hand, there was the recognition of innate ideas as a fixed form of understanding coming from God, and the postulation of the soul as a separate substance interactive with the body in Man. As Cassirer concludes: ". . . the general tendency in the new science . . . (is that) the concept of substance be substituted and overcome by the concept of function. This fundamental thinking is grasped and clearly exposed by Descartes for the first time in his logic and his theory of science, although afterwards he is unable to maintain it in relation to the problem of psychology (p512)."

We have examined in detail the contribution of Descartes to modern scientific thinking because of the impact that his metaphysical conception of the soul interacting with the body had on succeeding Western thought.

Objectivistic analyses of behaviour as movement and brain activity incorporated the methodic approach of the new science, mechanics, as well as the conceptual representation of this special kind of movement, the paradigm of the reflex. The conception of behaviour in terms of the reflex passed from biology to psychology (Sechenov, 1866, 1978 Spanish translation; Bekhterev, 1913; Pavlov, 1927; Skinner, 1931, 1938) incorporating not only the assumptions about a subject matter foreign to behaviour, but also the dualistic concern for the interaction between mind and body as substances. The inversion made by Descartes of relations to substances raised the existence of two different entities, mind and behaviour. Relations were reified into substances, and behaviour as interaction was isolated into two aspects; behaviour as action or movement, and mind as the representation of interactions within the body. Because of this, the theories of behaviour based on the reflex paradigm, irrespective of their inclusion or otherwise of the particular term, are prone to dualistic interpretation. In discussing the exclusion of consciousness from the domain of scientific psychology, Vygotsky (1925) pointed out that this fact ". . . considerably preserves all the dualism and spiritualism of earlier subjective psychology. . . . The main premise of reflexology, namely, the purported possibility in principle of explaining all human behaviour without any recourse to subjective phenomena and of constructing a psychology without mind, is the hand-me-down dualism of subjective psychology in its attempt to study pure, abstract mind. This is the other half of the old dualism: then there was mind without behaviour, now we have behaviour without mind; in both cases mind and behaviour are not one but two (p8)." We might add that there is sometimes evidence of what appears to be a transformation of behaviour into mind, as the acceptance of private events in the form of internal stimuli seems to suggest (Kantor, 1981; Ribes, 1982).

Behaviourism is not a theory in psychology, but a theory about psychology, that is to say, a philosophy of this special science. Nevertheless, behaviourism has been expressed as a special theory in psychology through particular developments that, although founded in one or another version of this philosophy of science, seem to have adopted categories, assumptions, and the basic logic of theories prescribed for a different subject-matter and anchored in the philosophies of other sciences (mechanics, biological evolution). Operant conditioning as a special set of categories has been formulated historically within the reflex paradigm, in spite of the fact that this particular term was abandoned after the early forties. We claim that the internal logic of the reflex has limited the conceptual and empirical scope of operant theory and that it is time to recognise that a critical examination of fundamentals has to be done to provide meaning to present and future research. This is especially critical for the case of human behaviour.

What is the internal logic of the reflex paradigm that is transferred to conditioning conceptions such as operant theory? Since we have already examined this issue in a different paper (Ribes, in press), we shall summarise the main conceptual features of the reflex paradigm insofar as they have affected the special formulations of operant categories. Three issues seem crucial in this regard: (1) causality relations; (2) the postulation of atomistic discontinuous behavioural states; and (3) neglect of contextual and historical conditions.

1. Causality Relations

Although movement in Galilean and Cartesian Mechanics was represented as geometrical movement, the reflex concept described empirical movement as the impulsed reflexion of the action of one body on the state of a different body. Mechanical causation was to be interpreted as external, immediate, contiguous body contact. Distal causation required intermediate contacts filling the location gap. This conception as incorporated by biology and psychology took two forms. One consisted of explaining movements as the direct effects of stimuli. The other account conceived of movements in terms of a double-state mechanism, either as a sequence of impulses and effects (as in contiguous association and chaining) or as the mechanical relation between external and internal impulses producing the effect (energetic and mechanical interaction as in drive theories). Both descriptions had their origins in the reflex action accounts given by Descartes and Willis respectively (Canguilhem, 1955).

In any of these causal interpretations, movement as behaviour was the effect to be explained, and causes resided in the external environment or in a sequence involving an external stimulus plus an internal organic event, either a response-produced stimulus or an energy state producing the necessary interacting causal condition with the external event. Behaviour as movement was the effect to be explained, and became the dependent variable of psychology (cf. Skinner, 1957, Chapter 2). Causality was to be found by the analysis of linear relations in time between stimulus and response. Even when some of the stimulus variables were consequences of behaviour (reinforcers and punishers), the linearity demanded by mechanical causation transformed the analysis of interdependencies in the search for forward effects. Stimulus consequences were not examined as dependent events, but on the contrary their reciprocal influence on future responding was emphasised to maintain behaviour as the dependent variable or phenomenon to be explained by stimulus events. Although operant behaviour, as emitted behaviour, seemed to break with the stimulus-response tradition, theoretical accounts continued looking for forward effects of stimulus changes.

Mechanical linearity imposed a sophisticated delayed stimulus-response causation on operant behaviour. Multiple causation was understood as an algebraic interaction of preceding variables acting linearly on behaviour, and functional relations were reduced to mechanical relations. Mach (1905, 1948, Spanish translation), stressed that "... in general, cause and effect are the two most relevant parts of a phenomenon, and the most accurate analysis shows that the assumed cause is nothing else than the complement of a whole set of circumstances, which determine the effect.... When sciences are well developed, the concepts of cause and effect are rarely employed. Such concepts are provisory, incomplete, and inaccurate ... the notion of function allows for a better representation of the reciprocal relation among the elements.... It seems that all immediate dependencies could be considered as reciprocal and simultaneous. The obverse takes place in the vulgar notions of cause and effect: the effect follows the cause and its relation is not reversible (pp218–220). If operant theory actually looked for functional relations, the response rate or any other response measure would not be *the* dependent variable. Reinforcement and response rate interactions would become the relations to be analysed in terms of the parameters and contextual constants under which behaviour takes place. Marr (1982) recently pointed out the convenience of abandoning mechanical causation for the analysis of non-linear interdependencies. To do so, nevertheless, implies awareness of the paradigmatic assumptions that have guided theoretical practice and the correlated conceptual changes required in a field approach, which an account stressing complex functional relationships demands.

2. Atomistic Discontinuous-State Categories

Geometrical descriptions of mechanics were based upon the possibility of calculating any magnitude, taking the point as ultimate element. The atomistic conception of the magnitude of bodies and their relations was additional to the discontinuous nature of mechanical actions, changing between two states: rest and motion. The reflex in biology was conceived of as a point-to-point relation between impulses, as a stimulus, and the effect, as movement. The reflex relation, though, was described as a discrete, discontinuous relation of stimulus-response, non-stimulus no-response. Physiological language was adapted to this conception in talking about neural impulses, all-or-none transmission, rest-state, refractory period, etc. Conditioning theories did not escape this representational model. Atomism and discontinuity in behavioural states were the conceptual framework for theoretical and empirical descriptions. Responses and stimuli were defined as punctate events in time in terms of the maximal possible restrictions, analogous to the neuromuscular plate isolated preparation (Skinner, 1931). Punctate events, in order to be quantified, had to be integrated into classes; no replicability would be possible for isolated single events (Schoenfeld, 1976). The reflex—and afterwards the respondent and the operant—became a class concept, and responses and stimuli, as single instances, had to be measured in terms of repetition as discrete, discontinuous events in time.

Repetitive single responses were taken as the basis for analysis of the patterning of behaviour. Theoretical accounts of behaviour segments were formulated in terms of principles describing interactions of these punctate response events. Instances of these principles were found in chaining, conditioned reinforcement, induction and differential reinforcement. When experimental or natural conditions consisted of more than a single response in time, constraints forcing temporal incompatibility among these response events were introduced, e.g., changeover delays in concurrent schedules. Punishment, avoidance, and extinction procedures became relevant examples of the two-state conceptual analysis prevalent in behaviour theory; responses were suppressed, extinguished, or stimulus events were postponed or eliminated. Responses and stimuli happened to occur in a continuum in space and time of non-responding and non-stimulation. Nevertheless, it was claimed that these punctate events selected for analysis were representative of all those events logically considered as non-events.

3. Contextual and Historical Conditions

Cartesian Mechanics saw the movement of bodies as changes in their location. Location changes were represented as different points in geometrical space. Space was not identical, in this sense, with concrete location. When the mechanistic conception was transferred to biological thinking, the reflex was conceived of as taking place in an invariant pathway consisting of afferent fibres, neural centres, and efferent fibres. No location concepts were required besides those procured by the morphological description of neural structures. In psychology, the reflex paradigm was adopted as a purely temporal representational system. Punctate events occurred in time, and location was neglected. The bar position in the operant chamber, for example, was fixed, so responding was assumed to have constant spatial properties. The linear conception about relationships between events brought about perforce the selection of successive events in time: the event preceding the selected response; a predetermined response; and the event consequent to the response, as set in train by pre-arranged manipulations. The analysis of the so-called three-term contingency relation excluded any other event that could not fit into the mechanistic formulation of causality.

Ryle (1949) has distinguished between events as occurrences or happenings, and dispositions or tendencies as a collection of events. Causal or functional relation statements may be established in regard to happenings. Dispositional concepts are only amenable to law-like statements. Nevertheless, as Popper (1972) points out, these statements provide the necessary initial grounds upon which to account for relations among events sufficiently well for scientific description. The omission of initial conditions necessary for the occurrence of systematic relations between events, leads to the replacement of functional relations by linear causal statements regarding antecedent and consequent events. In operant theory and research, no conceptual provision has been made for the formulation and description of dispositional variables, although recently, Michael (1982) has stressed the need to separate what he calls "establishing operations" from discriminative stimuli. Michael's suggestion, however, falls short of accounting for the fact that past discriminative relations may, and indeed do, become dispositional conditions in regard to actual contingencies. Kantor's (1933) setting factor concept is best suited to take into account both past interactions (or behavioural history) and situational conditions (both in the organism and the environment) as a collection of events that interact in the form of propensities or tendencies facilitating or interfering with particular interdependencies among events.

In summary, the paradigmatic characteristics of the reflex concept and its later transformation in the operant-respondent dichotomy imposed severe conceptual restrictions on operant theory. These restrictions survived the abandonment of the reflex term as such, and persisted in the form of a stress on discrete, punctate, repetitive events and a neglect of contextual and historical concepts. Because of the fundamental role of theory in scientific knowledge, these unrecognised limitations influenced not only the interpretation of phenomena but also the key process of selecting data and designing experimental situations.

HUMAN BEHAVIOUR, JUST OPERANT BEHAVIOUR?

In the previous discussion we have tried to demonstrate that in examining human behaviour as operant behaviour, it is necessary to determine whether the categories of operant theory are adequate to cope with the general issue of behaviour. There is enough evidence to claim, at least, that the conceptual features of operant theory provide a limited view of behaviour as an interactive process. In this respect, we could maintain that operant theory, as a special case of conditioning theory, emerged from a paradigmatic structure which did not provide the special properties that behaviour as subject-matter demands.

Therefore, the discussion should not be centred on the question of whether concepts and data obtained with infra-human organisms are representative and sufficient to cope with human behaviour as a special case. The argument developed here is that present operant concepts are poorly suited to cope both with animal and human behaviour. This, obviously, does not put aside the issue about specific features of human behaviour and the possibility that concepts and principles obtained in simpler situations might be useful to account for it.

What were the conceptual innovations introduced by operant theory for the study of behaviour? We shall concentrate on what should be considered the two most revolutionary contributions by Skinner. These contributions were unable to produce radical changes in behaviour theory to the extent that they were part of the mechanistic conceptual framework of conditioning formulations. In any case, revisiting them may allow us to find new ways to deal with the problem of behaviour analysis and, especially, the determinants of human behaviour.

The first contribution to stand out is the particular relation among events that the operant, as an interaction between the organism and the environment, involves. Although Thorndike in his *Law of Effect* had shown the importance of effects on behaviour, it was Skinner's concept of the operant that stressed environmental events as being dependent on behaviour. Not only did stimulus consequences affect behaviour, but behaviour also produced changes in the environment. The operant relation as an empirical description involved a double dependency: the presentation of stimulus events contingent upon the response of the organism, and the functionality of the response (operant or instrumental) dependent on the stimulus changes produced—and the new conditions for responding thus emerged. This double dependency between responding and consequent stimulus changes represented a level of functional relationship between the organism and the environment qualitatively different from the one illustrated in classical conditioning—or in later times by the superstition experiment. In the respondent situation, the organism is differentially reactive to contingency relations among environmental events. Nevertheless, the reactivity to these relations does not change them. Behaviour enters into the contingencies of the contextual variables in the environment, but does not produce changes in the relations between events. On the other hand, the operant relation describes a contingency relation in which the dependencies between events in the environment are contingent upon the behaviour of the organism. That is, in the operant relation not only is the consequent stimulus dependent on the response of the organism but on the whole of the stimulus dependency relations in the environment (SD–SR, or CS–UCS). The operant relation is more complex than the respondent relation because it includes within it the contingency relations defining stimulus dependencies. The consequent stimulus is just part of the dependency. In this sense, we may claim that the process described by the respondent relation is simpler than, and is included in, the operant relation.

The concept of *contingency* is the second key innovation introduced by Skinner into modern behaviour theory. Unfortunately, this concept was ill defined. Signifying conditionality in the description of reciprocal relations among events, it might have led to the analysis of mutual dependencies or interdependencies as recent discussions about schedule performance suggest (Morse, 1966; Schoenfeld & Farmer, 1970; Zeiler, 1979). But it was confined to a causal-type of interpretation. Contingencies were restricted to the analysis of contingencies of reinforcement, and this consisted of looking for the future effects of consequent stimuli on responding (Skinner, 1938, p62), and the contiguity relations beween responses and subsequent stimuli (Skinner, 1948, p168). Linearity was imposed on the interpretation of the operant relation, in such a way that, given an implicit or explicit occasion, a response was to be followed by a simulus that on similar occasions in the future would increase the probability of that response occurring again. Increase or decrease in frequency of behaviour became in this way the basic measure of this linear conception of probability (Skinner, 1950, pp200–201). The three-term contingency of operant conditioning was depicted as a linear relation between three events: the antecedent stimulus; the response; and the subsequent stimulus. The contingency was described as a double-dependency between the antecedent condition and the response, and the response and the stimulus consequence, or better stated, as the dependency between the occurrence of the response-stimulus relation given an antecedent stimulus or occasion. The difference in regard to the respondent relation was based on the assumed provoking function of the antecedent stimulus, and the occurrences of subsequent stimuli, even when their presentation might be adventitious, as in superstition.

Looking at the contingencies working in both relations, a distinctive critical factor stands out. As already has been suggested by other authors (Rescorla & Wagner, 1972), there is a contingency relationship between stimuli in the respondent situation. This relationship, however, involves a double dependency. On one side, the UCS is contingent upon CS presentation. On the other side, what has been called the "signal" function of the CS is dependent upon the UCS presentation. Both are interdependent. The response of the organism is not just an "anticipation" of the UCS occurrence, but the differential reaction to a contingency in the environment. The operant situation is distinctively different from the respondent, not because the antecedent stimulus has a non-provoking role, since no clear-cut differences are to be found between the CS and SD functions, but because the contingency between stimuli becomes dependent on the organism responding. This new element introduces a radical change in the contingencies. Not only are new dependencies established, but the parameters that hold for some of those relations in the respondent situation change their operation due to the mediating function of the operant response in the contingency field. The operant situation, thus, includes the contingencies of the respondent relation, but the parameters of the simpler dependency described by contextual stimulus relations become functionally subordinated to the variations introduced by their dependency on the organism responding. Complex contingencies imply not only new dependency relations, but also changes in the parametric properties of those relations.

In summary, we think that operant behaviour is important not because a consequent stimulus following the response is taken into account, but because this stimulus change is produced by the organism and introduces a new set of contingency relations compared with situations in which the organism is only reactive to stimulus dependencies. Contingency relations do not limit themselves to the temporal parameters involved, but consist of reciprocal functional dependencies, which have to be considered as a whole in order to provide a sound account of the behaviour under analysis. Operant relations include more than a three-term contingency, and do not interact with or exclude respondent relations. Stimulus-stimulus contingencies are always present in the operant situation, but they are functionally dependent on the critical mediating role of the organism's responding which establishes and changes contingencies.

Apart from in the early stages of its development, human behaviour involves active transformation of the environment, and thus requires a description involving contingencies produced by the individual. In that sense, Skinner's (1957) claim that human behaviour is behaviour transforming the environment is correct. Nevertheless, to claim that human behaviour includes processes related to contingencies such as those involved in operant situations, does not necessarily mean that it is governed by those sorts of contingencies alone. Human behaviour includes operant contingencies, but it is not operant behaviour, in the same way that operant behaviour includes respondent contingencies but is itself not respondent behaviour.

Why do we think that human behaviour is not *just* operant behaviour? Several arguments may be advanced:

1. There are contingency relationships described in animal behaviour that seem to be more complex, and therefore, to go beyond the operant relation, i.e., matching-to-sample (Cumming & Berryman, 1965), conditional discrimination (Sidman & Tailby, 1982), and social inter-organism relations (Hake, Donaldson & Hyten, 1983).

2. Human behaviour is based upon conventional repertoires or reactional systems in contrast to biological situation-bound responding in infrahuman organisms.

3. Natural and formal languages, as human social products, consist of

contingency systems restricting and limiting the functionality of conventional responding.

4. Conventional responding lacks any morphological correspondence with physico-chemical and biological events, and therefore, allows for functional detaching of the individual behaviour from situational, immediate contingencies. This fact is central for a reinterpretation of self-control and rule-governed behaviour analyses that reduce substitutional interactions and contingencies to simpler relations such as those of operant discrimination or delayed reinforcement and punishment.

5. Human behaviour consists of responding and interacting with the behaviour of other individuals and their products. These events and relations, due to their conventional nature, do not seem to obey the same parameters as physico-chemical event contingencies.

6. Human behaviour is an interactive process whose parameters can not be synthesised from the analysis of single components.

7. Conventional responding does not involve only the possibility of interaction in different time and space dimensions from those of situational contingencies, but also the fact that contingencies are introduced and created through convention. Linguistic responding replaces aspects of contingency operation, setting aside the physico-chemical relations acting in the situation. Social psychology has been very generous in examples of this.

8. Conventional contingency systems introduce consequences mediated by behaviour that because of their arbitrary condition are not amenable to being described in terms of operant reinforcers and punishers. The behaviour involved in doing science, logic, music, poetry, and so on, cannot be reduced to simple stimulus control and reinforcement descriptions. Behavioural contingencies may be identified in terms other than those employed by operant theory. To do so, in any case, it is necessary to abandon the reflex paradigm conceptions, and to look for complete contingency relations mediated by the individual behaving in non-linear ways with the environment.

To recognise critical differences between human behaviour and non-human behaviour does not mean to recognise the need to postulate internal variables or emergent principles unrelated to the processes studied under respondent and operant situations. Behaviour as interaction represents distinctive sorts of mediation of contingencies, that is, dependencies among the various events and organisms participating in a relationship. Looking at differential complexity in the mediation of contingencies allows for the recognition of hierarchical levels in the organisation of behaviour, without the need to postulate internal entities or autonomous emergent principles. Human behaviour is different from animal behaviour, just as animal behaviour can be differentiated among the diversity of *phyla*, because reactional systems, environmental contingencies and stimulating conditions are different. The differences do not reside only in the form of behaviour; they exist in the processes of mediating contingencies by the human individual. To identify such mediational processes, which are external, interactive processes, means to begin with the analysis of simpler contingency fields including behaviour, proceeding gradually to higher levels on the basis of the formulation of concepts, grasping the interdependencies between behaviour, stimulus events, and contextual factors. Nevertheless, the analysis of simpler elements and relationships does not provide the concepts or knowledge necessary to cope with more complex contingency settings. The analysis of non-human behaviour is necessary but not sufficient for the understanding of human behaviour, that is, behaviour organised within conventional contingency systems. The inclusion of simpler relations within human interactions does not mean that human behaviour is amenable to reduction to those descriptions. New relations, new parameters and new forms of behaving demand specific conceptual tools.

Behaviour theory and particularly conditioning theory—including the operant conception—served a major role in the development of psychology as a science. Nevertheless, the progress thus achieved has shown the limitation of the theory in coping with the complexity of behaviour. It may well be the case that, in the construction of a science of behaviour, conditioning theory has outlived its usefulness, and that it is time to look for innovative propositions to emerge from behaviourism as a philosophy of scientific psychology, allowing for new conceptual and experimental strategies for studying behaviour, particularly human behaviour. Otherwise our discipline will end as hermeneutic practice within a closed, stereotyped description of behaviour.

REFERENCES

Baron, A. & Galizio, M. (1976) Clock control of human performance on avoidance and fixed-interval schedules. *Journal of the Experimental Analysis of Behavior*, **26**, 165–180.

Baron, A. & Perone, M. (1982) The place of the human subject in the operant laboratory. *The Behavior Analyst*, **5**, 143–158.

Bekhterev, W. von (1913) *Objektive psychologie oder psychoreflexologie*. Leipzig.

Bradshaw, C. M., Szabadi, E., & Bevan, P. (1976) Behavior of humans in variable-interval schedules of reinforcement. *Journal of the Experimental Analysis of Behavior*, **26**, 135–141.

Bradshaw, C. M., Szabadi, E., & Bevan, P. (1978) Effects of variable-interval punishment on the behavior of humans in variable-interval schedules of monetary reinforcement. *Journal of the Experimental Analysis of Behavior*, **29**, 161–166.

Buskist, W. F. & Miller, H. L. Jr. (1982) The analysis of human operant behavior: A brief census of the literature: 1958–1981. *The Behavior Analyst*, **5**, 137–142.

Canguilhem, G. (1955) *La formation du concept de reflexe: Au XVIIe et XVIIIe siecles*. Paris: Presses Universitaires de France.

Cassirer, E. (1953) *El problema del conocimiento, Volume I*. (German original 1906). Mexico: Fondo de Cultura Economica.

Cumming, W. W. & Berryman, R. (1965) The complex discriminated operant: Studies of matching-to-sample and related problems: In D. I. Mostofsky (Ed.), *Stimulus generalization*. Stanford: Stanford University Press.

Dietz, S. M. (1978) Current status of Applied Behavior Analysis. Science versus Technology. *American Psychologist*, **33**, 805–814.

Duvinsky, J. D. & Poppen, R. (1982) Human performance on conjunctive fixed-interval fixed-ratio schedules. *Journal of the Experimental Analysis of Behavior*, **37**, 243–250.

Fearing, F. (1930) *Reflex action: A study of the history of physiological psychology*. Baltimore: Wilkins & Wilkins.

Hake, D. F. (1982) The basic-applied continuum and the possible evolution of human operant social and verbal research. *The Behavior Analyst*, **5**, 21–28.

Hake, D. F., Donaldson, T., & Hyten, C. (1983) Analysis of discriminative control by social behavioral stimuli. *Journal of the Experimental Analysis of Behavior*, **39**, 7–23.

Harzem, P., Lowe, C. F., & Bagshaw, M. (1978) Verbal control in human operant behavior. *The Psychological Record*, **28**, 405–424.

Kantor, J. R. (1933) *A survey of the science of psychology*. Bloomington: Principia Press.

Kantor, J. R. (1981) Concerning the principle of psychological privacy. *The Psychological Record*, **31**, 101–106.

Lowe, C. F., Beasty, A., & Bentall, R. P. (1983) The role of verbal behavior in human learning: Infant performance on fixed-interval schedules. *Journal of the Experimental Analysis of Behavior*, **39**, 157–164.

Mach, E. (1948) *Conocimiento y error*. (German original 1905). Buenos Aires: Espasa-Calpe.

Marr, J. (1982) Determinism. *The Behavior Analyst*, **5**, 205–207.

Michael, J. (1982) Distinguishing between discriminative and motivational functions of stimuli. *Journal of the Experimental Analysis of Behavior*, **37**, 149–155.

Morse, W. H. (1966) Intermittent reinforcement: In W. K. Honig (Ed.), *Operant behavior: Areas of research and application*. New York: Appleton Century Crofts.

Pavlov, I. P. (1927) *Conditioned reflexes*. Oxford: Oxford University Press.

Poppen, R. (1982) The fixed-interval scallop in human affairs. *The Behavior Analyst*. **5**, 127–136.

Popper, K. R. (1972) *Objective knowledge*. Oxford: Clarendon Press.

Rescorla, R. A. & Wagner, A. R. (1972) A theory of Pavlovian conditioning: Variations in the effectiveness of reinforcement and non-reinforcement: In A. Black and N. Prokasy (Eds.), *Classical conditioning II: Current theory and research*. New York: Appleton Century Crofts.

Ribes, E. (1977) Relationship among behavior theory, experimental research and behavior modification techniques. *The Psychological Record*, **27**, 417–424.

Ribes, E. (1980) Consideraciones metodologicas y profesionales sobre el analisis conductual aplicado. *Revista Mexicana de Analisis de la Conducta*, **6**, 89–102.

Ribes, E. (1982) Los eventos privados gun problema para la teorfa de la conducta? *Revista Mexicana de Analisis de la Conducta*, **8**, 11–29.

Ribes, E. (in press) Is operant conditioning sufficient to cope with human behavior? In P. Chase & L. Parrott (Eds.), *Psychological aspects of language: The West Virginia Lectures*. Hillsdale: Lawrence Erlbaum Associates.

Ryle, G. (1949) *The concept of mind*. New York: Barnes & Noble.

Schoenfeld, W. N. (1972) Problems of modern behavior theory. *Conditional Reflex*, **7**, 33–65.

Schoenfeld, W. N. (1976) The "response" in behavior theory. *Pavlovian Journal*, **11**, 129–149.

Schoenfeld, W. N., & Farmer, J. (1970) Reinforcement Schedules and the "behavior stream": In W. N. Schoenfeld (Ed.), *The theory of reinforcement schedules*. New York: Appleton Century Crofts.

Sechenov, I. (1978) *Los reflejos del cerebro*. (Russian original 1866). Barcelona: Fontanella.

Shimoff, E., Catania, A. C., & Matthews, B. A. (1981) Uninstructed human responding: Sensitivity of low-rate performance to schedule contingencies. *Journal of the Experimental Analysis of Behavior*, **36**, 207–220.

Sidman, M. & Tailby, W. (1982) Conditional discrimination *vs.* matching-to-sample: An expansion of the testing paradigm. *Journal of the Experimental Analysis of Behavior*, **37**, 5–22.

Skinner, B. F. (1931) The concept of reflex in the description of behavior. *Journal of General Psychology*, **5**, 427–458.

Skinner, B. F. (1938) *The behavior of organisms*. New York: Appleton Century Crofts.

Skinner, B. F. (1948) "Superstition" in the pigeon. *The Journal of Experimental Psychology*, **38**, 168–172.

Skinner, B. F. (1950) Are theories of learning necessary? *Psychological Review*, **57**, 193–216.

Skinner, B. F. (1953) *Science and human behavior*. New York: Free Press.

Skinner, B. F. (1956) A case history in scientific method. *American Psychologist*, **11**, 221–233.

Skinner, B. F. (1957) *Verbal behavior*. New York: Appleton Century Crofts.

Skinner, B. F. (1969) *Contingencies of reinforcement: A theoretical analysis*. New York: Appleton Century Crofts.

Vygotsky, L. S. (1979) Consciousness as a problem in the psychology of behaviour. (Russian original 1925). *Soviet Psychology*, **17**, 3–35.

Zeiler, M. D. (1979) Output dynamics. In M. D. Zeiler & P. Harzem (Eds.), *Advances in the analysis of behavior, Volume 1: Reinforcement and the organization of behavior*. Chichester: Wiley.

9 Rule-governed Behaviour and the Origins of Language

A. Charles Catania
University of Maryland Baltimore County

> *. . . it may be suspected that languages, far less perfect than any now spoken, aided by gestures, might have been used, and yet have left no traces on subsequent and more highly developed tongues.*
>
> Charles Darwin (1871, Chapter 7)

How do we trace the origins of human language? We might seek its roots in non-human organisms, as when we teach analogues of human verbal behaviour to primates (Gardner & Gardner, 1969; Premack, 1970; Savage-Rumbaugh & Rumbaugh, 1978). We might follow the acquisition of language by children (Brown, 1973; de Villiers & de Villiers, 1978; Lamendella, 1976), on the assumption that ontogeny may provide clues to phylogeny even though not recapitulating it (Gould, 1977). We might explore the emergence of new human languages, as when a creole language develops at the meeting of two populations without a common tongue (Bickerton, 1981). We might examine language pathologies (Luria, 1961; Sidman, 1971), on the assumption that aphasias and other deficits may uncover simpler processes upon which language depends. We might see how much language can be modified by various methods of teaching, recalling that Darwin (1859) learned from the artificial selection used in horticulture and animal husbandry as well as from the observation of species in nature. Any account of the origins and evolution of language must be consistent with the facts generated by these approaches.

In undertaking this task, we have to our advantage the precedents set by Darwin (1859, 1871) and the subsequent achievements of evolutionary theory (Catania, 1978; Dawkins, 1982; Mayr, 1982). But these are outweighed by some disadvantages. We have no access to prehistoric verbal behaviour, nor methods for dating the beginnings of speech among humans (or infra-humans). Even worse, we have no consensus on what constitutes language.

It is almost true that behaviour leaves no fossils. We may protest that a written text is a record of verbal behaviour, but a record of verbal responses preserves features of their topography rather than the stimulus conditions by which they were occasioned. In any case, there is little doubt that written language is a relatively recent human invention in comparison to speech, and even if a written text were more directly related to the verbal behaviour that produced it than fossils are to the organic matter they replaced, the text would not reveal the derivation of writing from speech.

Recognising these constraints, we can do little more than consider some of the possibilities. This paper will review the history of theories of language origin and will examine some alternatives suggested by an experimental analysis of verbal behaviour. But let us first consider what is required of an effective account of the origins of language.

LANGUAGE ORIGINS AND PHYLOGENIC CONTINGENCIES

One issue in evolutionary theory has been whether evolution is continuous or saltatory. But it is not unreasonable to assume that some features may be selected in a relatively continuous way while the selection of others is punctuated. Human language, involving complexities both of behaviour and of the physiologies of the vocal and auditory apparatuses and the central nervous system, is not likely to have emerged full-blown. Even Chomsky, as close to linguistic creationism as anyone in the contemporary behavioural sciences, has come some way from arguing that the assumption of "an evolutionary development of language from simpler systems of the sort that one discovers in other organisms" has as little justification as "assuming an evolutionary development from breathing to walking" (Chomsky, 1968, p60; cf. Midgley, 1978, p239). Chomsky (1980) has since moved away from that position, treating language as the consequence of a set of interacting cognitive modules that develop in a manner analogous to the growth of anatomical organs; thus, language according to this view is at least decomposable into components that presumably evolved separately (cf. Bickerton, 1981; Darwin, 1859, p481: "We are always slow in admitting any great change of which we do not see the intermediate steps").

To speak of the origins of language, therefore, is to speak of an evolution from non-verbal to verbal behaviour, of a series of continuous or discontinuous historical stages, rather than of an abrupt and unique creation. This evolution is to be distinguished from that of individual languages. Once verbal behaviour is established, the evolution of particular vocabularies and grammars, as in the inferred descent of most European languages from a common Indo-European ancestral tongue, is a separate issue, though a treatment in terms of selection remains appropriate: "Languages, like organic beings, can be classed . . . naturally according to descent . . . . Dominant languages and dialects spread widely, and lead to the gradual extinction of other tongues. . . . We see variability in every tongue, and new words are continually cropping up. . . . The survival or preservation of certain favoured words in the struggle for existence is natural selection (Darwin, 1871, Chapter 3)."

The steps taken in the evolution from non-verbal organisms to contemporary speakers and listeners may have been large or small. Whatever their size, each of them must have provided a selective advantage. The problems this raises for an evolutionary account are illustrated by the following (Dawkins, 1982):

> The designers of the first jet engine started with a clean drawing board. Imagine what they would have produced if they had been constrained to "evolve" the first jet engine from an existing propeller engine, changing one component at a time, nut by nut, screw by screw, rivet by rivet. A jet engine so assembled would be a weird contraption indeed. It is hard to imagine that an aeroplane designed in that evolutionary way would ever get off the ground. Yet in order to complete the biological analogy we have to add yet another constraint. Not only must the end product get off the ground; so must every intermediate along the way, and each intermediate must be superior to its predecessor. (p38)

These constraints have at least two important implications. First, a plausible account must be able to deal simultaneously with the behaviour both of speakers and of listeners, because verbal behaviour cannot occur if there are speakers but no listeners, or listeners but no speakers. If some aspect of the speaker's behaviour is to provide a selective advantage and therefore is to be maintained, appropriate behaviour must already be available on the part of the listener. Similarly, if some aspect of the listener's behaviour is to provide a selective advantage and is to be maintained, appropriate behaviour must already be available on the part of the speaker. Second, to the extent that these interactions have been shaped over phylogenic time, we cannot count on finding their evolutionary predecessors in contemporary behaviour. If each intermediate was "superior to its predecessor," then many of the predecessors will not have survived.

Consider the effects of intra-specific competition in cases in which the largest members of a population have some selective advantage (Simpson, 1953):

> . . . in the population as a whole there is a constant tendency to favor a size slightly above the mean. The slightly larger animals have a very small but in the long run, in large populations, decisive advantage in competition. . . . Thus, populations that are regularly evolving in this way are always well adapted as regards size in the sense that the optimum is continuously included in their normal range of variation, but a constant asymmetry in the centripetal selection favors a slow upward shift in the mean (p151; cf. Dawkins 1982, p104).

This is, of course, a phylogenic analogue of shaping, the production of new topographies of behaviour through the reinforcement of successive approximations (cf. the account by Skinner, 1975, of the evolution of homing and migration as instances of phylogenic shaping). In both ontogenic and phylogenic shaping, the vestiges of the past may not be obvious in current behaviour. For example, once capture by predators has shaped fast escape in a population, we should not expect to find many slow runners in it, even if that speed had provided a selective advantage at a much earlier time when it was fast relative to the population mean. If we cannot count on the survival of intermediate cases when shaping has produced changes in single dimensions of behaviour such as size or speed or distance migrated, the problems become even more difficult when we try to deal with language, a class of behaviour with multiple and complexly interacting dimensions. The current functions of language may not be a basis for inferring past functions (cf. Bickerton, 1981, pp216–220). Perhaps the problem is intractable, but no progress is likely to follow if we start with that assumption.

SOME HISTORY

Theories of the origin of language have a long and varied history. One bibliography on language origins has about 11,000 entries (Hewes, 1975). Some issues are traceable to Plato (e.g., *Cratylus*) and other Greek thinkers; these and additions to them had become subjects of lengthy debate by the 18th century (Condillac, 1746/1974; Rousseau, 1753/1966; Herder, 1771/1966), though without the benefit of Darwin's account of human origins (cf. Tweney, 1980). Although Condillac spoke in terms of understanding and the communication of ideas, he recognised limits on these processes: "There are few perhaps . . . who do not feel some inclination to refer all the names of substances to unknown realities. . . . This is certainly one of the most extensive causes of the errors we fall into. It is sufficient to suppose that words correspond to the reality of the things, in order to confound them with those things (p149)."

Rousseau offered the two apparent contradictions that society depended on language whereas language could not have developed except in society, and that reason required language whereas language could not have developed without reason. Herder's essay was influential in that it "presupposed the natural origin of language . . . and gave to the question of language origin a scholarly respectability it had not previously possessed (Tweney, 1980, p508)."

By the mid-19th century, answers to the question of human origins had been affected by revisions of the estimated age of the earth and other findings that challenged traditional views (e.g., the literal interpretation of the Bible: Mayr, 1972); discussions of language were affected in turn. Speculations about language origins were so common that in 1866, between the publications of *On the Origin of Species* and *The Descent of Man* (Darwin, 1859, 1871), the Société de Linguistique de Paris changed its bylaws to bar communications dealing with this topic (cf. Sprinker, 1980).

Müller (1861/1864; 1878), and subsequent reviewers of the field (cf. Thorndike, 1943/1949; Farb, 1974; Sprinker, 1980, p117) gave picturesque names to the several hypotheses of language origin that dominated debate from the 18th to the 20th century. The "ding-dong" theory, which held that things in the world evoked characteristic sounds from humans, was a theory consistent with the divine origin of language. The "bow-wow" theory was based on the imitation of sounds (onomatopoeia) and in particular on the imitation of natural cries of animals; these imitated cries evolved into the animals' names. The "pooh-pooh" theory saw the origins of speech in natural human interjections, such as grunts of pain. The "yo-he-ho" (or yo-heave-ho) theory assumed that language began with the coordinated sounds of men working together at strenuous tasks (Noiré, 1877).

These four were to some extent classic accounts, but they were soon supplemented by others. A source of language in love songs and rhythmic chants was advocated by the "sing-song" theory (Jespersen, 1922): "There once was a time when all speech was song, or rather when these two actions were not yet differentiated (p420)"; "Language . . . began with half-musical unanalyzed expressions for individual beings and solitary events (p441)." The "ha-ha" theory assumed that language evolved from laughter, and the "yum-yum" theory that it began with the smacking of the lips and other sounds related to eating. A more elaborate version of the latter, in which movements of the tongue followed movements of other parts of the body, was dubbed the "tongue-tied" theory (cf. Thorndike, 1943/1949): "What drove man to the invention of speech was, as I imagine, not so much the need of expressing his thought (for that might have been done quite satisfactorily by bodily gesture) as the difficulty of 'talking with his hands full' " (Paget, 1930, p132; cf. Whitney, 1875, p293: "The voice may fairly be said to have been given us for the purpose of speech; but it is only as the hands have been given us to write with . . . the voice is, on the whole, the most available means of communication . . . it acts with least expenditure of effort; it leaves the hand . . . at leisure for other work . . . ; and it most easily compels attention from any direction").

On the whole, these accounts were concerned with the sorts of behaviour that might have been the precursors of speech. In some instances, the evolution of the precursors posed problems as formidable as the evolution of speech itself (e.g., what phylogenic contingencies produced laughter?). Furthermore, the accounts typically had little to say about the functions of language and the ways in which such functions might have evolved. Thorndike (1943/1949), in his "babble-luck" theory, was more explicit: Once humans engaged in babbling or vocal play, for whatever reason, the chance connection between a particular sound and some object or event in the behaviour of one individual would sooner or later be established for another, and at that point the utterance could be "used by one of them" to "produce or favor certain behavior in the other (Thorndike, 1949, p290)." To capture the progression from one person to two, from "words used privately to purposive use of speech in the full speaker-hearer relation (p291)," Thorndike provided an alternative name, "onety-twoty," for his theory.

More recent theories have looked not at the origins of vocal behaviour, but rather at relations between language and behaviour of other sorts (cf. Harnad, Steklis & Lancaster, 1976). For example, what might be called the "hack-yack" theory ties the origins of language to the parallel development of tool use by hominids (Hewes, 1976; Hockett, 1960; Leakey & Lewin, 1977; Linden, 1981). The acceptance of sign languages as examples of verbal behaviour did not occur as a matter of course (cf. Gardner & Gardner, 1969), but to the extent that it did occur it went hand in hand with the exploration of analogies between vocal and manual dexterity, between speech and gestures.

Another specific skill that has been invoked is that of aimed throwing, on the assumption that complex coordinations of the sort required by this activity are prerequisites for language (the "throwing" theory: Calvin, 1981; but see Ross, 1982, on the "thrown-out" theory). There have also been various "knowing" theories, relating language to the development of intelligence in conjunction with food-getting and other activities, or to generalised cognitive development, as in the Piagetian stages (Bickerton, 1981; Parker & Gibson, 1979). In a more fanciful account, even leisure time has been implicated, in the "campfire" theory: Early hominids stayed awake all night guarding against predators, but after the discovery of fire they had idle time; the campfire kept them safe, and thus they invented language as a diversion, to occupy their waking time with the telling of stories.

MISLEADING COMMUNICATIONS

But despite the variety of these accounts, few have been built upon a functional analysis of verbal behaviour and few have acknowledged instructional control as the central function of language. Again and again they have appealed to the metaphor of communication: Language is a medium for transmitting something (ideas, feelings, meanings, thoughts, etc.) from one person to another. This metaphor is embedded in everyday talk, as when we say that we "put ideas into words" or "get something across," or as when we speak of words as "carrying meaning" or writings as "packed with information" (cf. Lakoff & Johnson, 1980; Reddy, 1979). Yet "idea," "feeling," "thought" and "meaning" are not well-defined terms, and even "information" rarely implies the quantifiable stuff of information theory (Catania, 1984):

> The metaphor of words as containers for meanings is well established, and yet the magnetic patterns that correspond to a tape-recorded voice or the patterns of pigment on a page that correspond to a hand-written message have no meaning unless someone listens to the recording or reads the note; the meaning is not waiting to be released from the tape or the paper. If anything is transmitted in language, it is the verbal behavior itself; in listening and reading our own behavior duplicates or recreates some features of the behavior of the speakers and the writers that constitute our verbal community (p222).

But the metaphor of communication leads to a different description of language and its functions. According to this view, language is "a purely human and noninstinctive method of communicating ideas, emotions, and desires by means of a system of voluntarily produced symbols (Sapir, 1921, Chapter 1)." The consequences of communication, typically taken for granted, have rarely been made explicit.

The metaphor has pervaded theories of language origin. Consider Whitney (1875), who speaks of "the main determining element in the whole history of production of speech; it is the desire of communication (p284)"; "We speak so as to be intelligible to others; we hear and learn that we may understand them (p287)." The term "communication" can function in a more neutral way, as in the following: "Examples of communication are numerous: song in birds, frogs, and crickets; tail-wagging and hackle-raising in dogs; 'grinning' in chimpanzees; human gestures and language. A great number of survival-machine actions promote their genes indirectly by influencing the behaviour of other survival machines. Animals go to great lengths to make communication effective (Dawkins, 1976, p67, see also Dawkins & Krebs, 1978)." Nevertheless, the language of communication soon tempts the question of what is communicated, and it may then become just as misleading to speak of words as carriers of meaning as it is to speak of genes as carriers of information about phylogenic contingencies (Dawkins, 1982, Chapter 9).

The simplest and most obvious function of verbal behaviour is instructional: it is a way in which one organism can make another do something. By talking, one organism can change another organism's behaviour. Yet even those who have recognised this function have typically turned away from it and instead have given their attention to communication. Consider Bréal (1897/1964): "Speech was not made for the purposes of description, of narrative, of disinterested considerations. To express a desire, to intimate and order, to denote a taking possession of persons or of things—these were the first uses of Language" (cf. Diamond, 1959, p122). In the final analysis, however, those uses become secondary: "The goal of Language is to be understood (Bréal, 1897/1964, p7)."

Russell (1948) provides another illustration, in his discussion of the uses of language:

> Philosophers . . . have been interested in language chiefly as a means of making statements and conveying information, but this is only one of its purposes, and perhaps not the most primitive. What is the purpose of language to a sergeant-major? On the one hand there is the language of the words of command, designed to cause identical simultaneous bodily movements in a number of hearers; on the other hand there is bad language, designed to cause humility in those in whom the expected bodily movements have not been caused. In neither case are words used, except incidentally, to state facts or convey information. . . . Language can be used to express emotions, or to influence the behaviour of others. Each of these functions can be performed, though with less adequacy, by pre-linguistic methods (p57).

Unfortunately, Russell then dropped the topic of command and moved on to language as expression and communication, or the giving of information.

Révész (1956) is another who argued that language evolved from the imperative form. But in that account the imperative is soon subordinated to other functions:

> When a human being enters into linguistic contact with his fellows he can order them to do something or invite or encourage them to some sort of activity (imperative, vocative, optative); indicate or communicate something

> to them (indicative); or ask them something (interrogative). The principle purpose of language is mutual understanding; its aim, the communication of facts, circumstances, intentions and wishes, and the inviting of others to action and communication; the means for the attainment of these aims are chiefly constructions of symbolic signs (pp124–125).

In the end, little is left of the instructional function (Révész, 1956): "the basic function of language *the utterance or communication of words or groups of words for the purpose of mutual understanding* (p16)"; "language is a specially developed and unique means of communicating, thinking, conveying meaning, and facilitating self-consciousness and self-expression (p105)."

Even when other functions have been offered in place of communication, they have often involved some kind of transmission. For example (Leakey & Lewin, 1977):

> Perhaps the pressures of natural selection planted in the heads of primitive *Homo* the ability for spoken language, not so that one individual could tell another what he should be doing next in the practical matters of daily life, but so that everyone could *think* more effectively about the world in which they made a living. Perhaps too the complex operation of an advanced gathering-and-hunting economy would be impossible without a series of *social rules* that could be elaborated and transmitted only through the medium of the spoken word (p170).

Language is then said to be "more a tool of individual imagery and group cohesion than simply an implement of communication (p170)," but given that thoughts and rules are said to be transmitted it is not clear how much this view differs from that already implied by the ubiquitous metaphor of communication.

To be understood and to be understanding, to be able to convey one's feelings and to appreciate the feelings of others, to express one's emotions, to think, to communicate: All of these are typically regarded as important capabilities in contemporary Western culture (Jespersen, 1948):

> Language is purposive activity on the part of one human being in order to come in mental contact with a fellow-man or fellow-men. But we should not one-sidedly think of the purpose of language as being predominantly, or even exclusively, the intellectual one of communicating thoughts; not even if we include volition (commands, wishes, prayers, imprecations, etc.) is that definition sufficiently comprehensive. Language often serves as an outlet for intense feeling, but very often also people speak for the mere pleasure of speaking without having anything really to communicate. . . . Language is likewise important in social intercourse; when two friends meeting in the street ejaculate their "Good-morning!" their intention is not to communicate

ideas to one another, but merely by means of language to give vent to their feeling of good will (pp696–697).

But what selective advantages could have accrued to such practices? What phylogenic and ontogenic contingencies have kept them going (cf. Darwin, 1872)? The point here is not to argue for or against their value; instead, it is to ask whether an evolutionary account of the origins of language can be built upon them. If it is conceded that "knowing someone's feelings" makes it simpler to influence that person's behaviour, then understanding, conveying meaning and so on, might merely be special cases of a more general function of verbal behaviour, and we must wonder how such indirect means of influencing the behaviour of others could have developed; if it is not, then we must be explicit about what the other alternatives are (the issues are different from those of the advantages that may follow from indirect contact with remote events through the verbal behaviour of someone else, or from guaranteeing the availability of an audience through "keeping the lines of communication open," as in the *phatic communication* of Malinowski, 1938).

ONE EVOLUTIONARY SCENARIO

The Darwinian revolution altered our thinking about human origins, but with the acceptance of these views there also developed a conventional wisdom about the evolution of human behaviour and human language. It might be summarised in the following way (cf. Skinner, Chapter 3, this volume; Catania, 1985). Over the epochs of evolution, some organisms became responsive to their environments, developing reflexes and later simple varieties of conditioning that adapted them to survive and reproduce in a competitive world that gradually increased in complexity. Their behaviour also became sensitive to its consequences, in the operant relations of reinforcement and punishment, and then sensitive to different consequences in different settings, in discrimination learning or stimulus control. But still their behaviour was subject to the vagaries of accidental correlations among events and of changing natural contingencies. Then in one line of primates came verbal behaviour, and subsequent human history is a chronicle of how language brought reason to the world. Science and logic were now possible, and humans, through their new capacity to describe contingencies, could overcome the behavioural constraints by which other organisms were bound. Such higher-order capabilities as deliberation and self-control were now possible, and thus humans were no longer captives of the ways in which the immediate consequences of action could outweigh important but temporally more remote consequences:

"The exact point at which the animal ceases and man begins can be determined with precision since it coincides with the beginning of . . . language, and language is reason (Moncalm, 1905, p40)."

Is this a plausible account? We know that non-verbal organisms need not be lured by immediate consequences to become victims of more remote ones (Garcia & Koelling, 1966), and we know that non-verbal processes enter into self-control and related processes (Rachlin & Green, 1972). Perhaps the problems of human history are not in the slowness with which language has transcended non-verbal behaviour but in our assumptions about the role of language in the evolution of human behaviour.

What if the preceding scenario had it backwards? The Age of Reason was a short part of human intellectual history, and language has not been universally regarded as a source of reason: "Men believe that their reason is lord over their words, but it happens, too, that words exercise a reciprocal and reactionary power over our intellect. Words, as a Tartar's bow, shoot back upon the understanding of the wisest, and mightily entangle and pervert the judgment (Francis Bacon, quoted in Sprinker, 1980, p113)." We recognise only too well that language need not be an instrument of reason or a vehicle of truth, but it is more difficult to see that it probably did not even emerge as such a vehicle or instrument. It was not simply superimposed upon non-verbal behaviour that had evolved under the constraints of natural contingencies. Yet even some of those who warned of the traps created by verbal behaviour (Korzybski, 1941, on general semantics; Chase, 1938, on the tyranny of words) spoke of the problems of language as if they were temporary aberrations of recent origin.

Verbal behaviour more likely followed from the evolution of social control, in a progression from vocal releasers to varied verbal functions shaped by social consequences. We now call behaviour that is under the control of verbal behaviour rule-governed, distinguishing it from contingency-shaped behaviour or behaviour that has been shaped by its consequences (Skinner, 1966). With the development of language, rule-governed behaviour was available to supplement contingency-shaped behaviour. But what ontogenic and phylogenic contingencies entered into its origins?

IMPERATIVES

The idea that language originated as a variety of instructional control is not new: "Primitive speech, apart from mere emotional cries . . . , no doubt began with imperative verbs, differing only in their variety and fuller meaning from instinctive cries (Smith, 1927, quoted in Diamond, 1959, p122)." On similar grounds, Diamond (1959) claimed the emergence of verbs before nouns as a universal feature of language evolution, arguing that "our most primitive sentence (the request for action of only one term—e.g., 'Look!') is . . . the origin of language. . . . language emerged out of requests for assistance addressed by one (male) person to another (p7)"; "Language is the means whereby man in society influences his environment; it is the means whereby he enlists the efforts of his fellows for his benefit. . . . instead of using his own limbs, he is by language enabled to use the limbs of his fellows (p114)." Other functions then entered into his account: "We have only to compare the request for action with the 'statement' of later times to appreciate the difference. . . . The request for action is itself an action; the statement is an expression of cognition (p151)." But the main point survived even though the metaphor of communication obviously retained its influence: "We speak to impress the minds of others. Directly and fundamentally we do so in the request for action; but indirectly this is the whole purpose of language, and indeed all language is a request for help (p178)."

Although it discusses the issue in different terms, the present account shares the assumption that verbal behaviour evolved as a way in which one organism alters the behaviour of another. The implications are potentially far-reaching. If verbal behaviour begins as instructional control, that control does not stop at non-verbal behaviour. Once verbal behaviour is established, one individual can instruct what another says as well as what the other does. Giving a definition or stating a fact or asking a question instruct verbal behaviour just as much as giving an order or making a request instruct non-verbal. The term "instruction" has been broadened here well beyond its familiar uses. We cannot judge whether a particular instance of verbal behaviour is an instruction on the basis of its grammatical form; there are many senses in which all utterances are ways of telling someone else what to do (Jaynes, 1977):

> Consider what it is to listen and understand someone speaking to us. . . . To hear is actually a kind of obedience. Indeed, both words come from the same root and therefore were probably the same word originally. This is true in Greek, Latin, Hebrew, French, German, Russian, as well as in English, where 'obey' comes from the Latin *obedire*, which is a composite of *ob+audire*, to hear facing someone (pp97–99).

If other functions of language have since emerged, what could they be and how could they have been maintained? How persuasively can the argument be defended not only that the original and primary function of language was instructional but also that this function *has not changed*?

ANOTHER EVOLUTIONARY SCENARIO

Consider now a scenario based on the assumption that language evolved primarily through the elaboration of its instructional functions (cf. Jaynes, 1977, pp126–138). Its early stages are similar to those in the preceding scenario, so we can move past the early stages directly to a band of preverbal hominids. In this band, a minimal repertory of fixed action patterns elicited by vocal releasers has already evolved. Such classes of behaviour exist among many current species, so this development is plausible. Vocal calls affect the behaviour of conspecifics among a variety of mammalian and avian species (Kroodsma & Miller, 1982; Smith, 1977; Snowdon, Brown & Petersen, 1983). Some cries that occur in the presence of predators may produce freezing or flight or attack; others in different circumstances may be correlated with feeding or with sexual behaviour.

The details of such vocal control can be complex; for example, predator calls can vary with kind of predator, and the response to the call can depend on who the caller is and who the listener is (Gouzoules, Gouzoules & Marler, 1984; Seyfarth, Cheney & Marler, 1980; cf. Beer, 1976, p427, on the long-call of the laughing gull: "Firstly, utterance of a long-call conveys more than one kind of information; the caller identifies itself and it transmits a message which is of the nature of a warning, a command, an invitation or an advertisement. Secondly this message can be varied on different occasions of use of the long-call, through variation of features internal to the call"). But the complexity creates no problems for this account; the more complex the properties of the known calls of existing species, the easier it is to grant that more sophisticated cases shaped by phylogenic contingencies are feasible.

On these grounds, we will assume that the calls of a primate leader once controlled the behaviour of members of its band as reliably as any releaser elicits a fixed action pattern. At first the vocabulary of releasers was limited to just a few calls. These calls did not yet qualify as verbal behaviour, but they had effects corresponding to those of words such as "come" or "go" or "stop". With the differentiation of more varied vocal calls, a more extensive repertory of instructed classes of behaviour followed. The phylogenic contributions to this rudimentary instructional control were soon supplemented by ontogenic ones. Verbs, nouns, and various modifiers followed simply from the increasing complexity of instructions: "stop," "run," "dig," "watch" must eventually be supplemented by "catch rabbit," "build fire," "plant seed," "shapen blade," and so on (cf. Jaynes, 1976, for an argument that modifiers developed before rather than after nouns and verbs).

But speculations about the sequence in which various grammatical forms emerged or about the correlation of language origins with human activities such as tool-making, agriculture and the mastery of fire are not strictly relevant to this scenario. Many aspects of the human behaviour we call culture have been shaped by contingencies operating on behaviour that is non-verbal (Binford, 1983; Harris, 1977). The differentiation of instructional control from vocal releasers may have occurred through any of a variety of different routes, and perhaps it actually occurred in more than one way in different populations of prehistoric hominids. The critical point, however, is that it suggests plausible origins for many special features of human verbal behaviour.

What we have so far is at least one speaker, probably a dominant male, a restricted repertory of vocal releasers, and a population of listeners who responded to each of the items in the vocal repertory in consistent and characteristic ways. The responses were presumably those that gave the group a competitive edge relative to other similar groups, and therefore typically had social functions: keeping the group together during movement from one place to another; coordinating aggression or flight in encounters with other groups; etc.

A central question is that of how phylogenic and ontogenic contingencies combined in maintaining these behavioural relations. If phylogenic determinants weakened, then under some circumstances ontogenic ones might have supplemented them or taken their place. For example, the dominant speaker, or leader, might learn to attack a listener who does not respond in the characteristic way, thereby punishing disobedience. There have been many suggestions of how transitions from phylogenically determined patterns to operant behaviour might have occurred: "Two young herring-gulls compete for the remains of a fish lying on the shore. One opens his wings to their full height and span and menacingly moves a step towards the other, who retreats. . . . The first time he made that gesture he may have done so in instinct or anger, but he now knows from experience that the other will recoil (Diamond, 1959, p149)." The distinction between incidental and intentional calls may correspond to a distinction between phylogenic and ontogenic sources of behaviour: "The first stage and the *sine qua non* of language is the development out of incidental calls of *intentional calls*, or those which tend to be repeated unless turned off by a change in behaviour of the recipient (Jaynes, 1977, p131)." In any case, the question of ontogenic and phylogenic contributions must remain open. We can recognise many ontogenic contingencies that maintain the effectiveness of instructional control: The following of instructions is often reinforced and deviations from it are often punished. But we also should not rule out the possibility of phylogenic sources of such behaviour.

THE CONSEQUENCES OF INSTRUCTIONAL CONTROL

What may follow now from the continued differentiation of this prototypical version of instructional control? The reinforcers in those settings were complex but primarily social. For the leader and the leader's successors, access to an audience was a prerequisite for exerting instructional control, and the behaviour generated by that control produced consequences that helped to maintain the instructional verbal behaviour of the leader. Thus, the availability of an audience as a reinforcer was built in early in this evolution. For the others, the followers, access to the leader and to the leader's instructions was important at least for the simple reason that only if this was so did the group survive as a group. Obedience produced consequences, including some arranged by the leader, that helped to maintain obedience, but some of the leader's control over the audience may have had phylogenic origins, in that the effectiveness of instructional control depended on the leader's commanding look or the leader's quality of voice or those other aspects of individuals that we sometimes summarise by speaking of charisma.

This instructional control was asymmetrical, and the individual differences thus implied made some members of the band more susceptible to it than others. To the extent that this involved responses to particular calls as well as instructional control in general, some calls became effective only for particular individuals. The singling out of instructional control over individuals by distinctive calls was the beginning of the language evolution leading to names. Much later in human prehistory, when the sources of instructional control had become more diffuse, keeping one's name secret became a way to escape from the power of instructional control (Frazer, 1922/1951, pp284–289).

Once instructional control had expanded to an extensive repertory that included arbitrary as well as phylogenically determined calls, the idiosyncratic repertories developed by particular leaders were ordinarily lost to subsequent generations until some ways of establishing this verbal behaviour in the leaders' successors had evolved. The next step in this evolution was probably long in coming. Its most crucial aspect was the repetition by the follower of the leader's instruction; in this way, the follower truly became a listener.

The repetition presumably began in an overt vocal form, but the argument can also be made in terms of covert behaviour. The present scenario has much in common with that of Jaynes (1976), in which instructional control is extended by the listener's auditory hallucinations of the leader's utterances. Both remembered voices and hallucinated voices begin as repetitions of heard voices. The main difference between them is in the listener's discrimination between their sources: Remembered voices are discriminated from heard voices whereas hallucinated voices are not. In other words, the difference between remembering and hallucinating lies in this discrimination, which is one instance of a discrimination of the sources of one's own behaviour. The possibility of this discrimination was prepared by other discriminations of aspects of one's own behaviour essential to complex instructional control. Autoclitic verbal behaviour (Skinner, 1957) is verbal behaviour built upon other verbal behaviour; its function is to modify the effects on the listener of the other verbal behaviour (e.g., as the effects of the instruction "go" are modified by the word "not"; particles, words, phrases and grammatical structures can have autoclitic functions; cf. Catania, 1980).

The differentiation of the repetition of instructions became especially critical as instructions became more complex. Its significance, however, was not merely that it initiated relevant vocal behaviour in those who were to become the leader's successors. That contingency had relatively remote effects, and might not have been sufficient to maintain vocal repetitions over generations. The more important and more immediate consequence was that the repetition of the leader's utterances established conditions under which the leader could give instructions to be followed in the leader's absence, at later times and in other places. In effect, control was gradually transferred from the leader's instruction to the listener's own repetition of that instruction. The extended social organisation this development allowed maintained the advantages of instructional control. It expanded the influence of the leader and allowed coordinated human groups to grow outside the range of the human voice. It also created the precursors of human verbal memory. With this instructional control, a cohesive social group was created, the coordinated behaviour of which gave each of its members a survival advantage relative to those of competing groups, even though the instructed behaviour was inevitably relatively insensitive to modification by its natural consequences.

The instructional control discussed here can operate over long periods of time and in subtle ways. It is consistent with superstitions about the magic of words (Ogden & Richards, 1938), with assumptions about the relations between language and ritual (Haldane, 1953), and with observations about insidious controlling effects of verbal behaviour in contemporary culture (Fowler, Hodge, Kress & Trew, 1979). To consider a more far-fetched possibility, if speculations on the origins of language in song were off the mark only in that they did not invoke song as the original language of command, then perhaps some of the power of music lies in its earlier instructional functions, even if those functions have now become mainly vestigial.

To the extent that increases in population over human evolution gave competitive advantages to groups that were efficient in agriculture, effective in production and coordinated in combat, the pressure for more powerful instructional control led to further refinements of language. Once leaders were able to instruct the verbal behaviour of listeners who could in turn instruct the non-verbal behaviour of others, the prerequisites for human religious and political institutions were firmly in place. The invention of writing, perhaps initially a matter of record-keeping, further removed instructional control from the behaviour of individual leaders. The behaviour of a substantial proportion of the present human population of the world is influenced by records of the verbal behaviour of past generations: the Rig-veda, the Torah, the Koran, the Book of Mormon, the Analects of Confucius, Das Kapital, the Bhagavad-Gita, and the New Testament, to mention only a few. We can no longer sort out the phylogenic and the ontogenic sources of this control, but the control undoubtedly remains with us.

This account is consistent with what we know about contemporary human behaviour. In contrast to behaviour that has been shaped by contingencies, instructed or rule-governed behaviour is often insensitive to its consequences (Lowe, 1979; 1983). Apart from the area of motor skills, it is difficult to find examples of adult human behaviour that are unequivocally contingency-shaped. For example, the scheduling of presumably reinforcing consequences for simple human responses such as button presses does not maintain the performances typically generated when these schedules operate for the responses of non-human species (Matthews, Shimoff, Catania & Sagvolden, 1977), though characteristic performances can be obtained from preverbal children (Lowe, Beasty & Bentall, 1983). When verbal behaviour is shaped, it rather than current contingencies is likely to determine performance (Catania, Matthews & Shimoff, 1982; cf. Luria, 1959a, 1959b; Zivin, 1979). Verbal behaviour does not necessarily put humans in closer touch with contingencies. When people do what they are told, their behaviour is controlled by the instructions rather than by the natural consequences of their behaviour. Uninstructed human behaviour, not influenced by language, is most likely to be in close touch with environmental events, but instructional control ordinarily overrides the contingency-shaped behaviour. It is pervasive and often operates in subtle ways. It is a type of control from which it is difficult to escape.

UNRESOLVED PROBLEMS

Language is complex, and inevitably there are many aspects of it that we have not considered here (cf., Catania, 1983, 1984a). For example, we have not dealt with the ways in which the leader's verbal behaviour is shaped by contingencies. Instructional control will not be advantageous to the group if the leader's instructions have little relation to the circumstances confronted by the group. This contingency at least provides for stimulus control over verbal behaviour by events in the non-verbal environment (the tact relation: Skinner, 1957), and this account has simply taken it for granted.

We have also dealt little with the structure of language. For the present purposes, it matters little what form languages take, provided the appropriate behaviour is available to both speaker and listener. If universals of language have evolved, no more problem is raised for the present account than for accounts of the topography of non-verbal behaviour. For example, motor programmes determined phylogenically may restrict the properties of human bipedal locomotion or avian flight, but operant contingencies determined ontogenically are still critical determinants of when and where a human walks or a bird flies (cf. Fentress, 1978; Gallistel, 1980). In any case, few of the claims for biological universals of language (Lenneberg, 1967) have been claims about function.

Another omission is that we have not dealt with the repetition of instructions as a special case of imitation (Baer, Peterson & Sherman, 1967). The significant consequences of echoic speech are the correspondences between sounds one has heard and sounds one has produced oneself. It is not too great a leap to extend such correspondences to include other properties of verbal behaviour (Paniagua & Baer, 1982; Risley & Hart, 1968). If verbal repertories are to be maintained, the discriminative (tact) relations between events and verbal responses in one's own behaviour must correspond to those in the behaviour of others. The verbal community provides the discriminative stimuli as well as the consequences that shape verbal behaviour and maintain its consistency. This source of the development of correspondences between the verbal and the non-verbal may be strengthened instructional control and the insensitivity of instructed behaviour to contingencies; but the correspondences developed in the reciprocities of speaker and listener may also have set the stage for equivalence classes (Sidman, Rauzin, Lazar & Cunningham, 1982).

Others will no doubt expand the list of omissions, but perhaps they will also expand the list of implications. If instructional functions such as those advanced here were the foundations for the origin of language, recent human history might best be regarded as a chronicle of the emergence of other functions of language and their substitution for instructional control. Religious fanaticism and political dogmatism argue that strongly determined instructional components of language have not become vestigial. From this perspective, contemporary human achievement is not that of developing and refining language but rather is that of freeing language from its origins in social control. First the non-verbal environment controlled directly; then the verbal environment assumed control, through the instructions of others as leaders; eventually that control became more direct, in that listeners became their own speakers, but the verbal environment and not the non-verbal remained in control. In the transition to the "truth" functions of language, scientific verbal behaviour may return verbal behaviour to, and anchor it more firmly in, the non-verbal environment. In the evolving functions of language, therefore, the promise of science is that of bringing human behaviour back into contact with natural contingencies, perhaps in new and more effective ways, without losing the benefits of rule-governed behaviour. Language did not evolve as a vehicle of truth or as an instrument of reason, but perhaps it could become one. There is grandeur in this view of language.

REFERENCES

Baer, D. M., Peterson, R. F., & Sherman, J. A. (1967) The development of imitation by reinforcing behavioral similarity to a model. *Journal of the Experimental Analysis of Behavior*, **10**, 405–416.

Beer, C. (1976) Some complexities in the communication behavior of gulls. *Annals of the New York Academy of Sciences*, **280**, 413–432.

Bickerton, D. (1981) *Roots of language*. Ann Arbor, MI: Karoma.

Binford, L. R. (1983) *In pursuit of the past*. New York: Thames & Hudson.

Bréal, M. (1964) *Semantics* (N. Cust, translator). New York: Dover. (Original work published 1897.)

Brown, R. (1973) *A first language*. Cambridge, MA: Harvard University Press.

Calvin, W. H. (1981, December) The throwing theory for language origins. *Human Ethology Newsletter*, 17–22.

Catania, A. C. (1978) The psychology of learning: Some lessons from the Darwinian revolution. *Annals of the New York Academy of Sciences*, **309**, 18–28.

Catania, A. C. (1980) Autoclitic processes and the structure of behaviour. *Behaviorism*, **8**, 175–186.

Catania, A. C. (1983) Behavior analysis and behavior synthesis in the extrapolation from animal to human behavior. In G. Davey (Ed.), *Animal models of human behavior*. Chichester: Wiley. 51–69.

Catania, A. C. (1984) *Learning* (2nd ed.). Englewood Cliffs, NJ: Prentice-Hall.

Catania, A. C. (1985) The two psychologies of learning: Blind alleys and nonsense syllables. In S. Koch & D. Leary (Eds.), *A century of psychology as science*. New York: McGraw-Hill. (in press).

Catania, A. C., Matthews, B. A., & Shimoff, E. (1982) Instructed versus shaped human verbal behaviour: Interactions with nonverbal responding. *Journal of the Experimental Analysis of Behavior*, **38**, 233–248.

Chase, S. (1938) *The tyranny of words*. New York: Harcourt, Brace & World.

Chomsky, N. (1968) *Language and mind*. New York: Harcourt, Brace & World.

Chomsky, N. (1980) Rules and representations. *Behavioral and Brain Sciences*, **3**, 1–61.

Condillac, E. B. de (1974) *An essay on the origin of human knowledge* (B. Nugent, trans.). New York: AMS Press. (Original work published 1756).

Darwin, C. (1859) *On the origin of species*. London: John Murray.

Darwin, C. (1871) *The descent of man*. London: John Murray.

Darwin, C. (1872) *The expression of the emotions in man and animals*. London: John Murray.

Dawkins, R. (1976) *The selfish gene*. New York: Oxford.
Dawkins, R. (1982) *The extended phenotype*. San Francisco: Freeman.
Dawkins, R. & Krebs, J. R. (1978) Animal signals: Information or manipulation? In J. R. Krebs & N. B. Davies (Eds.), *Behavioral ecology*. Sunderland, MA: Sinauer.
de Villiers, J. G. & de Villiers, P. A. (1978) *Language acquisition*. Cambridge, MA: Harvard University Press.
Diamond, A. S. (1959) *The history and origin of language*. New York: The Citadel Press.
Farb, P. (1974) *Word play*. New York: Knopf.
Fentress, J. C. (1978) *Mus musicus*, the experimental orchestration of selected movement patterns in mice. In G. M. Burghardt & M. Bekoff (Eds.), *The development of behavior: Comparative and evolutionary aspects*. New York: Garland.
Fowler, R., Hodge, B., Kress, G., & Trew, T. (1979) *Language and control*. London: Routledge & Kegan Paul.
Frazer, J. G. (1951) *The golden bough* (abridged ed.). New York: Macmillan. (Original work published 1922).
Gallistel, C. R. (1980) *The organization of action*. Hillsdale, NJ: Lawrence Erlbaum Associates.
Garcia, J. & Koelling, R. A. (1966) Relation of cue to consequence in avoidance learning. *Psychonomic Science*, **4**, 123–124.
Gardner, R. A. & Gardner, B. T. (1969) Teaching sign language to a chimpanzee. *Science*, **165**, 664–672.
Gould, S. J. (1977). *Ontogeny and phylogeny*. Cambridge, MA: Harvard University Press.
Gouzoules, S., Gouzoules, H., & Marler, P. (1984) Rhesus monkey (*Macaca mulatta*) screams: Representational signalling in the recruitment of agonistic aid. *Animal Behaviour*, **32**, 182–193.
Haldane, J. B. S. (1953) Animal ritual and human language. *Diogenes*, **4**, 61–73.
Harnad, S. R., Steklis, H. B., & Lancaster, J. (Eds.). (1976) Origins and evolution of language and speech. *Annals of the New York Academy of Sciences*, **280**, 1–914.
Harris, M. (1977) *Cannibals and kings: The origins of cultures*. New York: Random House.
Herder, J. G. (1966) *Essay on the origin of language*. (J. H. Moran & A. Gode, Trans.) New York: F. Ungar. (Original work published 1771).
Hewes, G. W. (1975) *Language origins: A bibliography* (2nd rev. and enl. ed.). The Hague: Mouton.
Hewes, G. W. (1976) The current status of the gestural theory of language origin. *Annals of the New York Academy of Sciences*, **280**, 482–504.
Hockett, C. D. (1960, March) The origin of speech. *Scientific American*, **203**, 88–96.
Jaynes, J. (1976) The evolution of language in the late Pleistocene. *Annals of the New York Academy of Sciences*, **280**, 312–325.
Jaynes, J. (1977) *The origin of consciousness in the breakdown of the bicameral mind*. Boston: Houghton Mifflin.
Jespersen, O. (1922) *Language: Its nature, development and origin*. New York: Macmillan.
Jespersen, O. (1948) Language. In *Encyclopedia Britannica*. Chicago: University of Chicago.
Korzybski, A. (1941) *Science and sanity* (2nd ed.). Lancaster, PA.: The Science Press.
Kroodsma, D. E. & Miller, E. H. (Eds.). (1982) *Acoustic communication in birds*. (Volume 2) *Song learning and its consequences*. New York: Academic Press.
Lakoff, G. & Johnson, M. (1980) *Metaphors we live by*. Chicago: University of Chicago Press.
Lamendella, J. T. (1976) Relations between the ontogeny and phylogeny of language. *Annals of the New York Academy of Sciences*, **280**, 396–412.
Leakey, R. E. & Lewin, R. (1977) *People of the lake*. New York: Doubleday.
Lenneberg, E. H. (1967) *Biological foundations of language*. New York: Wiley.

Linden, E. (1981) *Apes, men, and language* (revised ed.). New York: Penguin.

Lowe, C. F. (1979) Determinants of human operant behaviour. In M. D. Zeiler & P. Harzem (Eds.), *Reinforcement and the organization of behaviour*. Chichester: Wiley. 159–192.

Lowe, C. F. (1983) Radical behaviorism and human psychology: In G. C. L. Davey (Ed.) *Animal models of human behavior*. Chichester, UK: Wiley. 71–93.

Lowe, C. F., Beasty, A., & Bentall, R. P. (1983) The role of verbal behavior in human learning. *Journal of the Experimental Analysis of Behavior*, **39**, 157–164.

Luria, A. R. (1959a) The directive function of speech in development and dissolution. Part I. *Word*, **15**, 341–352.

Luria, A. R. (1959b) The directive function of speech in development and dissolution. Part II. *Word*, **15**, 453–464.

Luria. A. R. (1961) *The role of speech in the production of normal and abnormal behavior*. New York: Liveright.

Malinowski, B. (1938) The problem of meaning in primitive languages. In C. K. Ogden & I. A. Richards, *The meaning of meaning* (5th ed.). New York: Harcourt, Brace. 296–336.

Matthews, B. A., Shimoff, E., Catania, A. C., & Sagvolden, T. (1977) Uninstructed human responding: Sensitivity to ratio and interval contingencies. *Journal of the Experimental Analysis of Behavior*, **27**, 453–467.

Mayr, E. (1972) The nature of the Darwinian revolution. *Science*, **176**, 981–989.

Mayr, E. (1982) *The growth of biological thought*. Cambridge, MA: Harvard University Press.

Midgley, M. (1978) *Beast and man*. Ithaca, NY: Cornell University Press.

Moncalm, M. (1905) *The origin of thought and speech* (G. S. Whitmarsh, trans.). London: Kegan Paul, Trench, Trübner.

Müller, M. (1861/1864) *Lectures on the science of language*. London.

Müller, M. (1878, February) On the origin of reason. *Contemporary Review*, **466**.

Noiré, L. (1877) *Der Ursprung der Sprache*. Mainz: Verlag von Zabern.

Ogden, C. K. & Richards, I. A. (1938) *The meaning of meaning* (5th ed.). New York: Harcourt, Brace.

Paget, R. (1930) *Human speech*. London: Routledge & Kegan Paul.

Paniagua, F. A. & Baer, D. M. (1982) The analysis of correspondence training as a chain reinforceable at any point. *Child Development*, **53**, 786–798.

Parker, S. T. & Gibson, K. R. (1979) A developmental model for the evolution of language and intelligence in early hominids. *The Behavioral and Brain Sciences*, **2**, 367–407.

Premack, D. (1970) A functional analysis of language. *Journal of the Experimental Analysis of Behavior*, **14**, 107–125.

Rachlin, H. & Green, L. (1972) Commitment, choice and self-control. *Journal of the Experimental Analysis of Behavior*, **17**, 15–22.

Reddy, M. J. (1979) The conduit metaphor. In A. Ortony (Ed.), *Metaphor and thought*. New York: Cambridge University Press.

Révész, G. (1956) *The origins and prehistory of language* (J. Butler, Trans.). New York: Philosophical Library.

Risley, T. R. & Hart, B. (1968) Developing correspondence between the non-verbal and verbal behaviour of pre-school children. *Journal of Applied Behavior Analysis*, **9**, 267–281.

Ross, J. A. (1982, June) The thrown out theory of language origins. *Human Ethology Newsletter*, 34–37.

Rousseau, J.-J. (1966) *Essay on the origin of language* (J. H. Moran & A. Gode, Trans.) New York: F. Ungar. (Original work published 1753).

Russell, B. (1948) *Human knowledge: Its scope and limits*. London: Allen & Unwin.

Sapir, E. (1921) *Language*. New York: Harcourt, Brace.

Savage-Rumbaugh, E. S. & Rumbaugh, D. (1978) Symbolization, language, and chimpanzees: A theoretical reevaluation based on initial language acquisition processes in four young *Pan troglodytes. Brain and Language*, **6**, 265–300.

Seyfarth, R. M., Cheney, D. L., & Marler, P. (1980) Vervet monkey alarm calls: Semantic communication in a free-ranging primate. *Animal Behaviour*, **28**, 1070–1094.

Sidman, M. (1971) The behavioral analysis of aphasia. *Journal of Psychiatric Research*, **8**, 413–422.

Sidman, M., Rauzin, R., Lazar, R., & Cunningham, S. (1982) A search for symmetry in the conditional discrimination of Rhesus monkeys, baboons, and children. *Journal of the Experimental Analysis of Behavior*, **37**, 23–44.

Simpson, G. G. (1953) *The major features of evolution*. New York: Columbia University Press.

Skinner, B. F. (1957) *Verbal behavior*. New York: Appleton-Century-Crofts.

Skinner, B. F. (1966) An operant analysis of problem solving. In B. Kleinmuntz (Ed.), *Problem solving: Research method, and theory*. New York: Wiley.

Skinner, B. F. (1975) The shaping of phylogenic behaviour. *Journal of the Experimental Analysis of Behavior*, **24**, 117–120.

Skinner, B. F. (1984) The evolution of behaviour. *Journal of the Experimental Analysis of Behavior*, **41**, 217–221.

Smith, W. J. (1977) *The behavior of communicating*. Cambridge, MA: Harvard University Press.

Snowdon, C. T., Brown, C. H., & Petersen, M. R. (Eds.). (1983) *Primate communication*. New York: Cambridge University Press.

Sprinker, M. (1980) Gerard Manley Hopkins on the origin of language. *Journal of the History of Ideas*, **41**, 113–128.

Thorndike, E. L. (1943/1949) The origin of language. *Science*, **48**, 1–6. Reprinted in *Selected writings from a connectionist's psychology*. New York: Appleton-Century-Crofts. 280–293.

Tweney, R. D. (1980) Review of "Inquiries into the origin of language: The fate of a question" by J. H. Stam. *Journal of Psycholinguistic Research*, **9**, 507–515.

Whitney, W. D. (1875) *The life and growth of language*. New York: D. Appleton.

Zivin, G. (Ed.). (1979) *The development of self-regulation through private speech*. New York: Wiley.

IV FUNDAMENTAL RESEARCH AND BEHAVIOUR MODIFICATION

10 Fundamental Research and Behaviour Modification

Jack Michael
Western Michigan University

The relationship between fundamental research on behaviour and its application should be like the relationship between research in biology and its application in medicine, agriculture, or forestry. At issue is simply the relationship between the science of behaviour and the various applications of this science to practical problems of social importance. The concepts, terms, principles, methods, etc. of basic research should provide the bases for applied research, for non-research applications, and for extrapolations by analogy; new findings in basic research should lead to new applications and to more sophisticated extrapolations; problems in application should feed back to prompt new directions in basic research. Such a beneficial inter-relationship can be described as the "normal" one. However, it can be contrasted with two departures, one which consists of a seemingly self-sufficient applied field, the other which consists of applied workers who seriously question the relevance or adequacy of basic behavioural research.

During the 50s and early 60s behaviour modification involved the direct use of the methods, but also the concepts and principles of the animal conditioning laboratory in order to alter socially important human behaviour. By the late 60s, however, the single-subject methods of the operant laboratory were being adapted to the study of human behaviour in such a way as to make the results interesting and valuable irrespective of their relation to basic principles and concepts. It is this development which would seem to have led to the first departure from the normal basic-applied relation. Much current applied behaviour analysis consists essentially of (1) a strong belief in the value of *behavioural* dependent variables and environmental independent variables (as contrasted with an interest in mental or cognitive processes); and (2) a self-corrective "systems" approach to research or implementation, with the following rules:

1. Define the problem in behavioural terms.
2. Develop some way to measure the relevant behaviour and be sure that the measure is reliable.
3. Obtain a sequence of baseline measurements prior to intervening and for long enough to be sure that the behaviour is not changing systematically before the intervention is introduced.
4. Intervene by altering the environment in some way that might produce desirable changes in the behaviour, while continuing to measure.
5. If changes in the desired direction occur and if they are of sufficient magnitude to be of value, then give proper consideration to the generality and durability of the effect, and if all is well, terminate the procedure. If adequate changes are not produced after an appropriate period of application, then alter some other aspect of the environment and continue trying.

This general approach involves an increasingly sophisticated "single-subject" methodology with respect to experimental design, and increasingly effective measurement systems involving human observers.

Those working from this perspective may use the terminology of the conditioning laboratory if it proves convenient, but they seem to have little real compulsion to relate their procedures or results to basic conditioning concepts and principles. From their perspective the substantive aspect of the experimental analysis of behaviour is little more than one of several possible sources of ideas for manipulating independent variables, along with "common sense" or other theoretical orientations.

Without denying the general effectiveness of such a behavioural systems approach, especially for purely outcome-oriented research or implementation, a number of workers within the area of applied behaviour analysis have questioned its long-term value in isolation from basic research in the experimental analysis of behaviour (Hayes, 1978; Dietz, 1978; Birnbrauer, 1979; Pierce & Epling, 1980; Michael, 1980). These commentators have argued that a technology separated from its basic science lacks a coherent rationale for its procedures or results. Unless applied achievements can be interpreted in terms of the basic science of behaviour, the bearing of those achievements on other theoretical and practical issues cannot be easily seen, and of course the achievements do not support the strengths of the basic science nor identify its weaknesses.

The second departure from the normal relation between basic and applied research is the belief that basic behaviour analysis, as presently conceived, is not adequate for many applied purposes. This dissatisfaction takes two different forms. The first accepts a behavioural orientation but questions the relevance to an understanding of human behaviour of basic concepts and principles derived from experiments with animals. The other rejects an exclusively behavioural approach in favour of inferred psychodynamic, physiological, ethological ("sociobiological"), or cognitive constructs.

There is no question that much basic research has been and still is being carried out with animals in laboratories, nor that applied workers are now dealing, either theoretically or practically, with increasingly complex human behaviour. The human verbal repertoire and extensive social history may indeed require new concepts and principles. But before one rejects or supplements (some might say "contaminates") fundamental research in behaviour analysis as the basis for behaviour modification there are three points that should be considered.

First, a person making such a judgement may have an oversimplified understanding of the area of behaviour analysis. It may be seen as essentially the study of rewards and punishments, or the three-term contingency of stimulus, response, and reinforcement. Such an appreciation of behaviour analysis is, of course, much too limited. Even to describe this area as the study of learning is to omit many important topics. It is true that the best known source of basic research results, *The Journal of the Experimental Analysis of Behavior*, because of its editorial policies and the preferences of researchers who submit their findings, has focused on a limited set of behavioural topics. But the scientists publishing in that journal do not conceive of their science in such limited terms. Basic behaviour analysis is concerned with *all* aspects of behaviour, including unlearned behaviour of the sort studied by ethologists and respondent (classical) conditioning, as well as operant relationships involving schedules of unconditioned and conditioned reinforcement and punishment, stimulus control, motivation (deprivation, aversive stimulation, etc.), and emotion. This breadth can be seen in Skinner's *Science and Human Behavior* (1953), *Contingencies of Reinforcement* (1969), and *About Behaviorism* (1974), as well as in recent textbooks such as Fantino and Logan's *The Experimental Analysis of Behavior: A Biological Perspective* (1979) and Catania's *Learning* (1984).

Unfortunately, the body of knowledge that currently constitutes the results of basic behavioural research is not easily accessible. Original research papers (for example, in *The Journal of the Experimental Analysis of Behavior*) are often comprehensible only to specialists in the same research area. Reviews (as in Honig & Staddon, 1977) are useful, but unless the reviewer has a special interest in extrapolation, the relevance of their material to the human situation is not elaborated. But papers in less specialised journals, such as *The Behavior Analyst*, are sometimes specifically concerned with extrapolation and interpretation of basic research findings (Epling & Pierce, 1983) and among the many textbooks devoted to application there are some that make a special point of using recent basic research findings (Kalish, 1981).

In any case, the area of behaviour analysis is extensive and complex, and to understand it well enough to appreciate its deficiencies requires much more exposure than is obtained in a six-hour workshop, or a one-semester college course, or for that matter, a bachelor's degree in psychology.

The second issue concerns the availability of behavioural research results with humans. If the applied worker's primary concern is practical the applied literature would seem to be most appropriate. *The Journal of Applied Behavior Analysis* is now in its 17th year of publication, and many other applied behavioural journals (*Behaviour Research and Therapy, Behavior Therapy, The Journal of Behavior Therapy and Experimental Psychiatry, Behavior Analysis and Modification, Behavior Modification, Progress in Behavior Modification*) are available. Much of this literature is technique and outcome oriented, but for most practical goals this is just what is needed. Information is now available concerning almost every conceivable kind of applied behavioural problem, and the research is all with human subjects. The extensiveness of these data is a possible limitation in itself, but with the increasing availability of computer information and search systems they are becoming highly accessible.

But goals are seldom purely practical. Scientists, basic and applied, typically want to "understand" their subject matter in a more general sense than knowing how to manipulate it. Some of the applied literature *is* concerned with this type of understanding. Basic concepts and principles, even though derived from results with lower animals, are also a useful source for such understanding. Fundamental research with humans is especially useful, and although the trend is relatively recent, such research results are increasingly available. An excellent general treatment of this trend and a plea for more such research is provided by Hake (1982); an extensive review of the field that is coming to be referred to as "human operant research" has been made by Lowe (1979); and a comprehensive review of basic behavioural research on human language has been produced by Salzinger (1978).

The third point to be considered before rejecting fundamental research in behaviour analysis as the basis for behaviour modification concerns the criticism of the results and concepts of basic behavioural research as being an insufficiently rich source of ideas for further investigations of human behaviour, or for hypotheses and theoretical speculation. Such a criticism would certainly be valid if the critic had an oversimplified understanding of basic behavioural research. From such a perspective cognitive or psychodynamic approaches clearly may seem to be much richer sources for hypothesis formulation or theorising (a possibly dubious virtue). Although not ordinarily considered to be research there is another type of behaviour analysis available, however, that should more than satisfy this need for richness and complexity. Starting in 1953 with *Science and Human Behavior*, Skinner has continued to produce an extensive literature interpreting human behaviour in terms of basic behavioural concepts. For example, Section III of that text, "The Individual as a Whole," is especially relevant to the kind of human behaviour that is increasingly of interest in applied work. "Self-control", "Thinking", "The Self", and especially "Private Events in a Natural Science" are chapters rich in speculative analysis by an unquestioned master of this approach in psychology. Rather than try to extend basic behavioural concepts to complex human behaviour in a vacuum, it is probably more fruitful to study Skinner's interpretations and to try to continue where he leaves off.

Also, the book *Verbal Behavior* (1957), 478 pages of interpretative analysis of human language, is a more than sufficient source for hypothesis derivation (in the area of aphasia, for example). And if that were not enough, the chapter on problem solving (with the first detailed consideration of rule-governed behaviour) in *Contingencies of Reinforcement* (1969), together with the chapter on teaching thinking in *The Technology of Teaching* (1968), are similarly rich sources for speculation about "higher mental processes". Skinner's more recent books and articles are also useful in this respect, although somewhat less technical than those already mentioned. In addition to Skinner's extensive interpretative works, there are similar extensions by other behavioural psychologists. The journal *Behaviorism* is an excellent source of such material, especially concerning the issue of private events. There is no shortage of complex interpretative behavioural material, but it is not normally to be found in a short workshop on behaviour modification, or in the ordinary introductory text.

Finally, there are undoubtedly some problems involving human behaviour for which the area of basic behavioural research and theory may be inappropriate. The science of behaviour as portrayed above is, after all, a science of the behaviour of individuals. The individual in interaction with the social and non-social environment also constitutes the subject matter of sociology, economics, and political science. But the principles of individual behaviour may not provide the easiest basis for understanding, predicting, and controlling the dependent variables in these other fields. To consider an analogy, there is no question that the organism is composed of biological cells whose interaction with each other and with the environment underlies the behaviour of the intact organism. It has proved easier, however, to develop behavioural principles by studying behaviour directly than to derive such principles from the existing knowledge of cell biology.

There seems to be no good reason for behavioural psychologists to question the value of the normal relationship between basic and applied science that is seen in other fields. An extreme split between basic and applied behaviour analysis would be costly to both, and the supposed inadequacy of the basic area for applied purposes is either imagined, or, in the case of fundamental research with humans, steadily being overcome.

REFERENCES

Birnbrauer, J. S. (1979) Applied behavior analysis, service and the acquisition of knowledge. *The Behavior Analyst*, **2**, 15–21.

Catania, A. C. (1984) *Learning* (2nd ed.). Englewood Cliffs, NJ: Prentice-Hall.

Dietz, S. M. (1978) Current status of applied behavior analysis: Science versus technology. *American Psychologist*, **33**, 805–814.

Epling, W. F. & Pierce, W. D. (1983) Applied behavior analysis: New directions from laboratory. *The Behavior Analyst*, **6**, 27–37.

Fantino, E. & Logan, C. A. (1979) *The experimental analysis of behavior*. San Francisco: W. H. Freeman.

Hake, D. F. (1982) The basic-applied continuum and the possible evolution of human operant social and verbal research. *The Behavior Analyst*, **5**, 21–28.

Hayes, S. C. (1978) Theory and technology in behavior analysis. *The Behavior Analyst*, **1**, 25–33.

Honig, W. K. & Staddon, J. E. R. (Eds.). (1977) *Handbook of operant behavior*. Englewood Cliffs, NJ: Prentice-Hall.

Kalish, H. I. (1981) *From behavioral science to behavior modification*. New York: McGraw-Hill.

Lowe, C. F. (1979) Determinants of human operant behaviour. In M. D. Zeiler & P. Harzem (Eds.), *Reinforcement and the organization of behaviour*. New York: John Wiley & Sons. 159–192.

Michael, J. L. (1980) Flight from behavior analysis. *The Behavior Analyst*, **3**, 1–21.

Pierce, W. D. & Epling, W. F. (1980) What happened to analysis in applied behavior analysis? *The Behavior Analyst*, **3**, 1–9.

Salzinger, K. (1978) Language behavior. In A. C. Catania & T. A. Brigham (Eds.) *Handbook of applied behavior analysis*. New York: Irvington. 275–321.

Skinner, B. F. (1953) *Science and human behavior*. New York: MacMillan.

Skinner, B. F. (1957) *Verbal behavior*. New York: Appleton-Century-Crofts.

Skinner, B. F. (1968) *The technology of teaching*. New York: Appleton-Century-Crofts.

Skinner, B. F. (1969) *Contingencies of reinforcement*. New York: Appleton-Century-Crofts.

Skinner, B. F. (1974) *About behaviorism*. New York: Alfred A. Knopf.

11 Autistic Behaviour: Fundamental Research and Applied Analysis

Arne Brekstad
University of Oslo, Institute of Psychology, Oslo, Norway

Fundamental research is of course the cornerstone upon which all applied behaviour analysis should rest. Reports of fundamental research may, however, give the impression that some of the problems discussed there, although interesting, are created in the laboratory and maintained by reinforcers dispensed by the laboratory community, and have sometimes dubious relevance to the problems met in applied situations. This is not to underestimate the importance of fundamental research, but rather to raise the question as to which problems fundamental research should primarily address itself. The persistent problems encountered in the application of behaviour analysis to psychotic children during the last 15 years or so might serve as a useful starting point for a dialogue between those engaged in the practical application of behaviour analysis and those engaged in fundamental research.

It is fascinating to work with psychotic and autistic children. Besides having a feeling of helping a fellow human being, one can also experience the professional gratification of staying fairly close to the basic scientific principles of behaviour analysis in a practical context. Nothing comes unearned with autistic children. They learn very little on their own. Target behaviours and programmes must be specified carefully at every step when building new behaviour—and much patience is required. But it is revealing to watch the child's behaviour develop in slow motion.

In applied situations the main objective is to devise programmes which in the shortest time possible will lead to maximum progress for the child. This situation offers few possibilities for research on the intricate basic problems encountered. But to solve some of the practical problems we must resort to laboratory conditions where relevant variables can be adequately controlled.

Working with autistic children involves two broad sets of problem. One is to build new behaviours, the other is to reduce the frequency of deviant behaviour.

In reducing deviant behaviour it is important to find techniques that work fast and which are acceptable to the parties involved, including the general public. This may rule out the use of time-out (Solnick, Rincover & Peterson, 1977), overcorrection (Marholin, Luiselli & Townsend, 1980), presentation of aversive stimuli (Lovaas & Simmons, 1969), etc. According to a Skinnerian view, extinction would probably be the method of choice for reducing rate of responding (Skinner, 1953). Extinction seems to be an acceptable technique to the public; requires little instruction for those who will apply the technique; and sometimes works very fast, presumably with behaviour that is maintained by a continuous reinforcement schedule. A good example may be operant crying in young autistic children, for their parents are often extremely sensitive to any sign of distress on the part of the child. Under these conditions extinction procedures may lead to a dramatic reduction of crying (Williams, 1959).

But with many psychotic children deviant behaviour is often very destructive, and maintained by highly intermittent schedules of reinforcement leading to prolonged extinction periods during which the child might hurt himself or others badly (Lovaas & Simmons, 1969).

Extinction procedures tend to produce variations in behaviour, and the most deviant forms may force an extinction programme to be terminated. The net result may be that the behaviour may be reinforced on an even more intermittent schedule than before, and in the process an even more deviant topography may be shaped. Such an unsuccessful application of extinction procedures may account for the characteristic development of self-destruction in some psychotic children where all the mild forms of self-destructive responses disappear and only the more dangerous forms remain. Consequently, ordinary extinction procedures can often not be used.

Is it possible to rearrange these conditions so that extinction procedures would lead to a more rapid reduction in rates of responding? One possibility might be to start, not by ignoring the behaviour, but by reinforcing it on a continuous reinforcement schedule for some time, and then to introduce an extinction procedure, hoping for the rapid fall in rate of responding associated with extinction of behaviour which has been continuously reinforced.

Some may question how wise it would be to provide a continuous reinforcement for deviant behaviour. But such a procedure would be quite feasible as continuous reinforcement tends to slow down the rate of intermittently reinforced responding.

In view of the considerable number of studies on intermittent reinforcement (over 8,000 studies during the last 15 years alone), it is amazing that so few of them have dealt explicitly with the problem raised here. A handful of studies have been located since the 1940s but, although they seem to be relevant, they deal primarily with this problem in slightly different contexts (Glavin & Moyer, 1975; Jenkins, 1962; Sutherland, Mackintosh & Wolfe, 1965).

Many factors are involved here, like the kind of schedule used and how intermittently the deviant behaviour is reinforced, and for how long. In applied settings, extinction may be successfully carried out without necessarily identifying the specific reinforcers maintaining behaviour. But introducing a period with continuous reinforcement naturally necessitates the identification of the reinforcing events. This may sometimes be very difficult, especially with psychotic and autistic children. Does the specific reinforcer maintaining the behaviour have to be identified? For how long will a continuous reinforcement schedule have to be sustained for any profit to be obtained from this procedure? Such problems can hardly be studied in field conditions, but they should lend themselves to investigation in the laboratory, preferably using concurrent schedules.

The reduction of the frequency of deviant behaviour may sometimes be very important. But the real challenge with psychotic and autistic children is to be found in the building of new patterns of behaviour. Psychotic children may be sensitive to different reinforcing stimuli than are normal children, and hence develop deviant behaviour even though the prevailing contingencies of reinforcement may be quite "normal." Events leading to an increase in behaviour in normal children may lead to a decrease in behaviour in psychotic children, and vice versa. This problem can partly be overcome by relying on the establishment of conditioned reinforcers (Ferster, 1961). The events serving as conditioned reinforcers can be controlled through the learning history of the child. In this way the same stimuli can be established as reinforcers for psychotic and normal children, and the children will react in the same way to the same contingencies of reinforcement. In its most simple form, this can be done with tokens.

Even though programmes using tokens as conditioned reinforcers usually work well, a number of programmes have reported a small but persistent percentage of participants who fail to respond favourably (Kazdin, 1982). Several factors may contribute to such failure, as, for example, the schedule and the kind of back-up reinforcers used. But one point has not been seriously considered in the literature on token reinforcement, and may be important. For token programmes to be effective, the tokens must first be established as conditioned reinforcers. Many hypotheses have been proposed to explain the establishment of conditioned reinforcers (Fantino & Logan, 1979). The most well known is probably the discriminative stimulus hypothesis proposed by Keller and Schoenfeld (1950) which suggests that a stimulus can be established as a conditioned reinforcer only by first being made a discriminative stimulus. Traditionally discriminative stimuli are established by differentially reinforcing responses with respect to the dimensions of stimuli in the presence of which responses occur.

In the context of this discriminative stimulus hypothesis, how can tokens be established as discriminative stimuli and consequently as conditioned reinforcers? Usually tokens are dispensed as if they were already conditioned reinforcers, and the child is free to exchange them for back-up reinforcers. This leaves the whole procedure of establishing them and maintaining them as discriminative stimuli unspecified. This might account for the occasional failure of token reinforcement programmes.

Perhaps the most difficult and challenging problem in applied settings is the establishment of adequate stimulus control over behaviour. Part of the standard treatment programmes for autistic children is to teach them to follow requests or commands like "put on your coat," "open the door," "sit on the chair," "fetch a glass of milk." If a child cannot respond correctly, it is important that it is helped to react adequately so that correct responses can be reinforced. If the child fails continuously, no reinforcers can be presented, and various kinds of deviant behaviours like aggression, self-destruction, and self-stimulation may intervene. The principle of errorless learning (Terrace, 1963) can be used here to help the child to respond correctly.

A crucial point appears to be what kind of help should be given. Very often we help the child by pointing at objects. Such pointing seems to be a particularly strong prompt, but regrettably this prompt can block shifts in stimulus control to a training stimulus or goal object. For example, a child can be trained to follow requests by presenting two objects, say a cup and a spoon, and asking for one of the objects. If the cup is requested, the correct response may come under the discriminative control not only of the auditory stimuli, but also of the visual stimulus, the cup itself.

The usual procedure is to prompt the correct response initially by pointing to the cup and reinforcing the correct choice. When this manual pointing prompt is gradually withdrawn, it turns out that the child is often looking more and more in the direction of one's finger and hand, and less in the direction of the object, and the child's behaviour is gradually brought under the control of subtle visual cues. The smallest movement of the finger in the direction of an object will lead to the choice of that object. If pointing is eliminated completely by literally sitting on one's hand, a child will often discover that one tends to look in the direction in which one points, and consequently the child may now look very attentively at one's eyes. The slightest glance in the direction of an object will often lead to the choice of that object.

If the trainer is not aware of this tendency to look at the object being requested, it might appear that the child is adequately following spoken requests. But this can be tested by looking at one object and asking for another. Even after several thousand trials with prompts in a task like this, a child may often be unable to respond correctly if the trainer sits on his or her hands; closes his or her eyes; and asks for an object. The establishment of adequate stimulus control may therefore be particularly challenging with regard to autistic children. They have been described as being over-selective, in the sense that when they are given a complex stimulus situation, only a limited aspect of that situation will come to control the child's behaviour (Schreibman, Koegel & Craig, 1977). Many studies have commented upon the problems of transferring stimulus control from the prompt to the training stimulus (Lovaas & Newsom, 1976; Risley & Wolf, 1967). Some studies have shown that autistic children may be taught correct responses more easily without help than with certain kinds of help (Koegel & Rincover, 1976).

Some encouraging leads stem from recent studies on conditional discrimination involving both stimulus fading and stimulus shaping (Schilmoeller, Schilmoeller, Etzel & LeBlanc, 1979), and the use of a within- as opposed to extra-stimulus prompt (Schreibman, 1975). But much more still needs to be known if any firm applied technology for establishing adequate stimulus control is to emerge. Can fundamental research help us specify the conditions under which blocking and overshadowing of discriminative stimuli will be eliminated? How can certain kinds of stimuli be made more salient than others? Which procedures and which stimuli used as prompts would facilitate shifts in stimulus control from the prompt to the training stimulus?

Finally the compulsive acts which sometimes occur with autistic children may be briefly considered. These may take the form of a child insisting on closing the door three to four times; negotiating stairs by going up two and down one; touching somebody's nose three times; picking up every grain of sand on the tarmac until his or her fingers bleed; etc. etc. These are patterns of behaviour which these children just seem to have to do. If they are stopped, they show signs of suffering. Even by carefully analysing the conditions under which such behaviour occurs, it seems impossible to discover what may serve as a reinforcing event for it. Several reports have commented upon this behaviour as being a puzzle (Birnbrauer, 1976), and it may sometimes be so prominent that it virtually bars any educational programme for the child.

Those engaged in fundamental research might well try to investigate what kind of learning history could lead to the establishment of such compulsive behaviour, and thus how it might be changed.

Not all the problems raised here may have been presented in such an explicit and precise form that they make sense to those engaged in fundamental research. But I hope that I have indicated certain problem areas where further progress in the application of behaviour analysis awaits the assistance of fundamental research.

REFERENCES

Birnbrauer, J. S. (1976) Mental retardation. In H. Leitenberg (Ed.), *Handbook of Behavior Modification and Behavior Therapy*. Englewood Cliffs, NJ: Prentice-Hall.

Fantino, E. & Logan, C. A. (1979) *The Experimental Analysis of Behavior. A Biological Perspective*. San Francisco: W. H. Freeman & Co.

Ferster, C. B. (1961) Positive reinforcement and behavioral deficits of autistic children. *Child Development*, **32**, 437–456.

Glavin, J. P. & Moyer, L. S. (1975) Facilitating extinction of infant crying by changing reinforcement schedules. *Journal of Behaviour Therapy and Experimental Psychiatry*, **6**, 357–358.

Jenkins, H. M. (1962) Resistance to extinction when partial reinforcement is followed by regular reinforcement. *Journal of Experimental Psychology*, **64**, 441–450.

Kazdin, A. (1982) The token economy: A decade later. *Journal of Applied Behavior Analysis*, **15**, 431–445.

Keller, F. S. & Schoenfeld, W. N. (1950) *Principles of Psychology*. New York: Appleton-Century-Crofts.

Koegel, R. L. & Rincover, A. (1976) Some detrimental effects of using extra-stimuli to guide learning in normal and autistic children. *Journal of Abnormal Child Psychology*, **4**, 59–71.

Lovaas, O. I. & Newsom, C. D. (1976) Behavior modification with psychotic children. In H. Leitenberg (Ed.), *Handbook of Behavior Modification and Behavior Therapy*. Englewood Cliffs, NJ: Prentice-Hall.

Lovaas, O. I. & Simmons, J. Q. (1969) Manipulation of self-destruction in three retarded children. *Journal of Applied Behavior Analysis*, **2**, 143–157.

Marholin, D., Luiselli, J. K., & Townsend, N. M. (1980) Overcorrection: An examination of its rationale and treatment effectiveness. In M. Hersen, R. M. Eisler, and P. M. Miller (Eds.), *Progress in Behavior Modification* (Volume 9). New York: Academic Press.

Risley, T. & Wolf, M. (1967) Establishing functional speech in echolalic children. *Behavior Research Therapy*, **5**, 73–88.

Schilmoeller, G. L., Schilmoeller, K. J., Etzel, B. C., & LeBlanc, J. M. (1979) Conditional discrimination responding after errorless and trial-and-error training. *Journal of the Experimental Analysis of Behavior*, **31**, 405–420.

Schreibman, L. (1975) Effects of within-stimulus and extra-stimulus prompting on discrimination learning in autistic children. *Journal of Applied Behavior Analysis*, **8**, 91–112.

Schreibman, L., Koegel, R. L., & Craig, M. S. (1977) Reducing stimulus overselectivity in autistic children. *Journal of Abnormal Child Psychology*, **5**, 425–436.

Skinner, B. F. (1953) *Science and Human Behavior*. New York: Macmillan.

Solnick, J. V., Rincover, A., & Peterson, C. R. (1977) Some determinants of the reinforcing and punishing effects of timeout. *Journal of Applied Behavior Analysis*, **10**, 415–424.

Sutherland, N. S., Mackintosh, N. J., & Wolfe, J. B. (1965) Extinction as a function of the order of partial and consistent reinforcement. *Journal of Experimental Psychology*, **69**, 56–59.

Terrace, H. S. (1963) Discrimination learning with and without "errors". *Journal of the Experimental Analysis of Behavior*, **6**, 1–27.

Williams, C. (1959) The elimination of tantrum behavior by extinction procedures. *Journal of Abnormal and Social Psychology*, **59**, 269.

12 Behaviour Modification and Neuropsychology

Xavier Seron
Unité de Neuropsychologie Expérimentale de l'Adulte (NEXA)
Cliniques Universitaires St. Luc, Brussels

Behaviour modification exercises only a modest influence on neuropsychological rehabilitation. As in other contexts, there has been irrational opposition to the behaviourist penetration into neuropsychology, though this opposition has never been very strong. One must look elsewhere for the reason for the meagre role of behaviour modification in neuropsychology. It is probable that two factors are responsible: (1) the naiveté of the first therapeutic projects inspired by behaviour modification; (2) the complexity of the disorders of the higher human functions after brain lesions. Before evaluating the limits encountered by behaviour modification when confronted with neuropsychology, it is necessary to present briefly some characteristics of neuropsychological disorders and analyse the incidence of various environmental variables on their evolution.

Neuropsychological disorders after a cerebral lesion vary in gravity, number, and quality; primarily as a function of biological parameters such as the age of the subject, the site, extension and nature of the lesion, manual laterality, and health status. A priori, therefore, neuropsychological disorders do not seem to be good candidates for a behavioural approach since the post-lesional pathology cannot be attributed chiefly to environmental influences. The cause lies inside the organism, more specifically inside the "black-box." Furthermore, neuropsychological disorders are clearly dependent on the localisation of the brain lesion (Hecaen & Albert, 1978): Nervous centres, although having some plasticity, are not, in a mature organism, interchangeable or, as has been suggested by Lashley (1928), equipotential. Thus, for a long time, the climate was not favourable to behavioural therapeutic enterprises in neuropsychology.

Nevertheless, alongside these negative elements, a robust clinical reality has always been obvious; after a cerebral lesion, the deficits are not stable. When lesions do not evolve or recur, the rule is spontaneous recuperation varying in time and quality. Several general theoretical models have been proposed to explain this recuperation (Jackson, 1932; Lashley, 1928; von Monakov, 1914; Munck, 1881). It is only recently, however, that researchers have identified some specific neurophysiological and neuroanatomical modifications that take place after the lesion. Various studies have shown that some axons can regenerate after the cerebral lesion, or more frequently that some adjacent neurons emit collateral axons, which reinnervate the lesioned side. These facts plus the hypersensibility of denervation and activation of silent synapses may play a role in the recovery processes, but these structural and functional reorganisations remain difficult to relate precisely to behavioural changes (Jeannerod & Hecaen, 1979). These facts have led researchers in neuropsychology to suggest that the mature brain is not devoid of regenerative and reorganisation capabilities.

Although the existence of such neural modifications points to a neuroanatomical and neurophysiological functional plasticity, it cannot be considered as a direct argument in favour of the utility of behavioural therapies.

The influence of environmental variables on brain lesion effects has been demonstrated in animal experiments before and after the onset of the cerebral lesion (Finger, 1978). Long exposure to an enriched environment before the onset of a cerebral lesion has a positive effect on the resistance of the organism as demonstrated by the maintenance or rapid recovery of the prelesional level of performance in different learning tasks. This was also observed when the enriched environment was presented after the lesion was induced. But the precise nature of the environmental influence is far from clear and much more empirical data must be assembled with regard to: the precise definition and duration of the various enriched environments; the adequacy of the behavioural measures used for the evaluation of the recuperation; and the nature and extension of the cerebral lesion. Moreover, the positive effects of environmental exposures were not very specific and applied only to learning tasks with supra-modal cues and not to specific and unimodal learning tasks. Thus, environmental effects principally could improve the adaptability and the control of emotional reactions in animals. But whatever the interpretation of these experimental investigations, these data have modified the general attitude of researchers in human neuropsychology. The idea that a therapeutic intervention may be efficacious does seem not unreasonable.

In this modified and more favourable climate we can evaluate the impact and results of behaviour modification in neuropsychological rehabilitation.

The contribution of the operant school to the analysis and treatment of neuropsychological disorders is manifold. Schematically, one can distinguish four main topics of research and application:

1. Fundamental research on verbal and non-verbal learning.
2. Development of remedial procedures based on programmed learning techniques.
3. Functional re-education in a social context.
4. Transference to the clinical setting of the visual-artificial language of Premack.

I briefly examine each of these topics and evaluate the contributions as well as the limits of the behaviour modification. I then present what seems to be the present evolution of the treatment of aphasic and neuropsychological disorders and discuss the implications of the development of cognitivist therapeutic approaches to behaviour modification.

1. Fundamental Research on Verbal and Non-Verbal Learning

In this kind of research, the explicit goal has been to assess the so-called general learning capabilities of aphasic patients. Most of the time, the tasks were of a non-verbal, visual nature (Brookshire, 1968, 1969, 1971; Filby & Edwards, 1963; Rosenberg, 1965; Rosenberg & Edwards, 1964, 1965) and the most commonly used paradigm was that of discriminative learning. Different variables were systematically manipulated in order to study their effect in the course of learning. These variables were, for example, the nature and complexity of the discriminative stimuli; the type of reinforcement; the delay between response and reinforcement; and modifications of reinforcement contingencies (reversal or, in probability learning tasks, change in the reinforcement ratio). The global results of these studies have not been very instructive. Positively, they demonstrated that aphasic patients are able to handle some discriminatory tasks, that during learning their behaviour is not random, and that they develop some idiosyncratic strategies (Brookshire, 1968). But these general conclusions have not often been clearly linked to the severity or the nature of the language disorders. Perhaps the most serious shortcoming of these studies is that they offer no sufficiently precise analysis of the verbal and cognitive mechanisms set in motion when normal subjects are confronted with such learning tasks. Actually, many of the so-called non-verbal learning tasks leave open the possibility of a verbal coding of the stimuli to be discriminated. And it is possible that such covert verbal coding may facilitate or, when there are semantic disorders, interfere with the aphasic subject's performance. Without more precise analysis, it seems difficult to interpret the residual performance of the aphasic subjects. Finally, as far as re-education is concerned, it is not at all clear what can be inferred for language re-education from performance on these tasks. Consequently, these learning studies have not had much influence on therapeutic approaches.

2. Behaviour Modification and Programmed-Instruction Approaches.

The first attempts at re-education by behavioural modifiers in aphasiology used programmed teaching techniques (Holland, 1970; Sarno, Silverman & Sands, 1970) with teaching machines and exercise books. The general principles of programmed teaching were observed: progression in small steps, immediate correction of errors, and self-administration. Sarno, Silverman and Sands conducted a programme with 30 global aphasic patients covering gestural imitation, visual recognition, and writing and oral expression, and compared the results obtained from this experimental group with those of two other groups of patients, one without re-education, the other with classic clinical re-education. The differences between the three groups were trifling. It was thus a defeat for programmed teaching, but Sarno, Silverman and Sands and Holland (1970) did succeed in introducing into neuropsychology some of the most important techniques of behaviour modification such as baseline measures; the precise definition of the terminal behaviour; and the quantitative comparison of different methods of re-education. In addition to the group therapy, Holland designed instruction programmes for single-case therapy (Holland, 1970; Holland and Harris, 1968). The principal elements of progress were: detailed analysis of the residual behavioural repertoire; adaptation of the exercise content to the patients' interests; and orientation of the therapy to daily-life difficulties. The trend is thus towards greater individualisation of therapy.

Yet the first generation of research can be criticized at a number of points. First, one may wonder about the practical relevance of machine-patient (or textbook-patient) relationships. Such particular and restrictive contexts seem remote from natural daily-life contexts of communication. Moreover, in these programmes, reinforcement is given according to the correctness of the verbal responses. This kind of reinforcement is only a sub-type of the wide range of reinforcements delivered when we produce or receive linguistic messages. Another difficulty inherent in any such programmed therapy is the definition of the progression of exercises. This fundamental question is too often neglected by the behaviourist. How can we define what is simple and what is complex for a patient? Where should the therapy begin, and what sequence should be used to progress from the first step to the pre-established objectives? I return to these questions discussing contemporary rehabilitation approaches in neuropsychology.

3. Behavioural Modification and Functional Re-Education of Verbal Behaviour

In addition to programmed therapies for individual cases, some therapies have been used in group situations. Here the objectives have been more functional in character, being generally the improvement of the communication abilities of the patients. Alongside the behavioural approaches, other therapies were also developed with psychotherapeutic or sociotherapeutic goals: to help patients face natural conversion situations; to eliminate avoidance behaviour; and to improve self-esteem and social adjustment (Aronson, Shatin & Cook, 1956; Godfrey & Douglass, 1959).

Both Holland (1970) and Bloom (1962) have adapted operant procedures to group therapy. The goal was clearly to enhance verbal behaviour. The theoretical basis of group work as emphasised by Bloom lies in the functional analysis of verbal behaviour as proposed by Skinner (1957). Verbal behaviour is thus considered to be a link between dependent and independent variables in an environment that includes a speaker and an audience. In this view, an individual's language affects his environment, which in turn reinforces his verbal behaviour. Bloom stresses that such functional relations are at work in aphasic language and that the same utterance (from a formal point of view) may or may not be emitted according to the eliciting situations (the well-known neuropsychological dissociation between automatic and voluntary behaviour). The aim of group therapy is thus to recreate and to structure daily-life situations which elicit routine forms of speech. Examples of situations which efficiently control speech are: greeting behaviours; yes/no questions; and the use of "up" and "down" in an elevator. For patients with higher levels of communicative language, more complex situations are structured with appropriate verbal patterns related to their interests and needs. For reinforcements, those usually found in natural conversation are employed. The therapist employs repetition of these situations in order to maintain and increase response strength. In the same line is the work devoted to the amelioration of the spouse-patient verbal communication by Diller's team in New York (Diller, Ben-Yishay, Gerstman, Goodkin, Gordon & Weinberg, 1974). In this original programme the re-educator positively reinforces or informs the spouse about the inadequacy of his or her verbal comments during free, natural conversation with the patient. The spouse has headphones and the re-educator communicates instructions from another room through a microphone, without disturbing the conversation. Surprisingly, this method has not been applied by others in the behaviour modification school and therapeutic researches on functional communication are presently conducted in another, more powerful theoretical framework: the pragmatic approach (Davis & Wilcox, 1981; Schlanger & Schlanger, 1970).

4. Clinical Application of the Premack Visual-Artificial Language.

Another original contribution to aphasiology by the behaviour modification school is the technique developed with chimpanzees by Premack (Glass, Gazzaniga & Premack, 1973). Instead of reinstalling language on an auditory-phonatory basis, the Premack procedure consists of implementing, by means of an errorless learning programme, an artificial language made of arbitrary forms cut out of coloured cardboard. The first group of patients in this programme were all severe aphasics, and all of them made some progress in using the new code although with very different levels of proficiency. This procedure has also been extended to dyslexic children and to Broca's aphasics for the acquisition of locative prepositions (Smith, 1974). But since the work of Glass, Gazzaniga & Premack (1973), no general evaluation of Premack's language has been made. Consequently, some important questions remain unanswered. For example, it is far from clear if learning an artificial language is not a more complicated task than extending a residual verbal repertoire. The social utility of the Premack language is also questionable since anyone who wishes to communicate with the patient is obliged to learn it. New methods have been created to meet this objection: the Visual Communication System "VIC" of Gardner, Zurif, Berry and Bakker (1976), the Bliss method (Lane & Samples, 1981), the pantomime program of Helm-Estabrooks (Helm-Estabrooks, Fitzpatrick & Barressi, 1982) and so on. But these new therapies have not made use of behaviour modifiers.

What clearly emerges from this short summary of behaviour modification's contribution to neuropsychological therapy is that, after important and original contributions in different areas, the behaviour modification school lost its specificity and most of the new therapies which have appeared in neuropsychology are not explicitly linked to it. Among these new therapies, the cognitivist approaches deserve comment, in that they seem the most promising for the future, and their comparison with the classic behaviour modification approaches may be interesting in at least four respects: (1) in the pre-therapy analysis of disorders; (2) in the definition of the therapeutic strategy; (3) in the therapy administration; and (4) in the evaluation of the therapy effectiveness. I now briefly examine these four points in terms of the two schools.

5. Cognitivistic Behavoristic Approaches: A Comparison

In the pre-therapeutic analysis of the disorders, the behaviorist therapists have frequently limited themselves to descriptive evaluations. In some cases, they have used only the traditional semiological entities in neuropsychology, in others they added more precise quantitative criteria, and in rare cases they have gathered some functional measures in more natural situations. In doing so, either they quantified semiological units without sufficiently questioning their value, or they elaborated functional tests of a clearly pragmatic value but which were difficult to interpret since identical levels of success or failure could result from disorders of a very different nature. Furthermore, by limiting themselves to recovering the losses in the pre-therapeutic behavioural repertoires and by defining the goal of the programme for the most part as a filling-in approach, behavioural interventions have been reconstructive. But reconstruction is, as we see later, only one possible re-education strategy among several others.

Unlike the quantitative and phenomenological approach to the disorders, the cognitive neuropsychologist, in line with Luria's general approach to neuropsychology, tends to consider that, at least in some cases, overt disorders can be interpreted as the result of the disturbance of some specific mental sub-processes whose normal integration yields normal surface behaviour. A disorder is thus considered the result of a breakdown situated at a deeper and not directly observable level. As a consequence, two apparently identical disorders may in fact differ in that they result from different disturbances. Without entering into the details of this approach, which is sometimes called the information-processing approach, it may be noted that it has had some success in comprehending the nature of various neuropsychological disorders. This cognitivist approach has, for example, been recently successful in interpreting and identifying different reading behaviour disorders (Coltheart, Patterson & Marshall, 1980). Although the cognitivist approach is only in its infancy, its extension throughout neuropsychological semiology is maturing (Shallice, 1981; Marin, Saffran & Schwartz, 1976; Seron, 1982a).

Consider one example of such an approach to one of the most common language disorders: the anomia disorder or the incapacity to give a particular word in conversation or in picture- or object-confrontation tasks. Recent studies suggest that the inability to name pictures may result from the alteration of different mechanisms: a gnosis deficit or a gnosis weakening; a conceptual disorder; a disorganisation of the semantic lexicon; a deficient access to an otherwise intact lexicon; a modality-specific deficit as in selective anomia; a disturbance of the phonological representation of the word; a motor-output deficit; and of course any possible combination of these different deficits (see for anomia's models, Goodglass, 1980; Howes, 1979). All these specific disorders can impair the subject's performance in a confrontation naming task. To get an idea of the defective process responsible for the naming disorders, it is not, of course, sufficient to have a quantitative estimate as classically formed in pre-therapy evaluation batteries. What is necessary is to manipulate systematically the different dimensions of the stimuli and the responses. If, for example, one has evidence indicating a difficulty situated at the level of perceptive treatment of the stimuli, one can confirm it by manipulating physical dimensions of the stimuli (Bisiach, 1966). If there is reason to hypothesize a difficulty at the semantic level, one can explore this possibility by systematically modifying semantic aspects of the material, and so on. Of course, all these explorations are based on manipulation of the stimuli, the response and the stimulus-response relationships. At first sight, it seems that such manipulations are not beyond a behavioural perspective, but without any theoretical elaboration, without at least a rough model of the mental operations that may be involved in such a task, the modifications that can be made to test the variables are almost unlimited. Such a non-theoretical approach is not very economical. And when some behavioural approaches were used to test different variables influencing naming in neuropsychology, it was done without a theoretical framework, and thus one was not in a position to interpret the various naming disorders correctly.

Thus the first limitation of behaviour modification in neuropsychology is to have underestimated the structural complexity of the disorders and, by emphasizing quantitative assessment, to have neglected a more specific analysis of what precisely they measured. Unlike psychiatry, neuropsychology does not seek the cause of the disorder in the subject's past history, since the disorder is the result of an actual cerebral lesion. The rejection of an internal apparatus responsible for the overt disorder was one of the initial factors contributing to the success of behaviour modification approaches in psychopathology; in neuropsychology the contrary has occurred, as without elaboration of models depicting the mental operations responsible for the overt behaviour, one cannot interpret the disorders.

Second, with respect to strategies of re-education, the historical link between behavioural modification and the psychology of learning has caused re-education to be conceived of as a learning or teaching enterprise. Having identified the absence of a precise behaviour repertoire or the presence of inadequate behaviour, the general strategy has generally been to reconstruct adequate behaviour or to provoke the disappearance of deviant responses. Such an objective is, of course, perfectly legitimate, but interpretation of the nature of the disorder may have a profound influence on the re-education strategy. Basically, there are two schools of thought about re-education in neuropsychology. One proposes to re-establish behaviour in its original form, the other to reorganise the sub-processes responsible for the behaviour. In the first case, the interpretation of the disorder is that of a "loss of function," and the re-education strategy is to reconstruct the missing information. In the second case, the disorder is interpreted as a loss of access to preserved knowledge, and the re-education strategy is to reorganize the processes that permit access to this knowledge. For example, if one conceives of the disorder of anomia as a definitive loss of an identifiable part of the mental lexicon, the re-education strategy would be to reconstruct the missing vocabulary. But if one hypothesises that access to the mental lexicon is disturbed, the re-education strategy would be, first, to discover the processes of access to the lexicon that were best preserved or to elaborate new processes, and second, to enhance their role in naming. Because the behavioural modification school has stressed the observable repertoire, the first strategy was more frequently adopted. But the relationship between behavioural modification and re-establishment strategy is not a logical necessity but only a historical accident, and there are numerous examples in neuropsychology that indicate that some behavioural modification procedures can be used in reorganisation strategies.

Thus the critical difference is not between a learning strategy and a non-learning strategy. In all strategies there is something to learn; the critical difference is what is to be learned. A re-education strategy developed by Beauvois and Derouesné (1982) in a particular case of tacto-verbal anomia illustrates this. Their patient, who was unable to name objects after tactile inspection, was trained not to name a certain number of objects during each session, but to develop a compensatory strategy which, in this case, would consist, first, of inhibiting any attempt to verbalize after palpation, second, of elaborating during palpation a visual representation of the object, and third, of using this visual representation as a base for the naming activity. In the direct reconstruction strategy, learning is defined in terms of a number of objects to be named; in the second, learning is defined in terms of implementation between palpation and naming of a "covert visual behavior." In the cognitive lexicon, one would call this a "mental visual representation." But the fact that we are concerned with a reorganisation strategy does not signify that there is no learning, and thus all the procedures developed by the behaviour modification school may be helpful. For example, in the Beauvois and Derouesné re-education strategy, it may be interesting to choose, at the outset of the therapy, objects that are clearly visualisable, to repeat the exercises sufficiently so that the new strategy can be internalised, to reinforce each success positively, and so on.

Thus when we oppose a re-establishment strategy to a reorganising strategy, we question only the unnecessary association in neuropsychology between behavioural modification and the direct reconstruction approach. One difficult problem is to decide in which cases the reorganisation strategy is preferable and in which the re-establishment strategy would be better, but this is a problem for neuropsychology and not for behavioural modification.

Thirdly, we may consider the applications of cognitive and behavioural assumptions. Perhaps one of the most important virtues of the behaviour modification approach is its fine-graded organisation. In comparison with the intuitive and non-controlled progression of the more classic re-education schemes, behaviour modification procedures introduce a carefully controlled progression, and certain response criteria must be attained before moving on to each subsequent programme stage. But the construction of a programme requires having a good idea of what is simple and what is difficult at each step. Furthermore, the notion of complexity is crucial and in neuropsychology it arises from three major sources: the succession of acquisition during childhood (the developmental index of complexity); the structure of overt behaviours (the formal index of complexity); and the reappearance of behaviours during spontaneous post-lesional recuperation (the pathological index of complexity). But, as I have indicated elsewhere (Seron, 1979, 1982a, 1982b), none of these indices of complexity or difficulty seems satisfactory in that none can guarantee that the observed progressions have any psychological significance for the patient. The developmental index of complexity presupposes a parallelism between the acquired pathological condition and the progressive acquisition of a function during childhood, but there is no such parallelism, and there is thus no good reason to retrace the developmental stages in therapy. The indices of complexity based on the structure of overt behaviour are hardly more convincing, for what is difficult for a patient is not the structural complexity of the stimuli to be treated or the response to be produced, but rather the processes actually used when treating them. An index based on observation of spontaneous recovery is probably the most interesting candidate, but with two important reservations: First, we lack precise analyses of the processes of spontaneous recovery, and second, at least in some cases, the processes of spontaneous recovery are clearly different from those sustaining the re-education process.

The studies inspired by the behaviour modification methodology seem not to have analysed the problem of the index of complexity sufficiently. Indeed, several clinicians have questioned the rigid progression of exercises offered in behaviour modification programmes. It is regrettable that the programmes generally put forward in the clinical literature are presented in a completely ready-made fashion. Instead of critical discussions of different progressions from different points of view, programmes have been presented as if they were the only adequate ones. These re-educational schemes are far from the functional analysis of behaviour at the origin of behaviour modification, and here the cognitivist approaches may be useful in defining what progressions may be the more efficacious, since what is difficult is dependent upon what kind of processes one is trying to implement or enhance. The theoretical foundation for the progressions offered in classic neuropsychological therapy is generally just as inadequate as that of the behaviour modification school.

Fourthly, with respect to the evaluation of therapeutic effectiveness the behaviour modification influence in neuropsychology has been indisputably good. As was noted at the beginning of this chapter, the behaviour modification school has introduced rigorous control of the effectiveness of the therapy in neuropsychology and has kept attention focused on the transfer problems and on the long-term appraisal of therapy. No re-education research is published without pre- and post-therapeutic base-line measures. On this level, there is no reason to contrast behavioural modification and cognitivist approaches.

What can be concluded after this short comparison between the behaviour modification and the cognitive approaches in neuropsychological re-education? The problem is not choosing between them as if one were true and the other false, but rather determining their respective merits. The cognitive approach seems better able to generate hypotheses about the nature of the neuropsychological disorders, to propose adequate remedial procedures, and to determine the general re-education strategy. In this respect, behaviour modification has lost a great deal of its influence as the ideas underlying the various therapies derive from cognitive neuropsychological investigations.

But this does not imply that behaviour modification is passé in neuropsychology; its influence is essentially methodological. Behaviour modification gives us a useful tool for scientifically establishing that a change has occurred in therapy, and that this change was indeed due to the therapeutic intervention and not to extraneous variables. The present evolution of therapy in neuropsychology matches the evaluation I have given of the contribution of behaviour modification. If, in the last 10 years, several therapies have appeared without explicit reference to behaviour modification, the presence of methods and procedures from behaviour modification is obvious. This is true for the spectacular Melodic Intonation Therapy (Sparks & Holland, 1976; Sparks, 1981), for the gestural pantomime programmes of Helm-Estabrooks, Fitzpatrick & Barressi (1982), and for many other new methods (Seron, in press). Furthermore, in some pathological conditions such as traumatic injuries, the direct reconstruction approach is the most effective. In such cases, behaviour modification may be applied without limiting its influence to methodology.

REFERENCES

Aronson, M., Shatin, L., & Cook, J. C. (1956) Socio-psychotherapeutic approach to the treatment of aphasic patients. *Journal of Speech and Hearing Disorders*, **21**, 352–364.

Beauvois, M. F. & Derouesne, J. (1982) Recherche en neuropsychologie cognitive et rééducation: Quels rapports? In: X. Seron, & C. Laterre, (Eds.), *Rééduquer le cerveau*, Brussels: Mardaga.

Bisiach, E. (1966) Perceptual factors in the pathogenesis of anomia. *Cortex*, **2**, 90–95.

Bloom, L. M. (1962) A rationale for group-treatment of aphasic patients. *Journal of Speech and Hearing Disorders*, **27**, 11–16.

Brookshire, R. H. (1968) Visual discrimination and response reversal learning by aphasic subjects. *Journal of Speech and Hearing Research*, **11**, 677–692.

Brookshire, R. H. (1969) Probability learning by aphasic subjects. *Journal of Speech and Hearing Research*, **12**, 857–864.

Brookshire, R. H. (1971) Effect of delay of reinforcement on probability learning by aphasic subjects. *Journal of Speech and Hearing Research*, **14**, 92–105.

Coltheart, M., Patterson, K., & Marshall J. C., (Eds.) (1980) *Deep Dyslexia*, London: Routledge & Kegan.

Davis, G. A. & Wilcox, M. J. (1981) Incorporating parameters of natural conversation in aphasic treatment. In R. Chapey (Ed.), *Language Intervention Strategies in adult aphasia*. Baltimore: Williams & Wilkins.

Diller, L., Ben-Yishay, Y., Gerstman, L. J., Goodkin, R., Gordon, W., & Weinberg, J. (1974) Studies in cognition and rehabilitation in hemiplegia. *Rehabilitation Monograph*, No. 50. New York: University Medical Center.

Filby, Y. & Edwards, A. (1963) An application of automated teaching method to test and teach form discrimination in aphasics. *Journal of Programmed Instruction*, **2**, 25–33.

Finger, S. (1978) Environmental attentuation of brain-lesion symptoms. In S. Finger (Ed.), *Recovery from brain damage: Research and theory*, New York: Plenum Press.

Gardner, H., Zurif, E. B., Berry, Th., & Bakker, E. (1976) Visual communication in aphasia. *Neuropsychologia*, **14**, 275–292.

Glass, A. V., Gazzaniga, M. S., & Premack, R. (1973) Artificial language training in global aphasics. *Neuropsychologia*, **11**, 95–103.

Godfrey, C. & Douglass, E. (1959) The recovery process in aphasia. *Canadian Medical Association Journal*, **80**, 618–624.

Goodglass, H. (1980) Disorders of naming following brain injury. *American Scientist*, **68**, 647–655.

Hecaen, H. & Albert, M. L. (1978) *Human Neuropsychology*, New York: John Wiley & Sons.

Helm-Estabrooks, N., Fitzpatrick, P. M., & Barressi, B. (1982) Visual action therapy for global aphasia. *Journal of Speech and Hearing Disorders*, **47**, 385–389.

Holland, A. L. (1970) Case studies in aphasia rehabilitation using programmed instruction. *Journal of Speech and Hearing Disorders*, **35**, 377–389.

Holland, A. & Harris, A. (1968) Aphasia rehabilitation using programmed instruction: An intensive case history. In H. N. Sloane & B. D. Macaulay (Eds.), *Operant Procedures in Remedial Speech and Language Training*, New York: Houghton Mifflin Company.

Howes, D. (1979) The naming act and its disruption in aphasia. In D. Aaronson & R. W. Rieber (Eds.). (1979) *Psycholinguistic Research: Implications and Applications*, Hillsdale: Lawrence Erlbaum.

Jackson, H. (1932) In J. Taylor (Ed.), *Selected Writings of H. Jackson*. London: Hodder and Stoughton.

Jeannerod, M. & Hecaen, H. (1979) *Adaptation et restauration des fonctions nerveuses*, Paris: Simep.

Lane, V. & Samples, J. M. (1981) Facilitating communication skills in adult apraxics: Application of blissymbols in a group setting. *Journal of Communication Disorders*, **14**, 157–167.

Lashley, K. S. (1928) *Brain mechanisms and intelligence*, Chicago: The University of Chicago Press.

Marin, O. S. M., Saffran, E. M., & Schwartz, M. F. (1977) Dissociation of language in aphasia: Implications for normal function. *Annals of New York Academy of Sciences*, **280**, 868–884.

Monakov, von, C. (1914) *Die Lokalisation im Grosshirn und der Abbau der Funktion durch corticale Herde*, Wiesbaden: Berman.

Munck, H. (1881) *Ueber die functionen der Grosshirnrinde*, Gesammelte Mitleitungen aus den Jahren 1877–1880. Berlin: August Hiershwald.

Rosenberg, B. (1965) The performance of aphasics on automated visuo-perceptual discrimination, training, and transfer tasks. *Journal of Speech and Hearing Research*, **8**, 165–181.

Rosenberg, B. & Edwards, A. (1964) The performance of aphasics on three automated perceptual discrimination programs. *Journal of Speech and Hearing Research*, **7**, 295–298.

Rosenberg, B. & Edwards, A. (1965) An automated multiple response alternative training program for use with aphasics. *Journal of Speech and Hearing Research*, **8**, 415–419.

Sarno, M., Silverman, M., & Sands, E. (1970) Speech therapy and language recovery in severe aphasia. *Journal of Speech and Hearing Research*, **13**, 607–623.

Schlanger, P. H. & Schlanger, B. B. (1970) Adapting role playing activities with aphasic patients. *Journal of Speech and Hearing Disorders*, **35**, 229–235.

Seron, X. (1979) *Aphasie et neuropsychologie, approches thérapeutiques*, Bruxelles: Mardaga.

Seron, X. (1982a) Toward a cognitive neuropsychology. *International Journal of Psychology*, **17**, 149–156.

Seron, X. (1982b) The reeducation of aphasics: the problem of the reeducation strategies. *International Journal of Psychology*, **17**, 299–317.

Seron, X. (in press) Operant procedures and neuropsychological rehabilitation. In M. Meier, L. Diller & A. Benton (Eds.), *Neuropsychological rehabilitation*. New York: Churchill Livingstone.

Shallice, T. (1981) Neurological impairment of cognitive processes. *British Medical Bulletin*, **37**, 187–192.

Skinner, B. F. (1957) *Verbal Behavior*, New York: Appleton-Century-Crofts.

Smith, M. (1974) Operant conditioning of syntax in aphasia. *Neuropsychologia*, **12**, 403–405.

Sparks, R. W. (1981) Melodic intonation therapy. In R. Chapey (Ed.), *Language interventions strategies in adult aphasia*. Baltimore: Williams and Wilkins.

Sparks, R. W. & Holland, L. (1976) Method: melodic intonation therapy for aphasia. *Journal of Speech and Hearing Disorders*, **41**, 287–297.

V RECENT DEVELOPMENTS IN THE BEHAVIOURAL ANALYSIS OF DRUG EFFECTS

13 Treatment-behaviour Interactions in Activity/ Habituation and Avoidance: State Changes and Pre-exposure to CS, US, and Drug

Giorgio Bignami, Valerio Giardini and Enrico Alleva
Laboratorio di Fisiopatologia di Organo e di Sistema, Istituto Superiore di Sanità, Roma

More than 20 years ago, the late Robert McCleary (1961) warned experimental and physiological psychologists against using behavioural responses merely as convenient dependent variables. Fortunately, however, it has now become almost a truism that one should never extrapolate from an increased or decreased frequency of any given response after any given treatment to increased or decreased emotionality, or learning ability, or memory capacity, and so forth. Nevertheless, the more general question about which is the most appropriate approach in the behavioural analysis of treatment effects remains unsolved. Therefore, the various approaches should be carefully weighed on the heuristic balance rather than enthusiastically promoted or brutally rejected by *a priori* theoretical *fiats*.

Considering the more restricted domain of drug-behaviour interactions, it can now be affirmed that several different strategies have been successfully exploited over the past decades. One approach has been aimed mainly at providing a more accurate definition of drug effects in operational terms. For example, generic labels such as "stimulant" and "depressant" have been qualified by detailed analyses of the different effects of any given drug on various components of the organism's activity (Robbins, 1977). Another example can be found in the extensive literature on rate-dependent changes of schedule-controlled responding, showing the major role of the reinforcement contingencies and the resulting response baselines in determining the direction and the size of treatment effects (Kelleher & Morse, 1968).

A second approach has dealt mainly with possible mechanisms of action defined from a behavioural viewpoint, that is, in terms of assumed mediating processes. For example, there has been considerable heuristic value in the working models originally aimed at separating a motor deficit ("psychomotor retardation" or "impairment of motor act initiation") from more general associative or motivational changes in the neuroleptic syndrome (see discussion and examples in Bignami, 1978). Similarly, an impressive amount of data has been generated by more than two decades of conflict between associative, sensory, and motor ("disinhibitory") models of central muscarinic stimulation and blockade (Bignami, 1976; Giardini, Amorico, De Acetis, & Bignami, 1983).

Finally, still another approach—at present by far the most fashionable one—attempts to bridge the gap between behavioural and physiological-biochemical analyses of treatment effects. For example, considerable efforts have been made to correlate critical changes occurring at different levels during acute and extended exposure to various monoaminergic agents (Peters, Anisman, & Pappas, 1978). Furthermore, in parallel with some of the research already mentioned, the role of central cholinergic systems has been worked out in considerable detail by complex strategies including biochemical and physiological analyses of specialised neuronal networks, studies of the effects of localised intra-cerebral treatments, evaluation of drug-lesion interactions, and several other related methods (Bignami & Michałek, 1978; Jenden, 1977; Waser, 1975).

With more space it would be easy to show in considerable detail both the merits and the limitations of these different approaches. The first one, for example, can explore a fairly wide range of phenomena with relatively few constraints; therefore, it often takes the lead in illustrating new and important behavioural interactions which are subsequently exploited by other approaches. Inevitably, however, it creates a very large quantity of data to be explained since it must consider in its own right any response change occurring in any given subject in any given set of past and present contingencies. Therefore, it must leave to others those arbitrary selections which are needed, for example, in the analysis of brain-behaviour relations.

At the opposite end, the brain-behaviour approach must compromise between the complexities of the physiological-biochemical domain and those of the behavioural domain; consequently, some oversimplification of the latter becomes inevitable. Here the dividing line between a sound methodological reductionism and reductionism *tout court* is far from being well established. This explains why an important methodological chapter written several years ago by an eminent investigator and entitled "Some Traps and Pontifications" still appears to be quite topical (Weiskrantz, 1968), and why expressions such as "explanation of behaviour" can have so many different meanings (Rose, Lewontin, & Kamin, 1984).

As any person who has read the leading journals and attended meetings for two or three decades can witness, the approach which supports the heuristic value of working models for assumed mediating processes has been increasingly squeezed into an uncomfortable position between the phenomenological and the physiological schools. But two heuristically important points can be made in defence of the mediating processes approach. First, although this approach can work (and has actually worked) as a straightjacket, it has generated in these and other areas a wealth of critical data which would have had little chance of being produced by other approaches. Second, many of these data obtained by testing various sensory, motor, motivational, or associative models of treatment effects, are very far from being amenable to any kind of physiological analysis; therefore, either they are given an appropriate status in their own right (which rarely happens), or they are suppressed, resulting in a drastic and arbitrary curtailment of the overall reality.

It seems more useful, however, to illustrate an earlier stage of the mediating processes approach. Here the experimenter is confronted with complex interactions of uncertain significance, and attempts to use the touchstone of provisional model testing without knowing whether he or she is marching towards another substantial success, or plunging headlong into a quagmire. The work described in this article, although it has been in progress for some time, still belongs to this initial phase, and therefore is presented with all the reservations which are in order under such circumstances.

CHLORPROMAZINE, CHLORDIAZEPOXIDE AND ACTIVITY: PERFORMANCE VERSUS OTHER CHANGES

In spite of extensive work with neuroleptics and anxiolytics, some important treatment-behaviour interactions affecting the changes induced by these drugs are still poorly understood. For example, amount of prior experience seems to have little influence on neuroleptic-induced depression of locomotor and exploratory activity, except of course for quantitative differences related to differences in baselines between tests (Itoh & Takaori, 1968; Kumar, 1971). In contrast, several studies have shown that both the enhancing and the depressant effects of benzodiazepines on activity can be attenuated by prior experience in the untreated state, in a fashion which denies a major role of so-called floor or ceiling effects (Hughes & Greig, 1975; Itoh & Takaori, 1968; Marriott & Spencer, 1965; Nolan & Parkes, 1973).

Concerning carry-over effects (i.e., residual effects of treatments on subsequent activity and habituation in the no-drug state), the interactions so far reported appear to be even more complex. In the case of neuroleptics, for example, the use of a wheel activity test, previously habituated rats, and chronic treatments, revealed considerable residual effects of chlorpromazine (CPZ) and perphenazine after drug washout (Irwin & Armstrong, 1961). In constrast, the use of a Y-shaped apparatus, naive rats, and single depressant doses of either CPZ (up to 2 mg/kg) or thioridazine (up to 64 mg/kg), yielded activity levels comparable to those of appropriate controls in a second test performed 24 hours after the drug test (Shillito, 1967; for a similar absence of carry-over effects after five 1.5 mg/kg doses of CPZ in a comparable situation, see Kumar, 1971). After higher doses of CPZ (4 and 8 mg/kg), however, activity upon retesting in the undrugged state was as high as that of undrugged naive animals (Shillito, 1967).

In the case of benzodiazepines, carry-over effects in the direction of enhanced activity were shown both in mice after a single dose of chlordiazepoxide (CDX) in a hole-board apparatus (Dorr, Steinberg, Tomkiewicz, Joyce, Porsolt, & Summerfield, 1971), and in rats after a single dose of CDX in a Y-shaped apparatus (Marriott & Spencer, 1965). After more extended testing in the drug state, however, no carry-over effects of CDX treatment were observed in another Y-maze study (Kumar, 1971).

The traditional experimental design in this type of study involves a two-stage procedure in which four groups of animals receive the following treatment combinations: (1) No-Drug followed by No-Drug (ND – ND); (2) No-Drug followed by Drug (ND – D); (3) Drug followed by Drug (D – D); and (4) Drug followed by No-Drug (D – ND). Some important methodological analyses (e.g., Overton, 1974) have shown that it is often difficult to disentangle possible mechanisms of action—such as performance changes, associative changes, and state dependence—when using this paradigm. The mouse activity and habituation studies reported below were based on the tentative assumption that the power of this type of analysis may be enhanced by contrasting treatments which induce apparently similar changes from some viewpoints, but different changes from other viewpoints. The specific example illustrated below concerns the use of the aforementioned paradigm to study a neuroleptic (CPZ) and an anxiolytic (CDX) which at appropriate doses can induce apparently similar depressant effects in naive animals.

General Method

Male albino mice of a non-inbred Swiss stock (22–24 g) were housed in standard conditions in groups of four and used for brief (6 min) repeated daily measures of overall activity in a 37.5 × 32.5 × 30 cm photocell apparatus (Bignami, Pinto-Scognamiglio, & Gatti, 1974). All experiments reported here included an initial 5-day testing series, a 72- or 96-hr interval for drug washout, and a second 4-day testing series, and were completely balanced to account for various possible biasses. (For example, the four mice housed in the same cage were assigned to different groups—no drug to maximal dosage level in the initial experiments; ND – ND, ND – D, D – D, and D – ND schedules in subsequent single-dose experiments—

and tested simultaneously in the four available units, with equal representation of all groups in different units and different times.) All treatments, including vehicle (water), were given ip in a volume of 0.1 ml per 10 g body weight 15 min before testing, which was carried out in the housing room with the regular day-time artificial lighting (about 50 lux measured at floor level in the activity apparatus).

Dose-response Relations and Carry-Over Effects

This preliminary work was carried out as two independent experiments dealing with different doses respectively of CPZ and CDX. In each experiment one half of the mice were returned to their group cages, and the others isolated, during the interval between treatment and testing. The results are shown in Fig. 13.1. Overall day-to-day decrements of activity were clearly more marked in the CDX than in the CPZ experiment. Within-experiment comparisons, however, show that these decrements were in each case attenuated by the isolation procedure, except of course when a marked drug-induced reduction in activity created a floor effect. Furthermore, there was a clear contrast between the absence of carry-over effects over a wide range of doses of CPZ and the rebound of activity after CDX discontinuation. As a consequence, most former CDX groups showed day-to-day decrements of activity in the retest series, while the trend was flat in the former no-drug groups in this period. This type of effect, obviously, does not allow one to discriminate between an associative (learning and/or memory) deficit, a specific habituation impairment, and state dependence; but tolerance, if any, was negligible, indicating that the rebound of activity is unlikely to have been due to a genuine withdrawal syndrome.

Changes of State in Opposite Directions (high doses of CPZ and CDX)

Two independent experiments were carried out, one using 4 mg/kg doses of CPZ and the other using 40 mg/kg doses of chlordiazepoxide. At this stage of the work the safest way to equate the apparent effects of the two drugs in inexperienced animals—i.e., in the conditions generally employed in routine activity studies—was to use dosages reducing activity to nil or almost nil.

The results (Fig. 13.2) showed similar response reductions in both inexperienced animals (first series, D – D and D – ND groups) and experienced animals (second series, ND – D and D – D). Carry-over effects were again absent after CPZ washout, while rebounds of activity in former CDX-treated animals were apparently negligible when compared to those described above. Nevertheless, the D – D and the D – ND groups in the CDX experiment often showed deviations from a flat activity trend in the second test series similar to those observed in the previous experiment after treatment discontinuation (for the interaction between this carry-over effect and treatment-test interval condition see legend of Fig. 13.2). Such evidence for incomplete habituation suggested that some associative change, or interference with habituation mechanisms, might be more important than state dependence in the production of carry-over effects. (With a dissociative change only D – ND groups, but not D – D groups, should have shown rebound of activity and/or deviation from a flat trend in the retest series). The picture was somewhat confused by the influence of the treatment-test interval factor (see legend of Fig. 13.2). In view of the very high dose of CDX used, additional experiments were undertaken using different doses of the drug.

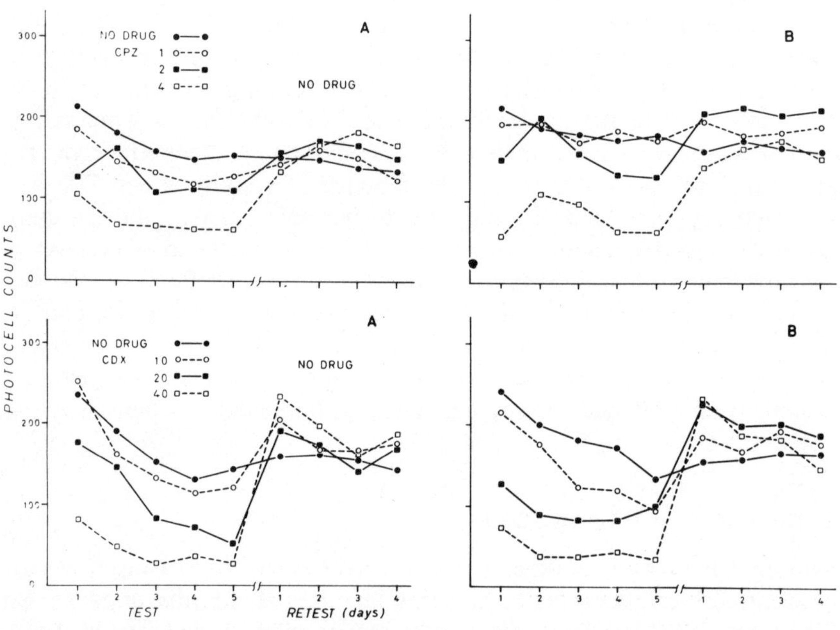

FIG. 13.1. Dose-dependent depression of mouse activity upon repeated exposure to chlorpromazine (CPZ, 1–4 mg/kg i.p. daily, upper graphs, N = 11 per group, drug $F[3, 80] = 25.96$, $p < .001$) or chlordiazepoxide (CDX, 10–40 mg/kg i.p., lower graphs, N = 10 per group, $F[3, 72] = 20.64, p < .001$). Housing conditions during the 15-min treatment-test intervals: A, "social" (animals remaining in groups of four, with one mouse in each treatment); B, "isolated" (animals housed singly). After drug washout former CPZ mice behaved similarly to controls, while CDX mice showed a rebound of activity followed by re-habituation (interaction between previous drug treatment and sessions significant only in the CDX experiment, $F[9, 216] = 1.99, p < .05$). The effect of temporary pre-test isolation was generally in the direction of an elevation of activity and an attenuation of day-to-day decrements in the first series of tests, although these effects reached statistical significance only in the CPZ experiment (treatment-test interval condition, first series $F[1, 80] = 7.03, p < .01$; retest series $F[1, 80] = 5.97, p < .025$).

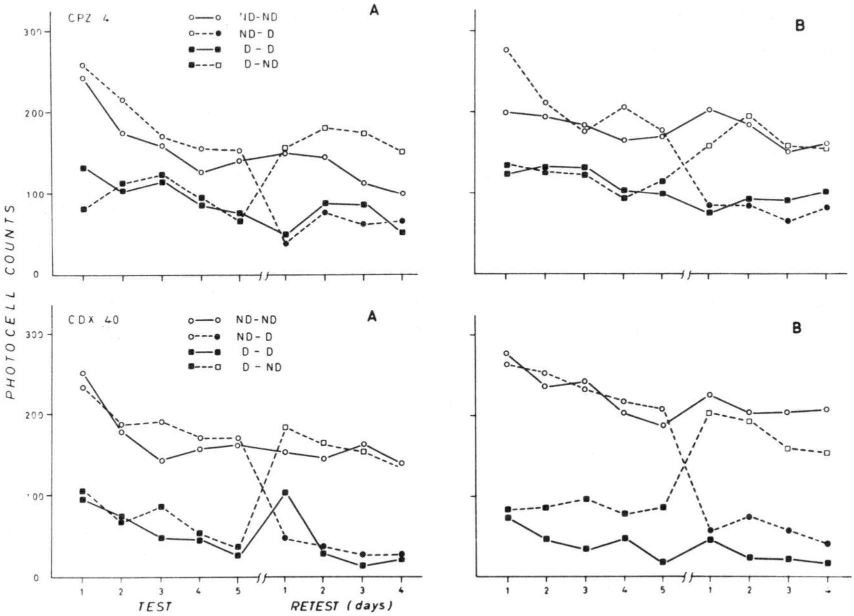

FIG. 13.2. Mouse activity experiments using a highly depressant dose of either CPZ (4 mg/kg, N = 10 per group) or CDX (40 mg/kg, N = 11 per group) and either no change or change in treatment conditions between the initial and the retest series (No Drug – No Drug, ND – ND; No Drug – Drug, ND – D; Drug – Drug, D – D; Drug – No Drug, D – ND). The CPZ experiment showed a similar drug depression in naive and experienced animals and no substantial carry-over effects (drug treatment, first series $F[1, 72] = 65.94$, $p < .001$; retest series $F[1, 72] = 75.68$, $p < .001$; no significant effects of previous drug treatment in the retest series). The CDX depression also appeared to be largely independent of time of treatment initiation (drug treatment, first series $F[1, 80] = 229.78$, $p < .001$; retest series $F[1, 80] = 233.34$, $p < .001$), and there was no clear-cut rebound of activity in the D – ND groups (see the equivalent groups in Fig. 13.1). However, day-to-day activity decrements in the retest series were generally more marked in the groups treated in the initial test series (D – D and D – ND), resulting in a significant interaction between previous drug treatment and sessions, $F[3, 240] = 3.17$, $p = .025$. The effects due to social vs. isolated treatment-test interval condition were statistically significant in each portion of both experiments. In addition, the CDX data showed that isolation between treatment and testing enhanced the drug–no drug difference (drug X treatment-test interval condition, first series $F[1, 80] = 5.78$, $p < .025$; retest series $F[1, 80] = 3.97$, $p < .05$) and attenuated the carry-over effect mentioned above (previous treatment X treatment-test interval condition $F[1, 80] = 4.88$, $p < .05$).

Changes of State in Opposite Directions (high vs moderate CDX dose)

This part of the study included two independent experiments on CDX, one with the same high dose used previously (40 mg/kg) and the other with a lower (10 mg/kg) dose (Fig. 13.3). The results obtained with the former confirmed the previous observation, showing both an activity rebound and a deviation from a flat activity trend in the retest series. An

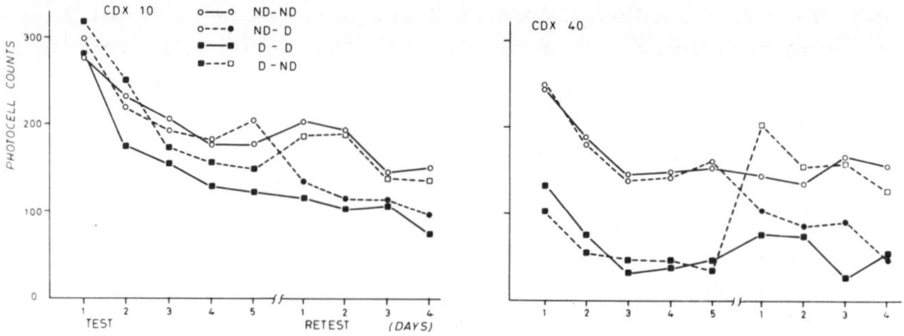

FIG. 13.3. Single-dose experiments with state changes in opposite directions and either a 10 mg/kg or a 40 mg/kg dose of chlordiazepoxide. The high-dose experiment confirmed the results shown previously, including a rebound of activity after treatment discontinuation (Fig. 13.1 and 13.2) and a flattening of activity trends in the retest series. The 10 mg/kg experiment yielded an entirely different profile of effects, including (a) a drug accentuation in the initial test series of the day-to-day activity decrement, without overall depression (drug X sessions $F[4, 160] = 3.34, p < .025$, in the absence of a main effect of drug treatment), (b) an appearance of a drug depression in experienced animals, independently of their previous treatment condition (retest series, drug $F[1,40] = 8.02$, $p < .01$), and (c) no carry-over effects after treatment discontinuation.

entirely different picture was obtained with the lower dose. Drug treatment apparently steepened the habituation slope in the initial test series. Prior experience with or without drug revealed a depressant effect in the second test series, which was absent in the initial sessions in the mice treated since their first exposure to the test.

These data will be discussed further in the next section, but one important point must be emphasised. The uniform depressant effects of the high dose of CDX in animals with different durations and different times of initiation of treatment, as well as the similar depression induced by the lower dose in both the D – D and the ND – D groups during the second testing phase, all tend to exclude any substantial role of either cumulation of effects or tolerance in the production of the changes so far described.

Some Provisional Inferences

The research reported above is still largely incomplete, and therefore the inferences can only be tentative and provisional. But, the results so far obtained indicate that the conventional two-stage approach to the analysis of behaviour modified both by experience and by drug treatments can be made remarkably more powerful by systematic comparisons between different treatments with at least one important element in common. The considerable complexity of the interactions observed with different doses of CDX provides a contrast which apparently strengthens some important inferences concerning the effects of CPZ over a wide dosage range. Specifically, it appears to be confirmed that this drug produces mainly a dose-dependent performance change, often called "psychomotor retardation" or "impairment of motor act initiation" (see discussion in Bignami, 1978), without any major associative change, habituation deficit, or state dependence.

On the other hand, the CDX syndrome does not appear to be amenable to a unitary explanation, since qualitatively different effects are observed at different doses, while even at a given dose a single type of change cannot account for the complex profile of effects. In the case of the lower dose used in the present experiments, the problem will be to test alternative explanations for two quite different effects, namely, apparent facilitation of habituation and increasing sensitivity to locomotor depression as experience progresses. (The problem of response enhancements at still lower dosage levels in several types of activity tests cannot be handled here.) In the case of the higher dose, a performance change (response depression) appears to go hand in hand with one or more of the other changes mentioned above, i.e., some general learning or memory deficit, a specific interference with habituation, or a sensory (dissociative) change. No small difficulties can be expected in further analyses of these points, considering, for example, that habituation is not a unitary phenomenon, and that opposite effects of CDX have been observed, depending on the habituation test (File, 1976, 1977). An important general caveat, however, is that multiple changes shown by an analysis conducted entirely from a behavioural viewpoint are likely to correspond to different types of physiological changes, or at least to different consequences of the same type of change occurring in different regulatory systems. In other words, refinements in the analysis of treatment-behaviour interactions apparently act in a direction opposite to that desired, i.e., they further widen the gap between behavioural and physiological models of treatment effects.

ACTIVITY AND AVOIDANCE LEARNING AFTER CS, US, AND AMPHETAMINE PRE-EXPOSURE

A considerable amount of work has been carried out in different laboratories in order to test various associative and non-associative hypotheses of punishment effects on subsequent behaviour modulation. For example, hypoactivity and impaired acquisition of escape and avoidance responses after exposure to strong inescapable shock has been explained: (1) by a widespread cognitive-associative-perceptual deficit ("learned helplessness") preventing the subject from learning the relations between its own responses and environmental events (Alloy & Seligman, 1979; Maier & Jackson, 1979; Maier & Seligman, 1976); (2) by more localised associative changes, such as learning the irrelevance of a particular response (Baker, 1976) or learning responses incompatible with those subsequently required for coping (Bracewell & Black, 1974; Glazer & Weiss, 1976); or (3) by a motor bias of a non-associative type ascribed to one or other of the many neurochemical changes induced by stressful experiences (Anisman, 1978; Weiss, Glazer, & Pohorecky, 1976; Weiss, Goodman, Losito, Corrigan, Charry, & Bailey, 1981). The latter model is also based on extensive pharmacological studies aimed either at mimicking, or at counteracting, the behavioural and biochemical effects of shock by treatment with a variety of monoaminergic agonists and antagonists (Anisman, Kokkinidis, & Sklar, 1981; Weiss, Bailey, Goodman, Hoffman, Ambrose, Salman, & Charry, 1982).

But the effects of pre-exposure to inescapable shock, with or without a discrete exteroceptive stimulus (i.e., a classical or Pavlovian CS), are not limited to hypoactivity and impairment of subsequent learning. Specifically, moderate intensities and durations of shock often fail to produce these effects, and sometimes produce an opposite type of change, particularly enhanced acquisition of escape-avoidance responding. In this instance the various types of possible mechanisms are not easily separated from each other. The clearest instances of facilitation have generally been obtained by pre-exposure to classical CS-US pairings (Anisman & Waller, 1973); therefore this effect may have resulted from either a motor change (proactive facilitation of activity) or an associative change (learning of the CS-US contingency transferred from the classical to the instrumental paradigm). Here also, pharmacological results have provided important additional evidence to support the role of non-associative (motor) changes, since for example pre-exposure to shock in the amphetamine state has been shown to produce opposite effects on active avoidance learning (facilitated) and passive avoidance learning (impaired) after drug washout (Anisman & Waller, 1971, 1973).

The work described here represents an attempt to elucidate further the nature of these interactions by studying the effects of various combinations of CS, US, and amphetamine pre-exposure on subsequent motor activity and active avoidance acquisition (for a more detailed description of part of this work see Alleva, De Acetis, Amorico, & Bignami, 1983).

General Method

The experiments used male albino rats of a Wistar-derived strain weighing 200–250 g and maintained in standard housing conditions. All pre-exposure, activity, and avoidance sessions were carried out using sound-insulated shuttle-boxes (49 × 41 × 22.5 cm) which were used with or without a central partition with a 7 × 7 cm opening at floor level. The boxes were equipped with two 10-W bulbs located on either side of the centre of the ceiling and a tilting floor which could be electrified to administer scrambled shock via a 70-KΩ resistor in series. Both the classical CS in pre-exposure (when present) and the avoidance CS in subsequent training consisted of turning on the lights 5 sec before the onset of shock. The CS and US terminated simultaneously both during classical pairings in pre-exposure and in avoidance tests, which were carried out according to a conventional delayed procedure (termination of CS and US together by an escape response after US onset; termination of CS and prevention of the scheduled shock by an avoidance response before US onset). Avoidance sessions consisted of 50 trials with 2.5 mA shock, 30-sec CS-CS intervals, and no inter-trial punishment. Four or five such sessions were given on successive days.

A Re-analysis of CS and/or US Pre-exposure Effects on Subsequent Avoidance

This part of the study consisted of an extensive series of preliminary experiments which can only be briefly summarised. In general, when the design included a single brief familiarisation session (6 min) and a single pre-exposure session, avoidance learning tended to be moderately facilitated by preshocks of different intensity and duration (12 presentations of 1.0–2.5 mA, 2.0–7.5 sec shock at 30-sec intervals to animals confined in one half of the cage). CS-US pairings produced a similar change, while pre-exposure to CS alone was followed by facilitation limited to sessions 2–4 (Fig. 12.4, left portion).

More extended pre-exposure (3 sessions), followed after a 48-hr interval by the first of a series of avoidance sessions, produced some interesting interactions (see right portion of Fig. 13.4). The longer period of handling and familiarisation with the apparatus elevated the performance of the no-CS, no-US group. Relative to this higher control baseline, avoidance acquisition was depressed by pre-exposure to either US alone or CS alone, both effects being in agreement respectively with the extensive literature already quoted, and with that on latent inhibition (reviews by Lubow, 1973; Weiss & Brown, 1974; also Feldman, 1977, for an analysis of this phenomenon in avoidance situations). Classical pairing of CS and US reversed these deficits, which confirmed that prior learning of the CS-US contingency can facilitate subsequent avoidance acquisition with the same warning signal.

Some of the experiments with a more limited pre-exposure also included groups treated with dl-amphetamine sulphate (1 mg/kg ip) either 15 min before the start, or immediately after the termination, of the pre-exposure session. The changes produced by the drug were generally small and

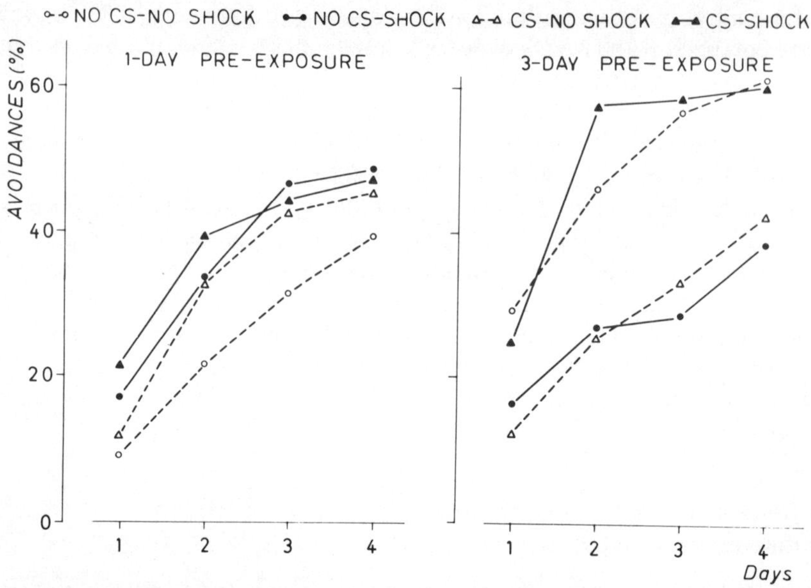

FIG. 13.4. Left portion: Facilitation of two-way avoidance acquisition in rats by limited pre-exposure to CS alone (light), US alone (shock), or CS-US pairings (pooled data from groups replicated in the same conditions in several experiments using a single pre-exposure session the day before the start of avoidance training). No CS – No shock = 6 min of pre-exposure to the apparatus in the absence of stimuli; No CS – Shock = 12 5-sec exposures (at 30-sec intervals) to 2.5 mA shock; CS – No shock = 12 10-sec exposures to the CS (light); CS – Shock = 12 CS-US pairings (light turned on 5 sec before shock). Total N = 41 to 56 rats in each of the four conditions. Right portion: More extended pre-exposure (three daily sessions followed after a 48-hr interval by the start of avoidance training) produced a CS-alone and a US-alone depression which was reversed in the group with CS-US pairings. N = 9 per group. (Repeated measures ANOVA on avoidance responses: Light X shock interaction $F[1,32] = 4.23$, $p < .05$).

variable from one experiment to another, with no instances of statistical significance.

At this point, it appeared that CS and/or US pre-exposure can lead to complex interactions between: (1) non-associative (motor) changes in different directions, depending on the severity of the punishment experience; (2) sensory changes of the latent inhibition type, depending mainly on the number of exposures to the CS presented alone prior to pairing with the US; and (3) associative changes, i.e., facilitation by prior learning of the CS-US contingency, producing effects which can either be confounded with those of a motor facilitation (limited pre-exposure) or counteract motor or sensory deficits (more extended pre-exposure). Therefore, the relative role of the various factors was further explored by the complex factorial experiments reported below.

Analysis of Critical Interactions Between CS, US, Apparatus, and Drug Treatment Factors

This part of the work included two large factorial experiments which investigated the proactive effects of various types of pre-exposure on subsequent activity in the shuttle-box (first experiment) and two-way avoidance acquisition (second experiment; for more details see Alleva, De Acetis, Amorico, & Bignami, 1983). All animals were given three days of pre-exposure as in the last of the experiments mentioned above, but they were allowed to move in the whole cage so as to measure the number of floor tilts (crossings) in pre-exposure sessions. These were followed by an extended interval (8 days) prior to retest for activity (three 6-min sessions without stimuli, first experiment) or avoidance (five sessions, second experiment).

The first experiment used 16 groups pre-exposed with or without CS, US, central partition in the shuttle-box, and drug treatment consisting of 1 mg/kg dl-amphetamine sulphate given ip 15 min before each session. (Based on previous work, the partition—no partition factor was used to manipulate the overall tendency to move from one to the other side of the apparatus [Bignami, Amorico, Frontali, & Rosić, 1971, Experiment 1, groups without inter-trial punishment]. Additional pilot experiments showed that this factor influenced in the expected direction the frequency of crossing in the absence of shock, as well as amphetamine effects thereon.) The second experiment used an identical design in pre-exposure, with, however, 32 groups since one half of the rats in each of the 16 treatment combinations was given avoidance training in the same apparatus condition, and the other half in the other condition (i.e., rats pre-exposed with partition were trained either with or without partition, and vice versa).

As expected on the basis of previous studies (e.g., Anisman & Cygan, 1975; Anisman & Waller, 1971), both experiments showed a marked hyperactivity in pre-exposure sessions in animals receiving both amphetamine and shock, as well as some interesting interactions between these and other factors leading to very high frequencies of crossing in the CS-US-Drug-No partition groups (for details see Alleva, De Acetis, Amorico, & Bignami, 1983). In retesting for activity (first experiment) the main effect was suppression of locomotion by prior punishment, which, however, was less marked in the CS-US-No partition animals. This suppression was not attenuated by amphetamine treatment in pre-exposure, i.e., former drug-shock groups showed low retest activity scores except in conditions which prevented a fully fledged suppression independently of drug treatment (Fig. 13.5).

In the second experiment, rats pre-exposed in the absence of stimuli had higher avoidance performances with the partition than without it (at least in the first session), while the CS-only groups showed differences in opposite

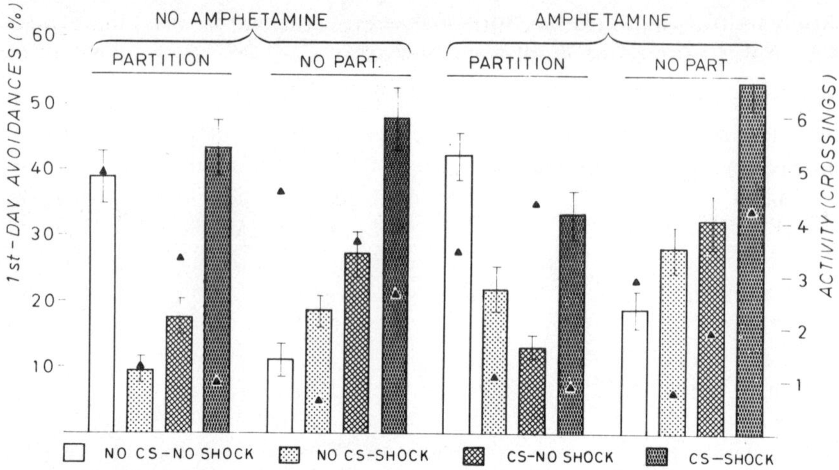

FIG. 13.5. Selected results from two experiments using three daily pre-exposure sessions with or without CS, US (for specifications see legend of Fig. 13.4), pre-session treatment by dl-amphetamine sulphate (1 ml/kg i.p.) and central partition in the shuttle-box (modified from Figs. 1, 2 and 3 in Alleva, De Acetis, Amorico, & Bignami, 1983, by permission; only data from groups without changes in apparatus conditions between pre-exposure and retest). In the first experiment (12 rats per group) retesting for activity in the absence of stimuli and treatment after an 8-day interval (triangles) showed the expected punishment suppression, except in the CS-US-No partition groups, and no substantial amphetamine effects thereon. In the second experiment (N = 11 per group), retesting for avoidance produced a uniform impairment by US-alone pre-exposure, opposite effects of CS-alone pre-exposure as a function of apparatus conditions, and facilitation by CS-US pairings (only first session data shown by the bars). Proactive amphetamine effects were again negligible, in spite of the considerable drug-shock hyperactivity measured in pre-exposure sessions (not shown; for more details and statistical data see Alleva, De Acetis, Amorico, & Bignami, 1983).

directions. In other words, the expected latent inhibition phenomenon occurred when the baseline in the no-CS group was high in the presence of the partition while CS pre-exposure elevated the low baseline obtained in the absence of the partition (for further discussion see Alleva, De Acetis, Amorico, & Bignami, 1983). The most consistent effect was an interation between US and CS pre-exposure, since the overall retardation induced by pre-shock alone was turned into a facilitation in the groups given CS-US pairings. Finally, the effects of amphetamine were again slight and not statistically significant (Fig. 13.5).

In general, the data profile in the retest phase of both experiments confirm a role of both non-associative (sensory and motor) and associative changes producing differential effects on subsequent activity and avoidance, as will be discussed in the following section. But the procedures demonstrate that there is not necessarily a correlation between activity in pre-exposure sessions and subsequent activity or avoidance, and between proactive effects of various pre-exposure conditions on subsequent activity and subsequent avoidance. In other words, the emphasis on this type of correlation in previous work may depend at least in part on the use of an insufficiently wide range of testing conditions.

Implications for Further Analyses

The peculiar combination of positive and negative results reported above suggests that previous work in this area has often led to overgeneralisations resting on insufficient analysis of interacting factors. For example, if only the partition groups in the last avoidance experiment reported above were considered, it would be easy to construct a relatively simple model using some well-known phenomena, i.e., latent inhibition by pre-exposure to CS alone (a sensory change), punishment suppression by pre-exposure to shock alone (a motor change), and favourable effects of prior learning of the CS-US contingency (an associative change). But the finding that CS pre-exposure exerted opposite effects depending on the apparatus factor indicates that additional elements may have to be taken into account; for example, differences in "coping style" (such as relative roles of response versus place learning), as a function of presence or absence of a partition located at a place which is critical with respect to the response criterion. Similarly, general inferences on CS-US interactions must await further analysis of the effects of different types of signals. There are data showing that conditioned freezing after classical CS-US pairings is easily obtained with acoustic, but not with visual signals (Sigmundi, Bouton, & Bolles, 1980). This may explain why pre-shock deficits were markedly enhanced, rather than reversed, by pairing with an acoustic CS in the experiments by Weiss, Krieckhaus, & Conte (1968).

One could further speculate about the generality of various associative and non-associative models which have so far shown considerable heuristic value in the analysis of amphetamine effects. In the work presented, the drug groups showed no changes suggestive of motor, sensory, or associative effects. But these experiments used a bidirectional response requirement, which is known to impede the acquisition of active avoidance. The potential relevance of this variable is shown by the fact that CS-US pre-exposure effects on subsequent learning of one-way avoidance are enhanced by amphetamine, with a direct relation between the drug-shock hyperactivity in pre-exposure and initial avoidance facilitation in the no-drug state (Anisman & Waller, 1971). Undoubtedly, as was underlined in our provisional conclusions about the activity and habituation data, it appears increasingly difficult to account for these interactions in physiological terms.

As indicated earlier in this paper, it is entirely possible that the heuristic value of the approach used in the work summarised has already been exhausted, which would strengthen the objections which are often raised by supporters of other approaches. Upon closer scrutiny, one could even question the very existence of a "mediating processes approach" as an autonomous entity in the study of behaviour. This line of work often oscillates between an open analysis of behavioural interactions, with little or no role of alternative models to be tested, and a reductionist analysis in which the definition of hypothetical mediating processes and the definition of brain mechanisms responsible for behavioural modulation come very close to each other. Further analysis of representative data from the literature, however, could show that premature attempts to close one or the other gap can have negative consequences, by suppressing a considerable portion of the overall reality, and by reducing the total explanatory and heuristic potential of all approaches taken together. Therefore, the problem is one of adequate standards and adequate integration into more comprehensive methods and models, which at present are still the object of considerable controversy.

ACKNOWLEDGMENTS

The authors wish to acknowledge the expert technical assistance of Luigi Amorico and Luigi De Acetis in the experiments described in this paper, and the help given by one of the editors (CMB) in restyling the manuscript.

REFERENCES

Alleva, E., De Acetis, L., Amorico, L., & Bignami, G. (1983) Amphetamine, CS, and non-debilitating preshock effects on activity and avoidance: Further evidence for interactions between associative and non-associative changes. *Behavioral and Neural Biology*, **39**, 78–104.

Alloy, L. B. & Seligman, M. E. P. (1979) On the cognitive component of learned helplessness and depression. *The Psychology of Learning and Motivation*, **13**, 219–276.

Anisman, H. (1978) Neurochemical changes elicited by stress. Behavioral correlates. In H. Anisman & G. Bignami (Eds.), *Psychopharmacology of aversively motivated behavior*. New York: Plenum. 119–172.

Anisman, H. & Cygan, D. (1975) Central effects of scopolamine and (+)-amphetamine on locomotor activity: Interactions with strain and stress variables. *Neuropharmacology*, **14**, 835–840.

Anisman, H., Kokkinidis, L., & Sklar, L. S. (1981) Contribution of neurochemical change to stress-induced behavioral deficits. In S. J. Cooper (Ed.), *Theory in psychopharmacology: (Volume 1)*. London: Academic Press. 66–102.

Anisman, H. & Waller, T. G. (1971) Effects of methamphetamine and shock duration during inescapable shock exposure on subsequent active and passive avoidance. *Journal of Comparative and Physiological Psychology*, **77**, 143–151.

Anisman, H. & Waller, T. G. (1973) Effects of inescapable shock on subsequent avoidance performance: Role of response repertoire changes. *Behavioral Biology*, **9**, 331–355.

Baker, A. G. (1976) Learned irrelevance and learned helplessness: Rats learn that stimuli, reinforcers, and responses are uncorrelated. *Journal of Experimental Psychology: Animal Behavior Processes*, **2**, 130–141.

Bignami, G. (1976) Nonassociative explanations of behavioral changes induced by central cholinergic drugs. *Acta Neurobiologiae Experimentalis*, **36**, 5–90.

Bignami, G. (1978) Effects of neuroleptics, ethanol, hypnotic-sedatives, tranquilizers, narcotics, and minor stimulants in aversive paradigms. In H. Anisman & G. Bignami (Eds.), *Psychopharmacology of aversively motivated behavior*. New York: Plenum. 385–453.

Bignami, G., Amorico, L., Frontali, M., & Rosić, N. (1971) Central cholinergic blockade and two-way avoidance acquisition: The role of response disinhibition. *Physiology and Behavior*, **7**, 461–470.

Bignami, G. & Michałek, H. (1979) Cholinergic mechanisms and aversively motivated behavior. In H. Anisman & G. Bignami (Eds.), *Psychopharmacology of aversively motivated behavior*. New York: Plenum. 173–255.

Bignami, G., Pinto-Scognamiglio, W., & Gatti, G. L. (1974) The evaluation of the behavioural toxicity of psychotropic agents: The case of lithium. In W. A. M. Duncan (Ed.). *Experimental model systems in toxicology and their significance in man*. Amsterdam: Excerpta Medica. 33–42.

Bracewell, R. J. & Black, A. H. (1974) The effects of restraint and noncontingent preshock on subsequent escape learning in the rat. *Learning and Motivation*, **5**, 53–69.

Dorr, M., Steinberg, H., Tomkiewicz, M., Joyce, D., Porsolt, R. D., & Summerfield, A. (1971) Persistence of dose related behaviour in mice. *Nature*, **231**, 121–123.

Feldman, M. A. (1977) The effects of preexposure to a warning or a safety signal on the acquisition of a two-way avoidance response in rats. *Learning and Motivation*, **5**, 21–24.

File, S. E. (1976) A comparison of the effects of ethanol and chlordiazepoxide on exploration and its habituation. *Physiological Psychology*, **4**, 529–532.

File, S. E. (1977) Effects of two anxiolytics on distraction, habituation and dishabituation. *Pharmacology, Biochemistry, and Behavior*, **7**, 105–109.

Giardini, V., Amorico, L., De Acetis, L., & Bignami, G. (1983) Scopolamine and acquisition of go–no go avoidance: A further analysis of the perseverative antimuscarinic deficit. *Psychopharmacology*, **80**, 131–137.

Glazer, H. I. & Weiss, J. M. (1976) Long-term and transitory interference effects. *Journal of Experimental Psychology: Animal Behavior Processes*, **2**, 191–201.

Hughes, R. N. & Greig, A. M. (1975) Chlordiazepoxide effects on reactions to novelty and activity with and without prior drug experience. *Psychopharmacologia*, **42**, 289–292.

Irwin, S. & Armstrong, P. M. (1961) Conditioned locomotor response with drug as the unconditioned stimulus: Individual differences. In E. Rothlin (Ed.), *Neuro-Psychopharmacology: (Volume 2) Proceedings of the 2nd International Meeting of the Collegium Internationale Neuro-Psychopharmacologicum*. Amsterdam: Elsevier. 151–157.

Itoh, H. & Takaori, S. (1968) Effects of psychotropic agents on the explanatory behavior of rats in a Y-shaped box. *The Japanese Journal of Pharmacology*, **18**, 344–352.

Jenden, D. J. (Ed.) (1977) *Cholinergic mechanisms and psychopharmacology*. New York: Plenum.

Kelleher, R. T. & Morse, W. H. (1968) Determinants of the specificity of behavioral effects of drugs. *Ergebnisse der Physiologie, Biologischen Chemie und Experimentellen Pharmakologie*, **60**, 1–56.

Kumar, R. (1971) Extinction of fear II: Effects of chlordiazepoxide and chlorpromazine on fear and exploratory behaviour in rats. *Psychopharmacologia*, **19**, 297–312.

Lubow, R. E. (1973) Latent inhibition. *Psychological Bulletin*, **79**, 398–407.

Maier, S. F. & Jackson, R. L. (1979) Learned helplessness: All of us were right (and wrong): Inescapable shock has multiple effects. *The Psychology of Learning and Motivation*, **13**, 155–218.

Maier, S. F. & Seligman, M. E. P. (1976) Learned helplessness: Theory and evidence. *Journal of Experimental Psychology: General*, **105**, 3–46.

Marriott, A. S. & Spencer, P. S. J. (1965) Effects of centrally acting drugs on exploratory behaviour in rats. *British Journal of Pharmacology*, **25**, 432–441.

McCleary, R. A. (1961) Response specificity in the behavioral effects of limbic system lesions in the cat. *Journal of Comparative and Physiological Psychology*, **54**, 605–613.

Nolan, N. A. & Parkes, M. W. (1973) The effects of benzodiazepines on the behaviour of mice on a hole-board. *Psychopharmacologia*, **29**, 277–288.

Overton, D. A. (1974) Experimental methods for the study of state-dependent learning. *Federation Proceedings*, **33**, 1800–1813.

Peters, D. A. V., Anisman, H., & Pappas, B. A. (1978) Monoamines and aversively motivated behaviors. In H. Anisman & G. Bignami (Eds.), *Psychopharmacology of aversively motivated behavior*. New York: Plenum. 257–343.

Robbins, T. W. (1977) A critique of the methods available for the measurement of spontaneous activity. In L. L. Iversen, S. D. Iversen, & S. H. Snyder (Eds.), *Handbook of psychopharmacology: (Volume 7) Principles of behavioral pharmacology*. New York: Plenum. 37–82.

Rose, S. P. R., Lewontin, R. C., & Kamin, L. (1984) *Not in our genes: Biology, ideology and human nature*. Harmondsworth: Penguin.

Shillito, E. E. (1967) The effect of chlorpromazine and thioridazine on the exploration of a Y-maze by rats. *British Journal of Pharmacology and Chemotherapy*, **30**, 258–264.

Sigmundi, R. A., Bouton, M. E., & Bolles, R. C. (1980) Conditioned freezing in the rat as a function of shock intensity and CS modality. *Bulletin of the Psychonomic Society*, **15**, 254–256.

Waser, P. G. (Ed.) (1975) *Cholinergic mechanisms*. New York: Raven.

Weiskrantz, L. (1968) Some traps and pontifications. In L. Weiskrantz (Ed.), *Analysis of behavioral change*. New York: Harper and Row. 415–429.

Weiss, J. M., Bailey, W. H., Goodman, P. A., Hoffman, L. J., Ambrose, M. J., Salman, S., & Charry, J. M. (1982) A model for neurochemical study of depression. In M. Y. Spiegelstein & A. Levy (Eds.), *Behavioral models and the analysis of drug action*. Amsterdam: Elsevier. 195–223.

Weiss, J. M., Glazer, H. I., & Pohorecky, L. A. (1976) Coping behavior and neuro-chemical changes. An alternative explanation for the original "learned helplessness" experiments. In G. Serban & A. Kling, *Animal models in human psychobiology*. New York: Plenum. 141–173.

Weiss, J. M., Goodman, P. A., Losito, B. G., Corrigan, S., Charry, J. M., & Bailey, W. H. (1981) Behavioral depression produced by an uncontrollable stressor: Relationship to norepinephrine, dopamine, and serotonin levels in various regions of rat brain. *Brain Research Reviews*, **3**, 167–205.

Weiss, J. M., Krieckhaus, E. E., & Conte, R. (1968) Effects of fear conditioning on subsequent avoidance behavior and movement. *Journal of Comparative and Physiological Psychology*, **65**, 413–421.

Weiss, K. R. & Brown, B. L. (1974) Latent inhibition: A review and a new hypothesis. *Acta Neurobiologiae Experimentalis*, **34**, 301–316.

14 Drug Discrimination and the Behavioural Analysis of Drug Action

F. C. Colpaert
Janssen Pharmaceutica, Beerse, Belgium

Behavioural pharmacology has evolved as an interdisciplinary science that studies the behavioural effects of drugs (Pickens, 1977). These effects of drugs on behaviour are being framed (Thompson & Dews, 1977, 1979; Thompson, Dews & McKim, 1981) into one of several different conceptual systems. Prominent conceptual systems are behavioural mechanisms (Thompson & Schuster, 1968), rate-dependency effects (Dews, 1958), and stimulus properties (Thompson & Pickens, 1971) of drugs.

Perhaps more so than many other biological sciences, behavioural pharmacology meets with an inherent difficulty; the conditions in which the effects of drugs on behaviour can be assayed empirically, are essentially unlimited (Skinner, 1959). As a result, the outcomes of drug testing can vary similarly, and it is often difficult to define behavioural drug actions that hold in more than a very limited range of conditions. The problem becomes particularly apparent when animal data are used to predict drug effects on human behaviour. The fact that virtually all discoveries in biological psychiatry have resulted from observations in humans that were not anticipated by laboratory work on animals (Ayd & Blackwell, 1970) indicates that the predictive power of animal data has been extremely limited. Thus behaviour is responsive to an immense variety of conditions (Skinner, 1959) and emerges (Bunge, 1980) from what is probably the most complexly organised form of matter, i.e., the nervous system. Variability is therefore a paramount feature of behaviour, and renders any analysis of the effects of drugs on behaviour extremely difficult.

The paradigms of behavioural pharmacology yield measurements of variable behaviour that are scaled along one of four general scales, i.e., the nominal, ordinal, interval, and ratio scales (Stevens, 1946). These different scales, or levels of measurement, define and limit the manipulations and operations which are permissible in handling the data (Siegel, 1956). It is commonly felt to be desirable that paradigms being used should achieve as high a level of measurement as possible. Interval and ratio scales are better than nominal and ordinal at allowing data to reflect changes of, and effects on, behaviour, and permitting sophisticated numerical analyses to be made. Even when a measurement is clearly nominal, as is the case with left or right turns in a T maze, the measurement is often transformed into a quantitative variate, such as the percentage of left turns, in an apparent attempt to achieve a higher level of measurement. But, while high levels of measurement do allow more penetrating statistical and mathematical analyses to be made of the behavioural response being studied, they also are susceptible to a greater multiplicity of different conditions that control behaviour. This susceptibility may be undesirable and make isolation of a possible drug effect from the additional sources of variability to which the measurement is responsive extremely difficult. In addition, the observed effect of the drug is invariably contaminated by additional sources of variability. It may be useful, therefore, to develop measurements of behaviour that are simple and which are only responsive to more limited ranges of conditions.

Drug discrimination is a paradigm of behavioural pharmacology that has evolved only recently. We briefly outline some of the characteristic features of the drug discrimination experiment and describe its pharmacological relevance. It will also be argued here that the dependent variable of the drug discrimination paradigm is nominal in nature, and that the paradigm can compress behaviour into the lowest possible level of variability, i.e., into a binary response. In doing so, the paradigm looses much of the behavioural sophistication that is characteristic of many other behavioural experiments; but it also gains a resolving capacity in analysing quantitative and qualitative characteristics of the behavioural effects of drugs that is perhaps unique among the available paradigms of behavioural pharmacology.

DRUG DISCRIMINATION

Drug discrimination (DD) is a technique that establishes drugs as discriminative stimuli (DS) for behavioural responses. The technique can be rendered complex by implementing several drug stimuli, by defining several responses, and by manipulating the reinforcing contingencies that are instituted between the drug stimuli and the behavioural responses (Järbe & Swedberg, 1982). But the intricacies of the outcomes that are being obtained from these more complex DD techniques are only poorly understood. The DD analysis of behavioural drug effects therefore starts with the use of a more elementary technique.

In its elementary, simple format, the DD paradigm involves the training of laboratory animals to discriminate a given drug from its vehicle, and has the following characteristic features (Colpaert, 1982, 1983). The drug and its dose which the animals are trained on, are referred to as the *training drug* and the *training dose*, respectively; physiological saline is the common vehicle. Perhaps the most widely used DD procedure is one in which food deprived rats press levers for food pellets in daily 15 min sessions (Colpaert, Niemegeers & Janssen, 1976). Pressing one of two levers (the drug lever, DL) is reinforced in sessions that are preceded by the administration of the training dose. Pressing the other lever (the saline lever, SL) is reinforced in saline sessions. Pellet delivery occurs after every 10th press on the lever that is appropriate to treatment (fixed ratio, FR 10, schedule); responses on the inappropriate lever have no programmed consequences. The discriminative response in this procedure is defined as the completion of the FR 10 schedule. The two discriminative responses are mutually exclusive; the schedule can be completed first within a session on only one of the two levers. The two responses are also operant, or instrumental, and similar in morphology, except that they differ in location (i.e., left or right). The response-reinforcement contingency is similar in the two stimulus conditions; it therefore is also symmetrical.

The total number of responses that occur on either lever before the FR 10 schedule is completed on the appropriate lever and, thus, before the first reinforcement is delivered, can vary from 10 to any larger number in training sessions (symbol: FRF). A correct discriminative response is said to occur if FRF assumes any value lower than 20. While DL and SL responding initially occur equally often in the two stimulus conditions, daily training results in the animal responding reliably on the SL in saline sessions, and on the DL in training drug sessions. The change in behaviour that is apparent in the course of training is similar to the acquisition of a discrimination between exteroceptive stimuli. The differential responding that develops therefore indicates that the animal discriminates between the training drug and saline, and permits stimulus generalisation tests to be conducted. For the purpose of such a test, the animal is given a novel pharmacological treatment, and its responding during a test session is recorded.

PHARMACOLOGICAL ANALYSES

Stimulus generalisation tests in animals trained to discriminate a given training drug from saline make it possible for a number of pharmacological experiments to be conducted in which the behavioural, discriminative response serves as the dependent variable. One type of experiment consists of determining how the response varies with different test doses of the training drug. The typical outcome is that lower doses yield responding which is appropriate to saline, whereas increasingly higher doses engender a response which is increasingly more appropriate to the training drug. The relation between training drug appropriate responding on the one hand, and test dose on the other, can often be described by an orderly function. This function is termed a dose-response curve or a stimulus generalisation gradient, depending on whether the focus is pharmacological or behavioural. A second type of experiment determines whether drugs other than the training drug will be generalised with the training drug. If the test drug does indeed produce generalisation, then it will be possible to establish its generalisation gradient. Further, a comparison of different gradients will reveal whatever differences in potency may exist among different drugs in producing the stimulus generalisation. A third type of experiment consists of pretreating the animal with some compound before administering the training dose; it may appear that the ensuing responding is appropriate to saline rather than to training drug, and the compound is then said to have antagonised the effect of the training drug. A dose-response curve can be obtained for the antagonist in antagonising the effect of the training drug. Different antagonists can be studied, and potency differences among antagonists can be established. One or several compounds can thus be examined and compared as potential antagonists of the effect of the training drug, and also of drugs that produced generalisation with the training drug. These three general types of experimental manoeuvers make it possible for the DD paradigm to resolve a number of differences in the possible effects of drugs on behaviour.

The body of DD data that has accumulated to date[1] reveals that the paradigm has a powerful resolving capacity in analysing behavioural effects of drug.

A first general feature of the DD analysis of drug action is that it can offer exquisite pharmacological specificity. A wealth of data to this effect is available with morphine-like drugs (Colpaert, 1978a, 1982; Herling and Woods, 1981; Holtzman, 1982a, 1982b). For example, rats trained to discriminate morphine from saline generalise other molecules that differ chemically, but which are known from other evidence to exert morphine-like, or opiate, effects. These animals do not generalise, i.e., will emit saline-appropriate responses, on injection of any non-opiate centrally acting drug. Non-opiate analgesics similarly fail to generalise in these animals.

---

[1]For references, the reader is referred to the proceedings of two international meetings (Colpaert & Rosecrans, 1978; Colpaert & Slangen, 1982) and to an extensive DD bibliography that has recently become available (Stolerman, Baldy & Shine, 1982).

Also, the opiate discriminative stimulus can be antagonised by naloxone, a specific antagonist of opiate drugs; and no drugs other than specific opiate antagonists have so far been found to antagonise the stimulus. Like many other pharmacological effects of opiates, the stimulus is stereoselective, and probably results from interactions with opiate receptors at central as opposed to peripheral sites in the organism. These sites are presumably neuronal.

A second feature is that the paradigm allows one to examine a wide variety of drugs in a uniform manner. This variety includes many classes of drugs whose relevance to medicine and the biological sciences has been chiefly behavioural. These include the opiates (Colpaert, 1978a, 1982; Herling & Woods, 1981; Holtzman, 1982a, 1982b), psychotomimetics (Shearman & Herz, 1982), central nervous system stimulants (Colpaert, Niemegeers & Janssen, 1979; Ho & Silverman, 1978), alcohol, barbiturates, and benzodiazepines (Barry & Krimmer, 1977) hallucinogens (Appel, White & Holohean, 1982; Glennon, Rosecrans & Young, 1982), and cannabinoids (Weissman, 1978).

Recent data reviewed elsewhere (Colpaert, 1982) also indicate that the pharmacological specificity of opiate DD data is variable. Specifically, the manipulation of several behavioural variables appears to produce orderly effects on the pharmacological specificity of the outcome of generalisation tests. The major variables that have been identified so far, are training dose, reinforcement of the operant, and dose-dose as opposed to drug-saline discrimination. The possibility of manipulating the pharmacological specificity of the outcome of drug testing is exceedingly important; it very much widens the dynamic range of the paradigm, and a broader range of agonist and antagonist drug effects becomes amenable to the analysis (Colpaert, 1982).

Studies (Colpaert, Niemegeers & Janssen, 1980a, 1980b) on the effects of training dose on the pharmacological specificity of opiate drug discrimination have revealed this specificity to be proportional to training dose; the naloxone-reversibility of the effect of the opiate fentanyl in fentanyl-saline discrimination increased as training dose was higher (Colpaert, 1982). This finding is of particular import because it challenges a view which is widely held in behavioural pharmacology. That is that the effects of low doses of behaviourally active drugs are more specific and, therefore, more relevant, than those of higher doses. The justification for this view is that higher doses exert a greater multiplicity and a broader variety of neurochemical, behavioural, and other effects. The DD finding that, at least in this paradigm, higher doses may yield greater pharmacological specificity, may suggest that this greater multiplicity and broader variety of effects are characteristic of, rather than being deleterious to, specific drug actions. Indeed, the multiplicity and variety of effects of drugs would seem to set the occasion for distinctiveness of drug action to become apparent. This latter view casts a new light on the definition of specificity of behavioural drug action, and suggests a reconsideration of the significance of a number of observed drug effects. For example, the significance of presumably analgesic effects of 0.1 mg/kg of morphine in the rat becomes questionable if it were to be found that a 3 mg/kg dose of the drug is required to achieve satisfactory specificity in this species.

THE DEPENDENT VARIABLE

It has been common practice in DD research to measure and express the drug discrimination and generalisation data by means of a quantitative variate. In the procedure described above, test sessions will reveal the animal to have made an observed number of responses on the DL, and an observed number of responses on the SL; either number of responses can vary from 0 to any number. Drugs may exert what are variously termed unconditioned, intrinsic, or unspecific effects on response rate, and DD procedures that yield only absolute rate measures (Winter, 1973) have for that reason been largely abandoned. The most commonly used variate, therefore, is one that measures the relative strength of DL responding, i.e., the percentage of all responses that occurred on the DL. This latter variate is free to assume any value from 0 to 100; it is quantitative and permits a large number of manipulations and operations to be made in handling the data. One popular operation consists of averaging this percentage across different tests or different animals. Averaging data at different test doses of the training drug, for example, will then result in a function that relates test dose to the measure of generalisation. The operation typically results in an orderly dose-response curve, or stimulus generalisation gradient.

The practice, in DD research, of using a quantitative variate for measuring stimulus generalisation, adheres to tradition in the experimental analysis of behaviour (Gilbert & Sutherland, 1969; Sutherland & Mackintosh, 1971). The tradition was set by the classic paper of Guttman and Kalish (1956). Guttman and Kalish introduced rate of responding as a major methodological innovation in a publication which marked the beginning of stimulus generalisation as an area of research. This proposal has remained essentially unchallenged, and rate of responding has continued since to feature as the principal measure of stimulus generalisation (Honig & Urcuioli, 1981). The wide acceptance of this innovation (Guttman & Kalish, 1956) may not be surprising in view of another tradition, set by Skinner. In designing what was referred to as a system of behaviour, Skinner (1938) argued that the main datum to be measured in the study of an operant is the rate of responding (Skinner, 1938, p58). For the study of behaviour to become a science, it seemed appropriate that behaviour be measured, and that the measure be quantitative. Consistent with this view, Skinner described the acquisition of a discrimination as two reflexes that draw apart in strength (p169). These changes in the strength of the reflexes were to be measured by means of response rate, and required no new dynamic process other than conditioning and extinction (p170). The current use of a quantitative measure in DD research thus seems to have evolved from an elementary cornerstone of Skinner's theory (Skinner, 1938).

While measuring behaviour along some quantitative scale is attractive because of the analytical sophistication that it permits (as already discussed) and although quantitative measures of behaviour may serve many practical purposes, there may be room to doubt the generalisation (Skinner, 1938, p58) that rate of responding is the principal, or perhaps even an adequate, measure of behaviour. Implicit in the use of a quantitative variate as a measure of the dependent variable, is the assumption that the dependent variable varies as a function of the independent variable(s) in a manner which is at least proportional[2]. Whether this assumption can be satisfied is almost always uncertain, and the issue is most frequently neglected altogether in the behavioural literature. We argue that this assumption is not being satisfied in the discrimination paradigm.

In the discrimination procedure described above, a particular relation is established between pharmacological stimuli and behavioural responses through what is termed acquisition, or training. Generalisation tests are conducted after training to determine how the dependent variable varies as novel, test stimuli are presented. The behaviour which ensues in these tests is free to vary in many diverse ways. But the variation in response which reflects variation in discriminative stimulus is that, and only that, which was defined by the relation between stimulus and response which was established by training. This relation can be described by the scheme (Colpaert, Niemegeers & Janssen, 1976):

$$R_1, R_2\ (S_1^D = S_I = S_2^\Delta;\ S_1^\Delta = S_{II} = S_2^D)$$

in which: S_I = training drug injection
S_{II} = saline injection
R_1 = DL response
R_2 = SL response
S^D = a stimulus which sets the occasion for the reinforcement of a specified response 1 or 2.
S^Δ = a stimulus which sets the occasion for withholding reinforcement of a specified response 1 or 2.

[2]This is the assumption which must be satisfied when the measure is ordinal; even stronger assumptions must be satisfied to justify the use of interval or ratio scales.

The scheme clarifies at least two important features of the paradigm. First, it defines only two values of behaviour, i.e., the DL and the SL response. These two values do not differ along any scale that is proportional to magnitude (i.e. ratio, interval, or ordinal scale); rather, they differ as categories (i.e., nominally). Second, it establishes a strict, all-or-none, correlation between S_I, S_{II} and R_1, R_2; R_1 is reinforced if, and only if, S_I applies, and R_2 is reinforced if, and only if, S_{II} applies. The following are some implications of this scheme. (i) It compresses all discriminative behaviour into a variate that assumes values that differ nominally: the dependent variable of the discrimination paradigm therefore is nominal in nature (Colpaert, 1977, 1978, 1982, 1983; Colpaert, Niemegeers & Janssen, 1976). It follows that the discrimination paradigm offers a measurement of stimulus (e.g., drug) effects which requires the most conservative of assumptions among all possible scales. (ii) The simple case being considered here defines no more than two responses; the dependent variable can assume only two values and is, therefore, binary. It follows that the paradigm is capable of compressing all complexity of behaviour into the simplest and clearest of all possible variates, i.e., the binary variate. (iii) That the dependent variable of the discrimination paradigm is nominal does not imply that some properties of the behaviour which is being observed in generalisation tests cannot be measured in terms of any of many additional parameters. These parameters may or may not be quantitative. They also may or may not to some extent correlate with the nominal dependent variable; but none of them can simply be taken to substitute for the dependent variable. The latency to making the discriminative response provides an example. Modal response latencies may differ between training drug and saline sessions (Colpaert, 1978b). Latency may also to some extent co-vary with test dose in test sessions (Colpaert, 1978b), and with training dose in saline sessions (Colpaert, Niemegeers & Janssen, 1980b). But these relations are very limited in range, and latency is responsive to drug effects on rate (Shannon & Holtzman, 1976). It would seem, therefore, that latency (Colpaert, Niemegeers & Janssen, 1980b; Colpaert, Maroli & Meert, 1982), and also FRF (Colpaert, Niemegeers & Janssen, 1978), may at times reflect variations of some intervening variable (e.g., doubt/certainty); but it cannot, at any point, be taken as a measure of the discriminative response.

While we have argued here and elsewhere (e.g. Colpaert, Niemegeers & Janssen, 1976) that the dependent variable of the DD paradigm is nominal in nature, it must be pointed out that the issue is particularly controversial. The percentage of drug-appropriate responding, a quantitative variate, has continued to be used almost unanimously as a measure of stimulus generalisation. Evidently, there has been a fair concordance of conclusions reached from using either nominal or quantitative measures, and the two measures co-vary in many (Koek & Slangen, 1982; Stolerman & D'Mello, 1981) if not all experimental conditions (Colpaert, 1977; Colpaert, Niemegeers & Janssen, 1977). What then is the importance of using the one as opposed to the other measure?

The importance of using a nominal rather than a quantitative measure of stimulus generalisation is at least two-fold. First, the scale being used defines and limits the statistical and mathematical manipulations and operations which are permissible in handling the data (Siegel, 1956). The use of the nominal measure prevents operations from being implemented which are not permissible and whose outcome can be particularly misleading. To recognise that the sex of mammals can assume only nominal values, prevents the conclusion that an observed population of a given mammal species shows no sexual differentiation because it features equal proportions of males and females. Similarly, to measure generalisation nominally prevents one from concluding that a given test treatment is generalised with neither saline nor training drug because the treatment generated an average of 50% of drug-appropriate responding. Second, the behavioural, pharmacological, and molecular conclusions that can be reached from DD data differ widely depending on whether the dependent variable is taken to be either nominal or quantitative. These differences have been apparent in considering complete generalisations (e.g., Colpaert, 1977, 1978b; Colpaert, Maroli & Meert 1982), but have become frankly decisive in recent studies of partial generalisation (Colpaert, 1983; Colpaert & Janssen, 1983; Colpaert, Niemegeers & Janssen, 1982). The nature of the dependent variable may therefore constitute perhaps the most important single issue in current DD research.

In summary, this chapter has outlined some features of drug discrimination as a paradigm of behavioural pharmacology. Available evidence indicates that the paradigm has a powerful resolving capacity in analysing the behavioural actions of a diversity of pharmacological agents. It is further argued that the dependent variable of the drug discrimination experiment is nominal rather than quantitative in nature, and that much of the paradigm's utility results from its ability to compress the complexity of behavioural drug effects into the simplest possible format of variation, i.e., a binary response. Some doubt is also raised about the generalisation (Skinner, 1938) that rate of responding is the principal datum in the study of an operant. Finally, it is suggested that the analysis and understanding of the behavioural, pharmacological, and molecular aspects of drug action depend greatly on the nature of the behaviours that serve as the dependent variables in the paradigms of behavioural pharmacology.

REFERENCES

Appel, J. B., White, F. J., & Holohean, A. M. (1983) Analyzing mechanism(s) of hallucinogenic drug action with drug discrimination procedures. *Neuroscience and Biobehavioral Reviews*, **6**, 529–536.

Ayd, F. J. & Blackwell, B. (Eds.) (1970) *Discoveries in biological psychiatry*. Philadelphia: J. B. Lippincott Company.

Barry, H. III & Krimmer, E. C. (1977) Discriminable stimuli produced by alcohol and other CNS depressants. In H. Lal (Ed.), *Discriminative stimulus properties of drugs*. New York: Plenum Press. 73–92.

Bunge, M. (1980) From neuron to behavior and meutation: an exercise in levelmanship. In H. M. Pinsker & W. D. Willis (Eds.), *Information processing in the nervous system*. New York: Raven Press. 1–16.

Colpaert F. C. (1977) Drug-produced cues and states: Some theoretical and methodological inferences. In H. Lal (Ed.), *Discriminative Stimulus Properties of Drugs*. New York: Plenum Press. 5–21.

Colpaert, F. C. (1978a) Discriminative stimulus properties of narcotic analgesic drugs. *Pharmacology, Biochemistry and Behavior*, **9**, 863–887.

Colpaert, F. C. (1978b) Some properties of drugs as physiological signals: The FR procedure and signal detection theory. In F. C. Colpaert & J. L. Slangen (Eds.), *Stimulus Properties of Drugs*. Amsterdam: Elsevier Biomedical Press. 217–242.

Colpaert, F. C. (1982) The pharmacological specificity of opiate drug discrimination. In F. C. Colpaert & J. L. Slangen (Eds.), *Drug Discrimination: Applications in CNS Pharmacology*. Amsterdam: Elsevier Biomedical Press. 3–10.

Colpaert, F. C. (1983) Drug discrimination: Behavioral, pharmacological, and molecular mechanisms of subjective drug effects. In S. R. Goldbert & I. P. Stolerman (Eds.), *Behavioral analysis of drug dependence*. New York: Academic Press, (in press).

Colpaert, F. C. & Janssen, P. A. J. (1983) Agonist and antagonist effects of prototype opiate drugs in rats discriminating fentanyl from saline: Partial generalization and opiate receptor theory (Submitted for publication).

Colpaert, F. C., Maroli, A. N., & Meert, T. (1982) Parametric effects in the discrimination of intracranial stimulation: Some methodological and analytical issues. *Physiology and Behavior*, **28**, 1047–1058.

Colpaert, F. C., Niemegeers, C. J. E., & Janssen, P. A. J. (1976) Theoretical and methodological considerations on drug discrimination learning. *Psychopharmacologia*, **46**, 169–177.

Colpaert, F. C., Niemegeers, C. J. E., & Janssen, P. A. J. (1977) Differential haloperidol effects on two indices of fentanyl-saline discrimination. *Psychopharmacology*, **53**, 169–173.

Colpaert, F. C., Niemegeers, C. J. E., & Janssen, P. A. J. (1978) Neuroleptic interference with the cocaine cue: Internal stimulus control of behavior and psychosis. *Psychopharmacology*, **58**, 245–255.

Colpaert, F. C., Niemegeers, C. J. E., & Janssen, P. A. J. (1979) Discriminative stimulus properties of cocaine: Neuropharmacological characteristics as derived from stimulus generalization experiments. *Pharmacology, Biochemistry and Behaviour*, **10**, 535–546.

Colpaert, F. C., Niemegeers, C. J. E., & Janssen, P. A. J. (1980a) Factors regulating drug cue sensitivity: Limits of discriminability and the role of a progressively decreasing training dose in fentanyl-saline discrimination. *Journal of Pharmacology and Experimental Therapeutics*, **212**, 474–480.

Colpaert, F. C., Niemegeers, C. J. E., & Janssen, P. A. J. (1980b) Factors regulating drug cue sensitivity: The effect of training dose in fentanyl-saline discrimination. *Neuropharmacology*, **19**, 705–713.

Colpaert, F. C., Niemegeers, C. J. E., & Janssen, P. A. J. (1982) A drug discrimination analysis of lysergic acid diethylamide (LSD): *In vivo* agonist and antagonist effects of purported 5-hydroxytryptamine antagonists and of pirenperone, a LSD-antagonist. *Journal of Pharmacology and Experimental Therapeutics*, **221**, 206–214.

Colpaert, F. C. & Rosecrans, J. A. (Eds.) (1978) *Stimulus properties of drugs: Ten years of progress*. Amsterdam: Elsevier Biomedical Press.

Colpaert, F. C. & Slangen, J. L. (Eds.) (1982) *Drug discrimination: Applications in CNS pharmacology*. Amsterdam: Elsevier Biomedical Press.

Dews, P. B. (1958) Stimulant actions of methamphetamine. *Journal of Pharmacology and Experimental Therapeutics*, **122**, 137–147.

Gilbert, R. M. & Sutherland, N. S. (Eds.) (1969) *Animal Discrimination Learning*. New York: Academic Press.

Glennon, R. A., Rosecrans, J. A., & Young, R. (1982) The use of the drug discrimination paradigm for studying hallucinogenic agents. A review. In F. C. Colpaert & J. L. Slangen, (Eds.), *Drug Discrimination: Applications in CNS Pharmacology*. Amsterdam: Elsevier Biomedical Press. 69–98.

Guttman, N. & Kalish, H. I. (1956) Discriminability and stimulus generalization. *Journal of Experimental Psycholology*, **51**, 79–88.

Herling, S. & Woods, J. H. (1981) Discriminative stimulus effects of narcotics: Evidence for multiple receptor-mediated actions. *Life Sciences*, **28**, 1571–1584.

Ho, B. T. & Silverman, P. B. (1976) Stimulants as discriminative stimuli. In F. C. Colpaert & J. A. Rosecrans (Eds.), *Stimulus Properties of Drugs: Ten Years of Progress*. Amsterdam: Elsevier Biomedical Press. 53–68.

Honig, W. K. & Urcuioli, P. J. (1981) The legacy of Guttman and Kalish (1956): 25 years of research on stimulus generalization. *Journal of the Experimental Analysis of Behavior*, **36**, 405–445.

Holtzman, S. G. (1982a) Stimulus properties of opioids with mixed agonist and antagonist activity. *Federations Proceedings*, **41**, 2328–2332.

Holtzman, S. G. (1982b) Discriminative stimulus properties of opioids in the rat and squirrel monkey. In F. C. Colpaert & J. L. Slangen, (Eds.), *Drug Discrimination: Applications in CNS Pharmacology*. Amsterdam: Elsevier Biomedical Press. 17–36.

Järbe, T. U. C. & Swedberg, M. D. B. (1982) A conceptualization of drug discrimination learning. In F. C. Colpaert & J. L. Slangen (Eds.), *Drug Discrimination: Applications in CNS Pharmacology*. Amsterdam: Elsevier Biomedical Press. 327–341.

Koek, W. & Slangen, J. L. (1982) The role of fentanyl training dose and of the alternative stimulus condition in drug generalization. *Psychopharmacology*, **76**, 149–156.

Pickens, R. (1977) Behavioral pharmacology: A brief history. In T. Thompson & P. B. Dews (Eds.), *Advances in behavioral pharmacology* (Volume I) New York: Academic Press.

Shannon, H. E. & Holtzman S. G. (1976) Evaluation of the discriminative effects of morphine in the rat. *Journal of Pharmacology and Experimental Therapeutics*, **198**, 54–65.

Shearman, G. T. & Herz, A. (1982) Generalization and antagonism studies with rats trained to discriminate an effect of the proposed sigma receptor agonist N-allylnormetazocine (SKF 10,047). In F. C. Colpaert & J. L. Slangen (Eds.), *Drug Discrimination: Applications in CNS Pharmacology*. Amsterdam: Elsevier Biomedical Press. 37–48.

Siegel, S. (1956) *Non parametric statistics*. New York: McGraw-Hill.

Skinner, B. F. (1938) The behavior of organisms: An experimental analysis. New York: Appleton-Century-Crofts.

Skinner, B. F. (1959) Animal research in pharmacotherapy of mental illness. In J. O. Cole & R. W. Gerard (Eds.), *Psychopharmacology: Problems in evaluation*. NAS-NRC Publication No. 583. Washington: National Academy of Sciences.

Stevens, S. S. (1946) On the theory of scales of measurement. *Science*, **103**, 677–680.

Stolerman, I. P. & D'Mello G. D. (1981) Role of training conditions in discrimination of central nervous system stimulants by rats. *Psychopharmacology*, **73**, 295–303.

Stolerman, I. P., Baldy, R. E., & Shine, P. J. (1982) Drug discrimination procedure: A bibliography. In F. C. Colpaert & J. L. Slangen (Eds.), *Drug Discrimination: Applications in CNS Pharmacology*. Amsterdam: Elsevier Biomedical Press. 401–441.

Sutherland, N. S. & Mackintosh, N. J. (Eds.) (1971) *Mechanisms of Animal Discrimination Learning*. New York: Academic Press.

Thompson, T. & Dews, P. B. (Eds.) (1977) *Advances in behavioral pharmacology* (Volume I) New York: Academic Press.

Thompson, T. & Dews, P. B. (Eds.) (1979) *Advances in behavioral pharmacology* (Volume II) New York: Academic Press.

Thompson, T., Dews, P. B., & McKim, W. (Eds.) (1981) *Advances in behavioral pharmacology* (Volume III) New York: Academic Press.

Thompson, T. & Pickens, R. (1971) *Stimulus properties of drugs*. New York: Appleton-Century-Crofts.

Thompson, T. & Schuster, C. R. (1968) *Behavioral pharmacology*. Englewood Cliffs: Prentice-Hall.

Weissman, A. (1978) Generalization of the discriminative stimulus properties of Δ^9-tetrahydrocannabinol to cannabinoids with therapeutic potential. In F. C. Colpaert & J. A. Rosecrans (Eds.), *Stimulus Properties of Drugs: Ten Years of Progress*. Amsterdam: Elsevier Biomedical Press. 99–124.

Winter, J. C. (1973) A comparison of the stimulus properties of mescaline and 2,3,4-trimethoxyphenyl-ethylamine. *Journal of Pharmacology and Experimental Therapeutics*, **185**, 101–107.

15 Rate-Independent Approaches to the Analysis of Drug Action

T. W. Robbins and J. L. Evenden
University of Cambridge, Department of Experimental Psychology

As Cooper (1981) has recently pointed out, two main approaches have been taken in the analysis of the behavioural effects of drugs. The first of these, the rate-dependency principle, is based on an empirical generalisation by Dews and his colleagues (Dews & Wenger, 1977) about data obtained on drug effects using operant techniques. The second approach, emanating from Neal Miller (Miller, 1964), has assumed that many psychoactive drugs act upon motivational or reinforcement mechanisms and that the changes in behaviour produced by drugs result indirectly from this action. There has been some interaction between these two levels of explanation, because one of the main measures of change in motivational state is, of course, response rate. The two main manipulations employed in experiments on motivation are to vary the motivational status of an animal, for example, by food deprivation or injections of testosterone, or to vary the nature of the terminal reinforcing event, for example, food, access to a sexual partner, or postponement of shock.

Response rate usually behaves in a predictable way in response to these manipulations, thus providing a consistent data base for comparing the effects of drugs. But most drugs do not have selective motivational effects. For example, d-amphetamine increases low rates of responding with many different reinforcers including intracranial stimulation, food, water, light, shock postponement, and shock presentation (see Robbins, 1981 for a review). One might then be tempted to argue that this drug generally enhances the effects of all reinforcers. But one problem with this account is the other side of the coin—that this drug reduces high control rates of responding maintained by the same events. On the basis of such evidence, it has been argued that amphetamine generally increases low rates of responding and reduces high rates. The effect of the drug therefore depends on the control rate of responding. This rate-dependency principle argues that the control rate of responding is the most important consideration when interpreting the behavioural effects of drugs. The strongest version of the principle is that the influence of all other variables (including motivational ones) can be assimilated to rate of responding (cf. Dews & Wenger, 1977), but it is evident that the nature of the reinforcer can modulate the effects of amphetamine and other drugs, if only in a minor way. For example, chlordiazepoxide tends to increase responding resulting in food presentation but to decrease responding resulting in shock presentation, with morphine having the opposite pattern of effects (McKearney, 1974; Barrett, 1976). In general, however, it is hard to deny that the existence of rate-dependent effects argues against monolithic actions of drugs on motivational processes.

This does not in turn imply that rate-dependency is a sufficient account of the behavioural effects of drugs. Although rate-dependency cannot be explained in terms of motivational constructs, it may well result from some other type of behavioural process. Previously, Robbins (1981) described and discussed the evidence for the three major explanations of rate-dependent effects, which can be summarised thus:

1. Impaired Stimulus Control (Ksir, 1981; McKim, 1981)

Either the drug itself acts as a stimulus which alters the environmental context controlling behaviour or the drug may impair the sensory processing of that environment (or both of these may occur). For example, loss of temporal control of responding would be responsible for the flattening of the fixed-interval scallop, or such changes in rate could result from the distracting or disinhibitory properties of extraneous or interoceptive stimuli, including the drug itself. Specifically, McKim (1981) invokes separate possible mechanisms for the rate-increasing and rate-decreasing effects of drugs—Pavlovian disinhibition, and external inhibition, respectively. Ksir (1981) emphasises the possible convergence of responding to a constant rate (also noted by Gonzalez & Byrd, 1977) as evidence for impaired stimulus control. This is the most general of the three hypotheses; the other two are designed more expressly to account for the rate-dependent effects of stimulants as opposed to other classes of drugs.

2. Conditioned Reinforcement (Hill, 1970)

This is an attempt to explain the apparently paradoxical effects subsumed under rate-dependency with a reinforcement-based model. Hill (1970) has suggested that stimulant drugs such as amphetamine, while not increasing the reinforcing value of stimuli such as food, do enhance the conditioned reinforcing properties of stimuli paired with such reinforcers. There is undoubtedly some evidence which is consistent with this hypothesis (Hill, 1970; Robbins, 1976) and it is possible, in theory, to extend it to rate-dependent effects. Animals responding under schedules of reinforcement receive many pairings of primary reinforcement with the proprioceptive and kinaesthetic feedback arising from responding, which may thereby gain conditioned reinforcing effects. Then, under amphetamine, for example, the animal may respond as though under a continuously-reinforced schedule with response feedback as the reinforcer. This would result in increases in low rates of responding or reductions in high rates, both of which are normally under scheduled control of the primary reinforcer.

3. Behavioural Competition

This hypothesis attempts to account for rate-dependency in amphetamine-treated animals by postulating that the drug increases the frequency of all responses having some minimal tendency, including "unconditioned" behaviour, such as locomotion, initially at the expense of behaviour requiring long pauses (Lyon & Robbins, 1975; Grilly, 1977). An increase in low control rates of operant behaviour will be seen, but high control rates may be reduced because of competition from other stimulated activities. This notion depends on considering the high rate activities as sequences of responses that are susceptible to shortening by the drug (cf. Lyon & Robbins, 1975). Similarly, at high doses of d-amphetamine, the effect on the operant behaviour which survives will depend on the compatibility of the operant with the other activities affected by the drug. At these high doses, the rate-dependency relationship may break down because even initially low rate activities may have been occluded by other stimulated behaviour. At very low doses, the drug effect may similarly deviate from rate-dependency because the shortening of other sequences of behaviour with longer pauses may enable rate-increasing effects of the drug upon target operants to be observed, even if the target behaviour is occurring at a high rate under control conditions.

In this article, we will mainly be concerned with the behavioural competition hypothesis, although we will also be alluding to the other hypotheses concerning stimulus control and conditioned reinforcement, in order to make not only the differences, but also the interrelationships, between the three positions clear, in attempting a more integrated account. We will be concerned primarily with the behavioural effects of amphetamine, not only because this drug and related compounds produce the most pronounced rate-dependent effects, but also because their neuropharmacological modes of action upon the catecholamine neurotransmitters, dopamine and noradrenaline, are relatively specific and well understood. Understanding the behavioural actions of these drugs may then provide us with insight into the functions of the catecholamines in the central nervous system.

BEHAVIOURAL COMPETITION

The behavioural competition hypothesis assumes that there are interactions between different responses and that the effect of amphetamine depends to a marked extent on the overall pattern of behaviour. In turn, this implies that measuring the average rate of a particular response is unlikely to provide a sufficient explanation of rate-dependent effects, or of the effects of amphetamine.

Although this strategy would appear to run counter to Dews' original argument (1958) that we study functional units of behaviour in isolation in a way perhaps analogous to physiological variables, this is not the case. For example, compared to the time of Dews' writing we now know enough about the effects of stimulant drugs on many of these isolated functional units of behaviour to determine their individual dose-response curves (cf. Grilly, 1977) and to begin to examine reasons for their differences and characteristic forms. The overall goal of the research is to specify the dose-response functions for the actual physiological or behavioural processes which underlie these functional units of behaviour.

A simple approach to this problem would be to measure the effects of amphetamine on several responses, and also concurrently to remove, by pharmacological means, the effect of the drug on one or more of these responses. It is by now quite well established that the locomotor stimulant effect of amphetamine can be attenuated by depletion of dopamine in the vicinity of the nucleus accumbens, using the neurotoxin 6-hydroxydopamine (6-OHDA) (Kelly, Seviour & Iversen, 1975). Recently, Robbins, Roberts and Koob (1983) examined the effects of such treatment upon the rate dependent effects of d-amphetamine. Simultaneously measuring locomotor activity and lever pressing under a fixed interval—60 sec (FI-60 sec) schedule of reinforcement in an operant chamber we found that d-amphetamine elevated the unconditioned locomotor activity in the operant setting and that lesions of the nucleus accumbens blocked this effect, as well as significantly attenuating both the rate-increasing and rate-decreasing effects of the drug. Because the lesion itself altered control levels of responding, it was necessary to take these altered rates themselves into account by calculating the slope of the regression line linking the drug effect to the control rate for each rat individually. The results are shown in Fig. 15.1. There were significant differences in the

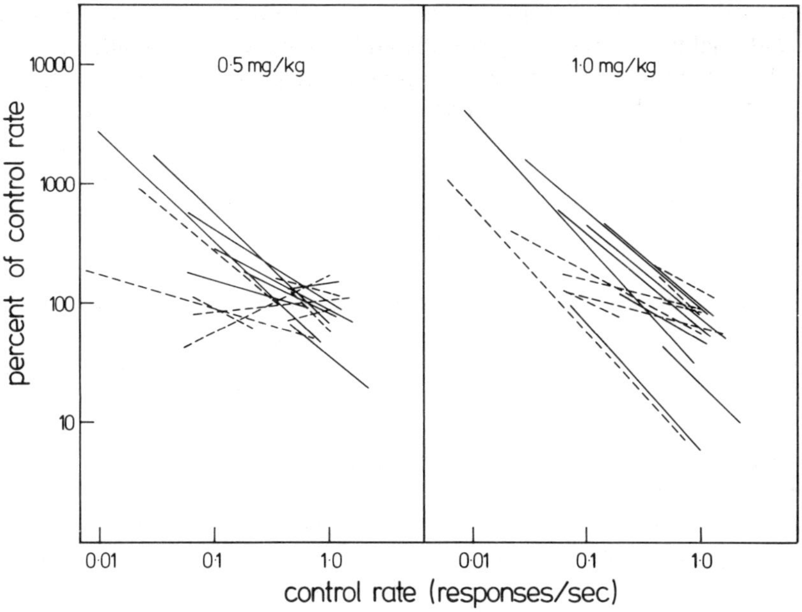

FIG. 15.1. Rate-dependency slopes for rats receiving 0.5 or 1.0 mg/kg of d-amphetamine following 6-OHDA lesions of the nucleus accumbens (dashed lines) or sham operations (solid lines). Abscissa; control rate of responding. Ordinate; drug effect. Each line represents an individual rat. The mean slope is significantly greater at 1.0 mg/kg of d-amphetamine for the sham group ($t = 2.31$, df 14; $p < 0.05$), but not at 0.5 mg/kg ($t = 1.35$, df 14). Data calculated from results reported by Robbins, Roberts & Koob, 1983.

rate-dependency slopes for the sham-operated and lesioned rats, so the altered effect of the drug on operant behaviour was not merely a result of changes in control rate but could be attributed directly to the lesion. In addition, it appeared that the reductions in amphetamine-induced locomotor activity caused by the lesion accompanied the attenuated rate-dependent effects of d-amphetamine, in support of the Lyon-Robbins hypothesis. Although locomotor activity was increased by the drug throughout the interval, this only competed effectively with the high terminal rates of lever-pressing. At the beginning of the interval presumably both locomotion and lever pressing competed with a third, unrecorded, form of behaviour.

Evidence from an earlier experiment with the same rats supports this conclusion. The FI-60 sec schedule was used not only to measure rate-dependent effects but also to generate adjunctive behaviour such as drinking at the beginning of the interval so that the characteristic positively-accelerated scallop of fixed interval responding was matched by the mirror image scallop of licking earlier in the interval. d-Amphetamine is known to reduce this adjunctive drinking (Sanger & Blackman, 1978). But 6-OHDA lesions of the nucleus accumbens, in addition to reducing the rate-dependent effects of d-amphetamine on operant behaviour, also reduced its attenuating effects upon adjunctive licking. There are several important points arising from this result. First, as shown in Robbins, Roberts and Koob (1983) it is difficult to see the changes in adjunctive licking as examples of rate-dependency—indeed the higher rates of licking occurring at the beginning of the interval were reduced proportionately less than lower rates later in the interval. This result argues that a simple rate-dependent analysis is insufficient to explain the overall pattern of results and that some additional principle is required. Second, coupled with the increases in low rates of operant responding occurring early in the interval, this suggests that rats treated with amphetamine were switching away from bouts of licking and were instead responding on the lever under the FI schedule of reinforcement. Therefore, it would appear that there is a competition between licking and lever-pressing, resulting in a more likely switching from the former to the latter. This tendency was evidently blocked to some extent by dopamine depletion in the nucleus accumbens.

This response switching is vectorial from licking in one location to lever pressing in another. This was evident from earlier work, for example by Nieto, Makhlouf and Rodriguez (1979) and could result of course from many factors. One plausible possibility, however, might be that switching between responses is controlled to some extent by factors associated with reinforcement: The drug-treated rat, as in the Nieto, Makhlouf and Rodriguez study, spending much more time in the vicinity of the reinforcer dispenser. Another possibility might be that the types of response topography involved (licking versus lever pressing) might be differentially susceptible to the effects of amphetamine. A further question might be whether the change in response switching itself depended upon the increase in locomotor activity produced by amphetamine (since movement from the water tube to the lever necessarily involves locomotion) or whether these increases in locomotion were simply expressions of a more fundamental process of response switching (given that all movement involves switching from one form of behaviour to another).

There have been a number of other studies suggesting that amphetamine does increase the likelihood of an animal switching from one form of behaviour to another, involving both unconditioned and conditioned forms of behaviour. For example, Norton (1973) reported that the bout duration of a large number of different categories of observed behaviour was reduced by amphetamine, suggesting an enhanced rate of transition from one category to another. Laties (1972) reported that pigeons trained to respond under fixed consecutive number (FCN) schedules for access to a second key showed an increased number of premature switches to this second key after amphetamine treatment, and Laties, Wood and Cooper Rees (1981) recently found similar results in rats. Moerschbaecher, Thompson and Thomas (1979) also found increased switching between keys in monkeys trained to respond under a fixed-interval schedule where responding could be distributed among six different keys. In this article we review some of our recent work on response switching with amphetamine and other drugs which attempts to characterise it systematically and to provide some behavioural explanation of this effect.

RESPONSE SWITCHING

In the present work, we have adapted a schedule devised by Morgan (1974) to measure the effects of amphetamine on response switching between two topographically similar responses, pressing levers situated on either side of a central food tray. We have measured the *probability* of switching as the number of switch responses divided by the total number of responses minus, of course, the first response after each delivery of food. We have also measured to the nearest 10 msec, the interval between the two lever presses constituting the switch. This inter-response time (IRT) provides an index of local *rate* of responding. The schedule is depicted schematically in Fig. 15.2.

Briefly, rats are trained to distribute responding between two levers with a random sequence of reinforcement. At the beginning of the session, following the delivery of a free food pellet, the computer selects with $p = 0.5$ which lever is next to provide reinforcement. No amount of responding on the unselected lever will produce reinforcement. Responding on the selected lever is reinforced according to a random ratio schedule. In some experiments, this ratio was varied, since the control level of switching is dependent upon this parameter, but in most of the experiments to be described here the probability of reinforcement was set at 0.30. Performance under this schedule also has several other important properties which make it useful for measuring the effects of amphetamine, and other drugs, as will become apparent later in the article. It is also, of course, feasible to measure basic aspects of performance, including rate of responding.

There have been a number of demonstrations (Evenden & Robbins, 1983a; Robbins & Watson, 1981) that amphetamine produces dose-dependent increases in the probability of switching under this schedule. Figure 15.3, for example, shows data reproduced from Robbins and Watson (1981). d-Amphetamine produced monotonic, dose-dependent increases in the probability of response switching even at doses which had no effect on average rate of responding. By contrast, the neuroleptic drug,

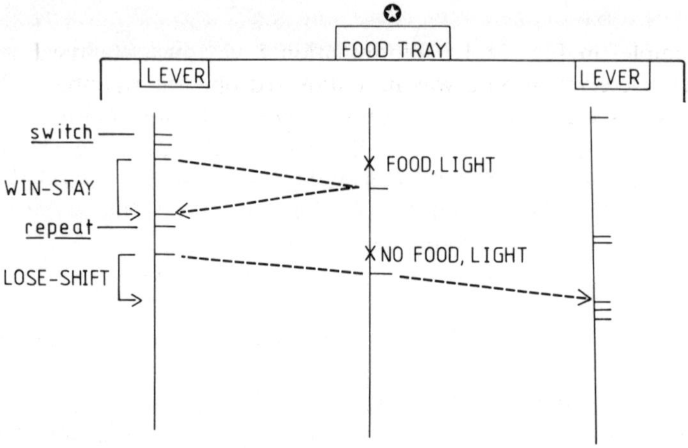

DEFINITIONS

1) Rate: total lever responses / time
2) Spatial Bias: return to SAME lever
3) Win-Stay: return to REWARDED lever
4) Lose-Shift: avoid NON-REWARDED lever
5) SI: sensitivity of response choice to reward
6) RI: repetition of last response regardless of reward
7) repeat: consecutive responses on SAME lever
8) switch: consecutive responses on OPPOSITE levers

FIG. 15.2. Schematic description of the standard schedule (cf. Morgan, 1974) used in this article, together with the definitions of various terms used. See text and Evenden and Robbins (1983a, 1983b) for more details. The rat begins with a non-rewarded response on the right hand lever and then switches to the left lever, making two repeat responses, the last one of which is reinforced. The rat then collects food at the food tray, which is illuminated and afterwards returns to the just-reinforced lever, thus showing win-stay behaviour. A repeat response follows before another switch to the right lever, a repeat and a switch back to the left lever which is given explicit non-reinforcement (tray light, but no food). The rat then lose-shifts to the right lever following its required visit to the food tray, and makes two repeated responses there. Perseverative responding (not illustrated) occurs when the rat continues to respond in the presence of the illuminated food tray.

α-flupenthixol, reduced response rate, while not affecting response switching. These effects on response switching were generally replicated in a later study by Evenden and Robbins (1983a) in a number of different situations in which the response topographies involved in switching were different. For example, in Fig. 15.4, Determination 1 was in a standard operant chamber. Determination 2 was in a standard operant chamber in which Perspex walls were added between the levers and the food magazine to increase the response cost of switching and thus reduce its probability. Determination 3 was in an apparatus with three holes monitored by infra-red photocell beams, in which the rat had to return to the central hole on each occasion to complete either a repetition or a switch. Thus, the response cost and topographies of repetition and switching were made similar. The apparatus for this experiment is shown schematically in Fig. 1 of Evenden and Robbins (1983a). The results again were quite clear. Parallel increases in response switching were obtained which peaked at about 0.8 or 1.6 mg/kg. Thus, over quite wide baseline values (0.10–0.55), d-amphetamine increased the probability of switching. Other studies have shown that this effect of d-amphetamine has a degree of pharmacological specificity. For example, Evenden and Robbins (1983b) showed that simi-

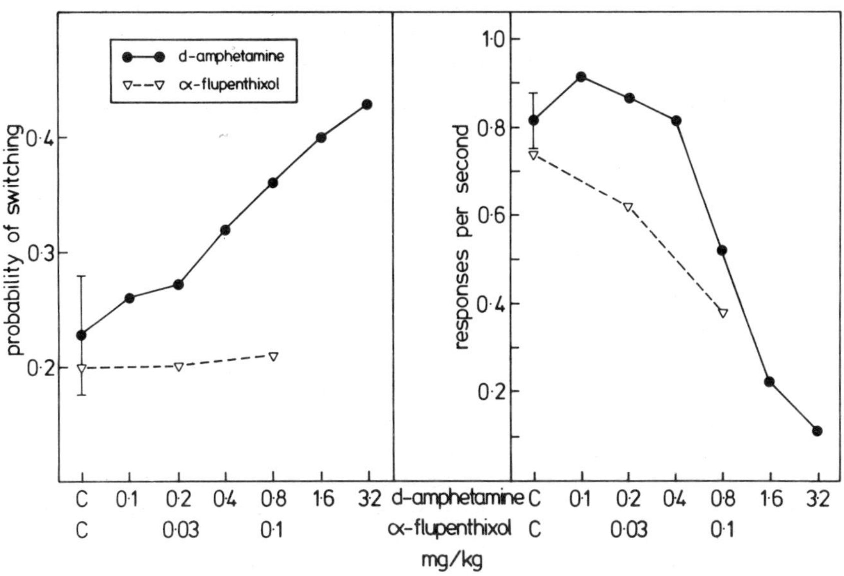

FIG. 15.3. Effect of *d*-amphetamine on behaviour in the rat under a schedule designed to measure different probabilities of repetition and switching across two levers. Left: the dose-dependent, monotonic increase in probability of response switching produced by d-amphetamine. Right: note the relative lack of effect by d-amphetamine at doses producing significant changes in switching. Values are plotted as means ± 1SD for 5 rats. Also shown are data for three of the same rats for two doses of the neuroleptic α-flupenthixol. (Data recalculated from Robbins and Watson, 1981).

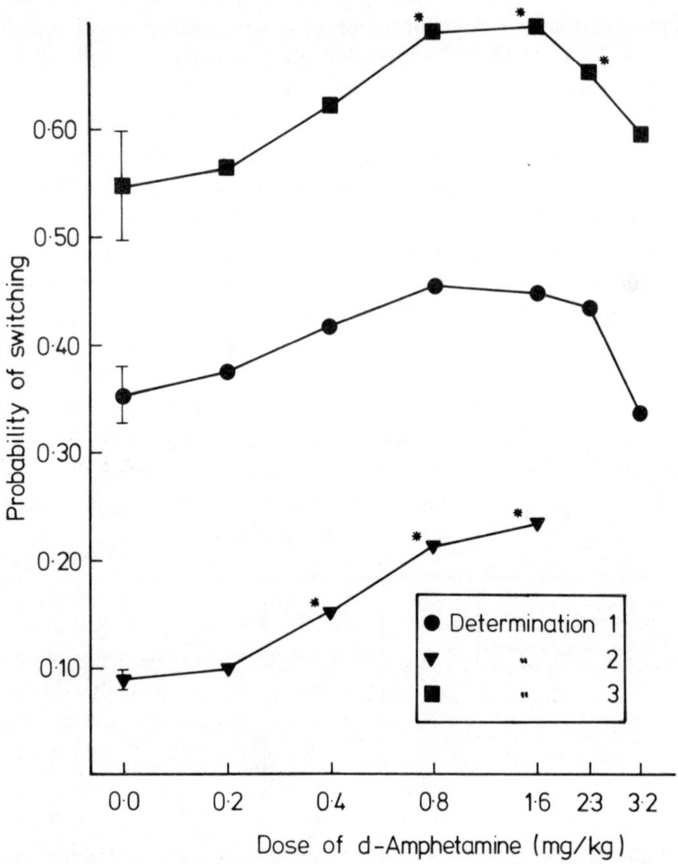

FIG. 15.4. The effect of d-amphetamine on the probability of switching in three different situations (Determinations 1–3). Data redrawn from Evenden and Robbins, 1983a. Asterisks indicate significant differences, compared with control. See text for further details.

lar effects could not be obtained with doses of chlordiazepoxide that significantly reduced response rate (Fig. 15.5) and other work has indicated that apomorphine, the direct dopamine receptor agonist, produces only increases in response repetition (Robbins, 1980).

Associated with the increased probabilities of switching following d-amphetamine are increased speeds of switching. For example Fig. 15.6 shows the relative frequency of IRTs of graded duration, either between two consecutive responses on the SAME lever or between two consecutive responses on DIFFERENT levers. Although there was little effect of d-amphetamine at low doses on SAME IRTs, there was an increased incidence of short DIFFERENT IRTs following low doses of the drug. But

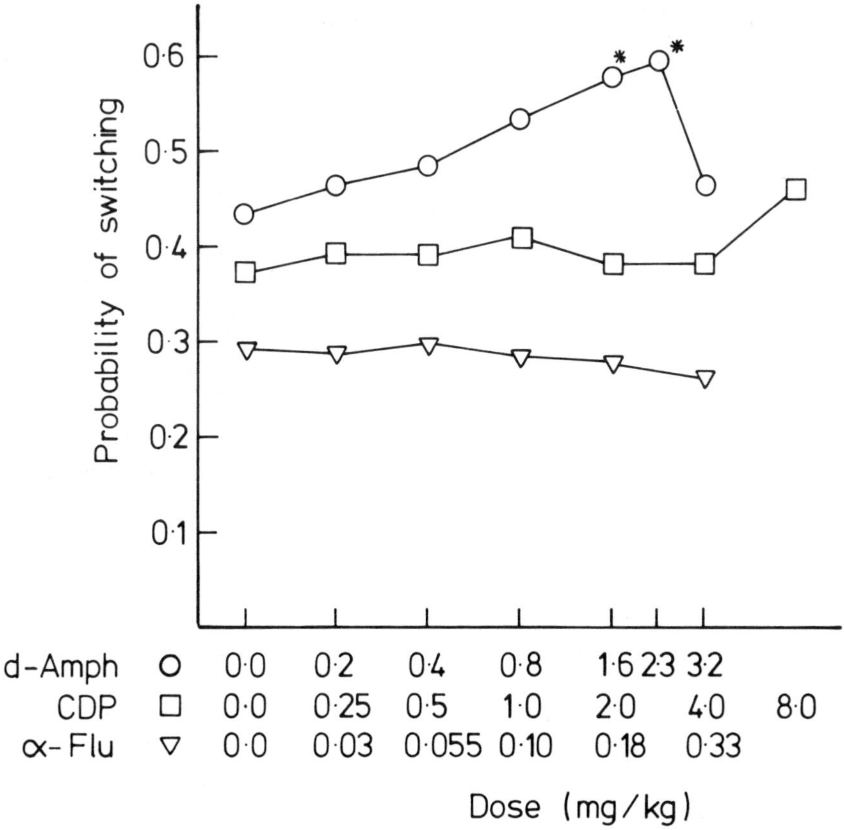

FIG. 15.5. Pharmacological specificity in the effects of d-amphetamine on response switching. CDP = chlordiazepoxide. Asterisks indicate significant differences, compared with control. Data redrawn from Evenden and Robbins, 1983b.

the increased probability of switching did not necessarily covary with shortened switch times. For example, at intermediate and high doses, the probability of switching increased at doses having no effect on switching speed (see also Evenden & Robbins, 1983a).

BEHAVIOURAL BASIS OF THE ENHANCEMENT OF RESPONSE SWITCHING

Although we have chosen to view the increased response switching produced by d-amphetamine as an example of shortened response chains arising from behavioural competition, many other questions could be

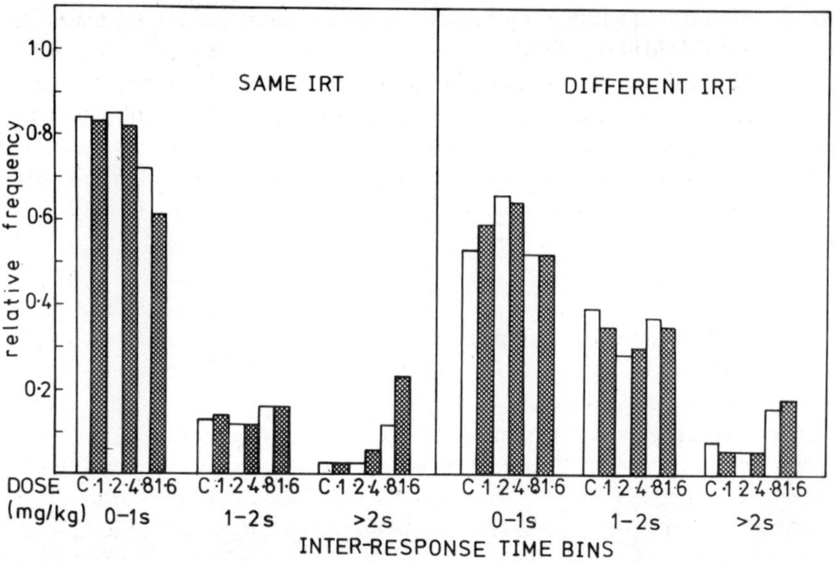

FIG. 15.6. Inter-response time (IRT) distributions for repetition (SAME IRT) and switching (DIFFERENT IRT) of responses on the two levers, under a random schedule (Robbins and Watson, 1981). These data were obtained for the same group of rats whose data on probability of switching are shown in Fig. 15.12, at the P(Rf) = 0.30, condition, which also resulted in increased probability of switching after d-amphetamine. Note the effects of low doses of d-amphetamine on DIFFERENT IRTs. The results should be compared with those for P(Rf) = 1.00 (Fig. 15.12, Robbins, 1981), which were associated with *increased* probabilities of responding.

asked about the interpretation of this effect. For example, does it arise simply because amphetamine increases the effect of the contingency between switching and reinforcement which this schedule entails? Lea and Morgan (1972) have previously shown through simulation that although increased switching is the optimum strategy (assuming zero response cost), it makes little difference in terms of the probability of reinforcement over quite a large range of switching probabilities. Therefore, it seems unlikely that amphetamine enhanced the effect of the contingency, since the efficiency of responding, in terms of procuring reinforcement, remains unchanged by the drug. In addition we have also ruled out this possibility by using concurrent random ratio (conc RR) schedules, where the switch contingency is absent. Amphetamine then still produces dose-related increments in the probability of switching, provided that the rats have some initial tendency to switch on this schedule. Of 12 rats trained under conc RR in the study by Evenden and Robbins (1983a) three rats showed no baseline switching tendency and no elevation in switching after d-amphetamine. Thus, for switching, as for response rate itself, it appears that some minimal tendency is necessary in order for amphetamine to increase it (McMillan, 1968).

Another possibility is that amphetamine in some way reduces the negative effect of response cost, and thus elevates switching, particularly as it is apparent from the control data shown in Fig. 15.4 that the switching is affected in a predictable way by manipulations altering response cost. The same figure, however, provides some evidence against this notion, because in Determination 3 the cost of switching and repetition was nearly equivalent, and yet the drug still increased switching significantly.

Related to the above two possibilities, of enhancing the effects of an implicit contingency of reinforcement and reducing response cost, would be the hypothesis that the drug is enhancing the effects of signals of non-reinforcement, or negative conditioned reinforcement. Thus, the rat may be avoiding the location momentarily paired with non-reinforcement. Conversely, the rat could be seen as tracking an undefined conditioned reinforcer, predictive of, or paired with, food presentation. This hypothesis therefore would seek to explain the elevated switching in terms of enhanced conditioned reinforcement. We have performed the following experiment to test this possibility (Evenden & Robbins, 1985).

Rats were placed under the basic schedule (with P(Rf) = 0.30), which was modified in the following way. Briefly, a light cue was introduced which explicitly signalled which lever was next to receive reinforcement from response to response (Fig. 15.7). Thus, although many responses on the illuminated lever might not necessarily result in food reinforcement, the latter would *only* be forthcoming after responding on the illuminated lever. Pressing the unilluminated lever was punished under the same schedule by explicit omission of the food. The single light and the contingency "moved" from one lever to the other following each non-reinforced response, with a probability set by the computer to be roughly equal to the rat's switching probability in the absence of the light (Fig. 15.7).

An obvious measure of efficiency of performance under this schedule following amphetamine treatment is the proportion of responses on the lit lever. d-Amphetamine increased this proportion significantly at certain doses (see Fig. 15.8). This result clearly suggested that performance following d-amphetamine was under greater control by conditioned reinforcers than usual. But other measures of performance indicated that this was not the case. For example, the proportion of switches made towards the illuminated lever actually decreased significantly (Fig. 15.8) suggesting that the elevated frequency of switching did not result from enhanced tracking of the conditioned reinforcer. Indeed, the reverse seems more likely, that the increased tracking of the conditioned reinforcer was caused by the increased frequency of switching.

A parallel can be drawn with other work apparently showing enhanced

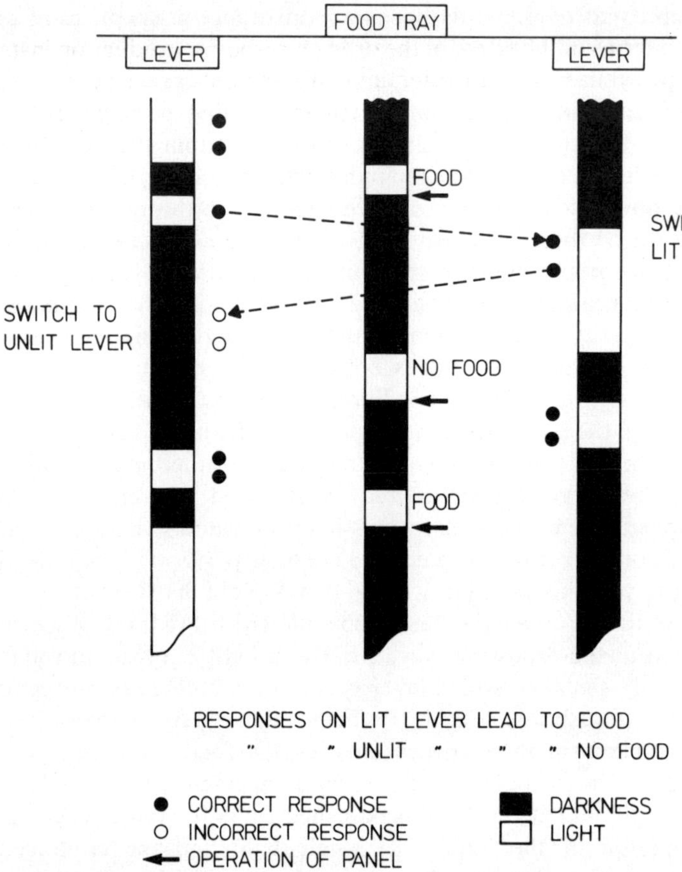

FIG. 15.7. Schematic representation of "light-tracking" experiment. Rats were reinforced only following a response on the illuminated lever, on an intermittent random ratio bias. Responses on the non-illuminated lever were explicitly non-reinforced (light, but omission of food), according to the same random ratio schedule. Hatched arrows show the rats' switching from one lever to another. See text for details.

effects of stimulants upon conditioned reinforcement. For example, Robbins (1976) found that although pipradrol (10mg/kg) increased responding on a lever providing conditioned reinforcement, this behaviour may have been perseverative in nature, with perseveration making some contribution towards the increased responding on the lever providing conditioned reinforcement. These experiments are important because they suggest that rather than directly interacting with reinforcement processes, stimulant drugs make behaviour somewhat autonomous with respect to reinforcement contingencies. Thus, it appears that the changes in response switching are unlikely to be accounted for by Hill's hypothesis and have to be explained in terms of the effect of the drug on response production instead. But it is always possible to offer a reinforcement-based account. For example, it could be argued that, by their frequent pairings with conditioned reinforcers such as the light in the aforementioned experiment, the response feedback from the lever itself gains higher-order conditioned reinforcing properties. These properties may extend even to the switch response itself, the performance of which may be enhanced to the detriment of other contingencies of conditioned reinforcement. This hypothesis is of course exceedingly difficult to test, and there is no ready explanation

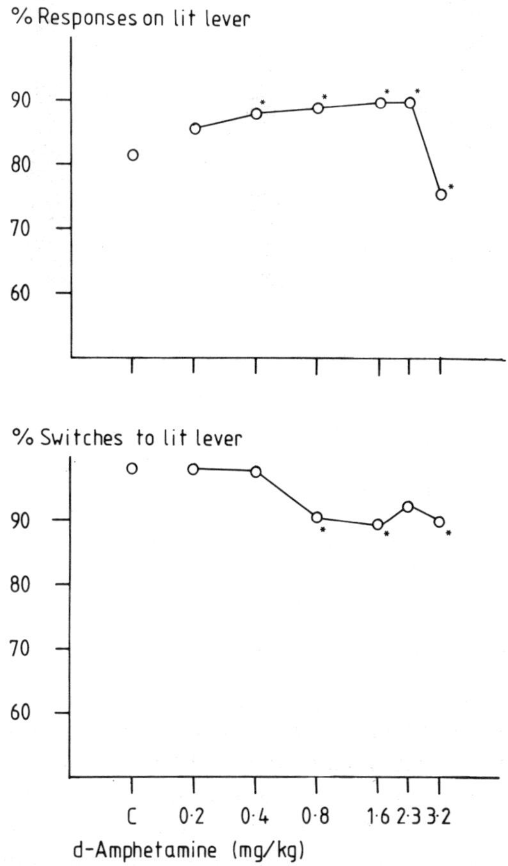

FIG. 15.8. Performance on "light-tracking" experiment following d-amphetamine. Top: Effects of amphetamine on proportion of responses made on the illuminated lever. Bottom: Effects of amphetamine on the proportion of switches made to the illuminated lever. Asterisks for both panels indicate significant differences compared with control.

for why certain conditioned reinforcers should be enhanced and others reduced. There would have to be a drift to control by conditioned reinforcers of interoceptive as opposed to exteroceptive origin, but Hill's hypothesis would seem to be driven into an ever tighter corner by these additional assumptions.

An alternative account of response switching following amphetamine might focus on the primary reinforcer. In all of the previously discussed experiments, food has been used as the reinforcer and amphetamine is well known to have anorectic effects. Increased switching might result from a decline in the motivational control over responding. Two obvious behavioural comparisons that can be made are with extinction and satiation. Extinction can be expected to have biphasic effects on response rate, first perhaps increasing responding in the very short term, and then completely attenuating responding. What happens to response switching under these conditions? Evenden and Robbins (1983b) in fact found that extinction failed to alter response switching either in the short or long term.

Additional pre-feeding resulting in satiation is another way of reducing the influence of food as a reinforcer and producing lower response rates. We have performed several experiments using different methods of satiation. The results are summarised in Fig. 15.9. In general, although various pre-feeding manipulations can be used to suppress response rate to quite low levels, there is little evidence for a specific effect on response switching. Only in one experiment (reported by Evenden & Robbins, 1983b) was there a suggestion that response switching was increased by a pre-feeding procedure. Here, the body weight of rats was maintained by giving access to food for 20 minutes following each day's testing. If this period of access was increased overnight to 12 hours, a marked reduction in response rate was observed, together with a small, but consistent and significant, increase in switching (Fig. 15.9). But in general, it seems unlikely that the large changes in switching produced by amphetamine can be mimicked by prefeeding, and this perhaps weakens the argument that the effects might arise because of the anorectic properties of the drug.

Turning from explanations of enhanced response switching based on motivation and reinforcement, it would seem appropriate to consider the data in terms of the behavioural competition hypothesis. The increased switching would indeed appear to be consistent with the hypothesis, but there are several questions still to be considered:

1. Does the drug produce a shortening of response sequences?
2. Does the drug impair the execution of the full sequence by omitting some of its elements?
3. Is the increased switching attributable to elevated locomotor activity?

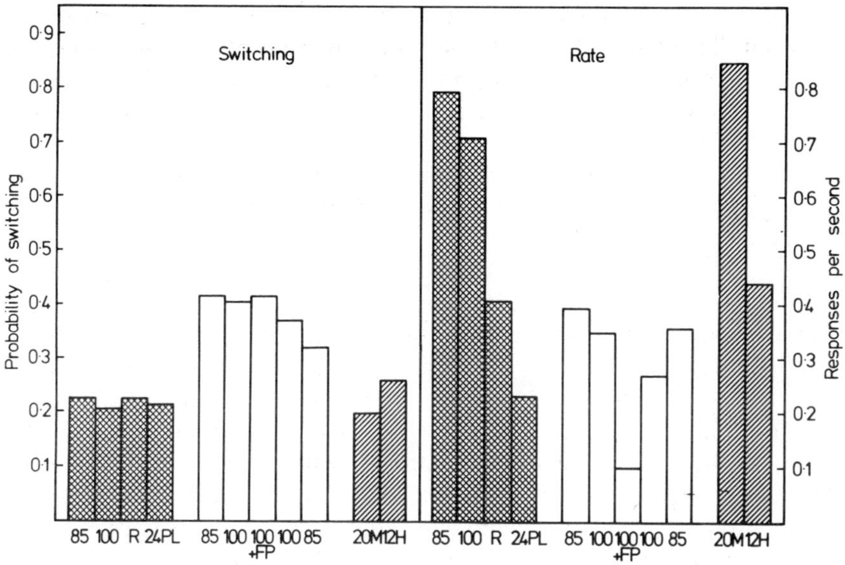

FIG. 15.9. Effects of various pre-feeding procedures on probability of switching (left) and average response rate (right). The three different types of column represent different experiments, with n = 5, 6 and 12 respectively. Key: 85 = 85% original ad lib body weight, 100 = 100% of original ad lib body weight, R = repeated sessions on the same day (after all rats run once, then run again) at 100% bwt. 24PL = access to laboratory chow in home cage for 24 hours preceding the session. 100 + FP = 100% body weight plus 30 min access to Noyes reinforcement pellets prior to the session. 20M = 20 minutes access of food in the night prior to testing. 12H = 12 hours access.

The only significant effects on switching were that there was an increase in 12H compared to 20M, and a decrease for the first 85 compared with the second 85 in the experiment with open histograms. Therefore, "satiation" procedures had much greater effects on rate of responding than on switching.

It may be difficult at this stage to provide definitive answers to these questions, but certainly some relevant evidence can be raised. First, it seems likely that there is generally a shortening of sequences of responses on a single lever at low doses. Direct evidence of shortening of response run lengths by amphetamine can be seen in Fig. 15.10 which presents in some detail the results of some of the determinations which generated the data for response switching shown in Fig. 15.4. Increased response switching produced by 0.4 mg/kg of d-amphetamine (Figs. 15.3 and 15.12) was accompanied by no change in the number of IRTs for SAME responses between 0 and 1 sec (which constitute about 80% of the total number of SAME IRTs). Hence, the duration of the entire sequence would be shortened mainly because there is a reduced number of responses in it which are

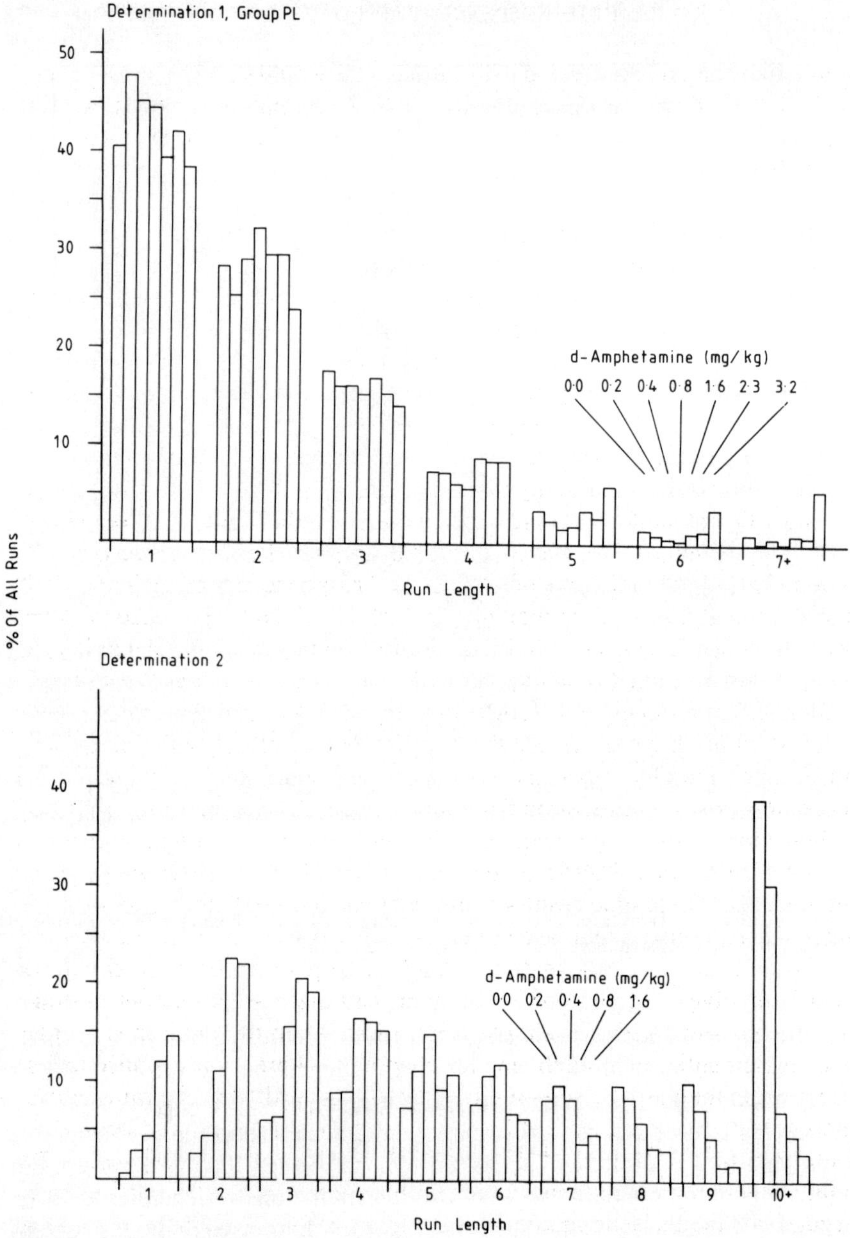

FIG. 15.10. Effects of d-amphetamine on run length (i.e., numbers of consecutive responses on a given lever without a switch). Top: one group (PL) of Determination 1 of Fig. 15.4 (and Fig. 15.11). Note the increased incidence of short (i.e., 1 response) runs at low doses and the increase in long runs, at high doses, of the drug. Bottom: Determination 2 of Fig. 15.4. Note the dose-dependent increases in short runs (1, 2, 3, 4 and 5) and the dose-dependent decreases in long runs (8, 9 and 10). The results illustrate that d-amphetamine generally shortens sequences of responding on either lever.

individually largely unaffected in duration. This would seem to be evidence in favour of behavioural competition. The alternative account would explain the apparent increased switching by postulating ineffective responses which are not registered, but do not necessarily shorten the time taken to complete the sequence. For example, instead of seven responses occupying 10 secs, six complete responses plus an ineffective "missing" response might occupy the same time. Thus, there is an apparent increase in response switching, but only because the proportion of switches to recorded repeat responses increases. Certainly, Weiss and Gott (1972), working with pigeons, found that there were changes in the harmonic distribution of IRTs for key pecks, suggesting that amphetamine increased the incidence of ineffective responses. But we can exclude a similar effect contributing to the present behavioural results, because although the incidence of long IRTs is markedly increased by higher doses of the drug, these are insufficient at lower doses to account for the change in response switching. Similarly, we have additional, unpublished evidence that no second harmonic, indicative of a "missing" response, develops in the IRT distribution at doses of amphetamine which significantly increase switching. The longer IRTs indicate breaks in responding, which a behavioural competition account would explain in the same way as it does the directly analogous rate-dependent reductions in high control baselines. The Lyon-Robbins hypothesis predicts both types of effect with increasing dose, since initially, response sequences are shortened, and then with increasing doses, competition from other, generally unconditioned, forms of behaviour causes significant gaps in conditioned responding to occur.

One of the critical questions remaining is whether the increased switching under amphetamine results from an enhanced tendency to locomote, since this response is increased over a similar dose-range in the rat (Segal, 1975), and as switching in the "standard" operant chamber situation clearly involves a locomotor component. But there are a number of findings inconsistent with this simple view. First, when the random schedule was implemented in a much smaller chamber, where two response holes (for nose-poking) were separated by about the width of the rat's body, increases in switching were still evident (unpublished results). Second, in Determination 3 of Fig. 15.4, repetition and switching had essentially equivalent motor components which both included locomotion. It might be argued that in this last experiment the rats developed a 'ballistic' tendency to continue their movement from one peripheral hole to the central hole towards the other peripheral hole, so that switching was artificially elevated. However, in Determination 2 (Fig. 15.4) it was necessary for the rat to change its direction of movement on at least two occasions. If amphetamine did indeed reduce the rat's ability to reverse its direction of movement, it would be expected that this complex response would decrease, but the reverse occurred. Thus, the strong suggestion from these experiments is that increased locomotion is unlikely to be a sufficient explanation of response switching.

PROBABILITY-DEPENDENCY

All of the effects described so far have been found with a single value of the probability of reinforcement (p = 0.30). Questions concerning the generality of the heightened switching must therefore be raised, especially given the lessons of rate-dependency. Does the response switching effect following amphetamine depend upon the control level of switching? Initial observations might suggest that it does not. Although only one probability of reinforcement has been employed, the use of different situations and response topographies has generated a range of different baseline values of switching. In each case, however, amphetamine has elevated switching significantly above control values.

More detailed observations, however, suggest that the size of the effect does sometimes depend on the control level of switching. Figure 15.11 shows data for the three different groups of rats comprising Determination 1 of Fig. 15.4. Rats were divided into these three groups for a separate experiment, the purpose of which is irrelevant to our present concerns and which will not be discussed here. Group NL had the houselight on during the trial, Group PL had a light turned on above the just-reinforced lever, whereas Group RL had the light turned on above the just-non-reinforced lever. For reasons not entirely clear to us, the three groups differed in their baseline probabilities of switching (Fig. 15.11). As can be seen from this figure, only the two groups with the lower levels of switching showed an elevated switching response. Indeed, while exhibiting no increase in switching at lower doses, Group PL actually showed reduced switching at 3.2 mg/kg.

Robbins and Watson (1981) obtained perhaps clearer evidence of probability dependency by varying the probability of reinforcement (P(Rft)) systematically in the same group of rats in order to generate different baseline probabilities of switching. After a stable baseline was obtained at each P(Rft) value (and the stability of the control values for individual rats was remarkably consistent, as can be seen from Fig. 15.12), a random sequence of doses of d-amphetamine was given. Increased switching was observed at all but the highest baseline probability of switching. At this control value, which was generated when P(Rft) = 1.00 on the selected lever, increased repetition was observed. These effects, like the increased switching seen at other values of P(Rft), occurred in each of the five rats (Fig. 15.12). The increased repetition could be explained by the Lyon and

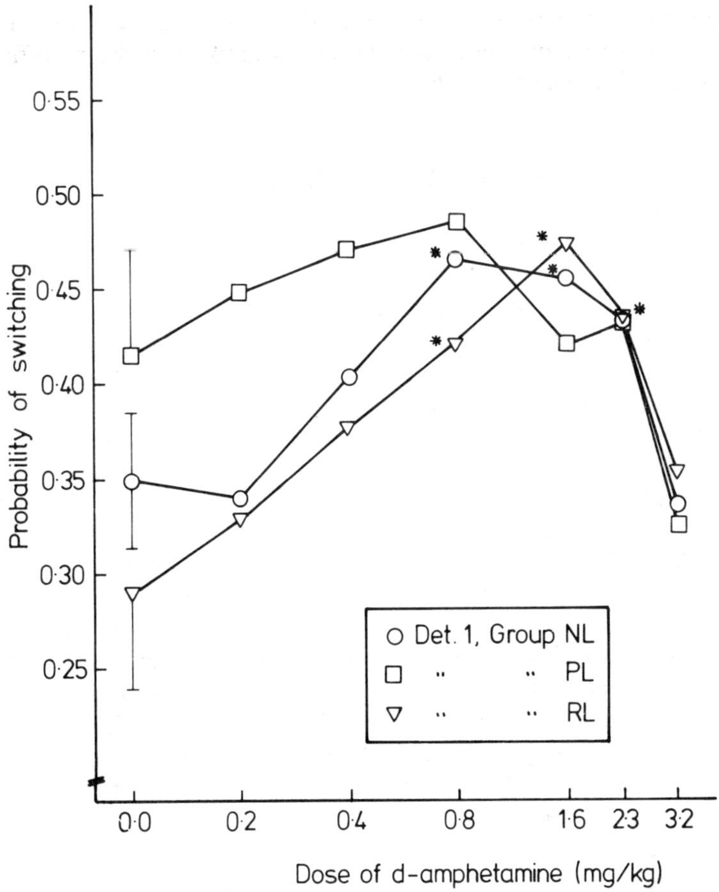

Fig. 15.11. Determination 1 of Fig. 15.4, divided into its three separate groups of rats which had different control (0.0) levels of switching. Note how the effect of d-amphetamine on this switching depends on the control level. Increases are seen at relatively low probabilities, but only decreases, at relatively high probabilities of switching. (Redrawn from Evenden & Robbins, 1983a).

Robbins hypothesis in that all low probability forms of behaviour are predicted to increase, thus allowing moderate increases in repetition. The increased probability of repetition is associated with lengthening of the IRT for the SAME responses, in roughly the same way as shown for the SAME IRTs in Fig. 15.6 (where P(Rft) = 0.30, and switching *increased*). Moreover, the same pattern of shortened DIFFERENT IRTs was seen as at P(Rft) = 0.30, at low and intermediate doses of d-amphetamine, despite the reductions in the probability of response switching (Fig. 15.12 of Robbins (1981)). Thus, although the rats are less likely to switch, when this response does occur, it is on average faster than usual at low doses of the drug. The similarity in IRT distribution changes at P(Rft) = 0.30 and 1.00 is to be contrasted with the opposite effects on the probability of response switching. This emphasises the fact that changes in local rate are probably somewhat independent of changes in response probability and also illustrates the gains of considering rate and probability as independent measures of performance.

Both the changes in local rate and in response probabilities can be squeezed into a classical rate-dependency account if switching and repetition themselves are considered as higher order response units occurring in real time and rate-dependent effects can operate in opposite directions depending on the definition of the response. Obviously, the utility of this description can seriously be questioned, particularly considering that switches and repetitions will not show monotonic dose-response functions as response rate declines at higher doses (Fig. 15.3). In addition, for Determination 3 of Fig. 15.4, switching occurred at an initially higher rate in real time than repetition, and yet was still enhanced.

The probability-dependent changes shown in Fig. 15.12 suggest that amphetamine induces a regression to an intermediate level of switching, regardless of the baseline value. This is strongly reminiscent of the point made by Gonzalez and Byrd (1977) and by Ksir (1981) about rate-dependent changes. Although high rates are reduced, and low rates increased, these absolute rates converge towards an intermediate constant value. This convergence, which has been linked with a "randomisation" of responding, has been used as evidence of impaired stimulus control, and hence lack of discriminability of responding, produced by amphetamine. In the context of the present measures, randomisation of switching and repetition should surely be represented by a dose-dependent convergence to a value of switching of $p = 0.5$. But several exceptions to this have been observed. For example, in Fig. 15.12 it is evident that rats 1, 3 and 4 at 1.6 mg/kg of d-amphetamine show convergence under some conditions but to a probability of switching which is greater than $p = 0.5$, even though in some cases the relevant control baseline was less than $p = 0.5$. To these results should be added the example of the rats in Determination 3, Fig. 15.4 which exhibited increased switching from a baseline of switching greater than $p = 0.5$.

Whereas these results run counter to the stimulus control hypothesis, the deviation from $p = 0.5$ to higher levels of switching is not necessarily inconsistent with the behavioural competition hypothesis, if a response run does indeed consist of repeated responses at one location, as has been assumed previously.

Evidence against the stimulus control hypothesis in terms of rate-dependent effects is obtained when the absolute rates beginning from low

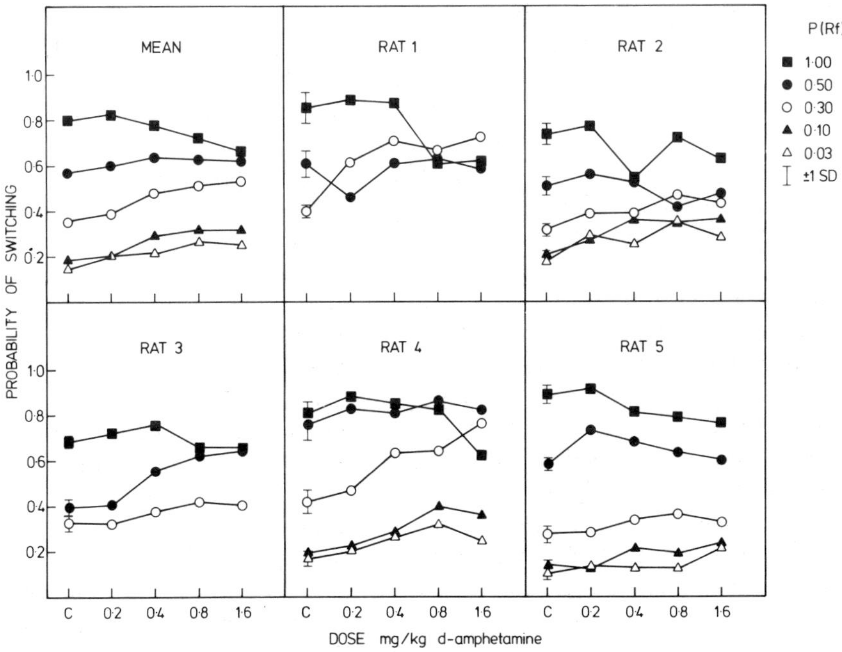

FIG. 15.12. Probability-dependency in five rats exposed to different probabilities of reinforcement from P(Rf) = 1.00 to 0.03, in sequential order over blocks of sessions. Significant increases in switching are seen in each rat, at all but the highest control probability of switching, where significant reductions are found. (Data recalculated from Robbins & Watson, 1981).

and high baselines actually converge but then cross over (Robbins, 1981). For behavioural competition, this can be accounted for by differential interference from unrecorded responses. In terms of probability dependency, there is a hint from the data of Rat 1 in Fig. 15.12 that analogous forms of cross-over can occur in individual rats following amphetamine. Additional evidence is shown in Fig. 15.13, which describes the unpublished results of an experiment with two rats designed explicitly to examine probability-dependency. Here, the first switch made after 20 responses resulted in reinforcement. Unlike for the FCN schedule (Laties, Wood & Cooper Rees, 1981) these responses could be completed on either lever, or as a mixture on both. The schedule generated almost a scallop-like pattern of increased probability of switching as a function of how much of the fixed ratio had been completed. Clearly, the low probabilities at the start of the ratio were increased more by amphetamine than the higher ones towards its end. Indeed, Rat 2 showed changes in switching strongly suggestive of a crossing over effect at 0.8 mg/kg where the probability of switching was

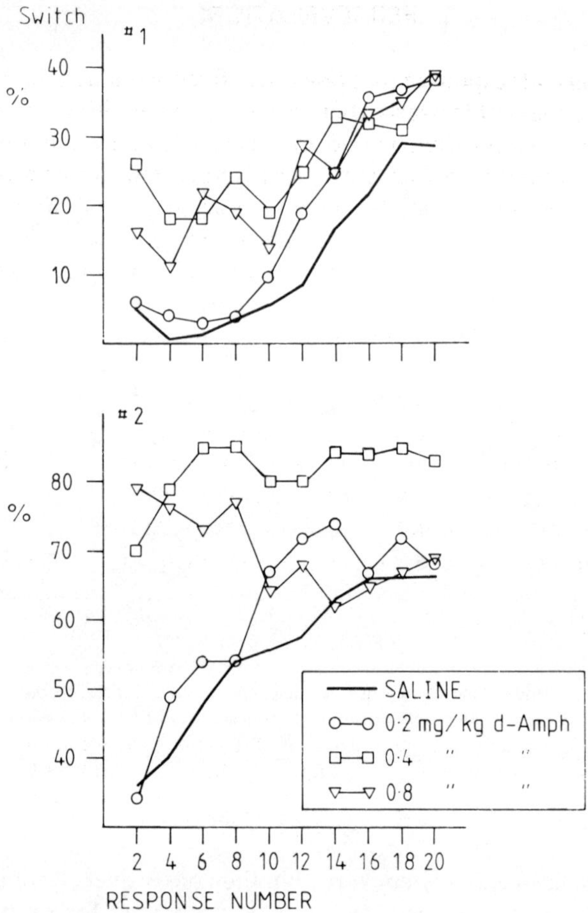

FIG. 15.13. Probability dependency in two rats subjected to the schedule described in the text. Rats were reinforced for the first switch made after 20 responses which could be distributed in any way across the two levers. Shown are the percentages of switches made as a function of the serial order of the response (unpublished results).

higher at the beginning of the ratio than at the end—the reverse of the control pattern.

Although the evidence for cross-over in the case of probability-dependency is as sparse as it is for rate-dependency (Ksir, 1981), it is a more important test of the behavioural competition hypothesis because with a choice between equivalent responses it is impossible to postulate interference by unrecorded, competing responses.

PERSEVERATION

Perseveration and response repetition are defined separately in this article, but there is an inevitable overlap between the two definitions. Repetition is simply repeated responding on one lever (Fig. 15.2). By contrast, perseveration is the continued performance of a response following the delivery of the reinforcer. This runs slightly counter to the normal definition of perseveration, which is generally in terms of the continuance of responding in the face of non-reinforcement. Specific instances of each of these cases can be provided. For example, responding to complete a fixed ratio requirement is a case of repetition whereas continued responding on the lever after the delivery of food is taken as the prime, unambiguous example of perseveration. Response repetition under the random schedule includes repeated responses following non-reinforcement and is clearly an ambiguous case because such responding is also dictated by the dual constraints of the schedule requirement and the response cost of switching.

Assuming a broader definition of perseveration than that used above, the two cases of increased response repetition seen thus far can be used to make the following points: (1) a weak tendency towards repetition can be seen at low doses of amphetamine, if there is a sufficiently low baseline; (2)

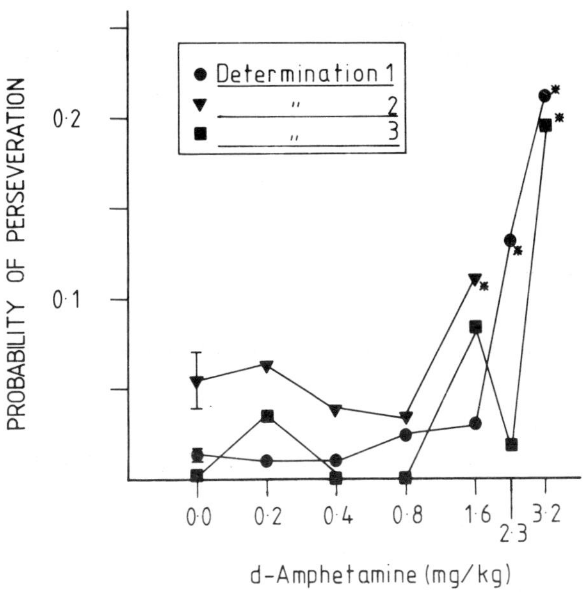

FIG. 15.14. Dose-dependent effects of d-amphetamine on probability of perseveration in the three Determinations described in Fig. 15.4. (Redrawn from Evenden & Robbins, 1983a.)

at higher doses (e.g., 3.2 mg/kg) just before conditioned behaviour is totally suppressed, the trend towards increased switching is often lost, sometimes being replaced with a reverse tendency, towards repetition (Fig. 15.11). This may begin to reflect the emergent predominance of responding on one lever combined with a gradual disappearance of response sequences on the other lever.

To these two admittedly ambiguous examples can be added the enhanced perseveration shown with increased doses of amphetamine, in the sense defined earlier, as continued ineffective responding following the delivery of food. For example, Fig. 15.14 shows the probability of perseveration in each of the three Determinations of Fig. 15.4. Doses of 1.6, 2.3 and 3.2 mg/kg of d-amphetamine are all seen to be capable of increasing perseveration significantly. A clear case of perseveration is shown in the cumulative record of Fig. 15.15. Here, the rat under amphetamine continued to respond at first on both levers and later only upon a single lever,

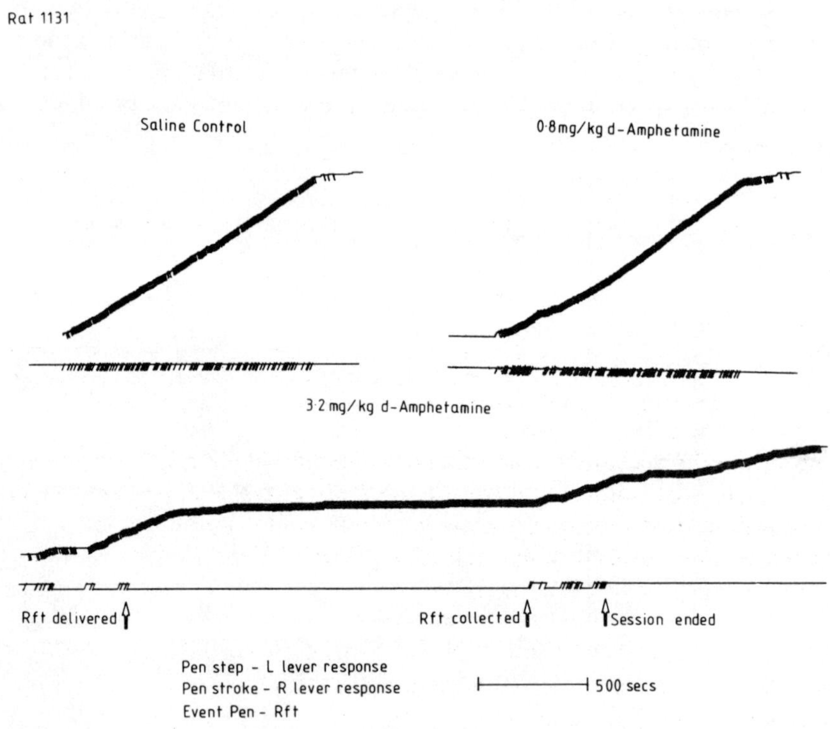

FIG. 15.15. Cumulative records of a rat to illustrate perseveration and perseverative switching produced by two doses of amphetamine compared with control. The event pen shows when food was delivered; the tray light was turned on (event pen) until the rat visited the food tray.

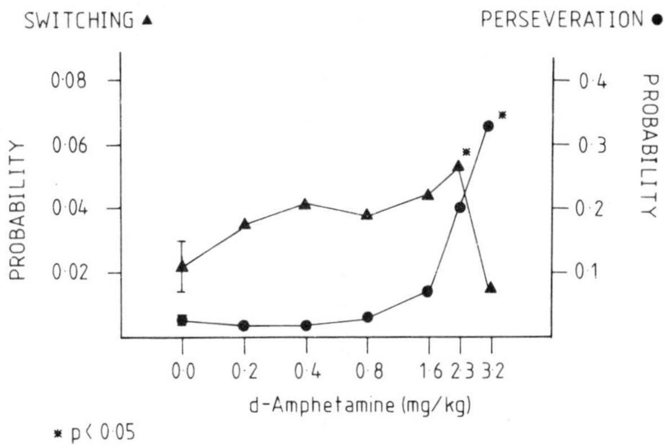

FIG. 15.16. Increased switching and perseveration as a function of dose of d-amphetamine under the concurrent random ratio schedule. (Redrawn from Evenden & Robbins, 1983a).

even though the light signalling the presentation of food was present (bottom trace).

By comparing Figs. 15.4 and 15.14, it can be seen that amphetamine first produces increased response switching, at low doses, and then increased perseveration, with some partial overlapping of these two effects. This is more evident from the results of the concurrent RR experiment described earlier (Fig. 15.16). Although switching and perseveration might reflect the action of amphetamine upon two different processes which compete at the behavioural level, we are arguing from the behavioural competition position that the two effects probably result from a single, cumulative action of the drug. Some evidence for the alternative position can be gleaned from the effect of apomorphine only to produce increased repetition, regardless of the baseline value (Robbins, 1980 & unpublished results). Clearly more work is required to address this problem. A possibly promising approach would be to use selective dopamine depletion in forebrain areas such as the neostriatum and nucleus accumbens, in a way which has already been employed to achieve a dissociation of the effects of amphetamine upon locomotor activity and stereotyped behaviour (Kelly, Seviour & Iversen, 1975). The contribution that the present studies makes is in providing some of the first controlled observation of biphasic changes in switching and perseverative responding.

Perseveration is a dominant theme of the Lyon-Robbins hypothesis because it is seen as a step on the path towards stereotypy. Its onset demarcates the transition between competition between different sequences and competition within a sequence. Thus, perseveration is viewed as a secondary effect of response sequence shortening. First, some competing sequences are so abortive that they are not discernible in the behavioural response. This may still leave intact relatively long response sequences, but they are now more likely to be performed in a perseverative manner. Thus, one would expect to see behaviour resembling some of the anecdotal reports of complex stereotyped behaviour such as route tracing in the rat (Segal, 1975) and the intricate rituals of amphetamine addicts (Randrup & Munkvad, 1967). Second, the perseverating response sequence begins to lose some of its elements because of competition of response elements within the sequences. Eventually this leads to outright stereotypy.

A particularly striking case of complexity in perseverative behaviour in the present studies is the "perseverative switching" between the two levers in which some amphetamine-treated rats continued to switch between the two levers and to press them, even though food had been delivered into the illuminated food tray (Evenden & Robbins, 1983a). Thus, lever-lever sequences were increased but lever-food tray sequences were concurrently reduced. This behaviour was dose-dependent and certain doses of d-amphetamine (e.g., 2.3 mg/kg), under certain conditions, could produce the seemingly paradoxical collection of effects, consisting of increases in switching, perseveration and perseverative switching. Therefore, perseverative behaviour in this case consisted of a complex sequence, but one which omitted its terminal elements, of approaching the food tray and eating. In the cumulative record shown in Fig. 15.15 it is shown how the relative complexity of "perseverative switching" becomes simple perseveration of one response as the drug effect progresses. This again is analogous to reports of progressive simplification of stereotyped rituals in amphetamine abusers (Kramer, Fischman & Littlefield, 1967).

Perseveration almost by definition connotes an increased autonomy of behaviour from its reinforcing consequences, and other measures of behaviour taken in this situation certainly endorse this conclusion. For example, whereas the latency to collect the food is increased (which is by no means wholly determined by increased perseveration), the latency to restart responding under the schedule (the post-reinforcement pause or PRP) is reduced. This suggests a drift away from behaviour oriented to food towards instrumental responding. Such a drift has also been observed following repeated injections of pipradrol in rats responding with conditioned reinforcement (Robbins, 1978). In this latter case the drug-treated rats showed increased responding on a lever providing a light previously paired with water, but reduced responding on a second lever providing no light, and importantly, a reduced frequency of visits to the reinforcement tray. This pattern of effects again supports the notion of an increased rate of responding within a reduced number of response categories (Lyon & Robbins, 1975). Whether first the increased switching and then the perseverative behaviour results in behavioural autonomy, or alternatively is caused by a loss of discriminative control by the reinforcer, remains a moot point, although we have been arguing that the first of these possibilities seems more likely. What is required is an independent measure of the discriminative control over behaviour exerted by reinforcement, so that its progressive weakening with increasing doses of amphetamine can accurately be assessed. We turn to this problem in the next section, because it can be tackled from a knowledge of some of the other important behavioural properties of Morgan's schedule.

WIN-STAY AND LOSE-SHIFT BEHAVIOUR

Performance under the schedule used throughout this work has an additional feature of great importance discovered by Morgan (1974). He found that rats under this schedule showed a significant tendency to repeat the just-reinforced response, even though there was no advantage, in terms of obtaining food, for doing so. This win-stay tendency, which is most evident for the first response following reinforcement (Fig. 15.2) seems to reflect a basic feature of reinforcement, that is, repetition of the just-reinforced response. We have modified the Morgan (1974) procedure in several experiments by including a component in which the reinforcer (food) is omitted, producing not only win-stay, but also the symmetrical effect of non-reinforcement (lose-shift), the animal responding on the lever alternative to the one just non-reinforced (Evenden & Robbins, 1984). We have also demonstrated that win-stay is not due to the adoption of asymmetric postures and that it is enhanced by reducing the frequency of reinforcement. By considering the first response following the delivery of food as analogous to a choice situation, and making certain assumptions, signal detection theory (TSD) can be employed to obtain indices of discriminative sensitivity (SI) to the reinforcer and an index of the overall bias of the animal to stay or shift following reinforcement (RI) can be obtained (Fig. 15.2).

Behavioural manipulations have very clear effects on win-stay, lose-shift and the associated TSD indices. Thus, for example, extinction eventually reduces both SI and RI (indicating an overall tendency to switch away from the lever last responded upon) (Evenden & Robbins, 1983b). Here, the change in win-stay undoubtedly occurs because the omission of food eventually reduces the discriminative control over the first response following reinforcement which is initially maintained by the conditioned reinforcer (the click of the empty food dispenser). Additional feeding, on the other hand, has no effect on these variables of choice behaviour although response rate is markedly reduced (Evenden & Robbins, 1983b).

d-Amphetamine reduces both win-stay and lose-shift at certain doses, resulting in significant reductions in SI but no change in RI (Fig. 15.17) thus suggesting, in accordance with the suggestion made earlier, that amphetamine eventually reduces the discriminative control by reinforcement over responding. These changes occur at doses higher than those producing effects on response switching, but at similar doses to those producing perseveration. The occurrence of enhanced switching before the change in win-stay supports our argument that the changes in switching are not necessarily caused by a reduction in the effects of reinforcement over behaviour.

Although perseveration (including perseverative switching) is generally correlated with the reduced win-stay tendency, it does not contribute in a direct fashion to the effect because win-stay is only assessed following trials in which the location of the reinforced lever press and the last perseverative lever press coincide. For some rats, amphetamine increased spatial bias on the first response following reinforcement (or non-reinforcement) and this may account in part for the reduction in SI (unpublished results). This is an important observation because it suggests that the

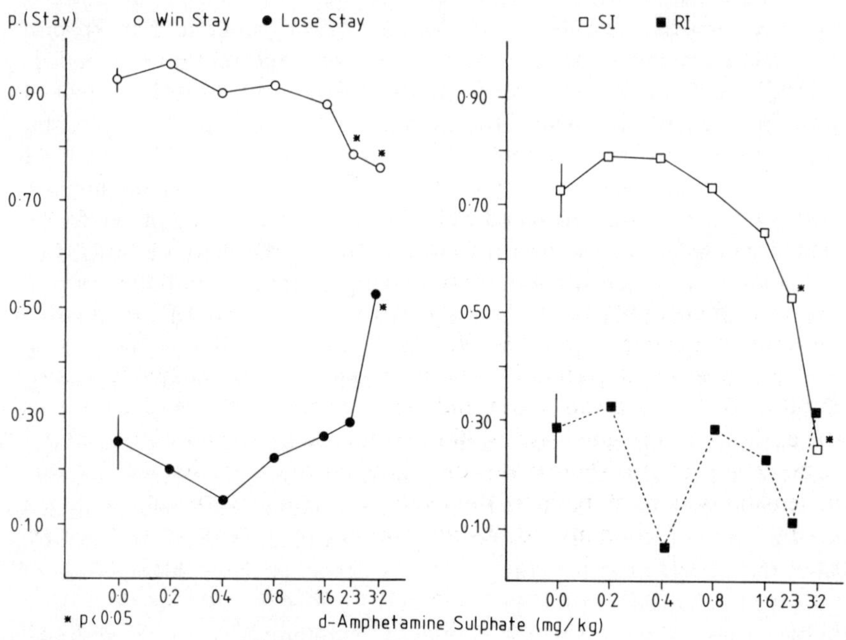

FIG. 15.17. Dose-dependent effects of d-amphetamine on win-stay, lose stay and the associated signal detection parameters SI and RI. (Data redrawn from Evenden & Robbins (1983b).

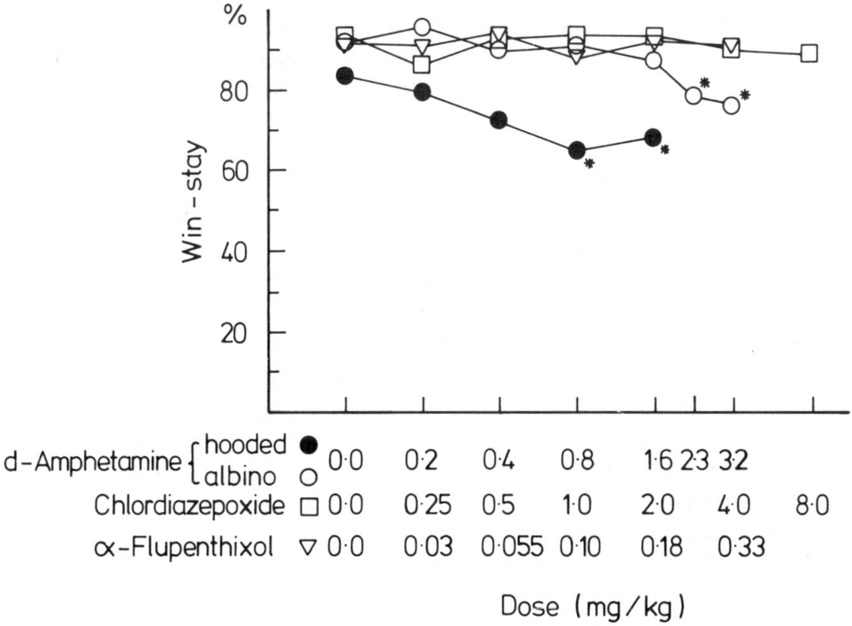

FIG. 15.18. Comparative effects of d-amphetamine, chlordiazepoxide and α-flupenthixol on percentage of win-stay responses in albino rats (Evenden & Robbins, 1983b) and in hooded rats, with d-amphetamine (Robbins & Watson, 1981), for purposes of comparison.

rat's choice was not randomised as an impaired stimulus control hypothesis might predict, but subjected to altered control and thus changed in an orderly way. But this effect on spatial bias has been observed in albino rather than hooded rats, and the latter still exhibit significant reductions in win-stay. Therefore, this question requires further analysis before it can be resolved. It might be argued, for example, that the spatial bias is an effect, rather than a cause of reduced SI.

The effect of d-amphetamine is replicable, although the hooded rats of the Robbins and Watson (1981) study showed effects on win-stay at lower doses than the Sprague-Dawley albino rats used by Evenden and Robbins (1983b) (Fig. 15.18). There was some additional evidence that the reduction in sensitivity to reinforcement followed panel entry by the rat and did not result from an inability to distinguish between reinforced and non-reinforced trials. The latency to enter the panel in the two types of trial differed significantly and this can be taken as an index of discrimination between them. Amphetamine made the difference between the two components greater (Evenden & Robbins, 1983b). This result again argues that the increases in perseveration were not caused by a general failure to discriminate the presence or absence of food.

In summary, responding under d-amphetamine clearly becomes independent of the effects of reinforcement to some degree, even though response rate might be unaffected. The behaviour seems autonomous of the delivery of food even though this event can still be discriminated. But the precise relationship of the reduction in win-stay and SI to the effects of amphetamine on switching and perseveration remains somewhat unclear.

The hypothesis that amphetamine makes behaviour more autonomous with respect to its consequences could be challenged on the grounds that win-stay is simply a more sensitive measure than average response rate. But results using other drugs such as the neuroleptic α-flupenthixol and chlordiazepoxide, do not support this view. Neither of these drugs have any effect on win-stay (or SI) over a wide dose range, even at doses which considerably reduce response rate (Evenden & Robbins, 1983b). These results may be relevant to suggestions that neuroleptics blunt the effects of reinforcement (Wise, 1981). In terms of discriminative control over responding, this appears not to be true. Nor are the effects of α-flupenthixol similar to those of extinction, an equivalence which has been claimed for neuroleptics by Wise (1981). Rather the effects of this neuroleptic mimic more those of additional feeding (Evenden & Robbins, 1983b). The results with amphetamine also challenge the generality of the assertion that this drug enhances reward, because in some aspects at least, the opposite is true. These considerations certainly underline the importance in general of using both rate-based and choice measures of reinforcement to assess the behavioural effect of drugs. The double dissociation of effects described above may also indicate a need to examine the concept of reinforcement more closely and to discuss its possibly separable components.

IMPLICATIONS

Rate-Dependency

Our title indicated that we wished to consider alternative approaches to rate-dependency as an empirical generalisation in explaining the behavioural effects of drugs. Because of their ubiquitous nature, it is desirable that any account has to begin by explaining the rate-dependent effects themselves. This has been attempted by the three main types of hypothesis described in the introduction but it is by no means certain that these hypotheses are mutually exclusive. First, the fact that so many drug classes have rate-dependent actions raises the possibility that the apparently similar behavioural effects actually depend on different mechanisms. Thus, for example, barbiturates may actually impair sensory processing and impair stimulus control, whereas the effects of amphetamine could arise from behavioural competition. Second, some of the hypotheses may be interrelated. For example, one version of the stimulus control hypothesis (McKim, 1981) has used a comparison between the effects of white noise and amphetamine to make the point that the drug may be acting merely as a disruptive stimulus. However, it is likely that this disruptive effect is produced by changes in responding which lead to behavioural competition. The white noise and the amphetamine could simply be acting at different levels on a mechanism which generates elevated activity. The fact that the effects of the noise rapidly abate whereas those of the drug persist after repeated administrations suggests that the noise might be acting at a level different from the drug; one that is susceptible to habituation, for example.

Despite these caveats, we have tried to reconsider the effects of amphetamine, like other authors (Branch & Gollub, 1974) by using probability as well as rate-based measures of performance. In our paradigm, we have deliberately chosen to work with intermediate control rates of performance in order to minimise rate-dependent effects and concentrate upon measures based on relative frequencies of different responses. By doing this, we have clearly uncovered effects of amphetamine and related compounds which would not be detectable using a simple rate or rate-dependent approach and which, for this drug class at least, may help us to discriminate between the three hypotheses described above. We have also looked at measures of local rate of responding such as IRTs between repeats and switches and latencies to collect food and the post-reinforcement pause. To a large extent, these measures of local rate do reveal rate-dependent like effects, but these changes were insufficient to account for the changes in structure of behaviour as revealed by the relative frequencies of different responses. Rather, it would appear that the rate-dependent changes themselves largely arose from the changes in relative frequencies of different responses. On the other hand, some changes in performance, such as the increased speed of switching from one manipulandum to the other may not depend on these probabilistic changes at all, and may represent somewhat orthogonal effects. Generating rate-dependency, of course, has relied largely upon the use of average rates of responding over time which are likely to include effects resulting from both speed and probability of performance. This would explain in part the nature of rate-dependency effects. By using the more exact measures of both speed and probability of performance we can perhaps achieve a finer dissection of pharmacological and behavioural effects.

Towards a Theory of Amphetamine Action

Initially, we drew a distinction between couching explanations of the behavioural effects of drugs in terms of motivational actions and the rate-dependency hypothesis. In the case of amphetamine, several lines of evidence contradict the hypothesis that its behavioural effects necessarily result from a direct modulation of motivational or reinforcement processes. However, there is little doubt that reinforcement of responses greatly enhances their capacity to be increased in frequency after amphetamine. This can be seen not only from the well-known requirement of rate-dependency that there should be a minimum rate of responding for the rate-increasing effects to be observed (McMillan, 1968), but also from the demonstration by the present set of experiments that there should be a minimum level of switching for the enhanced switching to be seen. Perhaps the effects of amphetamine apparently to enhance the effects of conditioned reinforcement (Hill, 1970; Robbins, 1976) can also be seen in these terms—the contingency providing conditioned reinforcement thus raising response rate to a level which becomes susceptible to the rate-increasing effects of the drug.

In terms of the stimulus control hypothesis, it has to be considered whether the obvious gradual weakening of the effects of programmed reinforcement on behaviour are primary or secondary to the general stimulant action of the drug. The weight of the evidence is in favour of the latter hypothesis. In particular, the demonstration of enhanced switching away from a random baseline (Fig. 15.4; Determination 3), and the various orderly progressions in the dose-response curves from increased switching to increased perseveration, seem unlikely to all be caused by a weakening of stimulus control.

Strong evidence for one form of the stimulus control hypothesis would be provided by demonstrating effects of amphetamine on discrimination performance which unequivocally could be attributed to effects on stimulus processing. This is much more difficult than one would think. Even signal detection theory, which provides independent measures of sensitivity and bias, is sometimes insufficient for this task. For a theory of impaired stimulus control adequately to explain changes in discrimination performance, a change in an index such as SI or A′, the sensitivity parameter, should be observed with no confounding consistent change in some form of response bias. Koek and Slangen (1983) recently showed that amphetamine impaired the discrimination of temporal frequency of rats and that significant reduction in A′ but no changes in B″, the response bias parameter (used to measure side preference) were produced. With foresight, however, the authors also measured the tendency of the animal to repeat the previous response regardless of which side it was on. This measure showed dose-dependent increases which were parallel to the reductions in A′, and which obviously could have been contributing to this apparently selective effect on stimulus sensitivity. Therefore, amphetamine may not have been exerting a specific effect on discriminative sensitivity, but rather was affecting performance by its effect on response output. This is a major prediction of the Lyon and Robbins hypothesis, and has been supported by other studies (Nielsen, 1981). It certainly cannot be assumed that changes in sensitivity necessarily lead to changes in response bias because in the Koek and Slangen study morphine, while also reducing A′, had no effect on response repetition. Therefore, this orderliness in output cannot easily be explained by the stimulus control hypothesis without extra assumptions.

If one assumes that behavioural competition does determine the form of the dose-response curve with amphetamine, then it is natural to ask which factors give certain responses an advantage over others. One of these is training, as emphasised above, and prepotency and the presence of eliciting factors may be factors of similar type and importance. But being a high probability response is in itself no guarantee of survival because the drug increases all responses exceeding some minimal probability and this inevitably will lead to behavioural competition. In that case, it is evident that long and complex response sequences with pauses will show considerable shortening, even if they are life-protecting responses such as eating. The question of which response elements in a sequence survive obviously will depend on a number of factors, and precise predictions are difficult to make. In general, responses which are short and not contingent upon particular conditions such as precise stimulus feedback and special postures, will be the ones most readily performed. The limited capacity for response output in time will constrain the variety of the different types of response which can easily be performed. These are all questions to be examined in more depth in later work.

Shortening of conditioned response sequences has received the most emphasis in this chapter, but unconditioned sequences have not been measured. Lyon and Magnusson (1982), however, have recently provided a framework for the detailed study of unconditioned response sequences affected by drugs such as amphetamine which substantiates our general case. They have been particularly rigorous in the definition of a response sequence and have developed a method (called THEME) for detecting "configurations" of response elements, which have a precise sequence, but are usually separated in time, the gaps being filled with other behaviour which is generally variable and independent of the configuration under study. Thus, these response sequences are not defined by their temporal contiguity as is the case for our studies. Nevertheless, preliminary results apparently suggest that amphetamine reduces both the length and the variation of the configurations which is analogous to the effects described here. THEME would probably be a powerful method for measuring unconditioned behavioural sequences in conjunction with operant behaviour.

In summary, the behavioural competition hypothesis still seems to be the most parsimonious explanation of the progression from switching to perseveration in response output. But precise mechanisms of these effects need to be specified. It is possible, for example, that switching, perseveration and changes in local rate might depend upon different neural mechanisms all activated by amphetamine rather than upon a single mechanism which works to produce a different pattern of output, depending on the level at which it is engaged. Moreover, it is by no means clear at present how behavioural competition could account for the cross-over effect described in the section on probability-dependency.

Implications for Abnormal Behaviour

Two of the major themes of the present article have been the sequential changes in switching and perseveration and probability-dependency. Both of these may have important clinical connections. First, the increases both in switching and perseveration following amphetamine may have precedents in the apparently opposed, but context-dependent overfocusing and heightened distractibility seen in frontal lobe patients (Norman & Shallice, 1980). Heightened perseveration (Boucher, 1977) and stereotyped alternation (possibly akin to perseverative switching) (Frith, 1970) have been observed in autistic children in tasks requiring response selection. But in none of these cases is there an obvious transition from switching to perseveration, perhaps as a function of a single underlying process, which may be the case in our experiments with increasing doses of amphetamine. If one assumes, however, that acute and chronic schizophrenics can form a continuum there is evidence that some of the attentional and response selection deficits of schizophrenics can be considered in this way. For example, Frith and Done (1983) have recently used the following task in testing groups of acute and chronic schizophrenics with both positive and negative symptoms, manic-depressives, senile demented patients and normal controls. Subjects were asked to guess at which of two locations a stimulus target would next occur on a screen. The programming of the event was random between the two locations and the non-schizophrenic groups generally responded in a way which tended towards randomness. However, acute schizophrenics (with negative symptoms) and chronic schizophrenics showed enhanced alternation between the locations, whereas chronic schizophrenics with intellectual impairment (defect state) showed an enhanced spatial bias. These deviations from random responding strikingly resemble the drift from switching to perseveration seen in the present studies, especially given the formal similarities between the paradigms employed.

The clinical utility of probability dependency may seem more obscure. It has been suggested, however, that the apparently paradoxical effect of amphetamine of reducing activity in hyperactive children might be an example of a rate-dependent action (Sahakian & Robbins, 1977; Robbins & Sahakian, 1979). It seems entirely plausible that the behavioural changes can be thought of in probability-dependent terms. The hyperactive child is said to have attentional disorders which might be examples of increased response switching. The drug might therefore act to reduce this excessively high level of switching.

This argument might seem a good deal more plausible if the converse was demonstrated, that is an increase in switching from a very low baseline. Recently, it seems that at least preliminary evidence of this type may be forthcoming. Patients with obsessive-compulsive neurosis, which almost by definition involves high levels of repetition, exhibited surprising improvement following medication with d-amphetamine (Insel, Hamilton, Guttmacher & Murphy, 1983). These examples perhaps strengthen the use of amphetamine as a tool in the analysis of psychopathology, and help to justify the "rate-independent" paradigms we have used.

ACKNOWLEDGEMENTS

We acknowledge JLE's MRC studentship and help with the manuscript from M. Gaskin and R. Hammans (figures) and Mrs S. Chandler and Miss L. Evans (typing).

REFERENCES

Barrett, J. E. (1976) Effects of alcohol, chlordiazepoxide, cocaine and pentobarbital on responding maintained under fixed interval schedules of food or shock presentation. *Journal of Pharmacology and Experimental Therapeutics*, **196**, 605–615.

Boucher, J. (1977) Alternation and sequencing behaviour and response to novelty in autistic children. *Journal of Child Psychology and Psychiatry*, **18**, 67–72.

Branch, M. N. & Gollub, L. R. (1974) A detailed analysis of the effects of d-amphetamine on behavior under fixed interval schedules. *Journal of the Experimental Analysis of Behavior*, **21**, 519–539.

Cooper, S. J. (1981) Prefrontal cortex, benzodiazepines and opiates: case studies in motivation and behaviour analysis. In S. J. Cooper (Ed.), *Theory in Psychopharamacology*, (Volume 1). London: Academic Press, 277–322.

Dews, P. B. (1958) Analysis of effects of psychopharmacological agents in behavioural terms. *Federation Proceedings*, **17**, 1024–1030.

Dews, P. B. & Wenger, G. R. (1977) Rate-dependency of the behavioural effects of amphetamine. In T. Thompson & P. B. Dews (Eds.), *Advances in behavioural pharmacology* (Volume 1). New York: Academic Press. 167–227.

Evenden, J. L. & Robbins, T. W. (1983a) Increased response switching, perseveration and perseverative switching following d-amphetamine in the rat. *Psychopharmacology*, **80**, 67–73.

Evenden, J. L. & Robbins, T. W. (1983b) Dissociable effects of d-amphetamine, chlordiazepoxide and α-flupenthixol on choice and rate measures of reinforcement in the rat. *Psychoparmacology*, **79**, 180–186.

Evenden, J. L. & Robbins, T. W. (1984) Win-stay behaviour in the rat. *Quarterly Journal of Experimental Psychology*, **36B**, 1–26.

Evenden, J. L. & Robbins, T. W. (1985) The effect of *d*-amphetamine, chlordiazepoxide and α-flupenthixol on food reinforced tracking of a visual stimulus by rats. *Psychopharmacology*, **85**, 361–366.

Frith, C. D. & Done, D. J. (1983) Stereotyped guessing by schizophrenic patients on a two choice guessing task. *Psychological Medicine*, **13**, 779–786.

Frith, U. (1970) Studies in pattern detection in normal and autistic children: II Reproduction and production of colour sequences. *Journal of Experimental Child Psychology*, **10**, 120–135.

Gonzalez, F. A. & Byrd, L. (1977) Mathematics underlying the rate-dependency hypothesis. *Science*, **195**, 546–550.

Grilly, D. M. (1977) Rate-dependency effects of amphetamine resulting from behavioural competition. *Biobehavioural Reviews*, **1**, 87–93.

Hill, R. T. (1970) Facilitation of conditioned reinforcement as a mechanism of psychomotor stimulation. In E. Costa & S. Garattini (Eds.), *Amphetamine and Related Compounds*. New York: Raven Press. 781–795.

Insel, T. R., Hamilton, J. A., Guttmacher, L. B., & Murphy, D. L. (1983) *d*-Amphetamine in obsessive-compulsive disorder. *Psychopharmacology*, **80**, 231–235.

Kelly, P. H., Seviour, P., & Iversen, S. D. (1975) Amphetamine and apomorphine responses in the rat following 6-OHDA lesions of the nucleus accumbens septi and corpus striatum. *Brain Research*, **94**, 507–522.

Koek, J. & Slangen, J. (1983) Effects of d-amphetamine and morphine in discrimination: Signal detection analysis and assessment of response repetition in the performance deficits. *Psychopharmacology*, **80**, 125–128.

Kramer, J. C., Fischman, V. S., & Littlefield, D. C. (1967) Amphetamine abuse. *Journal of the American Medical Association*, **201**, 305–309.

Ksir, C. (1981) Rate-convergent effects of drugs. In T. Thompson & P. B. Dews (Eds.), *Advances in behavioural pharmacology* (Volume 3). New York: Academic Press. 39–59.

Laties, V. G. (1972) The modification of drug effects on behaviour by external discriminative stimuli. *Journal of Pharmacology and Experimental Therapeutics*, **183**, 1–13.

Laties, V. G., Wood, R. W., & Cooper Rees, D. (1981) Stimulus control and the effects of d-amphetamine in the rat. *Psychopharmacology*, **75**, 277–282.

Lea, S. E. G. & Morgan, M. J. (1972) The measurement of rate-dependent changes in responding. In R. M. Gilbert & J. R. Millenson (Eds.), *Reinforcement; behavioural analysis*. New York: Academic. 129–145.

Lyon, M. & Robbins, T. W. (1975) The action of central nervous system stimulant drugs: a general theory concerning amphetamine effects. In W. B. Essman & L. Valzelli (Eds.), *Current Developments in Psychopharamacology* (Volume 2). New York: Spectrum. 80–163.

Lyon, M. & Magnusson, M. (1982) Central stimulant drugs and the learning of abnormal behavioural sequences. In M. Y. Spiegelstein and A. Levy (Eds.), *Behavioural models and the analysis of drug action*. Amsterdam: Elsevier. 135–153.

McKearney, J. W. (1974) Effects of d-amphetamine, morphine and chlorpromazine on responding under fixed-interval schedules of food presentation or electric shock presentation. *Journal of Pharmacology and Experimental Therapeutics*, **190**, 141–153.

McKim, W. A. (1981) Rate-dependency: a non-specific behavioural effect of drugs. In T. Thompson and P. B. Dews (Eds.), *Advances in behavioural pharmacology* (Volume 3). New York: Academic. 61–73.

McMillan, D. E. (1968) The effects of sympathomimetic amines on schedule-controlled behaviour in the pigeon. *Journal of Pharmacology and Experimental Therapeutics*, **160**, 315–325.

Miller, N. E. (1964) The analysis of motivational effects illustrated by experiments on amylobarbitone sodium. In H. Steinberg, A. V. S. De Reuck & J. Knight (Eds.), *Animal Behavior and Drug Action* London: Churchill. 1–18.

Moerschbaecher, J. M., Thompson, D. M., & Thomas, J. R. (1979) Effects of methamphetamine and scopolamine on variability of response location. *Journal of the Experimental Analysis of Behavior*, **32**, 255–263.

Morgan, M. J. (1974) Effects of random reinforcement sequences. *Journal of the Experimental Analysis of Behavior*, **22**, 301–310.

Nielsen, E. B. (1981) Effects of d-amphetamine and LSD on simultaneous discrimination. In C. M. Bradshaw, E. Szabadi & C. F. Lowe (Eds.) *Quantification of steady-state operant behaviour*. Amsterdam: Elsevier/North Holland. 461–464.

Nieto, J., Makhlouf, C., & Rodriguez, R. (1979) *d*-Amphetamine effects on behaviour produced by periodic food deliveries in the rat. *Pharmacology Biochemistry and Behavior*, **11**, 423–430.

Norman, D. A. & Shallice, T. (1980) Attention to Action: Willed and automatic control of behaviour. San Diego, CA: Center for information processing, University of California.

Norton, S. (1973) Amphetamine as a model for hyperactivity in the rat. *Physiology and Behavior*, **11**, 181–186.

Randrup, A. & Munkvad, I. (1967) Stereotyped activities produced by amphetamine in several animal species and man. *Psychopharmacologia*, **11**, 300–310.

Robbins, T. W. (1976) Relationship between reward-enhancing and stereotypical effects of psychomotor stimulant drugs. *Nature*, **264**, 57–59.

Robbins, T. W. (1978) The acquisition of responding with conditioned reinforcement: effects of pipradrol, methylphenidate, d-amphetamine and nomifensine. *Psychopharmacology*, **58**, 79–87.

Robbins, T. W. (1980) Stereotypy of a learned response after apomorphine. *British Journal of Pharmacology*, **69**, 275P–276P.

Robbins, T. W. (1981) Behavioural determinants of drug action: rate-dependency revisited. In S. J. Cooper (Ed.), *Theory in Psychopharmacology*, (Volume 1). New York: Academic Press. 1–63.

Robbins, T. W. & Sahakian, B. J. (1979) Paradoxical effects of psychomotor stimulant drugs in hyperactive children from the standpoint of behavioural pharmacology. *Neuropharmacology*, **18**, 931–950.

Robbins, T. W., Roberts, D. C. S. & Koob, G. F. (1983) Effects of *d*-amphetamine and apomorphine upon operant behaviour and schedule-induced licking in rats with 6-hydroxydopamine-induced lesions of the nucleus accumbens. *Journal of Pharmacology and Experimental Therapeutics*, **224**, 662–673.

Robbins, T. W. & Watson, B. A. (1981) Effects of *d*-amphetamine on response repetition and win-stay behaviour in the rat. In C. M. Bradshaw, E. Szabadi and C. F. Lowe (Eds.), *Quantification of steady-state operant behaviour*. Amsterdam: Elsevier/North Holland. 441–444.

Sahakian, B. J. & Robbins, T. W. (1977) Are the effects of psychomotor stimulant drugs on hyperactive children really paradoxical? *Medical Hypotheses*, **3**, 154–158.

Sanger, D. J. & Blackman, D. E. (1978) The effects of drugs on adjunctive behaviour. In D. E. Blackman & D. J. Sanger (Eds.), *Contemporary Research in Behavioural Pharmacology*. New York: Plenum Press. 239–287.

Segal, D. S. (1975) Behavioural characterisation of d- and l-amphetamine: neurochemical implications. *Science*, **190**, 475–477.

Weiss, B. & Gott, C. T. (1972) A microanalysis of drug effect on fixed ratio performance in pigeons. *Journal of Pharmacology and Experimental Therapeutics*, **180**, 189–202.
Wise, R. A. (1981) Brain dopamine and reward. In S. J. Cooper (Ed.), *Theory in Psychopharmacology*, (Volume 1). London: Academic Press. 104–122.

VI CONCLUSION

16 Contemporary Behaviourism: A Brief Overview

D. E. Blackman
University College, Cardiff

In this final chapter of *Behaviour Analysis* an attempt is made to place the preceding contributions in the broad context of contemporary behaviourism. The chapter does not set out to explore further new ground, but instead briefly surveys some of the points of growth and strain in contemporary behaviourism, many of which were addressed in the principal papers given at the first European Meeting on the Experimental Analysis of Behaviour held in Liège, Belgium, in 1983 and published in this book.

First it is necessary to be clear about what is meant by "contemporary behaviourism" here. Skinner (1974) has distinguished two types of behaviourism; methodological and radical. Methodological behaviourism is reflected in the reorientation of the discipline of psychology which developed from Watson's plea sixty years ago: "Why don't we make what we can observe the field of psychology?" (1924, p6). What we can observe is what people and animals do, how they behave, and the methodological impact of focusing on their behaviour as a legitimate domain for psychology is no longer contentious. Most contemporary psychologists would at least include behaviour in the definition of their study, though few would perhaps feel able to ignore the mysteries of a less tangible mental life and consciousness. The empirical study of behaviour has thus come to provide a central focus of contemporary psychology, and in that sense methodological behaviourism provides little by way of a distinctive forum for debate, and we are all behaviourists now. This latter claim may strike some psychologists as provocative, but I have noted before (Blackman, 1980, p100) that the term "behaviour*ist*" is still used without frisson or embarrassment by those in other fields who also include the behaviour of humans and animals in their studies, such as zoologists.

Radical behaviourism, on the other hand, is undoubtedly more contentious. Skinner (1974) defines it as a philosophical interpretation of the data resulting from the scientific investigation of behaviour. The interpretation of these data is certainly radically different from that which is favoured by many other psychologists. Some try to understand behaviour by relating it to physiological activities of the central nervous system, seeing such activities as the underlying determinants of behaviour. Others emphasise the primacy of mental life and its determining influence on what we do. Yet others appear to sit on the fence, explaining behaviour by recourse to hypothetical constructs which sound as if they might be physiological and/or mental in conceptual status, although in practice their bases in physiology or cognition can appear equivocal. Such programmes combine to conceptualise behaviour essentially as an appendage to events and processes occurring at some other level within the behaving organism. The interpretative scheme of radical behaviourism is boldly different, however. It attempts to construct an explanation and an understanding of behaviour by seeing it in its environmental context. The goal of radical behaviourism is the analysis of behaviour in relation to the physical and social world in which it occurs. In particular, radical behaviourists seek to identify functional relationships between the environment and behaviour which can be shown empirically to exert an influence on an observable behavioural repertoire. Thus the explanation of behaviour becomes couched in terms of the way in which it is nested in its environmental context, in relation to events occurring outside rather than inside the behaving organism.

I have considered elsewhere (Blackman, 1980) some of the objections to their programme which radical behaviourists, including B. F. Skinner himself, frequently encounter (c.f., Skinner, 1974). In particular it is often claimed that the approach is simplistic because it is based on a stimulus-response model of reflexes, that it has no place for the "person" or "self," and that it is, by its very nature, necessarily and dangerously manipulative. This is not the place to consider such general matters again, although some aspects of these objections will become relevant as the issues raised in the preceding chapters are addressed.

The programme of radical behaviourism, then, attempts to understand behaviour by identifying the effective components of its environmental milieu, those events which can be shown to influence it. In general there are two kinds of such influences. That which has perhaps attracted more attention is provided by the selective consequences of behaviour. If a pattern of behaviour can be shown to be increased in frequency, or sustained, by the consequences it produces, then those consequential events are defined as "reinforcers." It is always emphasised within this approach that determining whether in fact any event exercises a reinforcing influence over the frequency with which a behavioural act occurs is an empirical matter. It might perhaps be noted here that Azrin and Holz (1966) have advocated a similar functional definition of what they term "punishers"—consequences of behaviour that are responsible for maintaining the behaviour at a lower frequency of occurrence than would otherwise be the case. In this way functional analyses can incorporate two types of relationship between behaviour and its consequences, those which increase the behaviour (reinforcers) and those that decrease it (punishers). Interestingly however, Skinner himself has not favoured such a functional definition of punishment. In his discussions (e.g., 1974, pp61–64) he has tended to emphasise hedonic qualities of punishing events and the consequent emotional states which they induce, thus seeing punishment essentially as a disruptive influence on behaviour. Such emphases are markedly out of balance with his definition and discussion of reinforcement. Perhaps as a result, the historical precedent of Thorndike's truncated law of effect has to some extent endured in contemporary behaviour analysis, with a greater awareness of the selective effects of environmental consequences which lead to increases in behaviour than of those which lead to decreases.

The second class of functional relationship between environmental events and behaviour that is important in radical behaviourism is provided by the context that sets the occasion for behaviour to be affected by its consequences. Such contextual events can have marked modulatory effects on the frequency with which behavioural acts occur, and are described as discriminative stimuli. The choice of a term which includes the word "stimulus" here may be as misleading as is the use of the word "response" to characterise free-operant behaviour within functional analysis (see Blackman, 1980). The relationship between such a so-called "discriminative stimulus" and a so-called "operant response" is not as simple as is the case with those stimulus-response relationships which are termed "reflexes," since it can be expressed in a variety of ways and is essentially probabilistic.

In the functional analyses of behaviour favoured by radical behaviourists, therefore, three terms are considered:

1. a prior or antecedent environmental context, which sets the occasion for behaviour to be affected by its consequences and thus modulates the frequency at which the behaviour occurs;
2. the behaviour itself;
3. the consequences of that behaviour, which exert an influence on its rate of occurrence.

Skinner (1938, p178) originally termed these three elements a discriminative stimulus S^D, the response R^O, and the reinforcing stimulus S^1. However, in the light of the matters discussed briefly above, it might be clearer if the elements of the so-called "three-term contingency" were denoted as (A : B : C). Thus behaviour (B) is analysed in terms of the functional (i.e., effective) influences of environmental events which may be antecedent (A) to the behaviour or consequent (C) upon it. The colons used here to relate the antecedent environmental conditions to behaviour and behaviour to consequences are intended to reflect the fact that such relationships may be complex and infinitely variable. For example, consequences may reinforce behaviour even though they follow it only occasionally, as in schedules of intermittent reinforcement (Ferster & Skinner, 1957). The relationships between environment and behaviour may not be immediate, as for example when brief antecedent events set an occasion for behaviour to be emitted a little later, as in delayed-matching-to-sample procedures (see Shimp, 1976). The relationship between behaviour and environment may be expressed in relative rather than absolute terms, as for example in schedules of shock-frequency reduction (e.g., Herrnstein & Hineline, 1966) when the functionally significant environmental consequences occur at differing frequencies in the presence and absence of the behaviour. It can be seen then, that the relationships between behaviour and environmental antecedents and consequences may indeed be complex and subtle. Therein lies the power of the explanatory system provided by functional analyses of behaviour. Colons are used in the notation above, rather than, say, arrows, in order to allow for these subtleties and in an attempt to avoid an implication that the relationships are as simple as are those involved in reflexes.

The broad programme of radical behaviourism, then, can be pursued in two ways. The first of these may be described as the experimental analysis of behaviour, and the second as applied behaviour analysis. Both approaches are represented in the preceding chapters, and each is considered separately here before they are brought together in a more general conclusion.

THE EXPERIMENTAL ANALYSIS OF BEHAVIOUR

It was emphasised above that radical behaviourists seek to explain behaviour in terms of its environmental milieu, and that identifying the ways in which environmental events come to influence behaviour is an empirical matter. These dynamic influences can be investigated experimentally in the laboratory, and this is what "the experimental analysis of behaviour" sets out to do. Any success it might have may be used to evaluate the adequacy and potential subtlety of the broad interpretative approach of radical behaviourism.

In fact the experimental analysis of behaviour is a distinctive movement in experimental psychology which has three separable components. First, it is based on the philosophical stance of radical behaviourism, as discussed above. Second, it employs the experimental techniques of free-operant conditioning which have developed from Skinner's pioneering empirical studies (Skinner, 1938). Third, it adopts a strategy of experimental control over behaviour, which allows conclusions to be drawn from the intensive study of individual subjects rather than from the more conventional comparisons made between groups of subjects (see Sidman, 1960).

The paradigm case of operant conditioning experiments is provided by studies of behaviour such as lever-pressing by rats and key-pecking by pigeons in which this behaviour has been studied in relation to such environmental events as lights and noises used as antecedent conditions and food, water or shock as consequences. The patterns of behaviour and the environmental events favoured in operant conditioning experiments have provided a laboratory model of the ways in which behaviour can be influenced by environmental events. Experimental programmes have studied arbitrary behavioural acts which are readily performed at different rates by the experimental subjects and which can be easily recorded by the experimenter. The species of animals selected have been chosen for their tractability in laboratory conditions. The environmental events whose influences have been studied have been chosen because they are easily controlled and manipulated by the experimenter and often have some intrinsic biological significance for the experimental subject. However, the experimental analysis of behaviour seeks principles which can be generalised beyond the world of the rat or pigeon in a Skinner box. It provides an experimental foundation for the stance of radical behaviourism.

Functional relationships between behaviour and consequences have been studied in an extensive range of conditions in the experimental analysis of behaviour. Studies of the effects of schedules of intermittent reinforcement have so dominated the field as to lead some to think that they define it. As Zeiler (1984) has recently pointed out, schedules of reinforcement "represented the major unique contribution of the behavior-analytic approach to the field of learning, and they constituted the most powerful independent variables ever seen in psychology. It seemed obvious and appropriate that they should be a primary focus of research" (p485). Such research provides a descriptive account of the ways in which different schedules of reinforcement exert characteristic influences on behaviour and result in orderly patterns of behaviour (Ferster & Skinner, 1957; Zeiler, 1977). The main behavioural principle which can be generalised from such research is simply that an environmental event will influence behaviour in very different ways by virtue of the way in which it is scheduled and related to behaviour. This principle can be elaborated in many ways. Thus reinforcers may sustain very high frequencies of behaviour even if they occur only occasionally (e.g., as in variable ratio schedules) and characteristic *patterns* of behaviour in time can also be sustained (e.g., by fixed schedules). Events may come to influence behaviour because of the way they are scheduled with respect to other environmental events. For example, a brief light can sustain characteristic schedule control over behaviour even if it is never paired with a primary reinforcer but is delivered in a second-order schedule (Gollub, 1977), and thus satisfies the requirements necessary to be defined as a conditioned reinforcer. Similarly, in some circumstances even schedules in which the delivery of brief shocks is made consequent upon behaviour may sustain patterns of behaviour which are characteristic of those schedules, as can schedules in which behaviour is followed by the intermittent *removal* of an aversive or conditioned aversive event (Morse & Kelleher, 1970). Operant conditioning experiments have also investigated the conditions in which an event will serve as a punisher as defined above (Azrin & Holz, 1966).

Zeiler (1984) has suggested however that "schedule research, at least in a scientifically interesting form, is moribund" at present. He attributes its demise in part to the fact that it has not been possible to produce an integrated theoretical account of *why* or *how* schedules of reinforcement exert the effects they do, even though many researchers have tried to identify lower-order components or processes which may "explain" schedule control. Zeiler suggests that what he terms "the sleeping giant" of schedule research may be reactivated by a greater integration of such research with biological principles such as optimal foraging or optimisation theory. However, for the present purposes the point to be emphasised is rather that studies of reinforcement schedules have enriched the analytic power of the principle of reinforcement in radical behaviourism. Far from being a simple or rigid relationship between behaviour and consequence, the principle of reinforcement gains further potential explanatory force from such research.

A similar picture can be seen when we turn to consider how the experimental analysis of behaviour has studied relationships between antecedent environmental conditions and behaviour (so-called discriminative or stimulus control). Here too experiments have unravelled complex and subtle effects, and it is possible to make generalisations about the circumstances in which an antecedent event will come to modulate the frequency of operant behaviour and the extent to which such control will generalise to other events or be specific (see Nevin, 1973). In this area too, however, a recent reviewer (Williams, 1984) has suggested that experimental interest has declined in recent years. Williams suggests that the three-term contingency (A : B : C) provides only a descriptive framework and he argues that a greater interest in what he calls "the structure of associations" is necessary if further progress is to be made in understanding the dynamics of discriminative control. We shall return to this point, but again it should be emphasised that the experimental analysis of discriminative control over behaviour makes it possible to go beyond the simple rigidity of conventional stimulus-response relationships and thus enrich radical behaviourism's empirical and analytic base.

From this brief review it can be seen that the fundamental interest in schedules of reinforcement and in discriminative control which for long characterised the experimental analysis of behaviour have waned to some extent, though not before providing more subtle possibilities for functional analyses of behaviour. Some of the force of the experimental analysis of behaviour has been directed into more applied fields of research. For example, a growing interest in "behavioural economics" has emerged from research which has exposed the conceptual principles of economics to empirical scrutiny in operant conditioning experiments (e.g., Hursh, 1984); thus principles of behaviour have been introduced into a field which has conspicuously appeared to lack them.

A further example of this more applied approach is to be found in behavioural pharmacology, represented in this book in chapters 13–15. This field too has been reviewed recently (Branch, 1984). It can be characterised by two major emphases. In the first of these, operant conditioning techniques have been used to establish baselines of behaviour against which the effects of psychoactive drugs may be assessed. Following the early work of Dews (e.g., 1955) it became clear that the effects of drugs are often dependent on the nature of the behavioural baselines against which they are assessed. A given dose of a drug will often have differential effects on patterns of behaviour which are sustained by different schedules of reinforcement. Thus behavioural pharmacology was one of the first fields in which the importance of schedule-dependent effects was recognised. Zeiler (1984, p486) has emphasised that schedule dependencies are ubiquitous and are ignored at the risk of limiting any generalisations we may wish to make about the effects of further independent variables on behaviour. Zeiler also suggests that such schedule dependencies *are* ignored in many fields of contemporary research, but this is not true of behavioural pharmacology, for schedule-dependent effects have introduced an important psychological variable to this interdisciplinary study. For some time behavioural pharmacologists were lured towards an even more direct variable in drug-behaviour interactions, namely that of response rate. The rate-dependency hypothesis (see Branch, 1984) proposed that the behavioural effects of drugs depend principally on the rate of operant behaviour in control (non-drug) conditions. Such a simple organising principle appeared to capture the data from experiments in which different baseline rates resulted from different schedules of reinforcement, different rates characterised different parts of organised sequences of behaviour engendered by schedules of reinforcement, or similar patterns of behaviour were generated by intermittent schedules with different reinforcers. More recent research, such as that described in this book in Chapter 15, has ameliorated the rate-dependency hypothesis somewhat (see also Branch, 1984), but it should not be overlooked that the principle of *schedule*-dependent effects still remains, with undiminished importance, again providing further flexibility to the analytic system of functional analysis within radical behaviourism.

Behavioural pharmacology has also exploited the techniques of operant conditioning to investigate what have been termed the stimulus properties of drugs (see Stolerman, 1984). As with stimuli drawn from other domains, drugs can enter into the three-term contingency (A : B : C) either as reinforcers (C) or as discriminative stimuli (A). Drug infusions made dependent on operant behaviour according to some schedule of intermittent reinforcement can lead to the patterns of behaviour that are characteristic when other reinforcers are scheduled in that way; this finding makes obvious contact with research on drug addiction and abuse (e.g., Johanson, 1978). Such research emphasises that the self-administration of drugs is not a function simply of the pharamacological properties of the drug but also depends intimately on the environmental conditions in which the drug is related to behaviour. Similarly, drug infusions which set the occasion for operant behaviour to be reinforced by other events can serve as antecedents and exert discriminative control over that behaviour. Such research is reviewed in Chapter 13 of this book, and of course opens up the way to studies of the interoceptive properties of drugs. As Branch (1984) emphasises, this work has expanded along with increases in our knowledge of the pharmacological action of drugs and the ways they relate to specific receptors in the central nervous system. The so-called "drug-discrimination" procedures are now standard assay techniques in pharmacology laboratories which are studying drug receptors. Naturally enough, the need for standardised assay techniques has led to the use of relatively stereotyped procedures and measures in this field, and the analysis of environmental influences on drug discriminations is currently less forceful than is the pharmacological exploitation of the procedure. Zeiler's caution (1984) noted above concerning the ubiquitous importance of schedule dependencies should perhaps be borne in mind here. It is also perhaps worth noting that the emphasis on pharmacological mechanisms in drug-discrimination research removes this work from the philosophical stance of radical behaviourism by introducing physiological accounts of its phenomena. This emphasises in turn that the experimental techniques of operant conditioning and the single-subject research strategies that they make possible can be distinguished from the interpretative schemes in which they are used.

The above discussion has emphasised the importance of the experimental analysis of behaviour to contemporary behaviourism: Such empirical research provides a broader platform on which analyses of behaviour favouring the three-term contingency (A : B : C) may be developed. However, it was also noted that in recent years there has been some waning of the traditional research emphases in this field, namely the behavioural control exerted by schedules of reinforcement (B : C) and discriminative control of behaviour (A : B). At the same time the experimental techniques of operant conditioning have flourished in areas of psychology that are not necessarily conceptualised in environmentalistic terms, but which are complementary to that approach. Moreover, operant conditioning techniques are now also being used to identify and explore what some see as areas of strain for functional analyses of behaviour and thus to challenge rather than develop the interpretative scheme of radical behaviourism. Prominent in this challenge is the increased interest in phylogenetic influences on behaviour outlined and discussed in Chapters 4–6 of this volume.

The experimental analysis of behaviour was firmly rooted in the tradition within psychology of seeking general laws of behaviour by means of controlled experiments using a "model" of behaviour. This model, as was emphasised above, was based on the study of arbitrary patterns of behaviour in a limited range of species and in relation to a restricted range of environmental events. However, this long-dominant research strategy has of course been challenged in the last 15 years by an increasing awareness of the ways in which species differences can intrude in behavioural experiments. In the field of operant conditioning, for example, Shettleworth (1973) showed convincingly that different topographical aspects of the behavioural repertoire of hamsters, such as face-washing, digging and lever-pressing, are differentially susceptible to environmental control by contingencies of reinforcement. Staddon (1977) has reviewed the ways in which patterns of behaviour can be induced by procedures in which no formal dependency is programmed between behaviour and a reinforcer. Schedule-induced polydipsia, for example, takes the form of excessive and intrusive drinking after food reinforcement by animals that have not been deprived of water and for whom there is no contingency of reinforcement programmed for such drinking. Such patterns of behaviour appear to be non-functional in more senses than one. Similarly, studies of auto-shaping or sign-tracking behaviour have shown that pigeons will peck keys in conditions in which there is no dependency programmed between this behaviour and the delivery of food, a finding which challenges the assumption that key-pecking is an arbitrary and representative pattern of operant behaviour whose frequency of occurrence is a function solely of contingencies of reinforcement. Many investigations of sign-tracking behaviour have used a discrete-trials procedure in which a stimulus precedes the delivery (independently of behaviour) of a biologically significant event (Hearst & Jenkins, 1974), and it is not therefore surprising that the procedure has now come largely to be conceptualised in terms of Pavlovian rather than operant conditioning. However, the "auto-maintenance" procedure initially investigated by Gamzu and Schwartz (1973) has demonstrated that pigeons will peck a key at sustained and high rates when it is lit by a prolonged stimulus, which accompanies periods in which food is occasionally delivered independently of behaviour, if that stimulus alternates with one accompanying periods when food is never presented or is presented less frequently. While such a procedure does not necessarily remove the behavioural phenomenon from contemporary studies of classical conditioning, with their emphasis on differential frequencies of unconditional stimuli in the presence and absence of conditional stimuli, it is also strongly reminiscent of conventional multiple schedules of reinforcement in operant conditioning, with the one exception that no dependency is programmed between key-pecking and food.

"Phylogenetic intrusions" such as these have provided a focus for the enrichment of the data base of operant conditioning in recent years and, as Chapters 4–6 testify, there is certainly an increased awareness of the biological context of behaviour and the ways in which phylogeny interacts with environmental contingencies. Such data have placed constraints on the extent to which behaviour can be explained "simply" in environmentalistic terms. It should perhaps be emphasised that such a synthesis of phylogenetic and ontogenetic influences on behaviour, and thus of biology and psychology, is by no means anathema to contemporary behaviourists (see for example Skinner, 1966, 1977a). However, this development may also be thought to bring with it an important conceptual impact which has not been much addressed in the literature of radical behaviourism. To take but one example, the conventional language of behaviourism has defined reinforcers functionally, solely in terms of their effects on the behaviour to which they are related or on which they are dependent, and in turn it defines behaviour as operant behaviour only if it is affected by such contingencies. Increasing interest in the behavioural effects of procedures in which food is delivered independently of behaviour has led to the use of terms such as "response-*independent* reinforcement" (e.g., Sizemore & Lattal, 1977) which might be thought to contain something of a contradiction. If food delivery is not strictly a dependent consequence of behaviour, then perhaps it ought not to be defined as a reinforcer. Nevertheless (*given always the nature of the animal*), studies such as these identify the necessary and sufficient conditions for the behaviour to occur, and thus the conditions which are functionally responsible for the behaviour. The interpretative scheme of radical behaviourism ought therefore to be able to find a place for them. Perhaps one consequence of the increased awareness of the biological context of behaviour and the way in which it interacts with environmental influences should be a re-examination and redefinition of some of the basic concepts of functional analysis such as reinforcement and operant behaviour.

A similar conceptual point emerges from research on the effects of procedures in which correlations are established between behaviour and environmental events such as food or shock. Baum (1973), and Herrnstein and Hineline (1966) have shown that if such correlations are arranged experimentally so that the overall frequency of the events changes as a consequence of the occurrence of behaviour, then the behaviour may be sustained even though there may be no *immediate* consequence following it. This prompts the suggestion that the conventional three-term contingency may be liberalised beyond its normal emphasis on temporal (if occasional) contiguity between behaviour and functional consequences. Considered together with the issues raised by procedures such as "response-independent reinforcement," some profound ambiguities emerge in the term "contingencies of reinforcement," which has normally been used to describe dependent contiguities between behaviour and events, and these ambiguities need further attention if the full force of functional analyses of behaviour is to be sustained and developed.

Discussion of the correlation-based law of effect (Baum, 1973) leads towards another considerable point of tension in contemporary operant conditioning in relation to radical behaviourism, namely the increasing willingness of learning theorists to appeal to underlying cognitive mechanisms in order to explain the behavioural phenomena being currently studied. Such an appeal is of course certainly not consistent with the basic programme of radical behaviourism, and it is related to the theories of associative learning that now dominate the study of Pavlovian conditioning (e.g., Dickinson, 1980). The tension here can be illustrated by considering further the work by Herrnstein and Hineline (1966) discussed above. These researchers reported that the lever-pressing of rats occurred at higher frequencies if it led to an overall, but not necessarily immediate, reduction in the frequency with which brief shocks were delivered. When reporting these data, the authors emphasised that they had identified a functional relationship between the frequency of emitted behaviour and the (here dependent) frequency of environmental events, in this case an inverse correlation. For a radical behaviourist the explanation of such behaviour resides within the exposition of that functional relationship, i.e., in the account of the necessary and sufficient conditions for the behavioural phenomenon to occur. This is analogous to the explanation of conventionally reinforced lever-pressing by recourse to an account of the simpler relationships between the behaviour and its consequences. To others such as Mackintosh (1974), however, correlations between behaviour and consequence have made it seem necessary to look beyond the functional relationship in order to understand the behaviour. Thus an appeal may be made to the detection and processing of information by the rat (i.e., within the animal and underlying the behaviour): The rat calculates and compares the frequencies of events in the presence and absence of its behaviour, and its behaviour *reflects* these processes.

In this general vein there has been a remarkable and accelerating flight to cognitive theorising to "explain" the data of operant conditioning even with animal subjects, as shown for example in edited volumes by Hulse, Fowler and Honig (1978) and Roitblat, Bever and Terrace (1984). It should be noted that the move to cognitive explanations need not be, and has not been, confined to explaining why *complex* functional relationships have the effects they do. The contemporary literature of conditioning and learning abounds with discussions of such cognitive entities as memory (short-term, working, associative, visual, spatial, reference, long-term), cognitive processing, rehearsal, knowledge, attention, concept formation, form recognition, representation and the like, offered in an attempt to explain functional relationships between behaviour and the environment in which it occurs. It should not be thought that these cognitive processes are conscious, however, for "just as the modern rationale for using human cognitive terms is not based upon arguments that appeal to consciousness or introspective reports, the rationale for the study of cognitive processes in animals requires no reference to animal consciousness" (Terrace, 1984, p8). Nor can it be demonstrated (yet?) that they represent some physiological reality underlying behaviour. Nevertheless, it is claimed that "the research into animal behaviour has made it clear, however, that such cognitive states are real and necessary components of any adequate theory that seeks to explain animal behavior" (Roitblat et al., 1984, p1).

It has been suggested before (Blackman, 1983) that the precise conceptual status of these "real" and "unconscious" "cognitive states" is open to some doubt. Perhaps they will prove to be no more than daringly named intervening variables. Radical behaviourists might agree with Skinner, however, when he argues that he is not a cognitive psychologist principally because "The mental apparatus studied by cognitive psychology is simply a rather crude version of contingencies of reinforcement and their effects" which "goes no further towards an explanation of behavior than the external contingencies upon which it is modelled" (Skinner, 1977b, p9). The list of different forms of "memory" given above perhaps serves to emphasise the point. Radical behaviourists might also feel reminded of the doubts raised by Skinner (1950) about the *necessity* for theories which relate behaviour to events operating (or believed to be operating) within the organism. They might look askance too at the implication in some writings by cognitive theorists that the only alternative to their accounts is to be found in an inflexible and outmoded reflex model which offers a stimulus-response approach to the undoubted subtleties of environment-behaviour interactions.

Of course the current preference for cognitive explanations of behaviour does expose some considerable difficulties in the analysis of functional relationships of ever increasing complexity. Nevin (1984) has suggested that it is necessary for the experimental analysis of behaviour to move to an increasingly sophisticated use of mathematics if the orderliness of these relationships is to be adequately described. This might mean that a field which many outsiders already find daunting because of its technical language might become even less comprehensible. As the emphasis on the many forms of "memory" in cognitive theory suggests, there is also a particular need to deal more confidently with "the problem of action at a temporal distance," as Marr (1984) terms it. The point at issue here is that experimental programmes such as delayed-matching-to-sample have increasingly investigated the relationships between behaviour and antecedent events which were, but are no longer, present. Cognitive theories are perhaps particularly attractive here because they appear to provide a bridge in time, whereby the previously present stimulus is still present when the behaviour occurs, albeit as an internal representation. Marr (1984, p358) terms this "a kind of mental aether." The radical behaviourist would see no special problem in functional relationships which might be established between behaviour and brief events (either antecedent or indeed consequent events) which are no longer present, but it is true that the experimental analysis of behaviour has not tended to seek such relationships.

We may conclude this brief review by noting that the tensions resulting from the increased interest in phylogenetic influences on behaviour and from the current preferences of many theoreticians for cognitive accounts of behavioural data do not act on contemporary behaviourism in isolation. Indeed, they interact a good deal (see Roitblat et al., 1984), reflecting perhaps a general disposition in contemporary science to be drawn to information processing models of living organisms based on the analogy of the digital computer whose "behaviour" is often, in turn, conceptualised in terms of a comparison with a biological organism. This dominant and forceful trend in contemporary psychology (or cognitive science, as some would now prefer to call it) has clearly attracted many empirical researchers who are investigating behaviour by means of operant conditioning procedures. As a result, this effective experimental technology is now being used to challenge the philosophical stance of functional analysis in contemporary behaviourism quite as much as, perhaps even more than, to support it, as was largely the case in the past. In many ways this must be considered a healthy development even by those who prefer to retain the perspective of contemporary behaviourism, for it has enriched the data base on which competing explanatory systems may be evaluated.

APPLIED BEHAVIOUR ANALYSIS

The second main testing ground for the general programme of radical behaviourism is to be found in the field known as "applied behaviour analysis." As its name implies, applied behaviour analysis addresses patterns of behaviour that are exhibited in settings having potential applied significance rather than in the laboratory, and hence focusses directly on human behaviour. However, here too behaviour is conceptualised in terms of its functional relationships with environmental events, and the so-called three-term contingency (A : B : C) therefore provides its analytical key. Naturally many of the events which have an influence on the behaviour of a person can be expected to be provided by other people, and thus it is largely the *social* environment whose influences predominate in applied analyses of behaviour.

In general the approach favoured here leads to objective descriptions of what a particular person does (behaviour). An attempt is made to nest this behaviour in its social environmental context by seeking out any consequences of behaviour which may be functionally significant in sustaining it at its observed level of frequency. Thus, as in the experimental analysis of behaviour, one part of applied behaviour analysis attempts to unravel functional relationships between behaviour and its consequences. Taking a cue from experimental work, one might suppose that, in addition to those events which might occur directly and reliably after a pattern of behaviour is exhibited, social consequences which occur only occasionally, which are not necessarily immediately consequent upon the behaviour, and which occur merely at relatively higher or lower frequencies than otherwise, might be functionally significant and thus sustain behaviour. Applied behaviour analysis also, of course, seeks to identify social or environmental contexts which may modulate behaviour by setting the occasion for its occurrence to be followed by functionally significant consequences, i.e., to identify relationships between antecedent conditions and behaviour. Combined together, these features lead to an emphasis on objective description of behaviour and its social environment and the unravelling of potential relationships between them, thus applying the three-term contingency to human behaviour in the "real" world.

One problem immediately confronted by any attempt to conduct an applied behaviour analysis is that of being able to identify whether there are indeed *functional* relationships between behaviour and what appears to be its antecedents and consequences. Such relationships can only be identified unequivocally by manipulating the events within them, by changing the consequences or the way in which they occur in some way or by considering the behaviour in different social settings. This point brings us to the intimate relationship between attempts to understand behaviour in functional terms and attempts to change it by changing the environmental events surrounding it. This is of course normally only appropriate when some behavioural change is desired or desirable, often in clinical, educational, child-rearing or managerial situations. However, it should be noted that attempts to modify behaviour by manipulating events in the social environment do not necessarily have to be based on analyses of the natural contingencies of reinforcement which prevailed before the intervention was introduced. Herein lies a danger in the over-enthusiastic use of behaviour modification techniques by therapists who are not trained in or sympathetic to the perspective of applied behaviour analysis, for they may be led to superimpose insensitive procedures which are not likely to be effective because the natural contingencies influencing the problem behaviour have not been analysed and changed. It is no doubt partly because of this danger that Richelle (Chapter 1, this volume) draws attention to the frequent imbalance between enthusiasm for behaviour modification and appreciation of applied behaviour analysis, and why Michael (Chapter 10) also reiterates the importance of maintaining close links between fundamental research and applied practice.

The range of possible therapeutic manipulations of functional relationships between "problem" behaviour and its environmental and social context is extensive, and many of the techniques have been reviewed elsewhere and indeed some time ago (e.g., Leitenberg, 1976). They are perhaps most often directed to the (B : C) relationship, that between behaviour and its reinforcing or punishing consequences, as for example with methods of extinction by withholding functionally significant events (e.g., Glavin & Moyer, 1975), by reinforcing appropriate behaviour by introducing new consequences for behaviour as in token economies (e.g., Kazdin, 1977) or programmes of punishment (e.g., Lovaas & Simmons, 1969). Such techniques may be introduced gradually rather than peremptorily in order to shape target behaviours systematically by successive approximation. Once established, these behaviours can then be sustained by contingencies of reinforcement. However, the relationship between behaviour and its antecedent context (A : B) is also important and provides for further possibilities of therapeutic intervention, as for example with programmes which "fade" in discriminative control over behaviour (e.g., Sidman & Stoddard, 1966) or encourage generalisation of behavioural change which is produced initially within a constrained therapeutic setting (see Scott, Himadi & Keane, 1983). The terms "behavioural engineering" and "contingency management" have been used to describe procedures which manipulate potentially functional relationships between environment and behaviour rather than simply superimpose new ones. Some of the characteristics of this general approach are considered in Chapters 11 and 12.

One reason for the vigorous popularity of behaviour modification within applied psychology is doubtless to be found in the contingencies of reinforcement which relate to the behaviour of its practitioners. Its essentially pragmatic and non-invasive approach to dealing with behavioural problems has given behaviour modifiers an opportunity to develop a more therapeutic role for applied psychology than would emanate from the tradition of psychometric testing, for example, and its success with a wide range of clients and in a wide range of settings has surely provided reinforcing consequences to strengthen the behaviour of the behaviour modifiers. In this context it is noticeable, and in the light of the less developed appreciation of the stance of functional analysis it is perhaps not surprising, that the term "behaviour modification" has come to be used in an imprecise manner which is often far removed from its original roots in applied behaviour analysis. This becomes clear from a glance at the 15 volumes of the serial publication *Progress in Behavior Modification*, for example.

Lowe (1983, p73) has reflected on the way in which "the hydra-headed monster of mentalism . . . has resurfaced" in this area under the guise of "cognitive behavior modification" (e.g., Mahoney, 1974; Meichenbaum, 1977). This approach offers an alternative interpretation of the procedures used in the now diffuse field of behaviour modification and of the supposed reasons as to why some of them are effective, with correspondingly less appeal to functional accounts. Lowe (1983) has also pointed out that the extension of behaviour modification to less constrained clients and situations than mark the institutionalised schizophrenic in the closed back wards of a hospital has brought with it an awareness that "the power to predict and control complex human behavior . . . proved to be decidedly elusive" (p73). Behaviour modification is now diffuse and appears to be thought of as either trivial and often coercive in dealing with constrained problems, or ineffective in dealing with more complex aspects of human behaviour in less constrained settings (or both).

Much of the frustration and conceptual confusion here may result from the way in which what is now known as behaviour modification has drifted away from applied behaviour analysis. One of the key problems arises from the reluctance of radical behaviourists to address what Skinner has termed "rule-governed" as opposed to "contingency-shaped" behaviour, and it is here that Chapters 7–9 of the present volume perhaps have most force. Skinner (e.g., 1969) has provided extensive but relatively neglected discussions of rule-governed behaviour, which is seen by him as an extension of his functional analysis of verbal behaviour and its crucial role in the development of consciousness. He emphasises the central importance of verbal behaviour in the analysis of human behaviour, and enumerates ways in which behaviour that comes to be influenced by rules expressed in language may differ from behaviour which is merely shaped by environmental contingencies. It is important to emphasise here, of course, that the roots of language and thus of consciousness are in turn conceptualised in Skinner's account in terms of behavioural interactions within a social community, i.e., contingencies of reinforcement. The development of rules which may influence behaviour is therefore, as it were, a second-order reflection of environmental contingencies which shape verbal behaviour. Skinner argues that rules, however formulated, may be more influential in organising a person's behaviour than are contingencies of reinforcement: "the control exerted by directions, advice, rules and laws is more conspicuous than that exerted by (environmental) contingencies" (Skinner, 1974, p126). Thus when a person can formulate rules about a behavioural situation these may disrupt or enhance the environmental control that we have come to expect from the experimental analysis of animals' behaviour. Lowe (Chapter 7) provides empirical data which support this view.

The concept of rule-governed behaviour is seen by radical behaviourists as fundamental to an effective analysis of human behaviour, and so it is to behaviour modification too. Yet in the pragmatic applied field it seems almost to be believed that it is somehow cheating if a behaviourist talks to a client or if in a behaviour modification programme clients become, or are made aware of, the rules of an intervention, of how events are to be related to particular patterns of behaviour in particular contexts. Indeed, some have even argued that awareness negates the concept of conditioning in humans (e.g., Brewer, 1974), though this implies a narrower view of the meaning of the term "conditioning" than that of being able to specify the necessary and sufficient social and environmental conditions for behaviour to be changed. The advent of "behavioural contracting" (see Kirschenbaum and Flanery, 1983) exploits the concept of rule-governed behaviour and emphasises that it is both prudent and more ethical to discuss and negotiate the rules of an intervention with clients and others who may be involved than simply to impose changed or new contingencies of reinforcement in a cloak of furtive secrecy. It is this latter strategy which is exploitative, and, of course, it also allows the client's behaviour to become influenced by other and possibly incorrect verbal descriptions of the rules inherent in a reinforcement contingency.

It may be the case that behaviour modifiers will be increasingly drawn towards negotiating contracts with articulate clients and thus will move away from the earlier emphasis on contingency-shaped behaviour to a greater familiarity with the concept of rule-governed behaviour. Such a development would be entirely consistent with a central tenet of radical behaviourism. As well as extending the scope and effectiveness of interventions, a greater emphasis on rule-governed behaviour will allow for more meaningful *interactions* between behaviour modifiers and clients. Such interaction is another key concept in contemporary behaviourism. The approach is sometimes represented as being unidirectional, analysing the effects of environmental conditions on the behaviour of animals or of other target people. The behaviour of a person, however, is both influenced *by* the social environmental contingencies which are provided by another person and is itself an influence *on* the behaviour of that other person. Thus a dynamic interaction emerges which represents what Skinner has termed "control and counter-control". The analysis of such interactions forms the major theme in his book *Beyond freedom and dignity* (1971).

A consequent development which may perhaps be expected in the field of behaviour modification as a result of greater awareness of a rule-governed behaviour and the concept of *inter*action is an increased interest in conscious states and their modulation, such as pain, malaise, fears, emotions and the like. Such cognitions (unashamedly *conscious* states here, in contrast to those in the animal literature considered above) would in this case be seen not as the autonomous prime causes of behaviour but rather, like overt behaviour, as the product of social interactions. Since such interactions can be negotiated and structured, so too can their products in awareness. Early interests in the behavioural management of chronic pain (e.g., Fordyce, 1976) indicate a way forward, being sensitive in analysis as well as direct in intervention.

The field that calls itself "behaviour modification" currently appears to be at a choice point. It may continue to drift away from its early roots in radical behaviourism and applied analyses of behaviour, preferring instead merely to cater to the needs of pragmatism in developing effective techniques of behaviour change and incorporating these techniques in various interpretative schemata. Alternatively it may feed back and enrich the applied analysis of behaviour more than of late by opening up new interests which have long been emphasised at a theoretical level in contemporary behaviourism but which have not been exposed to a great deal of empirical scrutiny, such as the concept of rule-governed behaviour and the provenance of consciousness as a product of social interaction in a verbal community. As was noted earlier, applied analyses of behaviour require relationships between behaviour and potential controlling variables to be manipulated if they are to be shown to be functional, and thus applied behaviour analysis and behaviour modification have much to gain from a more symbiotic relationship than we have recently come to expect.

CONCLUSION

In this chapter an attempt has been made to consider some of the distinctive characteristics of contemporary behaviourism. The dominant theme has been its programme of explaining behaviour by focusing on its functional relationships with environmental events. This has not been the place to attempt a detailed critique or appraisal of the approach. However, a recent issue of the journal *The Behavioral and Brain Sciences* (Catania & Harnad, 1984) provides an excellent review of the field. Seminal papers by Skinner which address most of the key concepts are there republished, together with numerous commentaries both by critics and advocates of radical behaviourism. Furthermore, Skinner has in turn provided responses to these sets of reviews, and so for the student of behaviourism who wishes to identify the contemporary points of controversy and strain no finer source could be contemplated. Instead of attempting a comprehensive discussion, the present chapter has merely highlighted a few important topics which are to be found elsewhere in this book. Even then, a number of important issues identified in the first three chapters have not been discussed here, such as the place of individual differences and developmental processes, the evolution of the plasticity of behaviour, and the way in which the predominantly North American tradition of behaviourism can be interpreted from a more European perspective. Furthermore, some of the complex issues raised here cannot be given the detailed appraisal they demand, for example the current relationship between contemporary cognitive learning theory and contemporary behaviourism, and the place and role of private events in the Skinnerian system.

The experimental analysis of behaviour and applied behavioural analysis are both expressions of the perspective on psychology given by functional analyses of environmental influences on behaviour. In both traditions observable behaviour is explained in terms of the selective effects of functionally effective consequences (the B : C relationship) and in terms of the modulating effects of the antecedent environmental context (the A : B relationship). The experimental analysis of behaviour in particular emphasises that the nature of these relationships may be both subtle and complex, and is therefore not to be characterised in a simplistic manner. Identification of these relationships, it is claimed, provides an explanation and understanding of behaviour.

The experimental analysis of behaviour has been largely based on animal models of behaviour in a restricted range of environmental conditions, in the hope of being able to identify broad principles which may be extrapolated to behaviour in general. While the approach has indeed broadened the interpretative base of contemporary behaviourism, it is also noticeable that the most vibrant areas of research in operant conditioning at present are not to be found within this tradition. The techniques are being used in applied contexts such as behavioural pharmacology, in relation to an increased interest in the interactions between the phylogeny and ontogeny of behaviour, and even to support a surge of cognitive theorising that is deeply antithetical to the behaviourist programme. There is therefore considerable conceptual debate at present about the nature of adequate explanations of the behavioural data emanating from the conditioning laboratory, and this short chapter can do no more than identify some of the foci of that debate and hint at the depth of ferment in the debate at present.

Applied analyses of behaviour focus on human behaviour in the less structured world of social interaction. In order to ensure that observed relationships between behaviour and the social environment are indeed functional, applied behavioural analysis is intimately related to contingency management and behaviour modification in applied settings. At a pragmatic level, the success of direct manipulations of social and other influences on behaviour in a therapeutic context provides support for the view that functional analyses of human behaviour can be insightful and useful. However, "behaviour modification" as an applied discipline is not always closely tied to its roots in applied behaviour analysis, and here too there is considerable theoretical debate. But there is, nevertheless, reason to hope that developments in the applied field, such as the negotiation of contracts with articulate clients in far richer environments than the chronic hospital ward, may bring some of the key concepts of contemporary behaviourism more to the fore, for example, the importance of language in allowing rules to govern behaviour and in leading to consciousness as a product of social interaction. Perhaps such a development may lead more practitioners to become aware of the subtleties of contemporary behaviourism.

At the very least, the philosophical system of radical behaviourism as developed and advocated in particular by Skinner provides a coherent and unified approach to a very wide range of psychological phenomena. It leads to explorations of the important relationships between environmental events and behaviour, and these can be exploited in various fields by researchers of varying theoretical persuasions, in the laboratory and in the clinic, school and family. The chapters in the present book provide an indication both of the direction of current empirical research and also of the challenges and tensions such work offers to the conceptual system of behaviourism, which sees explanations of behaviour predominantly in terms of the interactions between it and environmental events.

The First European Meeting on the Experimental Analysis of Behaviour in 1983 was an unusually lively and pleasant conference which embraced both empirical research and theoretical debate. The papers, which form the chapters of this book, provided a focus on some major themes, and an attempt was deliberately made by the conference organisers to obtain contributions from a number of different countries. The predominance of North American workers in this field made it appropriate to include selected contributions from that quarter. However the conference was also attended by a large number of delegates drawn from most of the countries of Western Europe (as well as from many other countries in which a European influence has been dominant), and many other papers were presented. The pleasure and stimulation which was so clearly gained by the participants at this large conference in the sharing of their interests and the debating of current issues suggests that the rumour that behaviourism is dead is exaggerated.

REFERENCES

Azrin, N. H. & Holz, W. C. (1966) Punishment. In W. K. Honig (Ed.), *Operant behavior: Areas of research and application*. New York: Appleton-Century-Crofts. Pp380–447.

Baum, W. H. (1973) The correlation based law of effect. *Journal of the Experimental Analysis of Behavior*, **20**, 137–153.

Blackman, D. E. (1980) Images of man in contemporary behaviourism. In A. J. Chapman & D. M. Jones (Eds.), *Models of man*. Leicester: British Psychological Society. Pp99–112.

Blackman, D. E. (1983) On cognitive theories of animal learning: Extrapolation from humans to animals? In G. C. L. Davey (Ed.), *Animal models of human behavior*. Chichester: Wiley. Pp37–50.

Branch, N. M. (1984) Rate dependency, behavioural mechanisms, and behavioural pharmacology. *Journal of the Experimental Analysis of Behavior*, **42**, 511–522.

Brewer, W. P. (1974) There is no convincing evidence for operant or classical conditioning in adult humans. In W. B. Weiner & D. S. Palermo (Eds.), *Cognition and the symbolic processes*. Hillsdale, N.J.: Lawrence Erlbaum Associates. Pp1–42.

Catania, A. C. & Harnad, S. (Eds.) (1984) Canonical papers of B. F. Skinner (1984). *The Behavioral and Brain Sciences*, **7**, 473–724.

Dews, P. B. (1955) Studies on behavior: I. Differential sensitivity to pentobarbital of pecking performance in pigeons depending on the schedule of reward. *Journal of Pharmacology and Experimental Therapeutics*, **113**, 393–401.

Dickinson, A. (1980) *Contemporary animal learning theory*. Cambridge: Cambridge University Press.

Ferster, C. B. & Skinner, B. F. (1957) *Schedules of reinforcement*. New York: Appleton-Century-Crofts.

Fordyce, W. E. (1976) *Behavioral methods for chronic pain and illness*. St Louis: Mosby.

Gamzu, E. & Schwartz, B. (1973) The maintenance of key-pecking by stimulus-contingent and response-independent food presentation. *Journal of the Experimental Analysis of Behavior*, **19**, 65–72.

Glavin, J. P. & Moyer, L. S. (1975) Facilitating extinction of infant crying by changing reinforcement schedules. *Journal of the Experimental Analysis of Behavior*, **6**, 357–358.

Gollub, L. (1977) Conditioned reinforcement: Schedule effects. In W. K. Honig & J. E. R. Staddon (Eds.), *Handbook of operant behavior*. Englewood Cliffs, N.J.: Prentice-Hall. Pp288–312.

Hearst, E. & Jenkins, H. M. (1974) *Sign-tracking: The stimulus reinforcer relation and directed actions*. Austin, Texas: Monograph of the Psychonomic Society.

Herrnstein, R. J. & Hineline, P. N. (1966) Negative reinforcement and shock-frequency reduction. *Journal of the Experimental Analysis of Behavior*, **9**, 421–430.

Hulse, S. H., Fowler, H., & Honig, W. K. (Eds.) (1978) *Cognitive processes in animal behavior*. Hillsdale, N.J.: Lawrence Erlbaum Associates Inc.

Hursh, S. R. (1984) Behavioral economics. *Journal of the Experimental Analysis of Behavior*, **42**, 435–452.

Johanson, C. E. (1978) Drugs as reinforcers. In D. E. Blackman & D. J. Sanger (Eds.), *Contemporary research in behavioral pharmacology*. New York: Plenum Press. Pp325–390.

Kazdin, A. E. (1977) *The token economy: A review and evaluation*. New York: Plenum Press.

Kirschenbaum, D. S. & Flanery, R. C. (1983) Behavioral contracting. In M. Hersen, R. M. Eisler & P. M. Miller (Eds.), *Progress in behavior modification 15*. New York: Academic Press. Pp217–275.

Leitenberg, H. (1976) *Handbook of behavior modification and behavior therapy*. Englewood Cliffs, N.J.: Prentice-Hall.

Lovaas, O. I. & Simmons, J. Q. (1969) Manipulation of self-destruction in three retarded children. *Journal of Applied Behavior Analysis*, **2**, 143–157.

Lowe, C. F. (1983) Radical behaviorism and human psychology. In G. C. L. Davey (Ed.), *Animal models of human behavior*. Chichester: Wiley. Pp71–93.

Mackintosh, N. J. (1974) *The psychology of animal learning*. London: Academic Press.

Mahoney, M. J. (1974) Reflections on the cognitive-learning trend in psychotherapy. *American Psychologist*, **32**, 5–13.

Marr, M. J. (1984) Conceptual approaches and issues. *Journal of the Experimental Analysis of Behavior*, **42**, 353–362.

Meichenbaum, D. (1977) *Cognitive behavior modification: An integrative approach*. New York: Plenum Press.

Morse, W. H. & Kelleher, R. T. (1970) Schedules as fundamental determinants of behavior. In W. N. Schoenfeld (Ed.), *The theory of reinforcement schedules*. New York: Appleton-Century-Crofts. Pp139–185.

Nevin, J. A. (1973) Stimulus control. In J. A. Nevin (Ed.), *The study of behavior: Learning, motivation, emotion and instinct*. Glenview, Illinois: Scott, Foresman & Co. Pp 115–149.

Nevin, J. A. (1984) Quantitative analyses. *Journal of the Experimental Analysis of Behavior*, **42**, 421–434.

Roitblat, H. L., Bever, T. G., & Terrace, H. S. (Eds.) (1984) *Animal cognition*. Hillsdale, N.J.: Lawrence Erlbaum Associates Inc.

Scott, R. R., Himadi, W., & Keane, T. M. (1983) A review of generalization in social skills training. In M. Hersen, R. M. Eisler & P. M. Miller (Eds.), *Progress in behavior modification 15*. New York: Academic Press. Pp113–172.

Shettleworth, S. J. (1973) Food reinforcement and the organization of behavior. In R. Hinde & J. Stevenson-Hinde (Eds.), *Constraints on learning*. London: Academic Press.

Shimp, C. P. (1976) Organization in memory and behavior. *Journal of the Experimental Analysis of Behavior*, **26**, 113–130.

Sidman, M. (1960) *Tactics of scientific research*. New York: Basic Books.

Sidman, M. & Stoddard, L. T. (1966) The effectiveness of fading in programming a simultaneous form discrimination for retarded children. *Journal of the Experimental Analysis of Behavior*, **10**, 3–15.

Sizemore, O. J. & Lattal, K. A. (1977) Dependency, temporal contiguity, and response-independent reinforcement. *Journal of the Experimental Analysis of Behavior*, **22**, 119–125.

Skinner, B. F. (1938) *The behavior of organisms*. New York: Appleton-Century-Crofts.

Skinner, B. F. (1950) Are theories of learning necessary? *Psychological Review*, **57**, 193–216.
Skinner, B. F. (1966) The phylogeny and ontogeny of behavior. *Science*, **153**, 1205–1213.
Skinner, B. F. (1969) An operant analysis of problem solving (and notes). In B. F. Skinner (Ed.), *Contingencies of reinforcement: A theoretical analysis*. New York: Appleton-Century-Crofts. Pp133–171.
Skinner, B. F. (1971) *Beyond freedom and dignity*. New York: Knopf.
Skinner, B. F. (1974) *About behaviorism*. New York: Knopf.
Skinner, B. F. (1977a) Herrnstein and the evolution of behavior. *American Psychologist*, **32**, 1006–1012.
Skinner, B. F. (1977b) Why I am not a cognitive psychologist. *Behaviourism*, **5**, 3–10.
Staddon, J. E. R. (1977) Schedule-induced behavior. In W. K. Honig & J. E. R. Staddon (Eds.), *Handbook of operant behavior*. Englewood Cliffs. N.J.: Prentice-Hall. Pp125–152.
Stolerman, I. P. (1984) Internal stimulus effects of drugs. In D. J. Sanger & D. E. Blackman (Eds.), *Aspects of psychopharmacology*. London: Methuen. Pp57–83.
Terrace, H. S. (1984) Animal cognition. In H. L. Roitblat, T. G. Bever, & H. S. Terrace (Eds.), *Animal cognition*. Hillsdale, N.J.: Lawrence Erlbaum Associates Inc. Pp7–28.
Watson, J. B. (1924) *Behaviorism*. Chicago: University of Chicago Press.
Williams, B. A. (1984) Stimulus control and associative learning. *Journal of the Experimental Analysis of Behavior*, **42**, 469–483.
Zeiler, M. (1977) Schedules of reinforcement: The controlling variables. In W. K. Honig & J. E. R. Staddon (Eds.), *Handbook of operant behavior*. Englewood Cliffs, N.J.: Prentice-Hall. Pp201–232.
Zeiler, M. D. (1984) The sleeping giant: Reinforcement schedules. *Journal of the Experimental Analysis of Behavior*, **42**, 485–493.

Author Index

Subject Index